RAC Inspected
Guest Accommodation
Bed & Breakfast
Great Britain & Ireland 2000

Burghope Manor, Bath

Kirkton House, Helensburgh

Riversdale Farm, Ballinamore

rac

West One Publishing • London

First published 1904

© West One (Trade) Publishing Ltd. 1999

This book is sold subject to the condition that it shall not, by way of trade, or otherwise, be lent, re-sold, hired out or otherwise circulated without the publisher's prior consent in any form of binding or cover other than that in which it is published.

All rights reserved. No parts of this work may be reproduced, stored in a retrieval system or transmitted by any means without permission. Whilst every effort has been made to ensure that the information contained in this publication is accurate and up to date, the publisher does not accept any responsibility for any error, omission, or misrepresentation. All liability for loss, disappointment, negligence or other damage caused by reliance on the information contained in this guide, or in the event of bankruptcy, or liquidation, or cessation of trade of any company, individual or firm mentioned is hereby excluded.

ISBN 1-900327 39 2 paperback

A CIP catalogue record for this book is available from the British Library.

Cartography: © West One

Printed and bound in Slovenia.

Pictures reproduced with the kind permission of:
Ayrshire & Arran Tourist Board
(p165, Girvan, Ayrshire);
English Heritage
(pp18-19, Rievaulx Abbey, North Yorkshire);
Guernsey Tourist Board
(p213, St Peter Port, Guernsey);
Irish Tourist Board
(pp194-5, Halfpenny Bridge, Dublin);
The National Trust
(p181, Joe Cornish, Rossili Beach, Swansea);
NMEC
(p89, The Millennium Dome)

Published by
West One (Trade) Publishing Ltd,
Kestrel House
Dukes Place
Marlow
Bucks SL7 2QH

Telephone: 01628 487722
Fax: 01628 487724
Email: sales@west-one.com

Managing Editor	Stan Dover
Production Manager	Liz York
Editorial Team	Sara Foster
	Matthias Thaler
	Jack Gough
Finance and Administration Team	Cathy Seabrook
	Alex Wilson
	Alan Pearson
Chief Executive Officer	Martin Coleman

Contents

Foreword – Group Managing Director,
RAC Motoring Services   4

RAC Hotel Accreditation and Awards   7

Harmonised Quality Standards   8

New RAC Hospitality Awards   10

RAC Hotel Services   11

How to use this guide   12

Little Gems   14

Directory of Guest Accommodation

England	18
Scotland	165
Wales	181
Ireland	194
Channel Islands	214
Isle of Man	215

Great Britain & Ireland Maps   217

Momentum for the new millennium

Introduction by Graeme Potts
Group Managing Director
RAC Motoring Services

Writing the introduction to this guide gives me the opportunity to highlight a number of changes designed to serve our customers better as we begin a new century.

By the time you read this guide, one of the most significant developments in the history of the hotel industry will have been launched.

Unprecedented co-operation between the three main accreditation bodies – including RAC – has resulted in Harmonised Quality Standards, ending a confused situation where the consumer was often faced with several different ratings for the same property.

Clear definitions of the various types of accommodation and indications of the service quality which can be expected now provide the overseas and domestic guest with a framework for comparison - and a means of selecting the Hotel or Guest Accommodation which will best suit their needs.

With tourism a vital ingredient of the economies of both the UK and Ireland, this initiative will enable the hospitality industry to deliver a level of quality to match the consumers' expectations.

The aim of improving customer service was one of the principle reasons why Lex Service Plc bought RAC Motoring Services.

As part of a strong motor service based group, RAC can now offer a comprehensive service to its customers: Teaching learner drivers through BSM, providing an independent assessment of used cars, arranging lease or purchasing options as well as keeping vehicles on the road through servicing, repair and breakdown facilities. What's more, RAC Hotels and Travel services also help customers use their vehicle for the pleasurable things in life – like staying at RAC accredited properties.

Running a business like the new RAC group and running an Hotel or Bed and Breakfast shares an important aspect – satisfied customers are the ones who will tell their friends and neighbours – the best possible accolade.

This guide lists those properties which meet their guests' expectations and enjoy welcoming regular customers back.

I hope that you enjoy discovering them throughout Great Britain and Ireland and experiencing their own unique blend of quality and service.

Graeme Potts.

Maps

Leisure

Travel

Shoppin

www.WestOneWeb.com

West One

RAC Hotel Accreditation and Awards

New standards for the new millennium

To help tourists and business people identify the standard of accommodation they are looking for, Harmonised Quality Standards for all types of serviced accommodation have been launched.

Starting with extensive consumer research and with consultation within the hotel industry, the three main accreditation agencies – RAC, AA and English Tourist Council – have agreed a common set of inspection criteria to provide consistency for travellers looking for a place to stay.

Research shows that consumers are predominantly interested in two main types of accommodation – Hotels and Guest Accommodation (which includes guesthouses, farmhouses, inns, small private hotels, restaurants with rooms and bed and breakfast properties).

New inspection criteria have also been introduced for two newly recognised types of accommodation – Townhouses and Travel Accommodation – thus recognising the growing diversity in accommodation styles demanded by today's customers.

Inspections for the Harmonised Quality Standards have been taking place since January 1998 to meet the deadlines to get the accommodation shown in this guide into the new format, new signage on properties and all other material in place for the new century. However with the scale and complexity of the operation means inevitably there will still be some work outstanding to complete this task.

Properties with a harmonised quality rating will be identifiable as follows :

Hotels:

1-5 stars, with signs in a new format to help distinguish them from the previous rating system

Townhouses:

4 and 5 star Townhouses

Guest Accommodation:

1- 5 diamonds

Travel Accommodation:

the description depicts this category

RAC Inspectors have been working with Hotel and Guest Accommodation proprietors, throughout the UK and Republic of Ireland, advising of the impact of this important new initiative to help the domestic and overseas guest select the type and standard of accommodation that best suits their needs.

The RAC supports the

BRITISH
Hospitality
ASSOCIATION

the effective voice of the hospitality industry

Harmonised Quality Standards explained

The different types of accommodation in the UK and Republic of Ireland have been categorised into four categories with differing levels, the requirements for each being :

Hotels – Stars

★ Star
Hotels in this classification are likely to be small and independently owned, with a family atmosphere. Services may be provided by the owner and family on an informal basis. There may be a limited range of facilities and meals may be fairly simple. Lunch, for example, may not be served. Some bedrooms may not have en suite bath / shower rooms. Maintenance, cleanliness and comfort should, however, always be of an acceptable standard.

★★ Star
In this classification, hotels will typically be small to medium sized and offer more extensive facilities than at one star level. Some business hotels come into two star classification and guests can expect comfortable, well-equipped, overnight accommodation, usually with an en suite bath / shower room. Reception and other staff will aim for a more professional presentation than at one star level, and offer a wider range of straightforward services, including food and drink.

★★★ 3 Star
At this level, hotels are usually of a size to support higher staffing levels, and a significantly greater quality and range of facilities than at the lower star classifications. Reception and the other public rooms will be more spacious and the restaurant will normally also cater for non-residents. All bedrooms will have fully en suite bath and shower rooms and offer a good standard of comfort and equipment, such as a hair dryer, direct dial telephone, toiletries in the bathroom. Some room service can be expected and some provision for business travellers.

★★★★ Star
Expectations at this level include a degree of luxury as well as quality in the furnishings, decor and equipment, in every area of the hotel. Bedrooms will also usually offer more space than at the lower star levels, and well designed, co-ordinated furnishings and decor. En suite bathrooms will have both bath and fixed shower. There will be a high enough ratio of staff to guests to provide services such as porterage, 24-hour room service, laundry and dry-cleaning. The restaurant will demonstrate a serious approach to cuisine.

★★★★★ Star
Here you should find spacious and luxurious accommodation throughout the hotel, matching the best international standards. Interior design should impress with its quality and attention to detail, comfort and elegance. Furnishings should be immaculate. Services should be formal, well supervised and flawless in attention to guests' needs without being intrusive. The restaurant will demonstrate a high level of technical skill, producing dishes to the highest international standards. Staff will be knowledgeable, helpful, well-versed in all aspects of customer care, combining efficiency with courtesy.

Townhouse Accommodation

This classification denotes small, personally run town or city centre hotels which afford a high degree of privacy and concentrate on luxuriously furnished bedrooms and suites with high quality room service, rather than public rooms or formal dining rooms usually associated with hotels, they are usually in areas well served by restaurants. All fall broadly within the four or five Star classification.

Guest Accommodation – Diamonds

The term Guest Accommodation comprises guest houses, farmhouses, small private hotels, inns, restaurants with rooms and bed and breakfast properties, which in the UK and Ireland offer a style and warmth of accommodation envied around the world.

The Guest Accommodation scheme assesses establishments at five levels of quality from one

Diamond at the simplest, to five Diamonds at the luxury end of the spectrum.

To be recognised at all under the new Quality Standards, establishments must provide sufficient quality in all areas of operation covered under the following headings to merit a minimum score of 1 out of 5. If they do not achieve sufficient quality in one of these areas they cannot be awarded a quality rating at all:

Cleanliness and Housekeeping

Service and Hospitality (Guest Care)

Bedroom Facilities

Bathroom, Shower, WC and en suite Facilities

Food Quality and Service

Public Rooms

Safety and Security, Exterior and Interior Appearance and Up-keep (General Requirements)

The awards take into account the level of general cleanliness, the comfort and degree of style and quality of furnishings and decor throughout the establishment; the levels of service and hospitality displayed by owners and staff; the friendliness of the atmosphere; last but not least, the quality of the meals.

At all Diamond levels, cleanliness and good housekeeping are of the highest importance and the emphasis of the assessment for a Diamond rating is on guest care and quality rather than the provision of extra facilities.

The overall score in all areas of operation is then converted to a percentage, and this determines the quality rating awarded. The quality percentage bands at each level are listed below:

At 1 Diamond level:
Quality Percentage   20%-34%

At 2 Diamond level:
Quality Percentage   35%-49%

At 3 Diamond level:
Quality Percentage   50%-69%

At 4 Diamond level:
Quality Percentage   70%-84%

At 5 Diamond level:
Quality Percentage   85% plus

Travel Accommodation

This classification denotes budget or lodge accommodation suitable for an overnight stay, usually in purpose-built units close to main roads and motorways but could also include city centre locations. They provide consistent levels of accommodation and service, matching today's expectations.

Please Note
As Harmonised Quality Standards launches as this publication goes to print, direct comparison of properties with other inspection bodies may show some discrepancies as a result of different inspection dates.

The properties contained in this guide are accredited Guest Accommodation and Travel Accommodation, a full listing of Hotel and Townhouse properties can be found in 'RAC Inspected Hotels 2000', available at all good book stores price £13.99

New RAC Hospitality Awards

To reflect the increasing standards being achieved in the hotel industry, and to complement the new Harmonised Quality Standards, RAC has taken the opportunity to review its range of awards.

The range of awards celebrates excellence in both the Hotel and Guest Accommodation categories and a new award for dining recognises achievement at all that is good at all types of serviced accommodation.

Hotel Award

Gold Ribbon
For the past 13 years RAC has recognised excellence in hotel keeping with the RAC Blue Ribbon award. As hotel standards continue to rise, the best Blue Ribbon recipients are acknowledged by the introduction of the RAC Gold Ribbon accolade.

The new award is made to hotels who have raised their standards to even higher levels, continually demonstrating their commitment to superlative standards of customer care, service and accommodation.

Blue Ribbon
The RAC Blue Ribbon continues to stand for the high quality standards expected of the best in the industry. A Blue Ribbon award will only be presented to those properties who have achieved consistently high grades in all aspects of hotel keeping.

Both Gold and Blue Ribbon awards are made to Hotels in all classifications from 1 – 5 stars.

Guest Accommodation

RAC Little Gem
Now the highest accolade for Guest Accommodation, this award is presented to the best properties on a regional basis and recognises the all-round quality shown in hospitality, cleanliness, welcome and attention to detail that makes every stay memorable.

RAC Sparkling Diamond
This award is made to properties which achieve excellent standards of cleanliness, hygiene and attention to detail in their provision of guest comfort.

RAC Warm Welcome Award
Within the diamond scheme, only establishments that achieve excellent standards for hospitality and service in the overall inspection are put forward for this accolade.

RAC Dining Award

This new seal of quality assesses the entire dining experience at Hotel and Guest Accommodation, taking into account the quality of the cuisine as well as ambience, service and level of comfort.

The award reflects five levels of quality, starting at level one. The criteria for this award considers other guest meals available rather than purely concentrating on dinner and applies to both Hotel and Guest Accommodation categories.

RAC Hotel Services

Linda Astbury
Manager of Hotel Operations

This is the first guide using the new inspection criteria which takes the requirements of the guest as their basis.

This has meant that the RAC Inspection force underwent thorough and exhaustive re-training to allow them to assess each property to the new standards. Throughout the 19 month inspection process RAC Hotel Inspectors have been able to advise owners and managers of all styles of properties, of the requirements to ensure that consumer expectations are met at serviced accommodation throughout the UK and Republic of Ireland.

Of course each inspection is unique, with different styles of property serving differing clienteles and a major part of the Inspector's job is to take into account the individuality of each property. But, the bricks and mortar is only the beginning: in a service industry, it is the quality of the staff which makes the difference and that fact is reflected in the new Harmonised Quality Standards.

All Inspectors works incognito, observing the service received by other guests. The findings are discussed with the establishments and any areas for improvement are discussed. We believe that only in this way can RAC play its part in assisting properties to increase their standards on a constant basis.

Over the last few years we have noticed a marked improvement in the quality of properties in the RAC scheme. That fact, combined with the introduction of the Harmonised Quality Standards, has prompted us to review the range of our awards recognising excellence throughout the hotel industry.

We are particularly pleased to introduce the RAC Dining Award which acknowledges the quality of the dining experience not just at hotels but at Guesthouse, Bed and Breakfast and other Guest Accommodation where undoubtedly high standards are now abundant.

The award is not just about the food itself and recognises the atmosphere of the restaurant or dining room, the attention given to detail and service provided.

We hope that you will agree that the combination of a new rating scheme and new RAC awards will help you find the right property to suit your needs on every occasion.

12
An entry explained

Town, county and map reference. ——————— ALNMOUTH Northumberland 13F3

Hotel name, rating and contact details. ——————

♦♦♦♦ Marine House
1 Marine Road, Alnmouth NE66 2RW
📞 01665-830349

Short description with a picture of the hotel.

A 200 year old building of considerable charm, facing the sea. Ten individually appointed ensuite bedrooms, warm, homely atmosphere, delicious imaginative cooking, pets welcome, parking.

Bedroom information and facilities. ——————— 10 bedrs, all ensuite, TCF TV ✠ P 12 ⌂ Resid
No children under 7

Details of prices and credit cards accepted. ——————— HB £245-£259 D £13 CC MC Visa

Notes

Properties in this guide are listed alphabetically by their location within England, Scotland, Wales, Northern Ireland, the Republic of Ireland, the Channel Islands and the Isle of Man.

Properties are arranged by rating and then alphabetically within the classification.

The final entries for each town list those few establishments which, because of pressure of time, we have been unable to complete an inspection for Harmonised Quality Standards this year.

Cancellation of reservations

If you have to cancel a reservation of accommodation, you are advised to telephone the hotel at once, followed by a written confirmation of the cancellation. Please try to give the hotel as much notice as possible in order that they may have every opportunity to re-let the accommodation. If rooms which are reserved and not occupied cannot be re-let, the hotel proprietor may suffer loss and guests may be held legally responsible for part of the cost. This may also apply to table reservations in restaurants.

Arrival times

Small hotels and inns may close for part of the afternoon. It is wise to inform them of your expected arrival time when booking, and to telephone them if you are delayed, particularly after 6.00pm.

The Listing explained

Property Information

The listing for each property starts with its rating, followed by its name, RAC awards, address, telephone, fax number, e-mail address and details of any seasonal closing.

- ♦ Guesthouse classification
- ♛ Dining Award

Facilities at the property

♿	Facilities for the disabled – see notes below
🐕	Dogs permitted
🚭	No smoking anywhere in Establishment
▯	Lift
P	Parking
⚎	Conference facilities

Hotels do their best to cater for disabled visitors. Some, in old or converted buildings, find it difficult to make the necessary alterations. Those hotels which are considered by their proprietors or managers to have suitable facilities are indicated in the guide by the usual symbol. Disabled visitors are recommended to contact the hotel direct and ascertain whether the hotel can provide for their particular requirements and to let the hotel know what they will need in the way of extra service or facilities.

Licensing Information

⌬	Full licence
⌬ Rest	Restaurant or table licence. A licence whereby the sale of alcohol is restricted to customers taking meals
⌬ Resid	Residential licence. A licence whereby the sale of alcohol is restricted to residents at an establishment and to their friends entertained at their expense

Information on Charges

Where no return was received from the property, all prices have been removed.

SB	Rate for Single Room & Breakfast
DB	Rate for Double Room and Breakfast
HB	Rate for Half board
Room	Rate for Room only
D	Price of table d'hote dinner
CC	Credit Cards
MC	MasterCard
Amex	American Express
DC	Diners Club
JCB	Japan Card Bank
Vi	Visa

The prices given range from that for standard rooms in low season to that for superior rooms in high season. Tariffs given in the guide are forecast by the hoteliers of what they expect to charge in 2000. It is always advisable to check with the property before booking. All prices quoted should include VAT where applicable, they may or may not include a charge for service.

Sporting Facilities

	Indoor swimming pool
	Outdoor swimming pool
	Golf course
	Tennis
	Fishing
	Squash
	Riding
	Gymnasium
	Billiards/snooker
	Sauna

Fourposter bed

Over the past few years, many hoteliers have informed us that the item most frequently requested by their guests is a fourposter bed. Acting upon their advice we have introduced this new symbol, for the purpose of identifying the hotels in this guide, which provide this facility.

Maintenance of standards

All hotels listed in the guide are inspected regularly; nevertheless we welcome reports from readers on the standards being maintained. We are also glad to have reports about hotels which are not appointed by the RAC; such reports may enable the RAC to extend the number of hotels inspected.

Complaints

In cases of dissatisfaction or dispute, readers will find that discussion with the hotel management at the time of the problem/incident will normally enable the matter to be resolved promptly and amicably. Should the personal approach fail, the RAC will raise comments with the hotelier at the time of the next inspection.

Please write to RAC Hotel Services,
1 Forest Road
Feltham TW13 7RR

Please submit details of any discussion or correspondence involved when reporting a problem to RAC.

Little Gems 1999

Southern England

Widbrook Grange
Trowbridge Road
Bradford-on-Avon
Wiltshire BA15 1UH

Telephone: 01225 863173
John and Pauline Price
Five Diamonds

Every year we select one establishment from each of our regions which epitomises all those qualities which make for an outstanding small establishment. Not only does this include great style and comfort in the decor, furnishings and furniture, but it also includes original, high quality cooking and warm and caring hospitality. We believe that the seven establishments we have selected are truly the Little Gems of the year.

A warm welcome to an elegant, peaceful home personally run by John and Pauline Price, are unquestionably the initial, striking impressions. Set back within its own grounds of 11 acres the Georgian house and courtyard rooms have been lovingly restored to provide first class modern facilities, including televisions and telephones, yet with a myriad of antiques. Many rooms boast full and half-tester beds in addition to period furnishings, pictures and ornaments. Nice little additions of mineral water, fresh flowers and a varied tea selection add that personal touch with smart, well finished bathrooms adding to the degree of comfort. Two very comfortable, eclectically furnished lounges make the ideal relaxing retreat and for the more strenuous the indoor swimming pool and gymnasium should fit the bill.

One of the many strengths of Widbrook is the quality cooking complemented with a worthy wine list. Excellent use is made of quality, fresh produce with imaginative cooking of some depth. No formal breakfast menu, though John and Pauline to do their best to provide whatever guests' desire.

Eastern England

The Cooke House
78 Brookhouse Hill
Sheffield
South Yorkshire S10 3TB

Telephone: 0114 230 8186
Peter and Maureen Cooke
Five Diamonds

Situated in a quiet residential area, a stay at Peter and Maureen Cooke's very personal house is a must. Hospitality and customer care does not come any better with the level of friendliness. Squeaky clean this small, cosy retreat provides good sized and individually styled bedrooms with first class beds ensuring a good night's rest in addition to a host of personal touches which gel well with the range of modern facilities expected by today's traveller. Bathrooms are bright with welcome personal touches of disposable razors, tooth brush and tooth paste showing the attention to detail. Similar little touches of newspapers, magazines and books are always to hand in the comfortable lounges enhanced with fresh flowers, objet d' art and pictures. Commendable cooking features daily with excellent quality local produce resulting in bright, well executed dishes. Excellent quality with imaginative cooking are the hallmarks with a good wine list which is the personal pride of Peter. Breakfasts in particular are a treat, home made bread and preserves, dry cured bacon, black pudding and calves liver make a scrumptious start to the day. A distinctive, personal homely feel to Cooke House and considering the size of the house a wide choice of drinks is dispersed.

Midlands

Number Twenty Eight
28 Lower Broad Street
Ludlow
Shropshire S18 1PQ

Telephone: 01584 876996
Philip and Patricia Ross
Five Diamonds

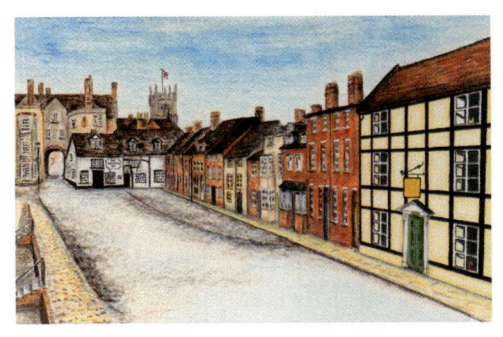

Where 'England meets Wales'. Number twenty Eight itself is early Georgian though the guesthouse comprises three houses all within a few yards of each other between the 13th century Broadgate and the ancient bridge over the River Teme. Broadgate Mews is in fact two tudor cottages combined to form a delightful secluded haven with Westgate part of a small Victorian terrace, which incidentally was built with the first recorded internal water closets in Ludlow. Delightfully and individually styled each boasts book lined walls, pictures and prints with the extra bonus of sittings rooms with open fires. First class hosts Philip and Patricia Ross ensure guests are cosseted with unobtrusive personal service and their team are to be congratulated for demonstrating equal enthusiasm and commitment. Breakfast, which can be taken at Number Twenty Eight, or continental in your room, provides the perfect start to the day. Traditional, freshly cooked English breakfasts, daily feature quality local produce, home-made preserves and a good range of teas and coffees. All in all an exceptional guest accommodation with many personal touches, dedication and a wealth of customer care.

Northern England

Rowanfield Country House
Kirkstone Road
Ambleside
Cumbria LA22 9ET

Telephone: 015394 33686
June and Philip Butcher
Five Diamonds

This no-smoking Lakeland period house is set in its own gardens surrounded by tranquil countryside in the heart of the Lake District. The beautiful view from the house is panoramic from 'the hundreds' to 'Coniston Old Man' and beyond including Lake Windermere and the village of Ambleside. Top marks for hospitality and sparkling surroundings, which are second to none. Mr and Mrs Butcher are very genial hosts with Chef Patron Mr Butcher equally impressive at the stove. Excellent use is made of quality fresh produce and first class ingredients resulting in innovative and tempting dishes. Poached poppy seed pears with cottage cheese and poppy seed vinaigrette followed by home made cauliflower soup are typical starters to the meal. Prime Aberdeen Angus fillet or poached fresh haddock served with saffron sauce continue with lemon barley pilaff with roasted fennel for the non-carnivores. Scrumptious home made puddings conclude the occasion. Cosy public rooms with wood burning stove, and individually styled and decorated bedrooms ensure a restful and enjoyable stay.

Scotland

Glenavon House
Kinchury Road
Boat of Garten
Inverness-shire PH24 3BP

Telephone: 01479 831212
Ian and Rosemarie Strain
Five Diamonds

Ian and Rosemarie Strain's handsome Victorian residence is a very special place to stay. Family owned and run it has been sympathetically restored and tastefully modernised yet still retains all the elegance and charm of the era. Set back within landscaped gardens with miles of forest walks outside the back gate yet in a central location in the pretty village of Boat of Garten. Sparkling standards of cleanliness are complemented by the exceptionally friendly approach and first class customer care. Bedrooms are individually styled, comfortable finished and complemented with a myriad of modern facilities and creature comforts yet boast a depth of character and charm. Nice little personal touches of fresh flowers, home-made short bread, complimentary newspaper and good hospitality trays emphasise that extra attention to detail which the Strain's pride themselves on. Commendable cooking, self described as 'Auld Alliance' – Scotland's finest produce cooked with a French influence – is another great strength of Glenavon. Dishes like brochettes of halibut and king prawns, tournedos of wild boar with juniper, port and redcurrant sauce or for fish lovers red snapper stuffed with spinach and basil are typical. Delicious home made puddings and tasty cheese conclude a very enjoyable dining experience. All in all Glenavon House makes the perfect location for a very enjoyable Highland holiday.

Wales

Penmachno Hall
Penmachno
Betws-y-Coed
Gwynedd L24 0PU

Telephone: 01690 760207
Ian and Modwena Cutler
Four Diamonds

If it's the absence of modernity you require, (yet quality standards in comfort), televisions, mobiles phones and a return to the dinner party and the art of conversation, Penmachno Hall is just the ticket. Tucked away in a very secluded and remote location this stylish house is the passion of owners Ian and Modwena Cutler who have now generated an enviable reputation and firm following. Guests are cosseted and encouraged to socialise with their fellow guests with introductions at 7pm cocktails to be followed by a delicious dinner on communal lines. Ian is a very genial 'mine host' ensuring nobody is missed or over-powered if a more intimate atmosphere is personally sought. Modwena's home cooking shows great depth with honest flavours and textures coming to the fore. Delicious soups, roast lamb, carved at the table and tempting home-made puddings feature daily. Public areas, adorned with antiques and period furnishings are cosy and pleasing to use. Bedrooms, again free of modern facilities, yet with a depth of comfort with well dressed beds, ensure guests receive peaceful surroundings. Bathrooms are smart with some boasting Victorian roll-top baths to add to the character and charm of the building.

Ireland

Ivyleigh House
Bank Place
Portlaois
Co. Laois

Telephone: 0502 22081
Dinah and Jerry Campion
Five Diamonds

Dinah and Jerry Campion are to be applauded for setting quality, homely standards for others to follow. Ivyleigh is a new business that has got off to a flying start with a tremendous amount of time, effort, commitment and capital invested into this delightful house. All the hallmarks of a superb and personally run retreat are there. Genuine hospitality, where nothing is too much trouble, combined with sparkling cleanliness and the scene is set for a relaxing and personal stay. This semi-detached Georgian family home, close to the town, has been sympathetically restored with not only modern quality standards in accommodation, but equally a depth of character with a profusion of antiques, period furnishings and objet d'art. Waterford glass table lamps and stunning chandeliers are just tasters of Dinah and Jerry's personal style. Comfortable bedrooms are individually styled with a commendable range of creature comforts and extra personal touches that gel well with smart bathrooms dripping with perfumed toiletries and first class towelling. Scrumptious home-made breakfasts are a treat in their own right. A selection of freshly baked breads, scones, perfect porridge or Dinah's muesli followed by either full Irish Breakfast or veggie fry, (French bread, potato cakes, tomatoes and mushrooms), for those more healthy conscious, promotes an enthusiastic start to the day. If you are looking for the ideal hospitable and relaxing retreat, Ivyleigh certainly fits the bill.

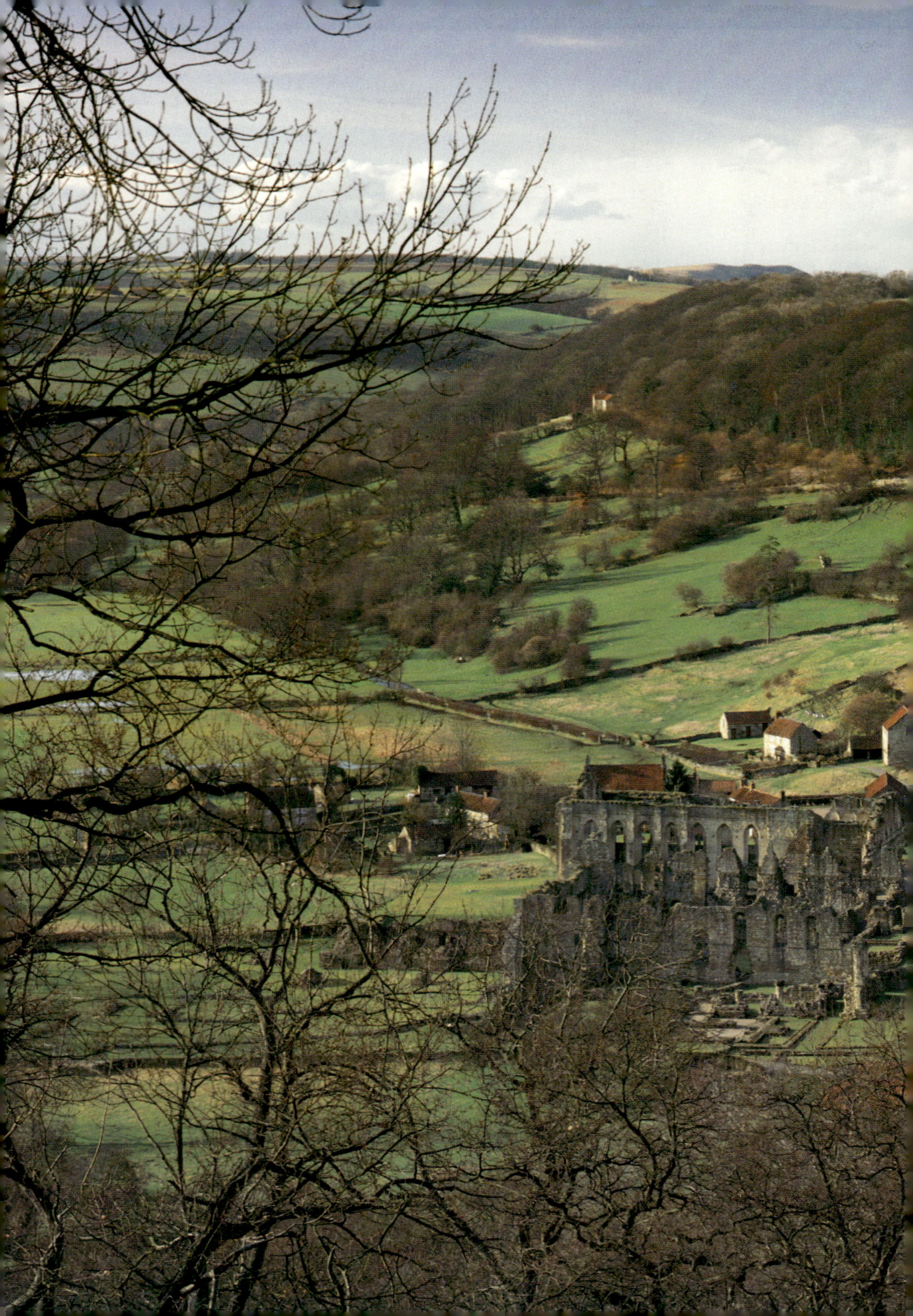

England

20 Almondsbury

ALMONDSBURY Gloucestershire   3E1

♦♦♦♦ Abbotts Way
Sparkling Diamond
Gloucester Road, Almondsbury BS12 4JB
📞 01454-613134 Fax 01454-613134
6 bedrs, all ensuite, TCF TV 📺 P 10 SB £29 DB £45
HB £200 CC MC Visa Amex DC

ALNMOUTH Northumberland   13F3

♦♦♦♦ Marine House
Sparkling Diamond
1 Marine Road, Alnmouth NE66 2RW
📞 01665-830349

A 200 year old building of considerable charm, facing the sea. Ten individually appointed ensuite bedrooms, warm, homely atmosphere, delicious. imaginative cooking, pets welcome, parking. Dinner included.
10 bedrs, all ensuite, TCF TV 🐾 P 12 No children under 7 ⊕ Resid SB £74-£80 DB £84-£90 HB £280 CC MC Visa
See advert on this page

ALNWICK Northumberland   13F3

♦♦♦ Bondgate House
20 Bondgate Without, Alnwick NE66 1PN
📞 01665-602025 Fax 01665-602025
8 bedrs, 5 ensuite, 1 🐾 TV P 8 ⊕ Rest Resid SB £23-£26 DB £43-£45 HB £150.50-£157.50 D £13 CC MC Visa JCB

ALTRINCHAM Cheshire   10C4

♦♦♦ Old Packet House
Navigation Road, Broadheath, Altrincham WA14 1LW
📞 0161-929 1331 Fax 0161-929 1331

4 bedrs, all ensuite, TCF TV P 12 ⊕ SB £47.50 DB £57.50-£67.50 D £14 CC MC Visa

Oasis
46 Barrington Road, Altrincham WA14 1HN
📞 0161-928 4523 Fax 0161-928 1055

Ensuite bedrooms with tea/coffee making facilities, ideally located for Manchester Airport, Cheshire, Altrincham town centre. Metro-link to Manchester. Local motorways (M6, M56, M60) are easily accessible.
33 bedrs, 32 ensuite, 2 🐾 TCF TV P 30 ♨ 150 ⊕ SB £30-£35 DB £40-£47.50 CC MC Visa

---

Marine House
Licensed
Private Hotel

A listed stone building of considerable charm, stands on the edge of the village golf links, faces the sea and overlooks a stretch of coastline of rugged natural beauty interspersed with long sweeping sandy beaches.
Pets are welcome.
Terraced garden with views over golf links and sea.

Alnmouth, Northumberland NE66 2RW
Tel: Alnmouth (01665) 830349

Arnside

AMBLESIDE Cumbria   10B2

♦♦♦♦♦ Rowanfield Country House
Little Gem
Warm Welcome, Sparkling Diamond
Kirkstone Road, Ambleside LA22 9ET
☎ 015394-33686 Fax 015394-31569
Closed mid Nov-Feb excl Xmas/New Year
7 bedrs, all ensuite, TCF TV ☒ P 8 No children under 8 SB £50-£60 DB £60-£80 HB £350-£420 D £22 CC MC Visa

♦♦♦♦ Borrans Park
Warm Welcome, Sparkling Diamond
Borrans Road, Ambleside LA22 0EN
☎ 015394-33454 Fax 015394-33003
12 bedrs, all ensuite, TCF TV ☒ P 15 No children under 7 ⊕ Rest Resid SB £60 DB £70-£90 HB £280-£375 D £20 CC MC Visa JCB ♿

♦♦♦♦ Elder Grove
Sparkling Diamond
Lake Road, Ambleside LA22 0DB
☎ 015394-32504 Fax 015394-32504
Closed Dec-Jan

Enjoy quality accommodation and service in our Victorian house, 10 pretty bedrooms with private bathrooms, relaxing bar and lounge, hearty Cumbrian breakfast, car park, no-smoking.
10 bedrs, all ensuite, TCF TV ☒ ⊢ P 9 ⊕ Rest Resid SB £23-£30 DB £46-£64 HB £280-£330 D £18 CC MC Visa JCB

♦♦♦ Lyndhurst
Wansfell Road, Ambleside LA22 0EG
☎ 01539-432421 Fax 01539-432421
8 bedrs, all ensuite, TCF TV P 8 ⊕ Resid SB £30-£50 DB £39-£45 HB £210-£245 D £14

Lyndale Awaiting Inspection
Lake Road, Ambleside LA22 0DN
☎ 01539-434244
Closed Christmas
6 bedrs, 2 ensuite, 2 ⇌ TCF TV ☒ SB £17.50-£18.50 DB £35-£45

AMPLEFORTH North Yorkshire   11D2

♦♦♦♦♦ Shallowdale House
Warm Welcome, Sparkling Diamond
West End, Ampleforth, York YO62 4DY
☎ 01439-788325 Fax 01439-788885
Closed Christmas-New Year

An elegant modern country house, stunningly situated on the southern edge of the North York Moors National Park, with wonderful views from every room. Outstanding food.
3 bedrs, all ensuite, TCF TV ☒ P 3 No children under 12 ⊕ Resid SB £32.50-£40 DB £65-£80 HB £31-£350 D £20 CC MC Visa

ARNSIDE Cumbria   10B3

♦♦♦♦ Willowfield
Sparkling Diamond
The Promenade, Arnside LA5 0AD
☎ 01524-761354
E-mail kerr@willowfield.netl.co.uk
10 bedrs, 7 ensuite, 2 ⇌ TCF TV ☒ ⊢ P 8 ⊕ Resid SB £20-£26 DB £48-£52 HB £220-£248 D £12.50
CC MC Visa JCB

Arundel

| ARUNDEL West Sussex | 4C4 |

♦♦♦♦ Mill House
Sparkling Diamond
16 Chichester Road, Arundel BN18 0AD
☎ 01903-882677 Fax 01903-884154

Refurbished bar and restaurant, completed 1998, offer memorabilia from yester-year. All 24 bedrooms ensuite with facilities. Function rooms can accommodate up to 150 people.
24 bedrs, all ensuite, TCF TV ★ P 100 ⌗ 140 ⌑
SB £44.50 DB £62.99 CC MC Visa Amex ⌑

| ASHBOURNE Derbyshire | 7F1 |

♦♦♦♦ Lichfield
Sparkling Diamond
Bridgeview, Mayfield, Ashbourne DE6 2HN
☎ 01335-344422 Fax 01335-344422
Closed 25-26 Dec

A family run, non-smoking Georgian guest house, standing in two acres of grounds on the Derbyshire/Staffordshire border and overlooking the River Dove and valleys beyond.
3 bedrs, all ensuite, TCF TV ⌑ P 10 DB £40-£45

| ASHBURTON Devon | 3D3 |

♦♦♦♦ Gages Mill
Buckfastleigh Road, Ashburton TQ13 7JW
☎ 01364-652391 Fax 01364-652391
E-mail gagesmill@aol.com
Closed Dec-Feb

Carefully converted former 14th century woollen mill, set in 1¼ acres on the edge of Dartmoor National Park. Delightful ensuite rooms, all with country views; home cooked food to a very high standard, licensed, ample parking.
8 bedrs, 7 ensuite, 1 ⌑ TCF TV P 8 No children under 12 ⌑ Rest Resid SB £24-£25.50 DB £48-£51 HB £231-£238 D £13

CROFT HOTEL

Country House located on A28 between Ashford and Canterbury.
An independent and well established family run hotel close to the M2 and M20.
28 comfortable ensuite bedrooms with Restaurant and Bar. A 'home away from home' atmosphere for business or pleasure, for business in Ashford or touring in Kent.
1 mile from Ashford International Station your gateway to and from Europe.

KENNINGTON, ASHFORD, KENT TN25 4DU
Tel: 01233 622140 Fax: 01233 635271

Barnstaple 23

| ASHFORD Kent | 5E3 |

♦♦♦ Croft
Canterbury Road, Ashford TN25 4DU
☎ 01233-622140 **Fax** 01233-635271
28 bedrs, all ensuite, TCF TV ⊁ P 30 ⊞ 12 ⊕ Resid
SB £42-£47 **DB** £52-£62 **D** £11 **CC** MC Visa Amex JCB
See advert on opposite page

| ASHOVER Derbyshire | 8A2 |

♦♦♦♦ Old School Farm
Sparkling Diamond
Uppertown, Ashover S45 0JF
☎ 01246-590813
4 bedrs, 2 ensuite, 1 ⇌ TCF TV P 10 **SB** £22 **DB** £44
HB £154 **D** £8

| ASHTON-UNDER-LYNE Lancashire | 10C4 |

Welbeck House Awaiting Inspection
324 Katharine Street, Ashton-under-Lyne OL6 7BD
☎ 0161-344 0751 **Fax** 0161-343 4278
8 bedrs, all ensuite, TCF TV ⊁ P 20 ⊕ Resid **SB** £33
DB £45 **D** £6.75 **CC** MC Visa DC

| AYLESBURY Buckinghamshire | 4C2 |

♦♦♦ B and B at 103
103 London Road, Aston Clinton, Aylesbury HP22 5LD
☎ 01296-631313 **Fax** 01296-631616
3 bedrs, 1 ensuite, 1 ⇌ TCF TV ⊠ P 6 No children under 7 **CC** MC Visa JCB

| BAINBRIDGE North Yorkshire | 10C2 |

♦♦♦ Riverdale House
Bainbridge DL8 3EW
☎ 01969-650311
Closed Nov-Jan

Beautiful situation in a peaceful village in the heart of Wensleydale. Enjoy a relaxing break in comfortable ensuite rooms and excellent food imaginatively cooked using all fresh ingredients.
12 bedrs, 11 ensuite, 1 ⇌ TCF TV P 4 ⊞ 30 ⊕ Rest Resid

| BANBURY Oxfordshire | 4B1 |

♦♦♦ Easington House
50 Oxford Road, Banbury OX16 9AN
☎ 01295-270181 **Fax** 01295-269527
E-mail easington@aol.com
12 bedrs, all ensuite, TCF TV ⊁ P 27 ⊞ 35 ⊕ Resid
SB £50-£55 **DB** £70-£75 **D** £12 **CC** MC Visa Amex DC

♦♦♦ La Madonette Country Guest House
North Newington, Banbury OX15 6AA
☎ 01295-730212 **Fax** 01295-730363
E-mail lamadonett@aol.com

Peacefully situated 17th century mill house, set in rural surroundings. Well located for the Cotswolds, Stratford-upon-Avon, Oxford and Blenheim. Gardens and swimming pool. Licensed.
5 bedrs, all ensuite, TCF TV P 20 ⊞ 15 ⊕ **SB** £40-£45
DB £58-£85 **CC** MC Visa DC JCB ⇌

| BARNSTAPLE Devon | 2C2 |

♦♦♦ Yeo Dale
Pilton Bridge, Barnstaple EX31 1PG
☎ 01271-42954 **Fax** 01271-42954
10 bedrs, 6 ensuite, 2 ⇌ TCF TV ⊕ Resid **SB** £20-£26.50 **DB** £39-£49 **CC** MC Visa

Home Park Farm Awaiting Inspection
Lower Blakewell, Muddiford,
Barnstaple EX31 4ET
☎ 01271-342955 **Fax** 01271-342955
Closed Christmas
3 bedrs, all ensuite, TCF TV ⊠ P 3 **SB** £20 **DB** £30-£40
HB £150-£195 **D** £8.50

ENGLAND

24 Basildon

BASILDON Essex   5D2

Campanile Basildon Lodge
A127 Southend Arterial Road, Pipps Hill, Basildon
SS14 3AE
☎ 01268-530810 Fax 01268-286710
98 bedrs, all ensuite, TCF TV ⊶ P 98 ⋕ 20 ⊞ Rest
Resid SB £42.50 DB £47 D £10.95 CC MC Visa Amex
DC &

BASSENTHWAITE Cumbria   10A1

♦♦♦♦ Lakeside
Bassenthwaite Lake, Cockermouth CA13 9YD
☎ 017687-76358 Fax 017687-76358
8 bedrs, 7 ensuite, 1 ⇌ TCF TV ⊠ P 10 No children
under 10 ⊞ Resid SB £21-£26 DB £46-£52

BATH Somerset   3F1

♦♦♦♦♦ Cheriton House
Warm Welcome, Sparkling Diamond
9 Upper Oldfield Park, Bath BA2 3JX
☎ 01225-429862 Fax 01225-428403
9 bedrs, all ensuite, TCF TV P 9 ⋕ 12 No children
under 12 SB £42-£48 DB £58-£74 CC MC Visa Amex
DC JCB
See advert on opposite page

♦♦♦♦♦ County
Warm Welcome, Sparkling Diamond
18/19 Pulteney Road, Bath BA2 4EZ
☎ 01225-425003 Fax 01225-466493
E-mail @county-hotel.co.uk
Closed 24 Dec-15 Jan
22 bedrs, all ensuite, TCF TV ⊠ P 50 No children
under 16 ⊞ ⊞ Club SB £76 DB £96-£180 D £25
CC MC Visa Amex DC

♦♦♦♦♦ Dorian House
Warm Welcome, Sparkling Diamond
1 Upper Oldfield Park, Bath BA2 3JX
☎ 01225-426336 Fax 01225-444699
E-mail dorian.house@which.net
8 bedrs, all ensuite, TCF TV P 8 ⊞ Resid SB £40-£47
DB £55-£80 CC MC Visa Amex JCB
See advert on opposite page

♦♦♦♦♦ Oldfields
Warm Welcome, Sparkling Diamond
102 Wells Road, Bath BA2 3AL
☎ 01225-317984 Fax 01225-444471
Closed Christmas, Jan 2-31

Elegant and traditional B&B in Victorian mansion
with views. English and wholefood breakfasts
available. Ample parking in own grounds. Ten
minutes walk to town centre.
14 bedrs, all ensuite, TCF TV ⊠ P 12 SB £48-£60
DB £55-£80 CC MC Visa Amex JCB &
See advert on next page

♦♦♦♦♦ Siena
Sparkling Diamond
24-25 Pulteney Road, Bath BA2 4EZ
☎ 01225-425495 Fax 01225-469029
E-mail siena.hotel@dial.pipex.com
Closed Christmas
15 bedrs, all ensuite, TCF TV ⊶ P 15 ⊞ SB £43-£58
DB £70-£95 CC MC Visa Amex DC JCB &
See advert on opposite page

♦♦♦♦ Ashley Villa
Warm Welcome, Sparkling Diamond
26 Newbridge Road, Bath BA1 3JZ
☎ 01225-421683 Fax 01225-313604

Comfortably furnished licensed hotel with relaxing,
informal atmosphere. Situated close to the city
centre, all bedrooms have ensuite facilities, colour
television, direct dial telephone, tea and coffee
making facilities.
14 bedrs, all ensuite, TCF TV P 10 ⊞ Resid SB £59
DB £59-£79 CC MC Visa ⋛
See advert on next page

Bath 25

ENGLAND

Cheriton House

Situated on the Southern slope of Bath with splendid views of the city, we have carefully restored and redecorated the house and our rooms are individually and attractively furnished.
All of our bedrooms have private bathrooms (en-suite) and offer standard, four poster or super king size beds. Colour TV and hot drink facilities are available in all rooms.
We offer a choice of delicious breakfasts including traditional English and a warm welcome is extended to all of our guests.
Guests are welcome to enjoy our beautiful peaceful garden.
RAC Highly Acclaimed.

**9 UPPER OLDFIELD PARK, BATH, AVON BA2 3JX
Tel: 01225 429862 Fax: 01225 428403
Email: cheriton@which.net**

THE SIENA HOTEL
Comfort Merit Award

An elegant Victorian Villa within a few minutes level walk of the City Centre. Set in landscaped gardens and overlooking Bath's medieval Abbey the Siena Hotel offers quality accommodation, excellent home cuisine, licensed bar, use of gardens and private car park.

**24-25 Pulteney Road
Bath BA2 4EX
Tel: 01225 425495 Fax: 01225 469029**

DORIAN HOUSE
BATH
✦ ✦ ✦ ✦ ✦

Enter an atmosphere of period charm in Dorian House. There is a small bar and cosy lounge where you can read a newspaper, or plan an evening meal using our book of menus collected from the excellent restaurants in town. Wine and champagne is available, also in half bottles.

Individually designed bedrooms. En-suite bathrooms, Egyptian cotton sheets, TV, tea/coffee, direct-dial telephone and hairdryer. Free parking. Ten minute walk into town.

NUMBER ONE, UPPER OLDFIELD PARK, BATH BA2 3JX
Telephone: 01225 426 336   Fax: 01225 444 699
E-mail <dorian.house@which.net>

Oldfields Hotel

A large, elegant 1870 Victorian house set in gardens overlooking the hills of Bath. Situated 10 minutes walk from the city centre with its own private car park. Individually decorated bedrooms, with a choice of four-poster and canopied beds, ensure your comfort, with ensuite facilities, CTV, d/d telephone, radio alarm, hairdryer, toiletries and hospitality tray. Traditional English a la carte and wholefood breakfast included.

102 WELLS ROAD, BATH, AVON BA2 3AL
Tel: (01225) 317984   Fax: (01225) 444471

Ashley Villa Hotel, Bath

26 Newbridge Road, Bath BA1 3JZ
Telephone: (01225) 421683 & 428887 Fax: (01225) 313604

Comfortably furnished licensed hotel with relaxing informal atmosphere, situated close to the city centre. All 14 well appointed bedrooms have ensuite facilities, colour television, direct dial telephone, tea and coffee making. Most credit cards welcome.

This small friendly hotel has recently been refurbished throughout. It has an outdoor swimming pool with garden patio and car park.
You can be sure of a warm welcome from the resident owners.
Rod and Alex Kitcher, M.H.C.I.M.A.

RAC
HIGHLY
ACCLAIMED

Bath 27

♦♦♦♦ Brompton House
Sparkling Diamond
St Johns Road, Bath BA2 6PT
📞 01225-420972 Fax 01225-420505
E-mail bromptonhouse@compuserve.com
Closed Christmas-New Year
16 bedrs, all ensuite, TCF TV P 18 No children under 15 Resid SB £32-£65 DB £55-£95 CC MC Visa Amex JCB
See advert on this page

♦♦♦♦ Burghope Manor
Winsley, Bradford-on-Avon, Bath BA15 2LA
📞 01225-723557 Fax 01225-723113
Closed Christmas-New Year

A historic 13th century country home set in beautiful countryside on the edge of the village of Winsley. Steeped in history, first and foremost a living family home, carefully modernised. A wealth of historical features complement present day comforts.
8 bedrs, all ensuite, TCF TV P 20 ⋕ 20 No children under 10 SB £60-£70 DB £70-£85 D £35 CC MC Visa Amex JCB

♦♦♦♦ Gainsborough
Sparkling Diamond
Weston Lane, Bath BA1 4AB
📞 01225-311380 Fax 01225-447411
E-mail gainsborough_hotel@compuserve.com
Closed 24 Dec-3 Jan
17 bedrs, all ensuite, TCF TV P 17 ⋕ 12 No children under 5 Rest Resid SB £34-£52 DB £50-£90 CC MC Visa Amex
See advert on next page

♦♦♦♦ Haute Combe
Sparkling Diamond
174-176 Newbridge Road, Bath BA1 3LE
📞 01225-420061 Fax 01225-446077
E-mail enquiries@hautecombe.com

Brompton House
St John's Road, Bath BA2 6PT
Tel: 01225 420972 Fax: 01225 420505
email: bromptonhouse@btinternet.com
website: www.bromptonhouse.co.uk

Charming Georgian country style house (former Rectory 1777). Family owned and run. Car Park and beautiful secluded gardens. 6 minutes level walk to main historic sights and restaurants. 16 tastefully furnished and fully equipped en-suite bedrooms. Delicious choice of breakfasts. No Smoking.

RAC ♦♦♦♦ *Sparkling Diamond Award*

Resident proprietors
David, Sue, Belinda & Tim Selby.

Old-style charm and warm hospitality combine with modern requirements of today's discerning guest. Well-appointed rooms, Sky TV, bar and restaurant, large private car park. Special winter rates. Families £12 per extra person.
12 bedrs, all ensuite, TCF TV ⊁ P 11 Rest Resid SB £42-£52 DB £52-£79 D £15 CC MC Visa Amex DC JCB ♿

♦♦♦♦ Highways House
143 Wells Road, Bath BA2 3AL
📞 01225-421238 Fax 01225-481169
E-mail hightways@toscar.clara.co.uk
Closed Christmas (4-days only)
7 bedrs, 6 ensuite, TCF TV P 8 SB £38-£55 DB £58-£70 CC MC Visa Amex

ENGLAND

28 Bath

The Gainsborough Hotel
BATH

RAC ♦♦♦♦ Sparkling Diamond Award

A spacious comfortable country house hotel in own attractive grounds near the Botanical gardens, Municipal golf course and park. The Abbey, Roman Baths and Pump Room are all within walking distance via the park, so most guests leave their cars and walk into town.

We provide a relaxing, friendly and informal atmosphere for our guests' stay. All of our tastefully furnished bedrooms are ensuite with colour TV, Satellite TV, tea/coffee facilities, telephones, hairdryers etc. The hotel has a small friendly bar, two sun terraces and our own large private car park. A warm welcome awaits.

WESTON LANE, BATH, AVON BA1 4AB
Tel: (01225) 311380 Fax: (01225) 447411
Email: gainsborough-hotel@compuserve.com
Website: www.gainsboroughhotel.co.uk

♦♦♦ Laura Place
Sparkling Diamond
3 Laura Place, Great Pulteney Street, Bath BA2 4BH
☎ 01225-463815 Fax 01225-310222
Closed 22 Dec-28 Feb

A Georgian town house centrally situated overlooking a fountain. Tastefully furnished with antiques and works of art. Brass and fourposter beds available. Rooms on four floors. Car parking. No smoking.
8 bedrs, 7 ensuite, 1 ⇌ TCF TV ☒ P 8 No children under 8 SB £50-£55 DB £66-£90 CC MC Visa Amex

♦♦♦ Oakleigh House
Sparkling Diamond
19 Upper Oldfield Park, Bath BA2 3JX
☎ 01225-315698 Fax 01225-448223
E-mail oakleigh@which.net

Quietly situated Victorian home only 10 minutes walk from the city centre, with splendid views over Georgian Bath. All luxury rooms ensuite. Tempting choice of breakfasts.
4 bedrs, all ensuite, TCF TV P 4 No children under 18
SB £40-£50 DB £60-£68 CC MC Visa Amex

Bath

♦♦♦♦ Sydney Gardens
Sydney Road, Bath BA2 6NT
☎ 01225-464818 Fax 01225-484347
Closed 24 Dec-1 Feb

In a unique parkland setting, Sydney Gardens Hotel offers superb bed and breakfast accommodation, with fine traditional English breakfast. A short stroll from the city centre, with delightful canal walks adjacent.
6 bedrs, all ensuite, TCF TV ✉ ✈ P 6 No children under 5 SB £49-£59 DB £59-£75 CC MC Visa Amex

♦♦♦♦ Villa Magdala
Warm Welcome, Sparkling Diamond
Henrietta Road, Bath BA2 6LX
☎ 01225-466329 Fax 01225-483207
E-mail villa@btinternet.com

Elegant town house hotel enjoying a peaceful location opposite Henrietta Park and with ample parking in own grounds. Just five minutes level walk to city centre.
18 bedrs, all ensuite, TCF TV ✉ P 18 No children under 7 SB £60-£75 DB £80-£110 CC MC Visa Amex

♦♦♦♦ Wentworth House
Sparkling Diamond
106 Bloomfield Road, Bath BA2 2AP
☎ 01225-339193 Fax 01225-310460
E-mail wentworthhouse@dial.pipex.com
Closed Christmas-New Year
18 bedrs, 17 ensuite, 1 ☞ TCF TV P 19 No children under 5 ☒ Resid SB £38-£60 DB £60-£95 CC MC Visa Amex ⚡
See advert on this page

♦♦♦ Bailbrook Lodge
35-37 London Road West, Bath BA1 7HZ
☎ 01225-859090 Fax 01225-852299
E-mail bailbrooklodge.demon.co.uk
Closed Christmas

A splendid Georgian house featuring 12 elegant bedrooms (some fourposters). The lounge and dining room overlook the lawns and patio. Personal service is guaranteed in this conveniently located hotel.
12 bedrs, all ensuite, TCF TV P 14 ♯♯♯ 10 ☒ SB £38-£50 DB £58-£75 HB £297.50-£367.50 D £13.95 CC MC Visa Amex DC

WENTWORTH HOUSE
106 Bloomfield Road, Bath BA2 2AP
Tel: (01225) 339193 Fax: (01225) 310460
e.mail: wentworthhouse@dial.pipex.com
web page: http://dspace.dial.pipex.com/wentworthhouse/

Built as a family home in 1887 Wentworth House is an imposing Victorian Mansion enjoying a peaceful location in secluded gardens with stunning views and is within walking distance of Bath centre. The tastefully decorated ensuite rooms, some with 4 poster beds offer colour TV, alarm, telephones, hairdryers and tea/coffee. Delicious breakfasts. Outdoor swimming pool.

LARGE FREE CAR PARK.
PRICES PER ROOM, PER NIGHT £60 TO £100

ENGLAND

30 Bath

♦♦♦ Lamp Post Villa
3 Crescent Gardens, Bath BA1 2NA
☎ 01225-331221 Fax 01225-426783
Closed Christmas
Situated close to Victoria Park in the city centre, this Edwardian house is 10 minutes from the Abbey and Roman Baths, close to the Royal Crescent and 5 minutes from the Theatre Royal.
4 bedrs, all ensuite, TCF TV ⌨ ⚹ P 4 SB £35-£40
DB £40-£55 CC MC Visa JCB

♦♦♦ Orchard Lodge
Warminster Road, Bathampton, Bath BA2 6XG
☎ 01225-466115 Fax 01225-446050
E-mail orchardlo@aol.com.uk

A modern purpose-built hotel, situated 1½ miles from Bath city centre, enjoying panoramic views of the Avon Valley.
14 bedrs, all ensuite, TCF TV ⚹ P 14 ⌘ 30 SB £39-£48
DB £49-£65 CC MC Visa

Edgar Awaiting Inspection
64 Great Pulteney Street, Bath BA2 4DN
☎ 01225-420619 Fax 01225-466916
E-mail snoo2@netgates.co.uk
Closed Nov-Feb
16 bedrs, all ensuite, CC MC Visa Amex

Paradise House
88 Holloway, Bath BA2 4PX
☎ 01225-317723 Fax 01225-482005
E-mail paradise@apsleyhouse.easynet.co.uk
Closed Christmas
8 bedrs, all ensuite, TCF TV P 6 CC MC Visa Amex
See advert on this page

Don't forget to mention the guide
When booking direct, please remember to tell the hotel that you chose it from RAC Inspected Guest Accommodation 2000

PARADISE HOUSE
BATH

Paradise House is a listed Georgian (1735) Bath stone house perfectly situated in a quiet cul-de-sac, only five minutes' walk from the centre of Bath. The rear-facing rooms and beautiful gardens command the most magnificent views of the city and surrounding countryside. Long established and highly recommended. Please contact us for fully illustrated brochure.

86/88 HOLLOWAY, BATH BA2 4PX
Tel: 01225 317723 Fax: 01225 482005
Email: paradise@apsleyhouse.easynet.co.uk
www.gratoon.co.uk/paradise

BATTLE East Sussex   5E4

♦♦♦ Little Hemingfold Hotel
Telham, Battle TN33 0TT
☎ 01424-774338 Fax 01424-775351
Closed 5 Jan-12 Feb

Part 17th century hotel, set in 40 acres of farm and woodland, with 2 acre trout lake, boat and grass tennis court. Renowned cuisine in relaxed informal atmosphere.
12 bedrs, all ensuite, TCF TV ⚹ P 50 ⌘ 20 ⌂ Rest
SB £38-£69 DB £76-£88 HB £350-£364 D £22.50
CC MC Visa Amex DC JCB

Beverley 31

♦♦ Moonshill Farm
The Green, Moons Hill, Ninefield, Battle TN33 9JL
☎ 01424-892645 Fax 01424-892645
Closed Dec

In the heart of '1066 Country'. Comfortable rooms, three ensuite, central heating, electric heaters, hospitality tray, TV lounge, large car park. Every comfort in this safe, quiet and peaceful home.
3 bedrs, all ensuite, TCF TV ⌇ P 6 SB £20-£25 DB £35-£40

BEDALE North Yorkshire	11D2

♦♦♦♦♦ Elmfield Country House
Sparkling Diamond
Arrathorne, Bedale DL8 1NE
☎ 01677-450558 Fax 01677-450557
9 bedrs, all ensuite, TCF TV P 25 ⌇ 20 ⌇ Resid
SB £35 DB £50-£55 HB £259-£287 D £12 CC MC Visa
⌇ ⌇ ⌇

BELPER Derbyshire	7F1

♦♦♦♦ Shottle Hall
Shottle, Belper DE56 2EB
☎ 01773-550203 Fax 01773-550276
Closed Nov-Christmas
10 bedrs, 6 ensuite, 2 ⌇ TCF TV P 30 ⌇ 10 ⌇ Rest Resid SB £28-£37 DB £50-£68 D £14 ⌇

BEVERLEY East Yorkshire	11E3

♦♦♦ Eastgate
Sparkling Diamond
7 Eastgate, Beverley HU17 0DR
☎ 01482-868464 Fax 01482-871899

Family run Victorian town house between the Minster and the pedestrianised town centre.
17 bedrs, 7 ensuite, 3 ⌇ TCF TV ⌇ SB £21-£34 DB £34-£48
See advert on this page

Rudstone Walk Farm Awaiting Inspection
South Cave, Brough HU15 2AH
☎ 01430-422230 Fax 01430-424552
E-mail office@rudstone-walk.co.uk
14 bedrs, all ensuite, TCF TV ⌇ P 60 ⌇ 50 ⌇ Resid
SB £45 DB £59 D £17 CC MC Visa Amex DC ⌇

Eastgate GUEST HOUSE

Situated in the centre of Beverley.
Beverley Minster, Museum of Army Transport and railway station all close by.

All rooms have colour TV, central heating, wash basins. Tea and coffee making facilities are also available. En suite rooms available.

7 Eastgate, Beverley, East Yorkshire HU17 0DR
Tel: 01482 868464   Fax: 01482 871899

Bexhill-on-Sea

BEXHILL-ON-SEA East Sussex   5E4

♦♦♦ Park Lodge
16 Egerton Road, Bexhill-on-Sea TN39 3HH
📞 01424-216547 Fax 01424-217460

Family run, informal hotel with character. Located in a quiet area of Bexhill but near shops, park and seafront. Rooms are very comfortable with ensuite, CTV, telephone and tea making.
10 bedrs, 8 ensuite, 2 ⌂ 1 ⇌ TCF TV P 4 ⊞ Resid
SB £22-£28 DB £45-£49 HB £175-£195 D £8 CC MC Visa Amex DC

BICKLEY Kent   5D2

♦♦♦ Glendevon House
80 Southborough Road, Bickley BR1 2EN
📞 0181-467 2183
11 bedrs, all ensuite, TCF TV P 7 No children under 2
SB £34-£39.50 DB £49.50 D £10 CC MC Visa

BIDEFORD Devon   2C2

♦♦♦♦ Pines at Eastleigh ☆
Warm Welcome, Sparkling Diamond
Eastleigh, Bideford EX39 4PA
📞 01271-860561 Fax 01271-861248
E-mail barry@barpines.demon.co.uk
6 bedrs, all ensuite, TCF TV ⊠ ⇌ P 20 ⊞ 20 ⊞ Rest
Resid SB £29-£40 DB £58-£80 HB £249-£309 D £15
CC MC Visa ♿

Facilities for the disabled

Hotels do their best to cater for disabled visitors. However, it is advisable to contact the hotel direct to ensure it can provide a particular requirement.

Anchorage Awaiting Inspection
The Quay, Bideford, Instow EX39 4HX
📞 01271-860655 Fax 01271-860767
15 bedrs, all ensuite, TCF TV ⇌ P 24 ⊞ SB £28 DB £56
D £17.50 CC MC Visa ♿

BINGLEY West Yorkshire   10C3

Five Rise Locks Awaiting Inspection
Beck Lane, Bingley BD16 4DD
📞 01274-565296 Fax 01274-568828
Closed New Year
9 bedrs, all ensuite, TCF TV ⇌ P 15 ⊞ 20 ⊞ Rest
Resid SB £45-£50 DB £50-£60 D £12.50 CC MC Visa JCB ⊠ ♿

BIRMINGHAM West Midlands   7F3

♦♦♦♦ Bridge House
Sparkling Diamond
49 Sherbourne Road, Acocks Green, Birmingham B27 6DX
📞 0121-706 5900 Fax 0121-624 5900
E-mail @bridgehousehotel.co.uk
Closed Christmas
50 bedrs, all ensuite, TCF TV P 60 ⊞ 150 ⊞ Rest
Resid SB £47-£50 DB £60-£65 CC MC Visa Amex DC JCB ⊠ ♿

♦♦♦ Central
1637 Coventry Road, South Yardley, Birmingham B26 1DD
📞 0121-706 7757 Fax 0121-706 7757
E-mail mmou826384@aol.com

Well established, family run guest house. Close to NEC, airport and city centre. All rooms ensuite with coffee/tea making facilities. Full English breakfast. Warm friendly atmosphere, home from home.
5 bedrs, all ensuite, TCF TV ⇌ P 4 SB £18.50-£22
DB £35-£40

Birmingham 33

♦♦♦♦ Chamberlain
Alcester Road, Birmingham B12 0TJ
☎ 0121-627 0627 Fax 0121-627 0628
E-mail info@chamberlain.co.uk

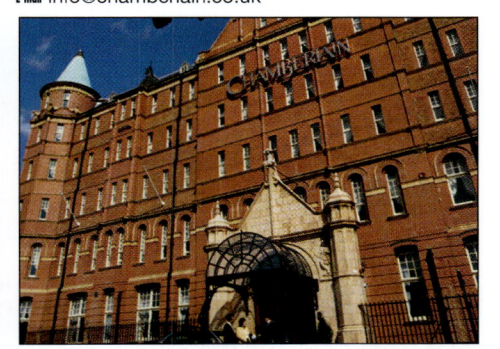

An imposing red brick Victorian Listed building of great character and style. Quality rooms designed for comfort and excellent facilities, including restaurant, bar, 24-hour patrolled parking and conference and meeting rooms. Outstanding value.
250 bedrs, all ensuite, TCF TV 🖥 P 200 ⋕ 400 SB £35 DB £40 D £10 CC MC Visa Amex DC ⚿

♦♦♦ Lyndhurst
135 Kingsbury Road, Erdington,
Birmingham B24 8QT
☎ 0121-373 5695 Fax 0121-373 5697
E-mail lyndhurst@fsbdial.co.uk
Closed Christmas
14 bedrs, 13 ensuite, 1 ⇌ TCF TV P 15 ⋕ 30 ⏃ Rest Resid SB £35-£42 DB £50-£56 HB £275-£295 D £12 CC MC Visa Amex DC JCB

Fairview Awaiting Inspection
1639 Coventry Road, South Yardley,
Birmingham B26 1DD
☎ 0121-708 2712 Fax 0121-708 2712

Friendly, family run guesthouse, situated near to the National Exhibition Centre, Birmingham Airport, Birmingham International Railway Station and within easy reach of city centre and Solihull. All rooms ensuite, with TV and tea/coffee making facilities.
4 bedrs, all ensuite, TCF TV ⇌ P 5 DB £40

Greswolde Park Awaiting Inspection
980 Warwick Road, Acocks Green, Birmingham
B27 6QG
☎ 0121-706 4068 Fax 0121-706 0649
11 bedrs, 10 ensuite, 1 ⌕ TCF TV ⇌ P 9 ⋕ 90 ⏃ Rest Resid SB £35 DB £44 D £6.30 CC MC Visa

Heath Lodge Awaiting Inspection
117 Coleshill Road, Marston Green, Birmingham
B37 7HT
☎ 0121-779 2218 Fax 0121-779 2218
E-mail reception@heathlodgehotel.freeserve.co.uk

Friendly family run hotel, less than 2 miles from the NEC Arena and Birmingham Airport. Good food, cosy bar and a comfortable lounge. We aim to please.
17 bedrs, all ensuite, TCF TV ⇌ P 20 ⋕ 16 ⏃ Rest Resid SB £40-£45 DB £54-£59 CC MC Visa Amex

Rollason Wood Awaiting Inspection
Wood End Road, Erdington, Birmingham B24 8BJ
☎ 0121-373 1230 Fax 0121-382 2578

Friendly family run hotel with 35 bedrooms. Choose from economy, with shower, or fully ensuite. Licensed bar and a la carte restaurant. Weekend and weekly reductions.
35 bedrs, 11 ensuite, 5 ⌕ 6 ⇌ TCF TV ⇌ P 40 ⏃ Resid SB £18-£36 DB £32-£50 D £8 CC MC Visa Amex DC

ENGLAND

34 Birmingham

Tri-Star Awaiting Inspection
Coventry Road, Elmdon, Birmingham B26 3QR
0121-782 1010 Fax 0121-782 6131

This licensed hotel is ideally situated on the A45, 1½ miles from NEC, airport and international station and 2 miles to jn 6 M42. A modern hotel with homely atmosphere.
15 bedrs, 11 ensuite, P 25 ₤ CC MC Visa Amex

Campanile Birmingham Lodge
Aston Lock South, Chester Street,
Birmingham B6 4BE
0121-359 3330 Fax 0121-359 1223
111 bedrs, all ensuite, TCF TV ⁂ ₤ CC MC Visa Amex DC ♿

BISHOP AUCKLAND Co. Durham 11D1

♦♦♦♦ Greenhead Country House
Sparkling Diamond
Fir Tree, Bishop Auckland DL15 8BL
01388-763143 Fax 01388-763143

A very well operated, squeaky clean, most comfortable, well sited and quiet hotel of distinction. Restricted to resident guests only. Located ten miles from Durham.
7 bedrs, all ensuite, TCF TV P 10 No children under 14 ₤ Resid SB £35-£40 DB £50-£55 CC MC Visa

BISHOP'S CASTLE Shropshire 7D3

♦♦♦ Boars Head
Church Street, Bishop's Castle SY9 5AE
01588-638521 Fax 01588-630126
E-mail grantboars@aol.com
4 bedrs, all ensuite, TCF TV ⋈ P 20 ₤ CC MC Visa Amex DC JCB ♿

BISHOP'S STORTFORD Hertfordshire 5D1

♦♦♦♦ Cottage
71 Birchanger Lane, Birchanger, Bishop's Stortford CM23 5QA
01279-812349 Fax 01279-815045
Closed Christmas & New Year

A 17th century listed property in a quiet village setting, yet near the M11 (jn 8) and Stansted Airport. Panelled reception rooms with wood burning stove and ensuite guest rooms. Conservatory breakfast room overlooks large mature garden.
15 bedrs, 13 ensuite, 1 ⇌ TCF TV ⊠ P 15 ₤ Resid
SB £35-£45 DB £55-£60 CC MC Visa JCB

BLACKPOOL Lancashire 10B3

♦♦♦♦♦ Old Coach House ⇋
Sparkling Diamond
50 Dean Street, Blackpool FY4 1BP
01253-349195 Fax 01253-344330
E-mail blackpool@theoldcoachhouse.freeserve.co.uk
7 bedrs, all ensuite, TCF TV P 14 ⋕ 36 ₤ Resid
SB £25-£35 DB £50-£65 HB £168.63-£328.65 D £8.95
CC MC Visa Amex

♦♦♦♦ Burlees
Sparkling Diamond
40 Knowle Avenue, North Shore,
Blackpool FY2 9TQ
01253-354535 Fax 01253-354535
E-mail burleeshotel@btinternet.com
Closed Nov-Mar

Blackpool

Attractive, comfortable, small hotel in peaceful North Shore. Highly recommended food and friendly atmosphere. Parking. Easy access to Blackpool's attractions.
9 bedrs, all ensuite, TCF TV P 5 ⊕ Resid SB £23.50-£26 DB £47-£94 HB £190-£221 D £9 CC MC Visa

♦♦♦ Garville
Sparkling Diamond
3 Beaufort Avenue, North Shore, Blackpool FY2 9HQ
☎ 01253-351004 Fax 01253-351004
Closed Jan
7 bedrs, all ensuite, TCF TV P 5 No children under 3 SB £18-£22 DB £32-£44

♦♦♦ Sunny Cliff
98 Queens Promenade, Blackpool FY2 9NS
☎ 01253-351155
Closed Nov-Easter

Ample parking. Quiet area overlooking sea, half a mile along Queens Promenade with attractive ensuite rooms, pleasant lounges, lovely homemade soups and puddings etc.
9 bedrs, all ensuite, TCF TV ⚰ P 6 ⊕ Resid SB £18-£22 DB £36-£44 HB £140-£155 D £7

♦♦♦ Windsor
21 King Edward Avenue, Blackpool FY2 9TA
☎ 01253-353735
Closed Nov-Mar
9 bedrs, all ensuite, TCF TV P 4 No children under 7
⊕ Resid SB £20 DB £39.80 HB £129-£159 D £6

♦♦♦ Windsor Park
96 Queens Promenade, Blackpool FY2 9NS
☎ 01253-357025
Closed 3 Nov-23 Dec, 2 Jan-Easter

The Windsor Park Hotel is situated in one of the most sought after areas of the Fylde coast. Queens Promenade overlooks the North Shore cliffs and looks out over the Irish Sea.
11 bedrs, all ensuite, TCF TV P 8 ⊕ Resid SB £17-£25 DB £34-£40 HB £136-£145 D £6 CC MC Visa

♦♦ Denely
15 King Edward Avenue, Blackpool FY2 9TA
☎ 01253-352757
Closed Christmas
9 bedrs, 2 ensuite, 2 ⚐ 1 ⚰ TCF P 6 ⊕

♦♦ Knowsley
68 Dean Street, Blackpool FY4 1BP
☎ 01253-343414

A friendly, family run hotel in a quiet area. Close to the Pleasure Beach, shops, M55 and the airport.
12 bedrs, 7 ensuite, 1 ⚰ TCF TV P 14 ⊕ Resid SB £10-£20 DB £20-£40 HB £119-£175 D £8 CC MC Visa

ENGLAND

36 Blackpool

♦ Roker
Sparkling Diamond
563 New South Promenade, Blackpool FY4 1NF
☎ 01253-341853
Closed Nov-Mar

A family owned hotel situated on the New South Promenade, close to the Sandcastle complex. Warm friendly atmosphere, comfort and service a top priority. Fully central heated, all rooms have colour tv and tea/coffee facilities. Large bar with dance area.
16 bedrs, 12 ensuite, 1 ⇌ TCF TV P 12 ⏣ Resid
SB £20-£25 DB £30-£55 HB £99-£165 D £6

Beaucliffe Awaiting Inspection
20-22 Holmfield Road, North Shore, Blackpool FY2 9TB
☎ 01253-351663
13 bedrs, all ensuite, TCF TV ⇌ P 10 ⏣ Resid &

Langwood Awaiting Inspection
250 Queens Promenade, Blackpool FY2 9HA
☎ 01253-351370
Closed Jan-Easter
26 bedrs, all ensuite, TCF 🖻 P 12 ⏣ 50 ⏣ SB £18-£20 DB £36-£40 HB £160-£170 D £8

Sunray Awaiting Inspection
42 Knowle Avenue, North Shore, Blackpool FY2 9TQ
☎ 01253-351937 Fax 01253-593307
Closed Christmas-New Year
9 bedrs, all ensuite, TCF TV ⇌ P 6 SB £25-£28 DB £50-£56 HB £225-£243 D £12.50 CC MC Visa Amex

Villa Awaiting Inspection
9-11 Withnell Road, Blackpool FY4 1HF
☎ 01253-343314
18 bedrs, 14 ensuite, 2 ⇌ TCF TV ⇌ P 10 ⏣ 40 ⏣ Resid SB £20-£22 DB £36-£40 HB £125-£140 D £5.95 CC MC Visa Amex DC

BOURNE Lincolnshire	8C3

♦♦♦ Angel
Market Place, Bourne PE10 9AE
☎ 01778-422346 Fax 01778-383990
14 bedrs, all ensuite, TCF TV ⇌ P 100 ⏣ 120 ⏣
SB £40-£50 DB £50-£60 CC MC Visa Amex

BOURNEMOUTH & BOSCOMBE Dorset	4A4

♦♦♦♦ Boltons
Sparkling Diamond
9 Durley Chine Road South, West Cliff, Bournemouth BH2 5JT
☎ 01202-751517 Fax 01202-751629
Closed Nov-Mar
12 bedrs, all ensuite, TCF TV ⇌ P 12 ⏣ 30 ⏣ Rest Resid SB £25-£29.50 DB £50-£59 HB £180-£230 D £12.50 CC MC Visa ⮕ &

♦♦♦♦ Holmcroft
5 Earle Road, Alum Chine Westbourne, Bournemouth BH4 8JQ
☎ 01202-761289 Fax 01202-761289
19 bedrs, all ensuite, TCF TV 🖻 P 12 No children under 8 ⏣ Resid SB £20-£25 DB £40-£50 HB £168-£210 D £10 CC MC Visa

♦♦♦♦ Tiffanys
Sparkling Diamond
31 Chine Crescent, West Cliff, BH2 5LB
☎ 01202-551424 Fax 01202-318559
Closed Jan
15 bedrs, all ensuite, TCF TV ⇌ P 15 SB £25-£30 DB £40-£50 CC MC Visa Amex

♦♦♦♦ Tudor Grange
Sparkling Diamond
31 Gervis Road, Bournemouth BH1 3EE
☎ 01202-291472
11 bedrs, all ensuite, TCF TV ⇌ P 11 ⏣ 20 ⏣ CC MC Visa Amex 🖻 🖻 🖻

♦♦♦♦ Valberg
Sparkling Diamond
1a Wollenstonecraft Road, Boscombe, Bournemouth BH5 1JQ
☎ 01202-394644
10 bedrs, all ensuite, TV P 7 ⏣ Resid

♦♦♦♦ Wood Lodge
Sparkling Diamond
10 Manor Road, East Cliff, Bournemouth BH1 3EY
☎ 01202-290891 Fax 01202-290892
Closed Jan-14 Mar

15 bedrs, 14 ensuite, 1 ⇌ TCF TV ⇻ P 14 ⌂ Resid
CC MC Visa ♿

♦♦♦ Dene Court
19 Boscombe Spa Road, BH5 1AR
☎ 01202-394874 **Fax** 01202-394874
20 bedrs, 18 ensuite, 1 ⇌ TCF TV P 12 No children
under 2 ⌂ **SB** £14-£25 **DB** £28-£49 **HB** £115-£150
D £6 **CC** MC Visa

♦♦♦ Dorset Westbury
62 Lansdowne Road, Bournemouth BH1 1RS
☎ 01202-551811 **Fax** 01202-551811
15 bedrs, 10 ensuite, 2 ⇌ TCF TV ⇻ P 16 ⌂ Resid
CC MC Visa JCB

♦♦♦ Durley Court
5 Durley Road, West Cliff, Bournemouth BH2 5JQ
☎ 01202-556857 **Fax** 01202-552455
Closed Jan
17 bedrs, 13 ensuite, 1 ⇌ TCF TV P 17 ⋕ ⌂ Resid
SB £22-£34 **DB** £44-£68 **HB** £162-£220 **D** £8.95 **CC** MC Visa JCB

♦♦♦ Hotel Sorrento
Warm Welcome
16 Owls Road, Boscombe, Bournemouth BH5 1AG
☎ 01202-394019
Closed Jan
19 bedrs, 17 ensuite, 1 ⇌ TCF TV ⇻ P 19 ⌂ Resid
SB £20-£24 **DB** £40-£48 **HB** £140-£195 **D** £7 **CC** MC Visa

♦♦♦ Ingledene
20 Derby Road, Bournemouth BH1 3QA
☎ 01202-555433
Closed Nov-Mar
8 bedrs, 7 ensuite, 1 ⇌ TCF TV ⇻ P 2 No children
under 14 ⌂ Resid **SB** £15-£20 **DB** £36-£45 **HB** £150-£175 **D** £7.50 **CC** MC Visa JCB

♦♦♦ Linwood House
11 Wilfred Road, Boscombe,
Bournemouth BH5 1ND
☎ 01202-397818 **Fax** 01202-397818
Closed Nov-Mar
10 bedrs, 8 ensuite, 1 ⇌ TCF TV ⇻ P 7 No children
under 6 ⌂ Resid **SB** £20-£24 **DB** £40-£48 **HB** £155-£189

♦♦♦ Ravenstone
36 Burnaby Road, Alum Chine Westbourne,
Bournemouth BH4 8JG
☎ 01202-761047 **Fax** 01202-761047
Closed Nov-Mar

Situated close to a wooded chine and beach yet
near to both Bournemouth and Poole town centres.
All rooms ensuite with TV and tea making facilities.
Four course dinner with a choice.
9 bedrs, all ensuite, TCF TV P 5 ⌂ Resid **SB** £17-£24
DB £34-£48 **HB** £135-£180 **D** £7 **CC** MC Visa Amex

♦♦♦ Thanet
2 Drury Road, Alum Chine, Bournemouth BH4 8HA
☎ 01202-761135 **Fax** 01202-761135
Closed Nov-Easter
8 bedrs, 5 ensuite, 2 ⇌ TCF TV P 6 No children under
7 ⌂ Resid **SB** £17-£20.75 **DB** £34-£45.50 **HB** £138-£176 **D** £5.75 **CC** MC Visa JCB

♦♦♦ West Dene
117 Alumhurst Road, Alum Chine, Bournemouth
BH4 8HS
☎ 01202-764843 **Fax** 01202-764843
Closed Nov-Feb
17 bedrs, 12 ensuite, 3 ⇌ TCF TV P 17 ⋕ 25 No
children under 5 ⌂ Resid **CC** MC Visa Amex DC

Carisbrooke Awaiting Inspection
42 Tregonwell Road, Bournemouth BH2 5NT
☎ 01202-290432 **Fax** 01202-310499
E-mail all@carisbrooke58.freeserve.co.uk
22 bedrs, 20 ensuite, 3 ⇌ TCF TV ⇻ P 18 ⋕ ⌂ Resid
SB £15-£30 **DB** £15-£30 **D** £11.50 **CC** MC Visa Amex ♿

East Cliff Cottage Awaiting Inspection
57 Grove Road, Bournemouth BH1 3AT
☎ 01202-552788 **Fax** 01202-556400
10 bedrs, 7 ensuite, 1 ⇌ TCF TV ⇻ P 8 **CC** MC Visa Amex DC

Mae Mar Awaiting Inspection
91-95 West Hill Road, Bournemouth BH2 5PQ
☎ 01202-553167 **Fax** 01202-311919
39 bedrs, 35 ensuite, 2 ⇌ TCF TV ⇻ ⬚ ⋕ 50 ⌂ Rest
Resid **SB** £18.50-£27.50 **DB** £37-£55 **HB** £150-£200
D £7 **CC** MC Visa ♿

38 Bournemouth

Washington Awaiting Inspection
3 Durley Road, West Cliff, Bournemouth BH2 5JQ
☎ 01202-557023 Fax 01202-315562

Large detached, sunny hotel ideally situated in a quiet position within 2 minutes of Bournemouth town centre, B.I.C., beaches and all amenities.
19 bedrs, 18 ensuite, 2 ⇌ TCF TV ✈ P 22 ⚲ Resid
SB £25-£30 DB £50-£60 HB £160-£180 CC MC Visa

BOURTON-ON-THE-WATER Gloucestershire 4A1

♦♦♦♦ Ridge
Sparkling Diamond
Whiteshoots, Bourton-on-the-Water GL54 2LE
☎ 01451-820660 Fax 01451-822448

Large country house set in two acres of mature grounds. Spacious bedrooms, two on the ground floor, are available with all facilities. Good pubs and restaurants nearby.
5 bedrs, all ensuite, TCF TV ⊠ No children under 6
SB £20-£30 DB £35-£40

♦♦♦ Polly Perkins
1 The Chestnuts, High Street,
Bourton-on-the-Water GL54 2AN
☎ 01451-820244 Fax 01451-820558

This 300 year old building is ideally situated in the centre of this beautiful village overlooking the river. Family run, offering a warm welcome all year round. Ample private parking.
8 bedrs, all ensuite, TCF TV P 15 No children under 3
⚲ Rest SB £30 DB £38-£48 CC MC Visa JCB

BOWBURN Co. Durham 11D1

Roadchef Lodge Lodge
Motorway Service Area, Thursdale Road, Bowburn DH6 5NP
☎ 0191-377 3666 Fax 0191-377 1448
Closed 25 Dec-2 Jan
38 bedrs, all ensuite, TCF TV P 130 ⦀ 8 Room £47.95
CC MC Visa Amex DC ♿

BRADFORD West Yorkshire 10C3

♦♦♦ Park Grove
28 Park Grove, Frizinghall, Bradford BD9 4JY
☎ 01274-543444 Fax 01274-495619
E-mail enquiry@parkgrovehotel.co.uk

Quietly positioned, two miles from the city centre. All rooms ensuite with satellite TV and all the latest facilities. Ample car parking, award winning food. Gateway to the Dales.
15 bedrs, all ensuite, TCF TV P 9 No children under 2
⚲ SB £41-£47 DB £58-£62 D £10 CC MC Visa Amex DC JCB ♿

Bridport 39

| BRADFORD-ON-AVON Wiltshire | 3F1 |

♦♦♦♦ Widbrook Grange
Little Gem
Warm Welcome, Sparkling Diamond
Trowbridge Road, Bradford-on-Avon BA15 1UH
☎ 01225-863173 Fax 01225-862890

A warm welcome to an elegant, peaceful home in its own grounds of 11 acres. The house and courtyard rooms have been lovingly restored, with ensuite facilities, colour TV, and telephone. Fourposter rooms. Indoor swimming pool and gymnasium.
19 bedrs, all ensuite, TCF TV P 50 ⋕ 40 ⚑ Resid
SB £62-£85 DB £95-£110 D £24.30 CC MC Visa Amex DC JCB

| BRAMPTON Cumbria | 10B1 |

♦♦♦ Abbey Bridge Inn
Lanercost, Brampton CA8 2HG
☎ 016977-2224 Fax 016977-2224
E-mail abbeybrid@aol.com
Closed 25 Dec
7 bedrs, 4 ensuite, 1 ⌂ 2 ⌁ TCF ⌁ P 20 ⋕ 10 ⚑
SB £22 DB £60 D £17 CC MC Visa Amex

| BRIDGWATER Somerset | 3E2 |

Castle of Comfort Awaiting Inspection
Dodington, Nether Stowey, Bridgwater TA5 1LE
☎ 01278-741264
5 bedrs, all ensuite, TCF TV ⌁ P 14 ⚑ Rest Resid CC MC Visa Amex

| BRIDLINGTON East Yorkshire | 11F3 |

♦♦♦ Bay Ridge
Summerfield Road, Bridlington YO15 3LF
☎ 01262-673425
14 bedrs, 12 ensuite, 1 ⌁ TCF TV ⌁ P 7 ⋕ 15 ⚑ Rest Resid SB £21-£22 DB £42-£44 HB £155-£165 D £7
CC MC Visa

♦♦ Park View
9-11 Tennyson Avenue, Bridlington YO15 2EU
☎ 01262-672140 Fax 01262-672140
16 bedrs, 4 ensuite, 3 ⌁ TCF TV ⌁ P 8 ⋕ 20 ⚑ Rest Resid SB £15-£16 DB £30-£32 HB £130 CC MC Visa Amex

| BRIDPORT Dorset | 3E3 |

♦♦♦ Park Farmhouse
Sparkling Diamond
Main Street, Chideock, Bridport DT6 6JD
☎ 01297-489157
Closed Christmas

A 250 year old, partly thatched house, Grade II Listed. Set in wonderful walking country with fourposter beds, log fires and good food.
6 bedrs, all ensuite, TCF TV ⌁ P 12 ⚑ Resid SB £25
DB £40 HB £140 CC MC Visa

Britmead House Awaiting Inspection
West Bay Road, Bridport DT6 4EG
☎ 01308-422941 Fax 01308-422516

Twixt Bridport and West Bay Harbour. Ensuite rooms (including one ground floor), all with many thoughtful extras. South facing lounge and dining room overlooking the garden to open countryside beyond.
7 bedrs, all ensuite, TCF TV ⌁ P 8 No children under 5 ⚑ Resid SB £26-£37 DB £42-£60 HB £217-£252
D £14 CC MC Visa Amex DC JCB

ENGLAND

Brighton

BRIGHTON East Sussex   5D4

♦♦♦♦ Adelaide
Sparkling Diamond
51 Regency Square, Brighton BN1 2FF
☎ 01273-205286 Fax 01273-220904

Regency town house hotel, quiet, informal, with the charm of yesteryear, in Brighton's premier seafront square convenient for all amenities. NCP car park beneath square.
12 bedrs, all ensuite, TCF TV ⊕ Resid SB £41-£60 DB £65-£82 CC MC Visa Amex

Regency Hotel

A hotel with history: once owned by a Marlborough, Churchill's great-grandmother. Smart, comfortable, family owned and professionally run. Licensed bar with snacks, direct sea views. Children welcome. Short breaks.

**28 Regency Square, Brighton BN1 2FH
Tel. 01273-202690 Fax. 01273 220438**

♦♦♦♦ Ainsley House
28 New Steine, Marine Parade, Brighton BN2 1PD
☎ 01273-605310 Fax 01273-688604
E-mail ahhotel@fastnet.co.uk.
Closed Christmas
11 bedrs, 8 ensuite, 1 ⇌ TCF TV SB £30-£35 DB £48-£70 CC MC Visa Amex DC JCB

♦♦♦♦ Arlanda
20 New Steine, Brighton BN2 1PD
☎ 01273-699300 Fax 01273-600930
E-mail arlanda@brighton.co.uk

The Arlanda stands in a Regency garden square, close to Brighton's main attractions. The proprietors take a personal interest in their guests' comfort, with good food and cleanliness being priorities.
12 bedrs, all ensuite, TCF TV ⅲ 16 ⊕ Resid SB £28-£40 DB £48-£80 D £12 CC MC Visa Amex DC JCB

♦♦♦♦ Regency
Warm Welcome, Sparkling Diamond
28 Regency Square, Brighton BN1 2FH
☎ 01273-202690 Fax 01273-220438
13 bedrs, 9 ensuite, 1 ⇌ TCF TV ⅲ 20 ⊕ Rest Resid SB £40-£50 DB £65-£80 CC MC Visa Amex DC JCB
See advert on this page

♦♦♦♦ Trouville
Sparkling Diamond
11 New Steine, Marine Parade, BN2 1PB
☎ 01273-697384
Closed Jan
8 bedrs, 6 ensuite, 1 ⇌ TCF TV ⊕ Resid SB £25 DB £53-£57 CC MC Visa Amex JCB

♦♦♦♦ Twenty One
Sparkling Diamond
21 Charlotte Street, Marine Parade, Brighton BN2 1AG
☎ 01273-686450 Fax 01273-695560
E-mail rooms@the21.co.uk
6 bedrs, all ensuite, TCF TV No children under 1 SB £40-£60 DB £55-£80 CC MC Visa JCB
See advert on opposite page

Brighton 41

ENGLAND

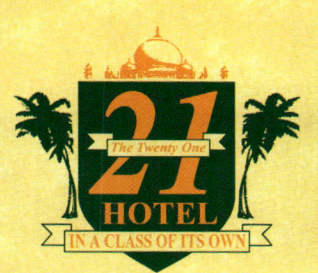

THE TWENTY ONE HOTEL
21 CHARLOTTE STREET
BRIGHTON BN2 1AG

Tel: 01273 686450/681617
Fax: 01273 695560/681617
E-mail: rooms@the21.co.uk
Web site: http://www.s-h-systrems.co.uk/hotels/21

The Twenty One
HOTEL
IN A CLASS OF ITS OWN

Celebrating 21 years as **Brighton's Premier Bed and Breakfast**. Just off the sea front, The Twenty One is ideally situated for all major attractions. All rooms are fully *en-suite and exquisitely* furnished and contain biscuits, chocolates, sweets and toiletries.

OUR COLLECTIONS OF "CLASSIC ROOMS" INCLUDE

The double **"Executive Victorian"** room with balcony.

The twin **"Executive Green"** room.

The double **"Oak"** room.

The double **"Champagne"** room.

RECOMENDED BY
TimeOut
&
The Daily Telegraph

"A Perfect surrounding for a refreshing and memorable stay"

Brighton

♦♦♦ Allendale
3 New Steine, Brighton BN2 1PB
☎ 01273-675436 Fax 01273-602603
Closed Christmas
13 bedrs, 9 ensuite, 1 ♠ 2 ➡ TCF TV ⌂ Resid SB £25-£36 DB £44-£70 D £13 CC MC Visa Amex DC

♦♦♦ Ascott House
21 New Steine, Marine Parade, Brighton BN2 1PD
☎ 01273-688085 Fax 01273-623733

Grade II Listed Georgian hotel in seafront garden square close to all amenities, where high standards and personal attention are paramount.
12 bedrs, 10 ensuite, 1 ♠ 1 ➡ TCF TV No children under 3 ⌂ Resid SB £22-£40 DB £42-£80 D £18
CC MC Visa Amex DC JCB

♦♦♦ Brighton Marina House
8 Charlotte Street, Marine Parade, Brighton BN2 1AG
☎ 01273-605349 Fax 01273-679484
E-mail the21@pavilion.co.uk
10 bedrs, 7 ensuite, 1 ➡ TCF TV ⌂ Rest Resid SB £17-£39 DB £35-£78 HB £224-£356.50 D £20 CC MC Visa Amex DC JCB
See advert on opposite page

♦♦♦ Cavalaire House
34 Upper Rock Gardens, BN2 1QF
☎ 01273-696899 Fax 01273-600504
E-mail cavalaire.hotel@virgin.net
Closed early Dec
9 bedrs, 3 ensuite, 3 ♠ 1 ➡ TCF TV No children under 5 SB £19-£21 DB £41-£45 CC MC Visa Amex DC JCB

♦♦♦ Fyfield House
26 New Steine, Brighton BN2 1PD
☎ 01273-602770 Fax 01273-602770
E-mail fyfield@aol.com
Closed Christmas

Homely, family run hotel with all rooms individually furnished. Peter and Anna are an English/Swiss combination and assure a nice stay.
9 bedrs, 6 ensuite, 1 ➡ TCF TV ♠ SB £15-£35 DB £35-£70 HB £150-£250 D £15 CC MC Visa Amex DC JCB

♦♦♦ Genevieve
18 Madeira Place, Brighton BN2 1TN
☎ 01273-681653 Fax 01273-681653
12 bedrs, 5 ensuite, 4 ➡ TCF TV SB £18.50-£25 DB £39.50-£50 HB £105-£140

♦♦♦ Kimberley
17 Atlingworth Street, Brighton BN2 1PL
☎ 01273-603504 Fax 01273-603504
15 bedrs, 7 ensuite, 8 ♠ 1 ➡ TCF TV No children under 2 ⌂ Resid SB £21-£25 DB £38-£50 CC MC Visa Amex DC JCB

♦♦♦ Melford Hall
41 Marine Parade, Brighton BN2 1PE
☎ 01273-681435 Fax 01273-624186
Closed Christmas
25 bedrs, 23 ensuite, 2 ♠ 2 ➡ TCF TV P 12 No children under 2 SB £30-£34 DB £50-£60 CC MC Visa Amex DC JCB
See advert on next page

Don't forget to mention the guide
When booking direct, please remember to tell the hotel that you chose it from RAC Inspected Guest Accommodation 2000

Facilities for the disabled
Hotels do their best to cater for disabled visitors. However, it is advisable to contact the hotel direct to ensure it can provide a particular requirement.

Brighton 43

ENGLAND

**Brighton Marina House Hotel
8 Charlotte Street
Brighton BN2 1AG**
Tel: 01273 605349
Fax: 01273 679484
E-mail: rooms@jungs.co.uk
www.s-h-systems.co.uk/hotels/brightma

Our Location:

Ideally situated just off the sea front. All major attractions are a maximum of ten minutes walk.

For your special comfort rooms are Charmingly furnished with en-suite facility and a hospitality tray.

We offer:

Single rooms • Double rooms - en-suite
4 Poster Double rooms - en-suite
Twin rooms - en-suite
Family rooms - en-suite
Triple rooms - en-suite

"You will love our beds"

Yummy Breakfast:

We offer an extensive breakfast menu. This will cater for Vegans, Vegetarians, Continental and the full English cooked.

Call us now with out obligation for information or take a look at our website.

Brighton

MELFORD HALL HOTEL

Seafront hotel overlooking the Palace Pier at the corner of a garden square. Furnished to a high standard, with the majority of rooms enjoying sea views. Forecourt parking.

41 MARINE PARADE, BRIGHTON BN2 1PE
Tel: 01273 681435
Fax: 01273 624186

11 bedrs, 11 TCF TV No children SB £18-£20 DB £36-£40 CC MC Visa

♦♦ Charlotte House
9 Charlotte Street, Brighton BN2 1AG
☎ 01273-692849
9 bedrs, all ensuite, TCF TV DB £40-£56 CC MC Visa

♦♦♦ Paskins Town House
19 Charlotte Street, Brighton BN2 1AG
☎ 01273-601203 Fax 01273-621973
E-mail welcome@paskins.co.uk

Welcome to this stylish, 'green' hotel in one of England's most perfectly preserved Victorian conservation areas. Organic and natural food. Delicious traditional and vegetarian breakfasts.
19 bedrs, 16 ensuite, 1 TCF TV Resid CC MC Visa Amex DC

♦♦♦ Rowland House
21 St George Terrace, Marine Parade, Brighton BN2 1JJ
☎ 01273-603639 Fax 01273-603639

BRISTOL 3E1

♦♦♦♦ Downlands House
Sparkling Diamond
33 Henleaze Gardens, Bristol BS9 4HH
☎ 0117-962 1639 Fax 0117-962 1639
E-mail mjdownlands@compuserve.com

Comfortable Victorian house set in a leafy road in north west Bristol, near M4 and M5.
9 bedrs, 6 ensuite, 1 TCF TV SB £30-£39 DB £45-£52 CC MC Visa Amex

♦♦♦♦ Westbury Park
Sparkling Diamond
37 Westbury Road, Bristol BS9 3AU
☎ 0117-962 0465 Fax 0117-962 8607

Detached late Victorian house in residential area on the edge of Durdham Downs. Easy access to Junction 17 of M5
8 bedrs, all ensuite, TCF TV P 4 Resid SB £32.50-£35 DB £49.50-£52 CC MC Visa JCB

Broadstairs

♦♦♦ Washington
11-15 St Paul's Road, Bristol BS8 1LX
☎ 0117-973 3980 Fax 0117-974 1082
Closed Christmas-New Year

Tasteful conversion of Georgian buildings situated close to shops and amenities.
46 bedrs, 40 ensuite, 4 ⇌ TCF TV ⌁ P 12 ⊕ Resid
SB £36-£58 DB £46-£72 CC MC Visa Amex DC

♦♦♦ Firwood
Sparkling Diamond
Main Road, Easter Compton, Bristol BS35 5RA
☎ 01454-633394 Fax 01454-633323
E-mail cgriff5720@aol.com
Closed Christmas
4 bedrs, 3 ⇌ TCF TV ✉ ⌁ P 5 SB £25-£28 DB £40-£45

♦ Downs View
38 Upper Belgrave Road, Clifton, Bristol BS8 2XN
☎ 0117-973 7046 Fax 0117-973 8169
15 bedrs, 7 ensuite, 2 ⇌ TCF TV ⌁ SB £28 DB £45
CC MC Visa JCB

Alcove Awaiting Inspection
508-510 Fishponds Road, Fishponds, Bristol BS16 3DT
☎ 0117-965 2436 Fax 0117-965 3886
9 bedrs, 5 ensuite, 2 ⇌ TCF TV ⌁ P 7 SB £28-£35
DB £38-£45 ♿

Oakfield Awaiting Inspection
52/54 Oakfield Road, Bristol BS8 2BG
☎ 0117-973 5556 Fax 0117-974 4141
Closed 24 Dec-2 Jan

A well-established immaculate hotel with high standards and personal attention. Set in a convenient location close to the BBC, the University and Clifton.
27 bedrs, 8 ⇌ TCF TV ⌁ P 6 SB £28.50-£30 DB £38.50-£40 HB £252 D £7.50

BRIXHAM Devon	3D4

♦♦♦ Harbour View
65 King Street, Brixham TQ5 9TH
☎ 01803-853052
8 bedrs, all ensuite, TCF TV P 5 SB £25-£28 DB £37-£42
CC MC Visa

BROADSTAIRS Kent	5F2

♦♦♦♦ Devonhurst
Sparkling Diamond
13 Eastern Esplanade, Broadstairs CT10 1DR
☎ 01843-863010 Fax 01843-868940
9 bedrs, all ensuite, TCF TV ⚌ 30 No children under 5
⊕ Resid SB £23.50-£25.50 DB £47-£53 HB £191-£210
D £10 CC MC Visa Amex DC JCB

♦♦♦♦ Oakfield
Sparkling Diamond
11 The Vale, Broadstairs CT10 1RB
☎ 01843-600659 Fax 01843-862506
10 bedrs, all ensuite, TCF TV P 12 No children under 1 ⊕ Resid SB £23-£25 DB £46-£50 HB £185-£205
D £10 CC MC Visa Amex DC JCB 🐾

♦♦♦ Bay Tree
Sparkling Diamond
12 Eastern Esplanade, Broadstairs CT10 1DR
☎ 01843-862502 Fax 01843-860589
11 bedrs, all ensuite, TCF TV P 11 No children under 10 ⊕ Resid SB £24-£27 DB £48-£54 HB £204-£222
D £10 CC MC Visa

Broadstairs

♦♦ East Horndon
4 Eastern Esplanade, Broadstairs CT10 1DP
☎ 01843-868306
Closed Nov-Mar
10 bedrs, 8 ensuite, 2 ⇨ TCF TV ✈ P 4 ⌂ Resid
DB £40-£44 D £8.50 CC MC Visa Amex

BROADWAY Worcestershire   4A1

♦♦♦♦♦ Old Rectory
Warm Welcome, Sparkling Diamond
Church Street, Willersey, WR12 7PN
☎ 01386-853729 Fax 01386-858061
E-mail beauvoisin@btinternet.com
Closed Christmas

A Georgian rectory in an idyllic position with a beautiful walled garden. Immaculately furnished rooms, fourposters. Elegant dining room with a real log fire. All amenities and ideal for honeymooners.
8 bedrs, all ensuite, TCF TV ✉ P 10 ⋮⋮⋮ 14 No children under 8 SB £45-£85 DB £65-£105 CC MC Visa Amex JCB ♿

♦♦♦ Olive Branch
78/80 High Street, Broadway WR12 7AJ
☎ 01386-853440 Fax 01386-859070
E-mail dine@theolivebrance.u-net.com
8 bedrs, 7 ensuite, 1 ⇨ TCF TV ✉ P 8 SB £25-£30
DB £47-£60 CC Amex ♿

Short Breaks

Many hotels provide special rates for weekend and mid-week breaks – sometimes these are quoted in the hotel's entry, otherwise ring direct for the latest offers.

Leasow House Awaiting Inspection
Laverton Meadows, Broadway WR12 7NA
☎ 01386-584526 Fax 01386 584596
E-mail leasow@clara.net

A 17th century Cotswold stone farm house in a peaceful countryside setting close to Broadway village. An ideal base for touring the Cotswolds, Oxford, Stratford-upon-Avon and Warwick.
7 bedrs, all ensuite, TCF TV ✉ ✈ P 14 DB £53-£65
CC MC Visa Amex ♿

BROCKENHURST Hampshire   4A4

Cottage Awaiting Inspection
Sway Road, Brockenhurst SO42 7SH
☎ 01590-622296 Fax 01590-623014
E-mail 100604.22@compuserve.com
Closed Dec-Jan

A delightfully converted 300 year old oak beamed forester's cottage with pretty gardens and residents cosy 'snug bar'. In summer, cream teas are served on the terrace.
6 bedrs, all ensuite, TCF TV ✈ P 12 No children under 10 ⌂ Rest Resid SB £49-£55 DB £69-£70 CC MC Visa

Bury St Edmunds

| BROMSGROVE Worcestershire | 7E3 |

♦♦♦♦ Avoncroft
Sparkling Diamond
77 Redditch Road, Stoke Heath,
Bromsgrove B60 4JP
☎ 01527-832819
4 bedrs, all ensuite, TCF TV ⌧ P 9 No children under 5 SB £26 DB £38-£40

| BUCKNELL Shropshire | 7D3 |

Bow Awaiting Inspection
Adleymoor, Bucknell SY7 0ES
☎ 01547-530878
1 bedr, ensuite, TCF ⌧ P 2 DB £55

| BUDE Cornwall | 2B2 |

Cliff Awaiting Inspection
Maer Down Road, Bude EX23 8NG
☎ 01288-353110 Fax 01288-353110
Closed Oct-Apr
15 bedrs, all ensuite, TCF TV ⌲ P 15 ⌷ Rest Resid
SB £25-£35 DB £50-£70 HB £240-£290 D £10 CC MC Visa JCB

| BUDLEIGH SALTERTON Devon | 3D3 |

♦♦♦♦ Long Range
Sparkling Diamond
Vales Road, Budleigh Salterton EX9 6HS
☎ 01395-443321 Fax 01395-445220
6 bedrs, all ensuite, TCF TV P 9 ⌷ Rest Resid

| BURFORD Oxfordshire | 4A2 |

♦♦♦♦ Bird In Hand
Whiteoak Green, Hailey, Burford OX8 5XP
☎ 01993-868321 Fax 01993-868702
16 bedrs, all ensuite, TCF TV ⌧ ⌲ P 150 ⌸ 10 ⌷
SB £55-£60 DB £60-£75 CC MC Visa ♿

♦♦♦♦ Elm House
Meadow Lane, Fulbrook, Burford OX18 4BW
☎ 01993-823611 Fax 01993-823937
7 bedrs, 6 ensuite, 1 ⌲ TCF TV ⌲ P 10 No children under 16 ⌷ Resid CC MC Visa JCB

| BURNHAM-ON-CROUCH Essex | 5E2 |

♦♦ Ye Olde White Harte
The Quay, Burnham-on-Crouch CM0 8AS
☎ 01621-782106 Fax 01621-782106

17th century building overlooking River Crouch, exposed brickwork and fireplaces in bars, restaurant and rooms. Private jetty over river.
18 bedrs, 11 ensuite, 3 ⌲ ⌲ P 18 ⌸ 15 ⌷ SB £20-£43 DB £36-£65 D £12.50 CC MC Visa

| BURTON-UPON-TRENT Staffordshire | 7F2 |

♦♦♦ Delter
5 Derby Road, Burton-upon-Trent DE14 1RU
☎ 01283-535115 Fax 01283-535115
6 bedrs, all ensuite, TCF TV P 8 ⌷ Rest Resid SB £30 DB £43 D £10.50 CC MC Visa

| BURY ST EDMUNDS Suffolk | 9E4 |

♦♦♦♦♦ Twelve Angel Hill
Warm Welcome, Sparkling Diamond
12 Angel Hill, Bury St Edmunds IP33 1UZ
☎ 01284-704088 Fax 01284-725549
Closed Jan

Award winning hotel set in a Georgian terrace on the north side of Angel Hill, close to the Cathedral and Abbey Gardens. Individually decorated rooms and a walled garden.
6 bedrs, all ensuite, TCF TV ⌧ P 3 No children under 16 ⌷ Rest Resid SB £50 DB £70-£85 CC MC Visa Amex DC

48 Buxton

BUXTON Derbyshire   7F1

♦♦♦♦♦ Coningsby ℞
Warm Welcome, Sparkling Diamond
6 Macclesfield Road, Buxton SK17 9AH
📞 01298-26735 Fax 01298-26735
E-mail coningsby@btinternet.com
Closed Nov-Jan

The best way to enjoy a break away from home is to stay where you feel special. We promise you just that. RAC Small Hotel of the Year 1998 (Midlands)
3 bedrs, all ensuite, TCF TV ⌦ P 6 No children ⌸ Resid DB £55 D £15.50

♦♦♦♦ Netherdale
16 Green Lane, Buxton SK17 9DP
📞 01298-23896 Fax 01298-23896
Closed Christmas-New Year

Quietly situated, stone-built Victorian house in a residential area, close to Pooles Cavern country park and Buxton town centre.
10 bedrs, 8 ensuite, 1 ⇌ TCF TV ⌦ P 12 ⋕ 16 No children under 5 ⌸ SB £23 DB £46 HB £248-£280 D £15 ▦

♦♦♦ Hawthorn Farm
Fairfield Road, Buxton SK17 7ED
📞 01298-23230
Closed winter
12 bedrs, 5 ensuite, 2 ⇌ TCF TV ⋔ P 12 SB £22-£23 DB £42-£50

♦♦♦ Roseleigh
19 Broad Walk, Buxton SK17 6JR
📞 01298-24904
E-mail enquiries@roseleighhotel.co.uk
13 bedrs, 10 ensuite, 3 ⌂ 2 ⇌ TCF TV ⌦ P 12 ⋕ 22 ⌸ SB £22 DB £48 CC MC Visa JCB

♦♦♦ Staden Grange Country House
Ashbourne Road, Buxton SK17 9RZ
📞 01298-24965 Fax 01298-72067
Closed Christmas & New Year

A carefully extended spacious residence enjoying magnificent uninterrupted views over open farmland, one and a half miles from Buxton.
11 bedrs, 10 ensuite, 1 ⌂ 1 ⇌ TCF TV ⋔ P 20 ⋕ 12 ⌸ Resid SB £40-£50 DB £50-£65 CC MC Visa Amex DC JCB ▦ ▦

♦♦♦ Westminster
21 Broad Walk, Buxton SK17 6JR
📞 01298-23929 Fax 01298-71121
E-mail cecelia@westminsterhotel.demon.co.uk

A quiet, friendly hotel overlooking the Pavilion Gardens. A short stroll from the Opera house and shops. Ensuite rooms. Special diets catered for. Ample parking.
12 bedrs, all ensuite, TCF TV P 12 ⌸ Rest Resid CC MC Visa

Cambridge

CADNAM Hampshire — 4A4

♦♦♦ Old Well
Romsey Road, Copythorne, Cadnam SO40 2PE
☎ 01703-812321 Fax 01703-814464
6 bedrs, 3 ensuite, 2 ⇌ TCF TV P 10 ⊟ ℂℂ MC Visa

CALLINGTON Cornwall — 2C3

Manor House Inn Awaiting Inspection
Rilla Mill, Callington PL17 7NT
☎ 01579-362354 Fax 01579-363305
12 bedrs, all ensuite, TCF TV ⊢ P 41 ⊞ 35 ⊟
SB £27.50 DB £50 ℂℂ MC Visa JCB 🛋 ▨ ◩

CAMBERLEY Surrey — 4C3

♦♦♦ Camberley
116 London Road, Camberley GU15 3TJ
☎ 01276-24410 Fax 01276-65409
Closed Christmas
7 bedrs, all ensuite, TCF TV P 10 SB £48 DB £60 ℂℂ MC Visa

CAMBRIDGE Cambridgeshire — 5D1

♦♦♦♦ Aylesbray Lodge
5 Mowbray Road, Cambridge CB1 7SR
☎ 01223-240089 Fax 01223-528678

We offer beautifully decorated individual rooms, all ensuite with complimentary extras; satellite TV, tea & coffee facilities. Convenient for town centre and Addenbrookes hospital. Car park.
7 bedrs, all ensuite, TCF TV P 6 SB £30-£35 DB £45-£55 ℂℂ MC Visa

♦♦♦♦ Cambridge Lodge
Warm Welcome
139 Huntingdon Road, Cambridge CB3 0DQ
☎ 01223-352833 Fax 01223-355166
15 bedrs, 12 ensuite, 3 ⋔ 1 ⇌ TCF TV ⊢ P 23 ⊞ 15
⊟ Rest Resid SB £60 DB £72.50 D £20.50 ℂℂ MC Visa Amex DC

♦♦♦ Ashtrees
Sparkling Diamond
128 Perne Road, Cambridge CB1 3RR
☎ 01223-411233 Fax 01223-411233
Closed first 3 weeks in Jan

A small family run guest house on a main bus route. Convenient for the city centre, railway station and Addenbrookes Hospital. A small garden is available for guests' use.
7 bedrs, 3 ensuite, 1 ⇌ TCF TV ▨ P 6 SB £19.50 DB £36-£43 D £9 ℂℂ MC Visa JCB

♦♦♦ Assisi
193 Cherry Hinton Road, Cambridge CB1 4BX
☎ 01223-211466 Fax 01223-412900
Closed 17 Dec-8 Jan
17 bedrs, all ensuite, TCF TV ▨ P 15 SB £28-£33 DB £39-£44 ℂℂ MC Visa
See advert on next page

♦♦♦ Bon Accord House
20 St Margarets Square, (off Cherry Hinton Road), Cambridge CB1 4AP
☎ 01223-411188
E-mail bon.accord.house@dial.pipex.com
Closed Christmas-New Year
9 bedrs, 1 ensuite, 2 ⇌ TCF TV ▨ P 9 ℂℂ MC Visa

♦♦♦ Brooklands
Sparkling Diamond
95 Cherry Hinton Road, CB1 4BS
☎ 01223-242035 Fax 01223-242035
5 bedrs, all ensuite, TCF TV P 5 SB £30 DB £40-£45 ℂℂ MC Visa Amex DC JCB ▨ ◩

ENGLAND

50 Cambridge

ASSISI GUEST HOUSE

Fine detached Victorian house ideally situated for the city centre and the famous Addenbrookes Hospital.
Family run guest house offering personal service. Spacious rooms complete with all modern facilities including shower, telephone and colour TV.
Full English breakfast, ample garden with large car park.

Single £33; Double £44; Family £75

193 CHERRY HINTON, CAMBRIDGE CB1 4BX
Tel: 01223 246648/211466 Fax: 01223 412900

♦♦♦ Lensfield
53 Lensfield Road, Cambridge CR2 1GH
☎ 01223-355017 Fax 01223-312022
Closed 2 weeks at Christmas

The Lensfield Hotel is a residential family run hotel, with over 45 years experience, offering high standards and comfort. Our aim is to provide personal service not only efficiently, but in a friendly and relaxed atmosphere.
30 bedrs, 29 ensuite, 1 ⋔ 2 ⇌ TCF TV P 5 ⊞ SB £42-£65 DB £70-£75 D £8.50 CC MC Visa Amex DC

♦♦♦ Suffolk House
69 Milton Road, Cambridge CB4 1XA
☎ 01223-352016 Fax 01223-566816

Small family run establishment, within walking distance of the historic city centre, colleges and the renowned Fitzwilliam museum. All rooms ensuite. Pleasant secluded garden. Private car park.
8 bedrs, all ensuite, TCF TV ✉ P 9 No children under 7 SB £48-£65 DB £58-£75 CC MC Visa Amex JCB

CANTERBURY Kent   5E3

♦♦♦♦♦ Thanington
Warm Welcome, Sparkling Diamond
140 Wincheap, Canterbury CT1 3RY
☎ 01227-453227 Fax 01227-453225
E-mail thanington_hotel@compuserve.com

Spacious Georgian bed and breakfast hotel, 10 minutes' walk to city centre and featuring fourposter beds, antique bedsteads, family rooms and indoor heated swimming pool. Walled garden and secure car park.
15 bedrs, all ensuite, TCF TV ✕ P 14 ⊞ Resid SB £48-£52 DB £68-£88 CC MC Visa Amex DC JCB ⊡ ⊞

♦♦♦♦ Oriel Lodge
Sparkling Diamond
3 Queens Avenue, Canterbury CT2 8AY
☎ 01227-462845 Fax 01227-462845

Castle Donnington 51

6 bedrs, 2 ensuite, 2 ⇌ TCF TV P 6 No children under 6 SB £25-£31 DB £43-£62 CC MC Visa DC JCB

♦♦♦♦ Waltham Court
Kake Street, Petham, Canterbury CT4 5SB
📞 01227-700413 Fax 01227-700317
E-mail sgw.chives.waltham@dial.pipex.com
4 bedrs, all ensuite, TCF TV P 60 ⌗ 50 ⌑ Rest Resid
SB £40-£45 DB £60-£65 HB £230-£250 D £17.50
CC MC Visa Amex DC

♦♦♦ Three Tuns
24 Watling Street, Canterbury CT1 2UD
📞 01227-456391 Fax 01227-785962
6 bedrs, 4 ensuite, TCF TV ⌑ DB £46-£61 CC MC Visa Amex DC

Ersham Lodge Awaiting Inspection
12 New Dover Road, Canterbury CT1 3AP
📞 01227-463174 Fax 01227-455482
Closed Jan
13 bedrs, 12 ensuite, 1 ⇌ TCF TV P 11 ⌑ Resid
CC MC Visa Amex

Pointers Awaiting Inspection
1 London Road, Canterbury CT2 8LR
📞 01227-456846 Fax 01227-452786
E-mail pointers.hotel@pop.dial.pipex.com
Closed 23 Dec-14 Jan
12 bedrs, all ensuite, TCF TV ⌖ P 8 ⌑ Rest Resid
SB £45-£55 DB £55-£65 HB £262-£280 D £14 CC MC Visa Amex DC JCB

CARLISLE Cumbria	10B1

♦♦♦♦ Avondale
Sparkling Diamond
3 St Aidans Road, Carlisle CA1 1LT
📞 01228-523012 Fax 01228-523012
Closed Christmas

Attractive Edwardian house in quiet situation, yet close to M6 (jn 43) and city centre. Well appointed and spacious rooms. Private parking.
3 bedrs, 1 ensuite, 1 ⇌ TCF TV P 3 SB £20-£40 DB £40 D £9

♦♦♦ Vallum House
Burgh Road, Carlisle CA2 7NB
📞 01228-521860
Closed 25 Dec, 1 Jan
9 bedrs, 5 ensuite, 2 ⇌ TCF TV ⌖ P 15 ⌗ 40 ⌑
SB £25 DB £45 CC MC Visa

East View Awaiting Inspection
110 Warwick Road, Carlisle CA1 1JU
📞 01228-522112 Fax 01228-522112

Friendly family run guest house, centrally situated. Private facilities, welcome tray and colour televisions in all rooms. Hair dryers available. Walking distance from city centre. 1 mile from M6 (jn 43).
8 bedrs, all ensuite, TCF TV P 4 SB £18-£25 DB £32-£35

CASTLE DONINGTON Leicestershire	8B2

♦♦♦ Donington Park Farmhouse
Warm Welcome
Melbourne Road, Isley Walton, Castle Donington DE74 2RN
📞 01332-862409 Fax 01332-862364
E-mail info@parkfarmhouse.co.uk
Closed Christmas
14 bedrs, all ensuite, TCF TV ⌖ P 18 ⌗ 20 ⌑ Rest Resid SB £55-£65 DB £68-£80 D £18 CC MC Visa Amex DC JCB ♿

ENGLAND

52 Charmouth

CHARMOUTH Dorset 3E3

♦♦♦♦ Hensleigh
Sparkling Diamond
Lower Sea Lane, Charmouth DT6 6LW
☎ 01297-560830 Fax 01297-560830
Closed Nov-Feb

Family run hotel offering comfort and hospitality with friendly service and a relaxing atmosphere. Situated just 300 metres from beach and coastal path.
11 bedrs, all ensuite, TCF TV ★ P 30 No children under 3 ⏛ Rest Resid SB £25-£27 DB £50-£54 CC MC Visa Amex

CHELMSFORD Essex 5D2

♦♦♦ Beechcroft
211 New London Road, Chelmsford CM2 0AJ
☎ 01245-352462 Fax 01245-347833
E-mail beechcroft.hotel@btinternet.com
Closed Christmas-New Year
19 bedrs, 13 ensuite, 3 ➛ TCF TV ★ P 15 SB £33-£44 DB £48-£61 CC MC Visa

♦♦♦ Tanunda
217-219 New London Road, Chelmsford CM2 0AJ
☎ 01245-354295 Fax 01245-345503
20 bedrs, 11 ensuite, 3 ➛ TCF TV P 20 ⌘ 30 ⏛ Resid SB £33-£50 DB £48-£56 CC MC Visa Amex DC JCB

Boswell House Awaiting Inspection
118-120 Springfield Road, Chelmsford CM2 6LF
☎ 01245-287587 Fax 01245-287587
Closed Christmas-New Year
13 bedrs, all ensuite, TCF TV P 13 ⏛ Rest Resid
CC MC Visa Amex DC JCB

Snows Oaklands Awaiting Inspection
240 Springfield Road, Chelmsford CM2 6BP
☎ 01245-352004
16 bedrs, 14 ensuite, 1 ☏ 1 ➛ P 14 ⏛ Rest Resid ♿

CHELTENHAM Gloucestershire 7E4

♦♦♦♦♦ Cleeve Hill
Sparkling Diamond
Cleeve Hill, Cheltenham GL52 3PR
☎ 01242-672052 Fax 01242-679969
Closed Christmas, New Year
9 bedrs, all ensuite, TCF TV ☒ P 12 No children under 8 ⏛ Resid SB £50 DB £65-£85 CC MC Visa Amex

♦♦♦♦ Hallery House ⓡ
48 Shurdington Road, Cheltenham GL53 0JE
☎ 01242-578450 Fax 01242-529730
E-mail hallery.house@bigfoot.com
15 bedrs, 10 ensuite, 2 ➛ TCF TV ★ P 20 ⌘ 20 ⏛ Rest Resid SB £25-£50 DB £45-£75 D £15.95 CC MC Visa Amex DC JCB

♦♦♦♦ Moorend Park
Sparkling Diamond
Moorend Park Road, Cheltenham GL53 0LA
☎ 01242-224441 Fax 01242-572413

Beautifully restored and refurbished Victorian house, personally run by an Austrian/Australian family. Situated within a short walk of Cheltenham's many cultural attractions and a short drive to charming Cotswold villages. 3.5 miles from the M5 (jn 11A).
9 bedrs, all ensuite, TCF TV P 25 ⌘ 25 ⏛ Rest Resid SB £42-£46 DB £52-£65 D £18 CC MC Visa Amex JCB

Facilities for the disabled

Hotels do their best to cater for disabled visitors. However, it is advisable to contact the hotel direct to ensure it can provide a particular requirement.

Cheltenham

♦♦♦ Abbey
16 Bath Parade, Cheltenham GL53 7HN
📞 01242-516053 Fax 01242-513034
E-mail manager@abbeyhotel.demon.co.uk

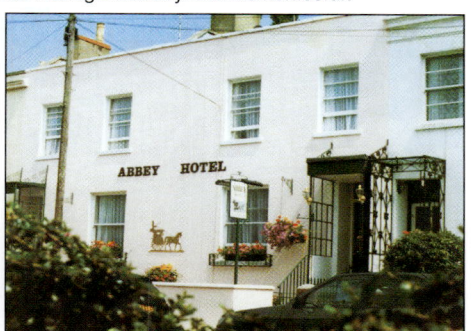

Ideally situated in a quiet road in the heart of Cheltenham, surrounded by its shopping streets, theatres, restaurants and parks, and offering a friendly, relaxed atmosphere.
13 bedrs, 9 ensuite, 2 ⁿ TCF TV ⌂ Resid SB £30-£40 DB £50-£65 HB £280 D £15 CC MC Visa Amex

♦♦♦ Broomhill
218 London Road, Cheltenham GL52 6HW
📞 01242-513086 Fax 01242-513086
3 bedrs, 1 ensuite, 1 ⁿ 2 ⇌ TCF TV ⌐ P 4 SB £19-£20 DB £36-£40 CC MC Visa Amex DC JCB

♦♦♦ Colesbourne Inn
Colesbourne GL53 9NP
📞 01242-870376 Fax 01242-870397
Closed Christmas
9 bedrs, all ensuite, TCF TV ⌐ P 50 No children under 10 ⌂ CC MC Visa JCB

♦♦♦ Ivydene Guest House
145 Hewlett Road, Cheltenham GL52 6TS
📞 01242-521726

Stylish but good value accommodation in grand Victorian house in quiet residential area, 7 minutes on foot from city centre. On main Cotswolds tourist routes. All rooms with CTV and tea/coffee facilities. Several languages spoken.
11 bedrs, 7 ensuite, 2 ⇌ TCF TV ⌐ P 5 SB £25-£35 DB £45-£55

♦♦♦ Montpellier
33 Montpellier Terrace, Cheltenham GL50 1UX
📞 01242-526009

A Grade II Listed building, facing a park and tennis courts. We are near the town centre and you are assured of a warm welcome.
5 bedrs, 4 ensuite, 1 ⁿ 1 ⇌ TCF TV ⌂ Resid SB £21-£26 DB £38-£45

♦♦ Beaumont House
Shurdington Road, Cheltenham GL53 0JE
📞 01242-245986 Fax 01242-520044
E-mail rocking.horse@virgin.net
Closed Christmas

Excellently situated where Cheltenham meets the Cotswolds. Close to good restaurants, the Montpellier antique area and secluded Cotswold walks. Enjoy gentle relaxation in our elegant surroundings, garden, private parking.
15 bedrs, all ensuite, TCF TV P 20 No children under 10 ⌂ Rest Resid SB £44-£50 DB £58-£78 D £27.50 CC MC Visa Amex JCB

54 Cheltenham

Hollington House Awaiting Inspection
115 Hales Road, Cheltenham GL52 6ST
01242-256652 Fax 01242-570280

A spacious, well equipped Victorian house, where excellent standards are maintained by the resident proprietors. Large garden. Conveniently situated near the town centre and 700 yards from the A40 with ample free parking. German and French spoken.
9 bedrs, 8 ensuite, 1 TCF TV P 16 15 No children under 3 Rest Resid SB £35-£45 DB £45-£65 D £12 CC MC Visa Amex

North Hall
Pittville Circus Road, Cheltenham GL52 2PZ
01242-520589 Fax 01242-261953
E-mail northhallhotel@btinternet.com

Charming early Victorian town house in a quiet tree lined road offering modern amenities.
20 bedrs, 16 ensuite, 3 TCF TV P 20 Rest Resid CC MC Visa

CHESTER Cheshire 7D1

♦♦♦♦♦ **Redland**
64 Hough Green, Chester CH4 8JY
01244-671024 Fax 01244-681309

A delightful hotel, with a unique Victorian ambience, conveniently situated only one mile from the city centre of Chester and with the advantage of ample parking.
13 bedrs, all ensuite, TCF TV P 13 Resid SB £45 DB £65-£75

Cavendish Awaiting Inspection
42-44 Hough Green, Chester CH4 8JQ
01244-675100 Fax 01244-678844
19 bedrs, all ensuite, TCF TV P 32 Resid SB £45-£50 DB £55-£65 CC MC Visa

Devonia Awaiting Inspection
33-35 Hoole Road, Chester CH2 3NH
01244-322236 Fax 01244-310881
10 bedrs, 1 ensuite, 3 TCF TV P 20 Resid

Edwards House Awaiting Inspection
61-63 Hoole Road, Chester CH2 3NJ
01244-319888 Fax 01244-310948
10 bedrs, all ensuite, TCF TV P 10 Rest Resid SB £22-£30 DB £35-£50 D £9.50 CC MC Visa

Malvern Awaiting Inspection
21 Victoria Road, Chester CH2 2AX
01244-380865
7 bedrs, 2 TCF TV No children under 2 SB £13.50 DB £27 HB £108

CHINLEY Derbyshire 7F1

Squirrels Awaiting Inspection
1 Green Lane, Chinley,
Chapel-en-le-Frith SK23 6AA
01663-751200 Fax 01663-750210
6 bedrs, all ensuite, TCF TV P 20 85 SB £28 DB £40 D £5.95 CC MC Visa Amex DC

Cirencester

CHIPPENHAM Wiltshire	3F1

♦♦♦ Oxford
32-36 Langley Road, Chippenham SN15 1BX
☎ 01249-652542
13 bedrs, 7 ensuite, 1 ☾ 1 ⇨ TCF TV ⊁ P 9 ⊞ Rest Resid

CHIPPING NORTON Oxfordshire	4A1

♦♦♦♦ Ascott House Farm
Whichford, Nr Long Compton, Shipston-on-Stour CV36 5PP
☎ 01608-684655 Fax 01608-684539
E-mail dp.haines.farms@farmpine.com
Closed Christmas

A 500 acre farm in an area of outstanding natural beauty. Ideal for Stratford, Oxford, Blenheim and the Cotswolds. Outdoor swimming pool, snooker room and guest lounge.
3 bedrs, 2 ensuite, 1 ⇨ TCF TV ⊁ P 12 SB £20-£25 DB £38-£40 ⊁ ⊞

♦♦♦ Southcombe Lodge
Sparkling Diamond
Southcombe, Chipping Norton OX7 5QH
☎ 01608-643068
6 bedrs, 3 ensuite, 2 ⇨ TCF TV ⊠ ⊁ P 10 ⊞ Resid
SB £24-£30 DB £42-£50 HB £220-£230 D £10

CHORLEY Lancashire	10B4

♦♦♦♦ Parr Hall Farm
Sparkling Diamond
Parr Lane, Eccleston, Chorley PR7 5SL
☎ 01257-451917 Fax 01257-453749
4 bedrs, all ensuite, TCF TV ⊠ P 20 SB £25-£35 DB £40-£50 ℂℂ MC Visa

CHURCH STRETTON Shropshire	7D3

♦♦♦♦ Belvedere
Warm Welcome, Sparkling Diamond
Burway Road, Church Stretton SY6 6DP
☎ 01694-722232 Fax 01694-722232
Closed Christmas week

Belvedere is a quiet guest house set in its own gardens, convenient for the town yet only 100 yards from 6,000 acres of National Trust hills.
12 bedrs, 6 ensuite, 3 ⇨ TCF ⊁ P 9 ⊞ Rest Resid
SB £24-£26 DB £48-£52 HB £224-£237 D £10.50
ℂℂ MC Visa

Travellers Rest Inn Awaiting Inspection
Upper Affcot, Church Stretton SY6 6RL
☎ 01694-781275 Fax 01694-781555
10 bedrs, 4 ensuite, 1 ⇨ TCF TV ⊁ P 30 ⊞ ℂℂ MC Visa Amex DC JCB ⊞

CIRENCESTER Gloucestershire	4A2

♦♦♦ Bungalow
Sparkling Diamond
93 Victoria Road, Cirencester GL7 1ES
☎ 01285-654179 Fax 01285-656159
6 bedrs, all ensuite, TCF TV P 6 SB £20-£22 DB £30-£33
♿

♦♦♦ Wimborne
91 Victoria Road, Cirencester GL7 1ES
☎ 01285-653890 Fax 01285-653890
Closed Christmas
5 bedrs, all ensuite, TCF TV ⊠ P 6 No children under 7

ENGLAND

56 Clacton-on-Sea

| CLACTON-ON-SEA Essex | 5E1 |

♦♦♦♦ Chudleigh
Agate Road, Marine Parade West, Clacton-on-Sea
CO15 1RA
📞 01255-425407 Fax 01255-425407
Closed 2 weeks Oct, 1 week Jan

Conveniently situated in a quiet side road near the central seafront gardens, pier and shopping centre, Chudleigh assures you of every comfort and personal attention. Renowned for its excellent cuisine. Fluent Italian and French spoken. Ample parking.
10 bedrs, all ensuite, TCF TV ✱ P 7 ⚑ 15 No children under 2 ⚐ Resid SB £32.50-£35 DB £48-£52 HB £225-£240 D £12 CC MC Visa Amex DC JCB ♿

♦♦♦ Sandrock
1 Penfold Road, Marine Parade West, Clacton-on-Sea CO15 1JN
📞 01255-428215 Fax 01255-428215

Private licensed hotel, 50 yards from the seafront, gardens and town centre. Some sea views, relaxed friendly atmosphere and high standards of accommodation and food. Free car park.
8 bedrs, all ensuite, TCF TV ✱ P 7 ⚐ Resid SB £22.50-£25.50 DB £44-£50 HB £185-£220 D £10 CC MC Visa DC JCB

| CLEETHORPES Lincolnshire | 11F4 |

♦♦♦ Holmhirst
3 Alexandra Road, Cleethorpes DN35 8LQ
📞 01472-692656 Fax 01472-692656
8 bedrs, 5 ensuite, 1 ✱ TCF TV No children under 3 ⚐ Rest SB £18-£25 DB £39-£42 HB £175 D £10 CC MC Visa

Burlington Awaiting Inspection
2-4 Albert Road, Cleethorpes DN35 8LX
📞 01472-699071 Fax 01472-699071
E-mail chesney@tesco.net
Closed 24 Dec-1 Jan
14 bedrs, 2 ⌂ 2 ✱ TCF TV ⚐ Resid SB £14 DB £26 HB £91

| CLIFTONVILLE Kent | 5F2 |

♦♦♦♦ Greswolde
Sparkling Diamond
20 Surrey Road, Cliftonville CT9 2LA
📞 01843-223956 Fax 01843-223956
6 bedrs, all ensuite, TCF TV ✱ ⚐ Resid SB £25 DB £38 CC MC Visa

| CLITHEROE Lancashire | 10C3 |

♦♦♦♦ Brooklyn
32 Pimlico Road, Clitheroe BB7 2AH
📞 01200-428268
4 bedrs, all ensuite, TCF TV ⚐ Resid SB £25-£27.50 DB £40-£43 HB £168-£199 D £10 CC MC Visa JCB

| CLOUGHTON North Yorkshire | 11E2 |

♦♦♦ Blacksmiths Arms
High Street, Cloughton, YO13 OAE
📞 01723-870244
10 bedrs, all ensuite, TCF TV ✉ P 30 ⚑ 34 No children ⚐ SB £30 DB £50 D £11 CC MC Visa

| CODSALL Staffordshire | 7E2 |

♦♦♦ Moors Farm Country Restaurant
Chillington Lane, Codsall WV8 1QF
📞 01902-842330 Fax 01902-847878

Coventry 57

Moors Farm is in a quiet picturesque valley, one mile from Cotswold village. The attractively decorated, comfortable bedrooms have lovely views. Cosy lounge and bar. Superb lounge.
6 bedrs, 4 ensuite, 2 ⇌ TCF TV ☒ P 20 No children under 4 ⌔ Rest Resid SB £25-£36 DB £45-£55 D £12 CC MC Visa JCB

COLESHILL Warwickshire	8A3

♦♦♦ Old Barn
Birmingham Road, Coleshill B46 1DP
☎ 01675-463692 Fax 01675-466275
9 bedrs, all ensuite, TCF TV ☒ P 25 ⌔ Resid SB £37.50 DB £63.50 CC MC Visa DC JCB ⌸

COMBE MARTIN Devon	2C2

♦♦♦ Blair Lodge
Moory Meadow, Seaside, Combe Martin EX34 0DG
☎ 01271-882294
Closed end Oct-Easter
10 bedrs, 6 ensuite, 2 ⇌ TCF TV P 10 No children under 8 ⌔ Rest Resid SB £22 DB £44 HB £195 D £10.50

CONISTON Cumbria	10B2

♦♦♦♦♦ Coniston Lodge ⍗
Sunny Brow, Coniston LA21 8HH
☎ 015394-41201 Fax 015394-41201

An 'RAC Small Hotel of the Year' winner. Beautiful scenery, peaceful surroundings, fine home cooking and a very warm welcome.
6 bedrs, all ensuite, TCF TV ☒ P 9 No children under 10 ⌔ Rest Resid SB £29.50-£44.50 DB £59-£77 D £19 CC MC Visa Amex

Crown Inn Awaiting Inspection
Coniston LA21 8EA
☎ 01539-441243 Fax 015394-41804
E-mail 113076.1551@compuserve.com
8 bedrs, 1 ensuite, 2 ⇌ TCF TV P 30 ⌔ SB £20-£35 DB £35-£50 HB £320-£400 D £9 CC MC Visa Amex DC ⌸

COOKHAM DEAN Berkshire	4C2

♦♦♦♦ Inn on the Green ⍗
The Old Cricket Common, SL6 9NZ
☎ 01628-482638 Fax 01628-487474
E-mail tim@theinnonthegreen.com

Charming country inn, with a renowned gourmet restaurant, in a secluded setting overlooking the old cricket common. Sunny courtyard, log fires, comfortable rooms and friendly service.
8 bedrs, all ensuite, TCF TV P 50 ⌗ 14 ⌔ SB £55-£80 DB £90-£95 D £21 CC MC Visa Amex

COVENTRY West Midlands	7F3

Campanile Coventry North Lodge
4 Wigston Road, Walsgrave (off junction 2, M6), Coventry CV2 2SD
☎ 01203-622311 Fax 01203-602362
51 bedrs, all ensuite, TCF TV ⚐ P 51 ⌗ 30 ⌔ Rest Resid CC MC Visa Amex DC ⌸

Campanile Coventry South Lodge
Abbey Road, Whitley, Coventry CV3 4BJ
☎ 01203-639922 Fax 01203-306898
50 bedrs, all ensuite, TCF TV ⚐ P 50 ⌗ 20 ⌔ Rest Resid CC MC Visa Amex DC ⌸

58 Crackington Haven

CRACKINGTON HAVEN Cornwall　　　　2B3

♦♦♦ Coombe Barton Inn
Crackington Haven EX23 0JG
☎ 01840-230345 Fax 01840-230788
Closed Jan-Feb
6 bedrs, 3 ensuite, 2 ⇌ TCF TV ✱ P 40 ⌁ SB £24-£28
DB £40-£50 HB £150-£250 D £10 CC MC Visa Amex

CREDITON Devon　　　　3D3

♦♦♦ Lower Burrow Coombe Farm
Cheriton Fitzpaine, Crediton EX17 4JS
☎ 01363-866220
Closed Oct
3 bedrs, 1 ensuite, 1 ⇌ TCF TV ☒ ♯ DB £30 HB £95

CROMER Norfolk　　　　9F2

♦♦♦♦ Westgate Lodge
Macdonald Road, Cromer NR27 9AP
☎ 01263-512840
Closed Christmas-New Year
11 bedrs, all ensuite, TCF TV P 11 No children under 3 ⌁ Resid DB £49-£55 HB £212-£220 CC MC Visa JCB

Birch House Awaiting Inspection
34 Cabbell Road, Cromer NR27 9HX
☎ 01263-512521
8 bedrs, 3 ensuite, TCF TV ☒ ⌁ Resid CC MC Visa

Chellow Dene Awaiting Inspection
23 Macdonald Road, Cromer NR27 9AP
☎ 01263-513251
7 bedrs, 5 ensuite, 1 ⇌ TCF TV ✱ P 6 ⌁ SB £19-£20 DB £38-£40 HB £164 D £6.50

Sandcliff Awaiting Inspection
Runton Road, Cromer NR27 9AS
☎ 01263-512888 Fax 01263-512888
23 bedrs, 16 ensuite, 2 ⇌ TCF TV ✱ P 14 ⌁ SB £21-£26 DB £42-£52 HB £170-£200 ♿

CROWBOROUGH East Sussex　　　　5D3

♦♦♦♦ Plough & Horses
Walshes Road, Crowborough TN6 3RE
☎ 01892-652614 Fax 01892-652614

Traditional inn offering excellent value accommodation in ensuite double/twin rooms. Near Ashdown Forest. Crowborough and East Sussex National golf clubs within easy reach.
15 bedrs, all ensuite, TCF TV ♯ 20 P 50 ⌁ CC MC Visa

CROYDE Devon　　　　2C2

♦♦♦♦♦ Croyde Bay House ▥
Warm Welcome, Sparkling Diamond
Moor Lane, Croyde EX33 1PA
☎ 01271-890270
Closed Nov-Feb
7 bedrs, all ensuite, TCF TV ✱ P 7 ⌁ Rest Resid SB £32-£42 DB £64-£84 HB £300-£353 D £20.25
CC MC Visa Amex JCB ♿

Denham Farm & Country House Awaiting Inspection
North Buckland, Braunton EX33 1HY
☎ 01271-890297 Fax 01271-890297
Closed Dec-Jan

A place for all seasons, this lovely farmhouse is situated amidst rolling Devon hills only two miles from the glorious coastline of Croyde and Woolacombe.
10 bedrs, all ensuite, TCF TV P 10 ⌁ Rest Resid SB £35 DB £50-£56 CC MC Visa ▦

Doncaster 59

CROYDON Surrey	5D3

♦♦♦♦ Kirkdale
Sparkling Diamond
22 St Peters Road, Croydon CR0 1HD
📞 0181-688 5898 Fax 0181-680 6001
Closed 25 Dec-1 Jan
19 bedrs, all ensuite, TCF TV 🖂 P 12 ⋕ 15 ⛶ Resid
SB £55 DB £68 CC MC Visa Amex DC JCB

DARLINGTON Co. Durham	11D2

♦♦♦♦♦ Clow Beck House 🍴
Warm Welcome, Sparkling Diamond
Monk End Farm, Croft on Tees,
Darlington DL2 2SW
📞 01325-721075 Fax 01325-720419
E-mail clow.beck.house@dial.pipex.com
13 bedrs, all ensuite, TCF TV P 30 ⋕ 30 ⛶ Resid
SB £45 DB £70 D £18 CC MC Visa Amex 🖂 ♿

DARTFORD Kent	5D2

Campanile Dartford Lodge
1 Clipper Boulevard West, Crossways Business Park, Dartford DA2 6QN
📞 01322-278925 Fax 01322-278948
80 bedrs, all ensuite, TCF TV 🛏 P 80 ⋕ 40 ⛶ Rest Resid CC MC Visa Amex DC ♿

DAWLISH Devon	3D3

♦♦♦♦ West Hatch
Sparkling Diamond
34 West Cliff, Dawlish EX7 9DN
📞 01626-864211 Fax 01626-864211
10 bedrs, all ensuite, TCF TV P 11 No children under 8 ⛶ Rest Resid SB £32-£38 DB £44-£68 CC MC Visa Amex JCB

DERBY Derbyshire	7F1

♦♦♦ European Inn
Sparkling Diamond
Midland Road, Derby DE1 2SL
📞 01332-292000 Fax 01332-293940
E-mail admin@euro-derby.co.uk
88 bedrs, all ensuite, TCF TV 🛏 🖃 P 88 ⋕ 60 ⛶
SB £49-£50.75 DB £55-£57 CC MC Visa Amex DC ♿

♦♦♦ Rangemoor Park
67 Macklin Street, Derby DE1 1LF
📞 01332-347252 Fax 01332-369319
Closed Christmas

A privately run hotel situated within Derby city centre. Traditional standards offering outstanding hospitality and comfort for guests. 13 ensuite rooms, 11 standard rooms. Car parking available.
20 bedrs, 13 ensuite, 2 ⇌ TCF TV 🛏 P 40 SB £25-£36 DB £40-£50 CC MC Visa Amex DC

Melbourne Arms Awaiting Inspection
92 Ashby Road, Melbourne, Derby DE73 1ES
📞 01332-864949 Fax 01332-865525
5 bedrs, all ensuite, TCF TV P 54 ⛶ SB £24-£32 DB £44-£52 D £10.25 CC MC Visa Amex JCB

Rose & Thistle Awaiting Inspection
21 Charnwood Street, Derby DE1 2GU
📞 01332-344103 Fax 01322-291006
13 bedrs, 2 ensuite, 4 ⇌ TCF TV P 8 SB £20 DB £34-£38 CC MC Visa

DONCASTER South Yorkshire	11DF

♦♦ Almel
20/24 Christchurch Road, Doncaster DN1 2QL
📞 01302-365230 Fax 01302-341434
30 bedrs, 14 ensuite, 10 🛁 4 ⇌ TCF TV 🛏 P 9 ⛶ Rest Resid SB £22-£30 DB £36-£40 D £7 CC MC Visa Amex DC

Campanile Doncaster Lodge
Doncaster Leisure Park, Bawtry Road, Doncaster DN4 7PD
📞 01302-370770 Fax 01302-370813
50 bedrs, all ensuite, TCF TV 🛏 P 60 ⋕ 20 ⛶ Rest Resid CC MC Visa Amex DC ♿

| DORCHESTER Dorset | 3F3 |

♦♦♦♦ Yellowham Farmhouse
Sparkling Diamond
Yellowham Wood, Dorchester DT2 8RW
☎ 01305-262892 Fax 01305-257707
E-mail b+b@yellowham.freeserve.co.uk
Closed Christmas

In the heart of Hardy Country. Peaceful and secluded set in 120 acres, 1½ miles east of Dorchester on the edge of idyllic Yellowham Wood. 3 bedrs, all ensuite, TCF TV P 8 No children under 8
SB £30 DB £45 ✉ ♿

Casterbridge Awaiting Inspection
49 High East Street, Dorchester DT1 1HU
☎ 01305-264043 Fax 01305-260884
Closed 25-26 Dec

A relaxed, essentially English, town house hotel with a modern annexe and fine period furnishings, situated in the heart of Thomas Hardy's Wessex. Weekend breaks from October to March, excl. Bank Holidays.
14 bedrs, all ensuite, TCF TV P 4 ⛔ Resid SB £36-£50
DB £52-£90 CC MC Visa Amex DC JCB ♿

| DOVER Kent | 5F3 |

♦♦♦♦ East Lee
Sparkling Diamond
108 Maison Dieu Road, Dover CT16 1RT
☎ 01304-210176 Fax 01304-210176

Elegant Victorian town house. Conveniently situated for port, tunnel, all amenities and historical attractions. A popular choice for the more discerning traveller in search of warm personal service.
4 bedrs, all ensuite, TCF TV ✉ P 4 DB £42-£48 CC MC Visa

♦♦♦♦ Number One
Sparkling Diamond
1 Castle Street, Dover CT16 1QH
☎ 01304-202007 Fax 01304- 214078
5 bedrs, all ensuite, TCF TV P 4 DB £38-£46

♦♦♦♦ Tower
Warm Welcome, Sparkling Diamond
Priory Hill, Dover CT17 0AE
☎ 01304-208212 Fax 01304-208212
E-mail jwraight@compuserve.com
2 bedrs, both ensuite, TCF TV ✉ P 2 DB £38-£46

♦♦♦ Ardmore
18 Castle Hill Road, Dover CT16 1QW
☎ 01304-205895 Fax 01304-208229
Closed Christmas-New Year

Next to Dover Castle, close to ferry, hovercraft, cruise liner terminals. Channel Tunnel 10 minutes. Internationally recommended establishment offers rooms with private facilities, tea/coffee making facilities and colour TV.
4 bedrs, all ensuite, TCF TV ✉ DB £38-£48 CC MC Visa

Driffield, Great 61

♦♦♦ Penny Farthing
Warm Welcome
109 Maison Dieu Road, Dover CT16 1RT
☎ 01304-205563 Fax 01304-205563

Centrally situated for both parts of town. Spacious and comfortable rooms, ensuite with hospitality trays and TV. Quality service at reasonable prices. Parking on forecourt to give you peace of mind. Overnight/short breaks/early departures catered for.
6 bedrs, 5 ensuite, 1 ฿ TCF TV P 6 SB £20-£25 DB £40-£46

♦♦♦ St Martins
17 Castle Hill Road, Dover CT16 1QW
☎ 01304-205938 Fax 01304-208229
Closed Christmas

Close to ferry, hovercraft, cruise liner terminals, Channel Tunnel 10 minutes. Ensuite rooms, CTV, tea/coffee facilities. In lee of Dover Castle. Internationally recommended.
6 bedrs, all ensuite, TCF TV ⊠ SB £25-£35 DB £35-£45
CC MC Visa

♦♦♦ Whitmore
Warm Welcome, Sparkling Diamond
261 Folkestone Road, Dover CT17 9LL
☎ 01304-203080 Fax 01304-240110
4 bedrs, all ensuite, TCF TV ⊠ P 4 SB £16-£25 DB £32-£44 CC MC Visa

Elmo Awaiting Inspection
120 Folkestone Road, Dover CT17 9SP
☎ 01304-206236

Family run guest house, two minutes from the town centre. Tea making facilities and colour TV with 50 channels in rooms. Private parking and garage. Early departure/late arrivals catered for.
6 bedrs, 2 ensuite, 2 ⇌ TCF TV P 7 CC MC Visa JCB

Gateway Hovertel Awaiting Inspection
Snargate Street, Dover CT17 9BZ
☎ 01304-205479 Fax 01304-211504
27 bedrs, all ensuite, TCF TV P 27 ⊟ Resid SB £35-£45
DB £45-£60 CC MC Visa Amex DC JCB

Hubert House Awaiting Inspection
9 Castle Hill Road, Dover CT16 1QW
☎ 01304-202253 Fax 01304-210142
6 bedrs, all ensuite, TCF TV P 6 SB £28-£32 DB £40-£50
CC MC Visa JCB

DRIFFIELD, GREAT East Yorkshire   11E3

White Horse Inn
Main Street, Hutton Cranswick, Great Driffield
YO25 9QN
☎ 01377-270383

An inn situated by the village pond and green, with proprietors Clive & Mary Tomlinson offering you a warm and friendly welcome. An ideal base for touring the Yorkshire Wolds.
8 bedrs, all ensuite, TCF TV ⇥ P 200 ⌗ 350 ⊟ CC MC Visa Amex

ENGLAND

62 Eastbourne

EASTBOURNE East Sussex	5D4

♦♦♦ Bay Lodge
61-62 Royal Parade, Eastbourne BN22 7AQ
☎ 01323-732515 Fax 01323-735009

Small friendly family run seafront hotel with sun lounges, non-smokers lounge and licensed bar. Two bedrooms sea-facing with balconies. Good traditional English cooking.
12 bedrs, 9 ensuite, 2 ⇌ TCF TV P 2 ⌺ Rest Resid
SB £20-£24 DB £40-£48 HB £196-£210 D £9 CC MC Visa Amex

♦♦♦ Chalk Farm
Cooper's Hill, Willingdon, Eastbourne BN20 9JD
☎ 01323-503800 Fax 01323-520331
9 bedrs, 6 ensuite, 1 ⇌ TCF TV ⊁ P 21 ⋕ 50 ⌺ Rest Resid CC MC Visa Amex DC

♦♦♦ Sherwood
7 Lascelles Terrace, Eastbourne BN21 4BJ
☎ 01323-724002
Closed 2 weeks late Sep or Oct
12 bedrs, 11 ensuite, 2 ⇌ TCF TV ⌺ SB £18-£22 DB £36-£44 HB £140-£160 D £7

♦♦ Courtlands
68 Royal Parade, Eastbourne BN22 7AQ
☎ 01323-726915
10 bedrs, 2 ensuite, 4 ⌂ 4 ⇌ TCF TV P 1 ⌺ Rest Resid SB £21-£23 DB £42-£46 HB £185-£210 D £7
CC MC Visa Amex

ECCLESHALL Staffordshire	7E2

Offley Grove Farm Awaiting Inspection
Adbaston, Eccleshall ST2 0QB
☎ 01785-280205 Fax 01785-280205
E-mail accomm@offleygrovefarm.freeserve.co.uk
3 bedrs, 1 ensuite, 1 ⇌ TCF SB £17-£20 DB £34-£40

EMSWORTH Hampshire	4B4

♦♦♦ Jingles
77 Horndean Road, Emsworth PO10 7PU
☎ 01243-373755 Fax 01243-373755
14 bedrs, 7 ensuite, 2 ⇌ TCF TV ⊁ P 14 ⋕ 20 ⌺ Rest Resid SB £26 DB £40-£56 D £12.50 CC MC Visa Amex ⌑

EPSOM Surrey	4C3

♦♦♦ Epsom Downs
9 Longdown Road, Epsom KT17 3PT
☎ 01372-740643 Fax 01372-723259

Epsom Downs Hotel is a privately owned hotel situated just outside of Epsom town centre. All rooms are ensuite and comfortably furnished. Easy access to London by 30 minute train journey from nearby Epsom train station.
15 bedrs, 13 ensuite, 2 ⌂ TCF TV P 10 ⋕ 20 ⌺
SB £45-£65 DB £65-£75 D £12.50 CC MC Visa Amex DC JCB

EVERCREECH Somerset	3E2

♦♦♦ Pecking Mill Inn
A371, Evercreech BA4 6PG
☎ 01749-830336 Fax 01749-831316
Closed 25-26 Dec
6 bedrs, all ensuite, TCF TV ⊁ P 26 ⋕ 12 ⌺ Rest Resid SB £35 DB £50 CC MC Visa Amex DC

Short Breaks

Many hotels provide special rates for weekend and mid-week breaks – sometimes these are quoted in the hotel's entry, otherwise ring direct for the latest offers.

Exeter 63

RECTORY HOUSE

Rectory House is an 18th Century listed building of great charm offering utmost comfort, fragrant rooms and antique furniture, a friendly atmosphere and delicious food.

Rectory House, Fore Street, Evershot, Dorset DT2 0JW
Tel: 01935 83273   Fax: 01935 83273

EVERSHOT Dorset   3E3

♦♦♦♦♦ Rectory House
Warm Welcome, Sparkling Diamond
Fore Street, Evershot DT2 0JW
☎ 01935-83273 Fax 01935-83273
Closed Dec-Jan

Lovely 18th century rectory in picturesque 'Hardy' village.
5 bedrs, all ensuite, TCF TV P 6 No children under 10 Rest Resid SB £40-£60 DB £70-£90 HB £287-£342 D £17 CC MC Visa
See advert on this page

EVESHAM Worcestershire   4A1

♦♦♦ Park View
Waterside, Evesham WR11 6BS
☎ 01386-442639
E-mail mike.spires@btinternet.com
Closed Christmas-New Year
26 bedrs, 7 ➡ ✈ P 30 ⋕ 30 ⊕ Rest Resid SB £21-£25 DB £37-£41 CC MC Visa Amex DC JCB

EXETER Devon   3D3

♦♦♦ Gledhills
Sparkling Diamond
32 Alphington Road, Exeter EX2 8HN
☎ 01392-430469 Fax 01392-430469
Closed Christmas

Family run, licensed hotel, close to the city, river and leisure centre. All modern comfortable bedrooms with full facilities. Own car park.
12 bedrs, 10 ensuite, 2 ⋔ 1 ➡ TCF TV P 12 ⊕ Resid SB £20-£34 DB £40-£46 CC MC Visa

---

ENGLAND

Don't forget to mention the guide

When booking direct, please remember to tell the hotel that you chose it from RAC Inspected Hotels 2000

Exeter

♦♦♦ Park View
Sparkling Diamond
8 Howell Road, Exeter EX4 4LG
☎ 01392-271772 Fax 01392-253047
E-mail philbatho@parkviewhotel.freeserve.co.uk

Family run Listed Georgian building, overlooking the park, close to the city centre, university and stations. From M5 follow B3183 into centre to clock tower roundabout. Take third exit into Elm Grove Road, at end turn left into Howell Road, hotel 100 m.
15 bedrs, 8 ensuite, 2 🛌 2 ⬌ TCF TV P 6 SB £22-£32 DB £38-£47 CC MC Visa Amex

♦♦ Braeside
21 New North Road, Exeter EX4 4HF
☎ 01392-256875
7 bedrs, 2 🛌 2 ⬌ 🐾

♦♦ Telstar
77 St David's Hill, Exeter EX4 4DW
☎ 01392-272466 Fax 01392-272466
E-mail telstar_hotel@compuserve.com
Closed Christmas
18 bedrs, 8 ensuite, 1 🛌 2 ⬌ TCF TV 🐾 P 9 SB £15-£19 DB £30-£40 CC MC Visa JCB ♿

FALMOUTH Cornwall   2B4

♦♦♦♦ Bosanneth
Warm Welcome, Sparkling Diamond
Gyllyngvase Hill, Falmouth TR11 4DW
☎ 01326-314649 Fax 01326-314649
Closed Nov-Mar
8 bedrs, all ensuite, TCF TV P 8 No children under 5
♨ Resid SB £23-£25 DB £46-£50 HB £178-£198 D £10

♦♦♦♦ Ivanhoe
Warm Welcome
7 Melvill Road, Falmouth TR11 4AS
☎ 01326-319083 Fax 01326-319083
E-mail berman.ivanhoe@talk21.com
7 bedrs, 4 ensuite, 3 ⬌ TCF TV P 5 No children under 2 SB £20-£25 DB £40-£50 CC MC Visa Amex

♦♦♦♦ Trevaylor
Sparkling Diamond
8 Pennance Road, Falmouth TR11 4EA
☎ 01326-313041 Fax 01326-313041
E-mail melsan@globalnet.co.uk
8 bedrs, 7 ensuite, TCF TV 📺 P 8 No children ♨ Resid SB £20-£22 DB £32-£36

♦♦♦ Gyllyngvase House
Gyllyngvase Road, Falmouth TR11 4DJ
☎ 01326-312956 Fax 01326-316166
E-mail gyllyngvase@btinternet.com
Closed Nov-Mar
15 bedrs, 12 ensuite, 2 ⬌ TCF TV P 13 ♨ Resid SB £24.50-£35.50 DB £49-£55 HB £240-£255 D £11.50 CC MC Visa Amex DC

Chellowdene Awaiting Inspection
Gyllyngvase Hill, Falmouth TR11 4DN
☎ 01326-314950
6 bedrs, all ensuite, TCF TV P 6 No children under 13 DB £40-£50 HB £190-£210

---

for hotels...

www.WestOneWeb.com

...great locations

Fowey

Rathgowry Awaiting Inspection
Gyllyngvase Hill, Falmouth TR11 4DN
01326-313482
Closed Oct-Apr
10 bedrs, all ensuite, **TV** 🛏 **P** 10 ⚐ Resid **SB** £17-£24
DB £34-£48 **HB** £157-£199 **D** £8

Tudor Court Awaiting Inspection
55 Melvill Road, Falmouth TR11 4DF
01326-312807 **Fax** 01326-312807

Family owned, licensed, eleven bedroomed mock Tudor hotel, set within pleasant gardens and ideally situated for Falmouth's three beaches, the town and harbour.
11 bedrs, 10 ensuite, **TCF TV P** 13 No children under 6 ⚐ Rest Resid **SB** £21 **DB** £40 **CC** MC Visa Amex DC

FAREHAM Hampshire 4B4

♦♦♦ Avenue House
22 The Avenue, Fareham PO14 1NS
01329-232175 **Fax** 01329-232196
17 bedrs, all ensuite, **TCF TV P** 17 ⚐ Resid **SB** £46
DB £53 **CC** MC Visa Amex DC ♿

Bembridge House Awaiting Inspection
Osborn Road, Fareham PO16 7DS
01329-317050
4 bedrs, 1 ensuite, **TCF TV DB** £40-£49

Short Breaks
Many hotels provide special rates for weekend and mid-week breaks – sometimes these are quoted in the hotel's entry, otherwise ring direct for the latest offers.

FELIXSTOWE Suffolk 5F1

♦♦ Dolphin
41 Beach Station Road, Felixstowe IP11 8EY
01394-282261 **Fax** 01394-278319
9 bedrs, 2 ensuite, 1 🛁 2 🚻 **TCF TV P** 35 ⚐ **SB** £18-£26 **DB** £32-£40 **D** £6 **CC** MC Visa Amex

FILEY North Yorkshire 11F2

♦♦♦ Seafield
9-11 Rutland Street, Filey YO14 9JA
01723-513715
13 bedrs, all ensuite, **TCF TV P** 9 ⚐ Resid **SB** £18.50-£20.50 **DB** £37-£41 **HB** £160-£174 **D** £5.50 **CC** MC Visa

FOWEY Cornwall 2B4

♦♦♦ Old Quay House
Fore Street, Fowey PL23 1AQ
01726-833302
9 bedrs, 7 ensuite, 1 🚻 **TCF TV** 🛏 ⚐ Rest Resid
CC MC Visa

---

for travel books...

www.WestOneWeb.com

...great value

ENGLAND

Gatwick Airport

GATWICK AIRPORT West Sussex	5C3

♦♦♦♦ Lawn
Sparkling Diamond
30 Massetts Road, Horley RH6 7DE
☎ 01293-775751 Fax 01293-821803
E-mail info@lawnguesthouse.co.uk

Luxury Victorian house set in a mature garden, four minutes to Gatwick, two minutes to the centre of Horley, and close to mainline rail station. Holiday parking. No smoking.
7 bedrs, all ensuite, TCF TV ⊠ ★ P 15 DB £45-£50
CC MC Visa Amex JCB

♦♦♦ Barnwood
Balcombe Road, Pound Hill, Crawley RH10 7RU
☎ 01293-882709 Fax 01293-886041
E-mail reception@barnwood.co.uk
Closed 25 Dec-3 Jan
35 bedrs, all ensuite, TV P 55 ⋕ 20 ⊟ CC MC Visa Amex DC JCB ⌧

♦♦♦ Prinsted
Sparkling Diamond
Oldfield Road, Horley RH6 7EP
☎ 01293-785233 Fax 01293-820624
E-mail prinsted @networkclub.co.uk
8 bedrs, 6 ensuite, 1 ☞ 1 ⇌ TCF TV ⊠ P 8 SB £32 DB £37-£45 CC MC Visa Amex

♦♦♦ Waterhall Country House
Prestwood Lane, Ifield Wood, Crawley RH11 0LA
☎ 01293-520002 Fax 01293-539905
Closed Christmas
10 bedrs, all ensuite, TCF TV ⊠ P 25 SB £35 DB £45
CC MC Visa JCB

♦♦ Melville Lodge
Warm Welcome
15 Brighton Road, Horley RH6 7HH
☎ 01293-784951 Fax 01293-785669
6 bedrs, 3 ensuite, 1 ⇌ TCF TV ★ P 15 CC MC Visa

Castle Lodge
28 Massetts Road, Horley RH6 7DE
☎ 01293-782738 Fax 01293-782738
Castle Lodge offers a variety of comfortable ensuite rooms and additional facilities such as car parking. Ideally situated just minutes away from Gatwick Airport and within easy walking distance of shops, pubs and restaurants.
10 bedrs, 8 ensuite, 2 ⇌ TCF TV P 15 ⋕ 20 CC MC Visa Amex DC JCB ⌧

GLASTONBURY Somerset	3E2

♦♦♦♦ Cradlebridge Farm
Sparkling Diamond
Glastonbury BA16 9SD
☎ 01458-831827
Closed Christmas
2 bedrs, both ensuite, TCF TV ⊠ P 10 No children under 3 SB £30 DB £40-£45 HB £120-£135 ⌧

Southtown House
Awaiting Inspection
West Pennard, Glastonbury BA6 8NS
☎ 01458-834552 Fax 01458-834494
E-mail trelawny@tesco.net
Closed mid Dec-mid Jan
2 bedrs, 1 ⇌ TCF TV ★ P 3 SB £23.50-£25 DB £36-£45

GLOSSOP Derbyshire	10C4

♦♦ George
34 Norfolk Street, Glossop SK13 9QU
☎ 01457-855449 Fax 01457-857033
9 bedrs, 6 ensuite, 1 ⇌ TCF TV ⋕ 40 ⊟ SB £25 DB £40 D £14 CC MC Visa ⌧

GLOUCESTER Gloucestershire	7E4

♦♦♦♦ Gilbert's
Gilbert's Lane, Brookthorpe, Gloucester GL4 0UH
☎ 01452-812364 Fax 01452-812364
E-mail jenny@gilbertsbb.demon.co.uk

Facilities for the disabled

Hotels do their best to cater for disabled visitors. However, it is advisable to contact the hotel direct to ensure it can provide a particular requirement.

Grange-over-Sands 67

This 400 year old Listed gem lies beneath the Cotswolds, central to Bath, Oxford, Stratford, etc. The organic smallholding contributes to the delicious British breakfast.
4 bedrs, all ensuite, TCF TV P 6 ⋮⋮ 10 SB £24-£29 DB £48-£57

♦♦ Rotherfield House
5 Horton Road, Gloucester GL1 3PX
☎ 01452-410500 Fax 01452-381922

Elegant, detached Victorian property, tastefully extended and sympathetically decorated to a high standard throughout. Neat and tidy.
13 bedrs, 8 ensuite, 2 ⇌ TCF TV ⊁ P 11 ⌂ Rest Resid SB £30-£36 DB £44-£48 HB £210-£240 D £10
CC MC Visa Amex DC

Pembury
9 Pembury Road, St Barnabas, Gloucester GL4 9UE
☎ 01452-521856 Fax 01452-303418

Licensed family run detached house, close to ski-slope and golfing facilities. Ideal base for Cotswolds, Gloucester docks and cathedral.
10 bedrs, 5 ensuite, 2 ⋔ 1 ⇌ TCF TV P 10 ⌂ Resid SB £20 DB £34 CC MC Visa

GODALMING Surrey	4C3

♦♦♦ Meads
65 Meadrow, Godalming GU7 3HS
☎ 01483-421800 Fax 01483-429313
15 bedrs, 7 ensuite, 3 ⋔ 2 ⇌ TCF TV ⊁ P 14 ⌂ Resid SB £45-£50 DB £55-£60 CC MC Visa Amex

GORLESTON-ON-SEA Norfolk	9F3

♦♦ Avalon
54 Clarence Road, Gorleston-on-Sea NR31 6DR
☎ 01493-662114 Fax 01493-661521
9 bedrs, 4 ensuite, 2 ⇌ TCF TV ⌂ Resid SB £15-£20 DB £30-£40 CC Amex DC

GRANGE-OVER-SANDS Cumbria	10B3

♦♦♦♦ Elton
Sparkling Diamond
Windermere Road, Grange-over-Sands LA11 6EQ
☎ 01539-532838

Our small, family run, licensed hotel prides itself in good food and hospitality. Set in peaceful surroundings, with the advantage of ground floor accommodation.
7 bedrs, 5 ensuite, 2 ⋔ TCF TV ⊁ P 4 ⌂ Resid SB £20-£29 DB £40-£48 HB £210 D £10 &

68 Great Yarmouth

GREAT YARMOUTH Norfolk	9F3

♦♦♦♦ Corner House
Warm Welcome, Sparkling Diamond
Albert Square, Great Yarmouth NR30 3JH
☎ 01493-842773
Closed Oct-Mar
8 bedrs, all ensuite, TCF TV P 8 ⌓ Resid SB £20-£25 DB £40-£50 HB £165-£209 D £8

♦♦♦♦ Grange
Yarmouth Road, Ormesby, NR29 3QG
☎ 01493-731877 Fax 01493-731877
7 bedrs, all ensuite, TCF TV P 50 ⌓ SB £37.50 DB £50 CC MC Visa

♦♦♦ Andover
28-30 Camperdown, Great Yarmouth NR30 3JB
☎ 01493-843490 Fax 01493-843490
Closed Nov-Mar
25 bedrs, all ensuite, TCF TV ‡‡‡ 70 ⌓ Resid SB £22-£25 DB £36-£44 HB £133-£185

♦♦♦ Arrandale
58 Wellesley Road, Great Yarmouth NR30 1EX
☎ 01493-855046 Fax 01493-855046
Closed Nov-Mar
9 bedrs, all ensuite, TCF TV P 6 ⌓ Resid SB £15-£20 DB £30-£40 HB £125-£163 D £6 CC MC Visa Amex JCB

♦♦♦ Belvedere
90 North Denes Road, Great Yarmouth NR30 4LN
☎ 01493-844200
9 bedrs, 5 ensuite, 2 ↤ TCF TV ↥ P 8 SB £13-£15 DB £26-£30 HB £115-£130

♦♦♦ Concorde
84 North Denes Road, Great Yarmouth NR30 4LW
☎ 01493-843709 Fax 01493-843709
13 bedrs, 9 ensuite, 1 ☏ 2 ↤ TCF TV ↥ P 8 ⌓ Resid SB £14-£20 DB £28-£40 HB £96-£158 D £7 CC MC Visa Amex

♦♦♦ Fairholme
23-24 Princes Road, Great Yarmouth NR30 2DG
☎ 01493-843447
19 bedrs, 12 ensuite, 6 ↤ TCF TV ✉ ⌓ Resid SB £15-£20 DB £30-£40 HB £115-£155 D £6

♦♦♦ Maryland
Sparkling Diamond
53 Wellesley Road, Great Yarmouth NR30 1EX
☎ 01493-844409
7 bedrs, all ensuite, TCF TV P 8 ⌓ Resid SB £16-£19 DB £32-£38 HB £128-£159 D £6

♦♦♦ Merivon
6 Trafalgar Road, Great Yarmouth NR30 2LD
☎ 01493-844419
7 bedrs, 4 ensuite, 1 ↤ TCF TV No children under 12

♦♦♦ Raynscourt
83 Marine Parade, Great Yarmouth NR30 2DJ
☎ 01493-856554 Fax 01493-856554
Closed Jan & Feb
55 bedrs, 54 ensuite, 4 ↤ TCF TV ✉ P 15 ‡‡‡ ⌓ Resid SB £20-£28 DB £20-£28 HB £140-£200 CC MC Visa

♦♦♦ Rhonadean
Sparkling Diamond
110-111 Wellesley Road, Great Yarmouth NR30 2AR
☎ 01493-842004
18 bedrs, all ensuite, TCF TV No children under 10 ⌓ Resid

♦♦♦ Russell
Sparkling Diamond
26 Nelson Road South, Great Yarmouth NR30 3TL
☎ 01493-843788 Fax 01493-843788
E-mail russellhotel@greatyarmouth18.freeserve.co.uk
Closed Oct-Apr
10 bedrs, all ensuite, TCF TV ⌓ Resid SB £17-£21 DB £34-£42 HB £126-£172 D £6 CC MC Visa

♦♦♦ Sienna Lodge
17-18 Camperdown, Great Yarmouth NR30 3JB
☎ 01493-843361
Closed Oct-Apr
14 bedrs, all ensuite, TCF TV ↥ ‡‡‡ 25 ⌓ Resid SB £18-£23 DB £36-£46 HB £115-£165

♦♦♦ Southern
46 Queens Road, Great Yarmouth NR30 3JR
☎ 01493-843313 Fax 01493-853047
20 bedrs, 16 ensuite, 3 ↤ TCF TV P 10 ⌓ Resid SB £15-£20 DB £30-£35 HB £110-£155 D £6.50

♦♦♦ Spindrift
36 Wellesley Road, Great Yarmouth NR30 IEU
☎ 01493-858674 Fax 01493-858674
Closed Christmas week
7 bedrs, 5 ensuite, 2 ↤ TCF TV P 1 No children under 3 ⌓ SB £18-£30 DB £30-£44 CC MC Visa Amex

♦♦♦ Thelton House
60 Wellesley Road, Great Yarmouth NR30 1EX
☎ 01493-843288

♦♦♦ Trotwood
2 North Drive, Great Yarmouth NR30 1ED
☎ 01493-843971
Closed Christmas-New Year

Great Yarmouth 69

Opposite bowling greens on seafront, giving unrivalled sea views. Close to Britannia Pier and all amenities. Bedrooms ensuite, licensed bar, own car park.
9 bedrs, 8 ensuite, 1 ☕ TCF TV ⛔ P 11 ⚷ Resid
SB £27.50-£34 DB £44-£54 CC MC Visa

♦♦♦ Winchester
12 Euston Road, Great Yarmouth NR30 1DY
📞 01493-843950 Fax 01493-843950
Closed Dec-Mar
14 bedrs, all ensuite, TCF TV P 14 No children under 5 SB £16-£21 DB £30-£42 HB £117-£161.50

♦♦♦ Woods End
49 Wellesley Road, Great Yarmouth NR30 1EX
📞 01493-842229 Fax 01493-842229
Closed 22 Dec-3 Jan
8 bedrs, all ensuite, TCF TV P 3 ⚷ Resid SB £16-£19
DB £32-£38 HB £130-£157 D £6

♦♦ Alclive
33-35 North Denes Road, Great Yarmouth NR30 4LU
📞 01493-844741
Closed Oct-Apr
21 bedrs, 17 ensuite, 4 ⚷ TCF TV ⛔ ⚷ Resid SB £15-£21 DB £30-£42 HB £125-£165 CC MC Visa Amex

♦♦ Anglia House
56 Wellesley Road, Great Yarmouth NR30 1EX
📞 01493-844395
Closed Nov-Mar
10 bedrs, 8 ensuite, 1 ⚷ TCF TV No children under 2 ⚷ Resid SB £16-£25 DB £32-£39 HB £120-£165 D £7

♦♦ Charron
151 Nelson Road Central, Great Yarmouth NR30 2HZ
📞 01493-843177
Closed Christmas
10 bedrs, 7 ensuite, 1 ⚷ TCF TV ⛔ ⚷ Resid SB £16-£18 DB £32-£36 HB £100-£165 D £7

♦♦ Chatsworth
32 Wellesley Road, NR30 1EU
📞 01493-842890
Closed End of Sept.
17 bedrs, all ensuite, TCF TV ⛔ P 17 ⚷ 65 ⚷ SB £25-£35 DB £36-£48 HB £144-£178 CC MC Visa

♦♦ Dene
89 North Denes Road, Great Yarmouth NR30 4LW
📞 01493-844181 Fax 01493-844181
Closed Oct-Easter
8 bedrs, 3 ensuite, 2 ⚷ TCF TV P 5 ⚷ Resid SB £12-£16 DB £20-£22 HB £99-£126 D £6

♦♦ Kingsley House
68 King Street, Great Yarmouth NR30 2PP
📞 01493-850948
6 bedrs, all ensuite, TCF TV No children under 2 ⚷

♦♦ Little Emily
18 Princes Road, Great Yarmouth
📞 01493-842515
11 bedrs, 6 ensuite, 1 ☕ 1 ⚷ TV ⚷ Resid

♦♦ Marine Lodge
19-20 Euston Road, Great Yarmouth NR30 1DY
📞 01493-331210 Fax 01493-332040
Closed Nov-mid Feb

Quality room only accommodation at seaside rates. Seafront location, all rooms ensuite. Free use of indoor pool close by.
39 bedrs, all ensuite, TCF TV ⛔ P 37 ⚷ Rest Resid
SB £29 DB £36 CC MC Visa Amex DC ♿

♦♦ Ravenswood
5/6 Nelson Road South, Great Yarmouth NR30 3JA
📞 01493-844117
Closed late Sep-Easter
18 bedrs, 16 ensuite, 1 ⚷ TCF TV P 15 ⚷ Resid
SB £16-£21 DB £32-£42 HB £105-£140 D £6

70 Great Yarmouth

♦♦ Sandholme
12 Sandown Road,
Great Yarmouth NR30 1EY
☎ 01493-300001 Fax 01493-300001
10 bedrs, 6 ensuite, 2 ⇌ TCF TV ⌑ SB £15-£20 DB £21-£35 HB £70-£100 D £6 CC MC Visa Amex

♦♦ Senglea Lodge
7 Euston Road, Great Yarmouth NR30 1DX
☎ 01493-859632
Closed Christmas & New Year
7 bedrs, 4 ensuite, 1 ⇌ TCF TV ⋔ ⌑ Resid SB £14-£15 DB £28-£32 HB £85-£135 CC MC Visa

♦♦ Sunnydene
83 North Denes Road, Great Yarmouth NR30 4LW
☎ 01493-843554 Fax 01493-332391
14 bedrs, 12 ensuite, 1 ⇌ TCF TV ⋔ ⌑ ▣ P 9 ⌑ Resid SB £14.50-£22 DB £28-£40 HB £76-£159 D £6 CC MC Visa Amex DC ♿

♦♦ Trevi
57 Wellesley Road, Great Yarmouth NR30 1EX
☎ 01493-842821
10 bedrs, 3 ensuite, 2 ⇌ TCF TV ⌑ Resid SB £12-£14 DB £24-£28 HB £100-£120 D £6

♦♦ Waverley
32-37 Princes Road, Great Yarmouth NR30 2DG
☎ 01493-842508 Fax 01493-842508
40 bedrs, 37 ensuite, 3 ⇌ TCF TV ▣ ⌑ Resid SB £25-£35 DB £45-£55 HB £190-£230 CC MC Visa

♦ Gladon
Sparkling Diamond
59 Clarence Road, Great Yarmouth NR31 6DR
☎ 01493-661067
8 bedrs, 2 ⇌ TCF SB £14-£15 DB £28-£30 HB £90-£120

Arch House Awaiting Inspection
14 Wellington Road, Great Yarmouth NR30 3AQ
☎ 01493-854258
8 bedrs, 7 ensuite, 1 ⇌ TCF TV ⋔ SB £14-£18 DB £28-£36 HB £95-£145 D £6

Armani Awaiting Inspection
14-15 Sandown Road, Great Yarmouth NR30 1EY
☎ 01493-843870 Fax 01493-843870
25 bedrs, 16 ensuite, 2 ⇌ TCF P 30 ⌘ 60 No children under 3 ⌑ DB £45-£56 D £6 ▣

Bramalea Balmoral Awaiting Inspection
114-115 Wellesley Road, Great Yarmouth NR30 2AR
☎ 01493-844722
Closed Nov-Apr
15 bedrs, all ensuite, TCF TV ⌑ Resid SB £16-£20 DB £32-£40 HB £99-£158 D £7

Clover Court Awaiting Inspection
15 Princes Road, Great Yarmouth NR30 2DG
☎ 01493-842175 Fax 01493-842175
12 bedrs, all ensuite, TCF TV ⌑ Resid SB £15-£23 DB £30-£46 HB £100-£160 CC MC Visa

Four Oaks Awaiting Inspection
82 North Denes Road, Great Yarmouth NR30 4LW
☎ 01493-844092
13 bedrs, 4 ⇌ TCF TV ⋔ P 7

Georgian House
Awaiting Inspection
17 North Drive, Great Yarmouth NR30 4EW
☎ 01493-842623
Closed Nov-Easter
19 bedrs, 17 ensuite, 2 ⇌ TCF TV P 19 No children under 5 ⌑ Resid DB £35-£50

Katena Awaiting Inspection
56 Albion Road, Great Yarmouth NR30 2JD
☎ 01493-852385
5 bedrs, all ensuite, TCF TV

Lyndhurst Awaiting Inspection
22 Princes Road, Great Yarmouth NR30 2DG
☎ 01493-332393
Closed Dec-Jan
12 bedrs, 5 ensuite, 2 ⇌ TCF TV ⌑ Resid SB £15-£16.50 DB £24-£28 HB £95-£135 D £6

Midland Awaiting Inspection
7-9 Wellesley Road, Great Yarmouth NR30 2AP
☎ 01493-330046
32 bedrs, all ensuite, TCF TV ⋔ ▣ P 25 ⌘ 16 ⌑ CC MC Visa

Richmond House Awaiting Inspection
113 Wellesley Road, Great Yarmouth NR30 2AR
☎ 01493-853995
8 bedrs, 6 ensuite, 1 ⇌ TCF TV No children under 2 ⌑ Resid CC MC Visa

Sands Awaiting Inspection
14 Paget Road, Great Yarmouth NR30 2DN
☎ 01493-844016
9 bedrs, 1 ⌂ 2 ⇌ TCF TV No children under 3 ⌑ Resid SB £12.50-£15 DB £30 HB £85-£95

Harrogate

Sedley House Awaiting Inspection
5 St Georges Road, Great Yarmouth NR30 2JR
☎ 01493-855409
7 bedrs, 2 ensuite, 2 ⋔ 1 ⇌ TCF TV P 6 No children under 15 SB £13-£17 DB £26-£34

Shemara Awaiting Inspection
11 Wellesey Road, Great Yarmouth NR30 2AR
☎ 01493-844054
9 bedrs, all ensuite, TCF TV ⊕ Resid

GUILDFORD Surrey	4C3

Carlton
36 London Road, Guildford GU1 2AF
☎ 01483-575158 Fax 01483-534669
E-mail hotelengland.com

Situated a few minutes walk from town centre, comfortable and friendly hotel offering good hospitality and a licensed bar. Reservations number 01483 303030
30 bedrs, all ensuite, TCF TV P 40 ⊕ Resid SB £28-£80 DB £44-£100 CC MC Visa Amex DC

Short Breaks

Many hotels provide special rates for weekend and mid-week breaks – sometimes these are quoted in the hotel's entry, otherwise ring direct for the latest offers.

HAMPTON IN ARDEN West Midlands	8A3

♦♦♦ Cottage
Kenilworth Road, Balsall Common, Hampton in Arden B92 0LW
☎ 01675-442323 Fax 01675-443323

Ideal location for NEC - 2½ miles, ICC - 9 miles, NAC - 6 miles, Birmingham City Centre - 9 miles, Birmingham International Airport - 3 miles. Local golf courses include Forest of Arden, English Open Venue - 2 miles and Belfry, Ryder Cup venue - 8 miles.
9 bedrs, all ensuite, TCF TV ⋔ P 15 ⋕ 10 SB £25-£28 DB £40-£44 ⟰

Hollies Awaiting Inspection
Kenilworth Road, Balsall Common, Hampton in Arden B92 0LW
☎ 01675-442941 Fax 01675-442941
8 bedrs, all ensuite, TCF TV ⋔ P 12 ⋕ 20 SB £25-£30 DB £40-£45

HARROGATE North Yorkshire	11D3

♦♦♦♦♦ Ruskin
Warm Welcome, Sparkling Diamond
1 Swan Road, Harrogate HG1 2SS
☎ 01423-502045 Fax 01423-506131
E-mail ruskin.hotel@virgin.net
6 bedrs, all ensuite, TCF TV P 9 No children ⊕ Rest Resid SB £50-£70 DB £70-£110 D £19.50 CC MC Visa Amex

♦♦♦♦ Alexa House
26 Ripon Road, Harrogate HG2 2JJ
☎ 01423-501988 Fax 01423-504086
13 bedrs, all ensuite, TCF TV ⊠ P 12 ⊕ Rest Resid SB £45-£48 DB £52-£63 D £13 CC MC Visa Amex DC ⟰

Harrogate

♦♦♦♦ Ashley House
Sparkling Diamond
36-40 Franklin Road, Harrogate HG1 5EE
☎ 01423-507474 Fax 01423-560858
E-mail ashleyhousehotel@btinternet.com

Only 5 minutes' walk from the town centre. Comfortable, well-equipped bedrooms and a cosy bar specialising in single malt whiskies. A warm welcome and friendly service await you. Contact Ron or Linda to reserve your room.
18 bedrs, all ensuite, TCF TV ✈ P 6 ⌬ Resid SB £35-£65 DB £55-£85 HB £299-£359 D £19.40 ℂℂ MC Visa Amex DC

♦♦♦♦ Shannon Court
Sparkling Diamond
65 Dragon Avenue, Harrogate HG1 5DS
☎ 01423-509858 Fax 01423-530606
E-mail shannon@hotel.harrogate.co.uk
Closed Christmas-New Year
8 bedrs, all ensuite, TCF TV ✉ P 3 ⌬ Resid SB £22.50-£29.50 DB £45-£55 HB £227-£245 D £15 ℂℂ MC Visa

♦♦♦ Abbey Lodge
31 Ripon Road, Harrogate HG1 2JL
☎ 01423-569712 Fax 01423-530570
17 bedrs, 13 ensuite, 2 ✈ TCF TV ✈ P 24 ⌬ Rest Resid SB £29.50-£52 DB £52-£62 D £12.25 ℂℂ MC Visa Amex

♦♦♦ Anro
90 Kings Road, Harrogate HG1 5JX
☎ 01423-503087 Fax 01423-561719
7 bedrs, 4 ensuite, 1 ✈ TCF TV No children under 7
SB £22.50 DB £45 D £13 ℂℂ MC Visa

♦♦♦ Arden House
69/71 Franklin Road, Harrogate HG1 5EH
☎ 01423-509224 Fax 01423-561170
E-mail arden@harrogate.com
Closed Christmas
14 bedrs, all ensuite, TCF TV ✈ P 9 ⌬ Resid SB £29.50 DB £54 HB £220 D £15 ℂℂ MC Visa Amex DC

♦♦♦ Gillmore
98 King's Road, Harrogate HG1 5HH
☎ 01423-503699 Fax 01423-503699
E-mail gillmoregh@aol.com
22 bedrs, 5 ensuite, 1 ⌂ 5 ✈ TCF TV ✈ P 14 ⌬ 45 ⌬
Resid SB £25-£40 DB £42-£55 HB £140-£210 D £8.50

Delaine Awaiting Inspection
17 Ripon Road, Harrogate HG1 2JL
☎ 01423-567974 Fax 01423-561723
Closed 25 Dec
10 bedrs, all ensuite, TCF TV P 12 ⌬ Resid ℂℂ MC Visa Amex

HARROW Middlesex 4C2

♦♦♦ Crescent
Sparkling Diamond
58-62 Welldon Crescent, Harrow HA1 1QR
☎ 0181-863 5491 Fax 0181-427 5965
E-mail jivraj@crsnthtl.demon.co.uk
21 bedrs, 13 ensuite, 3 ✈ TCF TV P 7 ⌬ Rest Resid SB £40-£50 DB £55-£65 HB £280-£350 D £20 ℂℂ MC Visa Amex

♦♦♦ Hindes
Hindes Road, Harrow HA1 1SJ
☎ 0181-427 7468 Fax 0181-424 0673
14 bedrs, 7 ensuite, 2 ✈ TCF TV P 25 SB £37-£45
DB £48-£55 D £10 ℂℂ MC Visa Amex DC JCB

♦♦ Central
6 Hindes Road, Harrow HA1 1SJ
☎ 0181-427 0893 Fax 0181-427 0893
14 bedrs, 5 ensuite, 1 ⌂ 3 ✈ TCF TV P 13 ℂℂ MC Visa

HARWICH Essex 5F1

♦♦♦ New Farm
Spinnells Lane, Wix, Nr Harwich CO11 2UJ
☎ 01255-870365 Fax 01255-870837
E-mail barrie.winch@which.net

Hemel Hempstead 73

Modern comfortable farmhouse in 4 acres. Relaxing atmosphere. Good food. Sailing, fishing, bird-watching, walking. Close to Colchester/Ipswich. 55 minutes by train to London. 11 bedrs, 9 ensuite, 1 ↤ TCF TV ⌧ ↥ P 15 ⊕ Resid SB £22-£30 DB £42-£48 HB £190-£250 D £7 ℂℂ MC Visa Amex JCB ♿

HASTINGS & ST LEONARDS East Sussex 5E4

♦♦♦♦ Eagle House
Sparkling Diamond
12 Pevensey Road, Hastings TN38 0JZ
☏ 01424-430535 Fax 01424-437771
19 bedrs, all ensuite, TCF TV P 14 No children under 5 ⊕ Rest Resid SB £29-£32 DB £44.50-£49 HB £233-£312 D £18.95 ℂℂ MC Visa Amex DC
See advert on this page

HAWKSHEAD Cumbria 10B2

♦♦♦♦ Buckle Yeat
Buckle Yeat, Hawkshead LA22 0LF
☏ 015394-36446 Fax 015394-36446
E-mail info@buckle-yeat.co.uk

Tastefully furnished guest house, all rooms ensuite with tea and coffee making facilities. Centrally heated and log fires. Ideally situated for walking and touring. Open all year.
7 bedrs, all ensuite, TCF TV ↥ P 8 SB £22-£25 DB £44-£50 ℂℂ MC Visa Amex JCB

♦♦♦♦ Ivy House
Sparkling Diamond
Ambleside, Hawkshead LA22 0NS
☏ 015394-36204 Fax 015394-36171
E-mail ivyhousehotel@btinternet.com
Closed Nov-Feb
11 bedrs, all ensuite, TCF TV ↥ P 16 ⊕ Rest SB £30-£32 DB £60-£64 HB £255.50-£269.50 D £12 🖼

EAGLE HOUSE HOTEL

A Victorian family house furnished in period style with large car park. All ensuite bedrooms, bar and restaurant overlooking large garden. Near main London Road but in a quiet residential area.

**12 Pevensey Road, St. Leonards-on-Sea, East Sussex TN38 0JZ
Tel: Hastings (01424) 430535/441273
Fax: (01424) 437771**

HAYLING ISLAND Hampshire 4B4

♦♦♦♦ Cockle Warren Cottage
Sparkling Diamond
36 Seafront, Hayling Island, PO11 9HL
☏ 01705-464961 Fax 01705-464838
Closed Christmas
5 bedrs, all ensuite, TV ↥ P 7 ⊕ Resid SB £35-£40 DB £60-£80 ℂℂ MC Visa JCB ♨

HEMEL HEMPSTEAD Hertfordshire 4C2

♦♦ Southville
9 Charles Street, Hemel Hempstead HP1 1JH
☏ 01442-251387
19 bedrs, 6 ↤ TCF TV ↥ P 10 SB £23.50-£29.38 DB £33-£38.78 ℂℂ MC Visa

Alexandra Awaiting Inspection
40-42 Alexandra Road,
Hemel Hempstead HP2 5BP
☏ 01442-242897
16 bedrs, 3 ensuite, TCF TV SB £29.50 DB £40-£50 ℂℂ MC Visa

74 Henfield

HENFIELD West Sussex　　　　　　　　　　4C4

♦♦♦♦ Tottington Manor ♜ ♜
Edburton, Henfield BN5 9LJ
☎ 01903-815757 Fax 01903-879331
E-mail tottington_manor@compuserve.com.uk
Closed 26-30 Dec
6 bedrs, all ensuite, TCF TV P 100 ⋕ 40 No children under 5 ⊞ SB £45-£50 DB £65-£85 D £28 ⊄ MC Visa Amex DC JCB

HEREFORD Herefordshire　　　　　　　　　7D4

♦♦♦♦ Aylstone Court
Aylstone Hill, Hereford HR1 1HS
☎ 01432-341891 Fax 01432-267691

Three storey Georgian building, Listed Grade II, tastefully renovated throughout. Spacious, comfortable public rooms and ensuite bedrooms. Lawns and gardens. 4 minutes walk to Hereford city centre.
9 bedrs, all ensuite, TCF TV P 25 ⋕ 40 ⊞ Rest Resid SB £55-£65 DB £70-£85 D £24.95 ⊄ MC Visa Amex DC JCB

HEXHAM Northumberland　　　　　　　　10C1

♦♦♦ Rose & Crown
Main Street, Slaley, Hexham NE47 0AA
☎ 01434-673263 Fax 01434-673305
3 bedrs, all ensuite, TCF TV P 32 ⊞ SB £25-£32.50 DB £45-£50 D £10 ⊄ MC Visa Amex JCB

♦♦♦ Westbrooke
Allendale Road, Hexham NE46 2DE
☎ 01434-603818
11 bedrs, 3 ensuite, 2 ⚐ 2 ⇌ TCF TV ⤳ P 6 ⊞ ⊞ Club SB £25 DB £49 ⊄ MC Visa

HIGH WYCOMBE Buckinghamshire　　　　4C2

♦♦♦ Bird in Hand
West Wycombe Road, High Wycombe HP11 2LR
☎ 01494-523502 Fax 01494-459449

A family run inn built in the 30's, with original oak panelling and log fire in winter. In summer the patio is popular. There is a fine range of bar meals, snacks and specials. Good choice of cask ales and a large range of fine malt whiskies.
6 bedrs, 5 ensuite, 1 ⇌ TCF TV P 30 ⊞ DB £50 D £6.80 ⊄ MC Visa JCB

♦♦ Drake Court
141 London Road, High Wycombe HP11 1BT
☎ 01494-523639 Fax 01494-472696
20 bedrs, 3 ensuite, 3 ⚐ 4 ⇌ TCF TV ⤳ P 30 ⊞ Rest Resid ⊄ MC Visa Amex DC JCB ⇗

Clifton Lodge
210-212 West Wycombe Road,
High Wycombe HP12 3AR
☎ 01494-440095 Fax 01494-536322

Situated two miles from the M40 and one mile from High Wycombe on the A40 towards Oxford and Aylesbury.
32 bedrs, 20 ensuite, 2 ⚐ 4 ⇌ TCF TV P 20 ⋕ 30 ⊞ Rest Resid ⊄ MC Visa Amex DC JCB

Horsham 75

| HINCKLEY Leicestershire | 8B3 |

♦♦♦ Kings
13-19 Mount Road, Hinckley LE10 1AD
📞 01455-637193 Fax 01455-636201
E-mail kingshinck@aol.com

This handsome privately owned hotel is in a central, yet quiet location, with its own car park and gardens. Lovely rooms and a much acclaimed restaurant ensure a memorable stay.
7 bedrs, all ensuite, TCF TV P 16 ⊞ 40 ⊕ SB £49.50-£69.50 DB £59.50-£79.50 HB £350-£450 D £17 CC MC Visa Amex DC

♦♦♦ Ambion Court
The Green, Dadlington, Hinckley CV13 6JB
📞 01455-212292 Fax 01455-213141
E-mail ambion@aol.com

Charming, modernised Victorian farmhouse overlooking tranquil village green. Luxurious ensuite bedrooms and excellent licensed restaurant. Convenient for Leicester, Coventry, Warwick, NEC and main motorways.
7 bedrs, all ensuite, TCF TV ⊶ P 8 ⊞ 10 ⊕ Rest Resid CC MC Visa

| HOLMFIRTH West Yorkshire | 10C4 |

♦♦ White Horse Inn
Jackson Bridge, Holmfirth HD7 7HF
📞 01484-683940
5 bedrs, all ensuite, TCF TV P 12 ⊕ SB £25 DB £40 D £6

| HOLT Norfolk | 9E2 |

♦♦♦ Lawn's
26 Station Road, Holt NR25 6BS
📞 01263-713390 Fax 01263-710642
10 bedrs, all ensuite, TCF TV P 10 No children under 8 ⊕ Rest Resid SB £35-£45 DB £56-£90 HB £175 D £9.50 CC MC Visa JCB

| HOPE COVE Devon | 2C4 |

Hope Cove Awaiting Inspection
Hope Cove, Kingsbridge, TQ7 3HH
📞 01548-561233 Fax 01548-561233
Closed Nov-Easter
7 bedrs, all ensuite, P 19 ⊞ 20 No children under 6 ⊕ Rest Resid SB £32.50 DB £45 HB £208 D £10.50 CC MC Visa

| HORNSEA East Yorkshire | 11F3 |

♦♦♦ Merlstead
59 Eastgate, Hornsea HU18 1NB
📞 01964-533068 Fax 01964-536975

A family owned and run hotel offering spacious, recently refurbished, accommodation. Our guests' comfort is our priority. Ideally situated only 150 yards from sea and shops.
6 bedrs, all ensuite, TCF TV ⊶ P 4 ⊕ Resid SB £30-£33 DB £45-£50 HB £258-£276 D £13 CC MC Visa

| HORSHAM West Sussex | 4C3 |

Quintrell House Awaiting Inspection
13 Warnham Road, Horsham RH12 2QS
📞 01403-260929
Closed Christmas & New Year
2 bedrs, both ensuite, TCF TV ⊠ P 2 No children under 10 SB £22 DB £44

ENGLAND

Hull

HULL East Yorkshire 11E3

♦♦♦ Earlsmere
76-78 Sunnybank, Off Spring Bank West, Hull HU3 1LQ
☎ 01482-341977 Fax 01482-473714
9 bedrs, 7 ensuite, 1 ⇌ TCF TV ✈ ⚑ Resid SB £20-£28 DB £30-£40 HB £200-£280 CC Visa DC ♿

Campanile Hull Lodge
Beverley Road, Freetown Way, Kingston-upon-Hull HU2 9AN
☎ 01482-325530 Fax 01482-587538
48 bedrs, all ensuite, TCF TV ✈ P 50 ⊞ 35 ⚑ Rest Resid SB £39.50 DB £45.50 HB £47.50 D £10.85 CC MC Visa Amex DC ♿

HUNGERFORD Berkshire 4B3

♦♦♦♦ Marshgate Cottage
Sparkling Diamond
Marsh Lane, Hungerford RG17 0QX
☎ 01488-682307 Fax 01488-685475

A small, friendly, family run hotel in superb countryside, adjoining the Kennet and Avon Canal. M4 (jn 14) just four miles away.
9 bedrs, all ensuite, TCF TV ✉ P 9 ⊞ 10 ⚑ Resid SB £35.50-£37.50 DB £48.50-£50 D £16 CC MC Visa ♿

HUNSTANTON Norfolk 9D2

Sunningdale Awaiting Inspection
3 Avenue Road, Hunstanton PE36 5BW
☎ 01485-532562
12 bedrs, all ensuite, TCF TV P 2 No children under 10 ⚑

HUNTLEY Gloucestershire 7E4

♦♦♦ King's Head
Birdwood, Huntley
☎ 01452-750348 Fax 01452-750348

6 bedrs, all ensuite, TCF TV P 50 ⊞ 120 No children under 3 ⚑ SB £25 DB £40 D £7

HYDE Cheshire 10C4

♦♦ Needhams Farm
Uplands Road, Werneth Low, SK14 3AQ
☎ 0161-368 4610 Fax 0161-367 9106
7 bedrs, 5 ensuite, 1 ⇌ TCF TV ✈ P 10 ⚑ Resid SB £19-£20 DB £30-£32 D £7 CC MC Visa

ILFRACOMBE Devon 2C2

♦♦♦♦ Southcliffe
Warm Welcome, Sparkling Diamond
Torrs Park, Ilfracombe EX34 8AZ
☎ 01271-862958
Closed Nov-Feb

Charming Victorian mansion, with quality refurbished ensuite bedrooms. Set in its own secluded grounds with superb views across the town to the sea. Adjacent to National Trust walks, and close to harbour and seafront. Totally non-smoking.
9 bedrs, all ensuite, TCF TV ✉ P 12 ⊞ 15 no children under 6 ⚑ Resid SB £21-£25 DB £43-£50 HB £213.50-£227.50 D £9 CC MC Visa Amex JCB

♦♦♦ Avalon
6 Capstone Crescent, Ilfracombe EX34 9BT
☎ 01271-863325 Fax 01271-866543
10 bedrs, 8 ensuite, 1 🅟 1 ⇌ TCF TV P 10 ⊞ 35 ⚑ Rest Resid SB £22.50-£32.50 DB £35-£45 HB £140-£185 D £10 CC MC Visa

♦♦♦ Greyven House
4 St James Place, Ilfracombe Ex34 9BH
☎ 01271-802505 Fax 01271-863928
E-mail greyvenhouse@btinternet.co.uk
7 bedrs, 4 ensuite, 2 ⇌ TCF TV P 6 ⚑ Rest Resid SB £17-£20 DB £34-£40 HB £145-£155 D £5.50 CC MC Visa Amex DC

Ipswich

♦♦♦ St Brannocks House
61 St Brannocks Road, Ilfracombe EX34 8EQ
☎ 01271-863873

St Brannocks House is a detached Victorian hotel set in its own grounds, with ample parking space. A few minutes level walk from the town and seafront and just 200 yards from the beautiful Bicclescombe Park and Cairn Nature Reserve.
16 bedrs, 10 ensuite, 2 ⇌ TCF TV ⊁ P 20 ⏣ Resid
SB £21-£23 DB £42-£46 HB £192.50-£210 D £10
CC MC Visa Amex

Capstone Awaiting Inspection
15-16 St James' Place, Ilfracombe EX34 9BJ
☎ 01271-863540 Fax 01271-862277
E-mail capstone@ilfracombe2000.freeserve.co.uk
Closed Nov-Mar
12 bedrs, 11 ensuite, 1 ⇌ TCF TV ⊁ P 4 ⏣ Rest
SB £16-£18.50 DB £32-£37 HB £155-£175 D £6 CC MC Visa Amex JCB

Strathmore Awaiting Inspection
57 St Brannocks Road, Ilfracombe EX34 8EQ
☎ 01271-862248 Fax 01271-864044
9 bedrs, 8 ensuite, 1 ⇌ TCF TV ⊁ P 7 ⏣ Resid
SB £16-£20 DB £36-£44 HB £185-£199 D £11.95
CC MC Visa Amex JCB

Trafalgar Awaiting Inspection
Larkstone Terrace, Ilfracombe EX34 9NU
☎ 01271-862145 Fax 01271-865193
25 bedrs, 24 ensuite, 1 ☇ TCF TV ⊁ P 8 ⌗ 60 ⏣
CC MC Visa Amex DC

INGLETON North Yorkshire	10B3

♦♦♦ Springfield Country House
Sparkling Diamond
Main Street, Via Carnforth, Ingleton LA6 3HJ
☎ 015242-41280 Fax 015242-41280
Closed Christmas

A family run detached Victorian villa with a fountain at the front, set in its own grounds, backing onto the River Greta, with panoramic views.
5 bedrs, all ensuite, TCF TV ⊁ P 12 ⏣ Resid SB £23
DB £46 HB £196 D £11 CC MC Visa Amex DC 🖼

Ferncliffe House Awaiting Inspection
55 Main Street, Ingleton LA6 3HJ
☎ 015242-42405
Closed Nov-Jan
5 bedrs, all ensuite, TCF TV ⊁ P 5 No children under 12 CC MC Visa Amex

IPSWICH Suffolk	5E1

♦♦♦ Highview House
56 Belstead Road, Ipswich IP2 8BE
☎ 01473-601620 Fax 01473-688659

Converted Victorian rectory, all 9 well equipped ensuite bedrooms have colour TV's, telephones, hair-dryers and hospitality trays. Smokers lounge, liquor licence, garden, ample parking. Accommodation and breakfast only. Close to station and town centre.
9 bedrs, all ensuite, TCF TV ⊁ P 9 ⏣ Rest Resid
SB £40 DB £56 CC MC Visa JCB 🖼

78 Ipswich

♦♦ Anglesea
Oban Street, Ipswich IP1 3PH
☎ 01473-255630 Fax 01473-255630

A large Victorian house in Suffolk brick, refurbished to a high standard and set in a conservation area.
7 bedrs, all ensuite, TCF TV P 9 No children under 8
⌂ Resid SB £35 DB £45 CC MC Visa Amex DC

ISLE OF WIGHT	4B4

♦♦♦♦ Aqua
Sparkling Diamond
The Esplanade, Shanklin PO37 6BN
☎ 01983-863024 Fax 01983-864841
Closed Nov-Mar
22 bedrs, all ensuite, TCF TV P 2 ⌘ 60 ⌂ SB £25-£30
HB £210-£245 D £9.95 CC MC Visa Amex DC JCB

♦♦♦♦ Lake
Sparkling Diamond
Shore Road, Bonchurch PO38 1RF
☎ 01983-852613
E-mail enquiries@lakehotel.co.uk
Closed Nov-Feb
21 bedrs, all ensuite, TCF TV ⌃ P 21 No children under 3 ⌂ Resid SB £24.50-£27.50 DB £45-£55
HB £205-£220 D £8

♦♦♦♦ Rooftree
Sparkling Diamond
26 Broadway, Sandown PO36 9BY
☎ 01983-403175 Fax 01983-407354
E-mail rooftree@netguided.co.uk
9 bedrs, all ensuite, TCF TV P 10 ⌂ Resid SB £22-£26
DB £44-£52 HB £178-£209 D £9 CC MC Visa

♦♦♦♦ St Catherines
Sparkling Diamond
1 Winchester Park Road, Sandown PO36 8HJ
☎ 01983-402392 Fax 01983-402399
Closed Christmas-New Year
20 bedrs, all ensuite, TCF TV ⌃ P 8 ⌘ 0 ⌂ CC MC Visa

♦♦♦♦ St Leonards
Sparkling Diamond
22 Queens Road, Shanklin PO37 6AW
☎ 01983-862121 Fax 01983-868895
E-mail les@stleonardsiw.freeserve.co.uk
7 bedrs, all ensuite, TCF TV P 6 ⌂ Resid SB £18-£21
DB £36-£42 HB £159-£179 D £8 CC MC Visa

♦♦♦ Bay House
8 Chine Avenue, Keats Green, Shanklin PO36 6AG
☎ 01983-863180 Fax 01983-866604
E-mail bay-house@netguides.co.uk

Located in a quiet position with one of the finest views over the bay, this family run hotel, serving exceptional cuisine, is just a five minute walk to the old village and beach.
21 bedrs, all ensuite, TCF TV ⌃ P 15 ⌂ Rest Resid
SB £23-£33 DB £46-£66 HB £203-£273 D £6 CC MC Visa

♦♦♦ Denewood
7 Victoria Road, Sandown PO36 8AL
☎ 01983-402980 Fax 01983-402980
15 bedrs, 13 ensuite, 1 ⌃ P 10 ⌂ Resid CC MC Visa

♦♦♦ Georgian House
22 George Street, Ryde PO33 2EW
☎ 01983-563588
6 bedrs, 5 ensuite, 1 ⌃ TCF TV P 10 SB £18-£20
DB £36-£38

♦♦♦ Glen Islay
Warm Welcome
St Boniface Road, Ventnor PO38 1NP
☎ 01983-854095
Closed Nov-Feb
5 bedrs, 4 ensuite, 1 ⌃ TCF TV P 6 No children ⌂
Resid SB £17.50-£19 DB £35-£38 HB £168-£189

♦♦♦ Littledene Lodge
Granville Road, Totland Bay PO39 0AX
☎ 01983-752411 Fax 01983-752411

Isle of Wight

A small, family run hotel with ensuite facilities in all rooms. Situated between shops and Totland Beach, with friendly staff, good food and relaxed atmosphere.
7 bedrs, 6 ensuite, TCF P 5 Resid SB £17-£22 DB £35-£44 HB £150-£199.50 D £10 CC MC Visa

♦♦♦ Mount House
20 Arthurs Hill, Shanklin PO37 6EE
☎ 01983-862556 Fax 01983-867551
E-mail mounthouse@netguides.co.uk
Closed Jan
9 bedrs, all ensuite, TCF TV P 8 Resid SB £18-£22 DB £36-£44 HB £154-£179 D £5.50 CC MC Visa JCB

♦♦♦ Nodes Country
Sparkling Diamond
Alum Bay Road, Totland Bay PO39 0HZ
☎ 01983-752859 Fax 01705-201621
11 bedrs, all ensuite, TCF TV P 15 Rest Resid CC MC Visa

♦♦♦ Osborne House
Esplanade, Shanklin PO37 6BN
☎ 01983-862501 Fax 01983-862501
Closed 15 Oct-2 Jan
12 bedrs, all ensuite, TCF TV No children under 13 Rest Resid SB £30 DB £50 CC MC Visa

♦♦♦ Richmond
23 Palmerston Road, Shanklin PO37 6AS
☎ 01983-862874 Fax 01983-862874
10 bedrs, 9 ensuite, 1 TCF TV P 5 Resid SB £22-£26 DB £44-£52 HB £220-£250 D £10 CC MC Visa JCB

♦♦♦ St Boniface House
Sparkling Diamond
6 St Boniface Road, Ventnor PO38 1PJ
☎ 01983-853109
E-mail stboniface@defiant9.freeserve.co.uk
Closed Nov-Feb

3 bedrs, all ensuite, TCF TV P 4 No children Resid SB £26-£30 DB £52-£60 HB £241-£250 D £9.50 CC MC Visa JCB

♦♦♦ White House
7 Park Road, Shanklin PO37 6AY
☎ 01983-862776 Fax 01983-865980
E-mail white-house@netguides.co.uk
Closed Nov-Dec

Situated on the famous cliff walk, with panoramic sea views. Comfortable informal atmosphere, sun lounge, bar and dining room, excellent choice of menu. Ample car parking.
11 bedrs, all ensuite, TCF TV P 11 Resid SB £24-£28 DB £48-£56 HB £204-£245 CC MC Visa Amex JCB

♦♦ Brackla
7 Leed Street, Sandown PO36 9DA
☎ 01983-403648
Closed Oct-Mar
16 bedrs, 9 ensuite, 2 TCF P 10 36 No children under 3 Resid SB £18.50-£23 DB £37-£46 HB £153-£182 D £7 CC MC Visa JCB

♦♦ Channel View
4-8 Royal Street, Sandown PO36 8LP
☎ 01983-402347 Fax 01983-404128
Closed early Dec & Jan
48 bedrs, all ensuite, TCF TV P 12 Resid

Belmore Awaiting Inspection
101 Station Avenue, Sandown PO36 8HD
☎ 01983-404189
9 bedrs, 7 ensuite, 2 1 TCF TV P 4 No children under 5 Resid SB £14-£16 DB £28-£32 HB £110-£127 D £6 CC MC Visa

Berry Brow Awaiting Inspection
9 Popham Road, Shanklin PO37 6RF
☎ 01983-862825 Fax 01983-865995
E-mail berrybrow@pswa.co.uk
Closed Nov-Feb
23 bedrs, all ensuite, TCF TV P 12 No children under 5 Resid SB £20 DB £36 CC MC Visa

80 Isle of Wight

Heatherleigh Awaiting Inspection
17 Queens Road, Shanklin PO37 6AW
☎ 01983-862503 **Fax** 01983-862503
7 bedrs, all ensuite, **TCF TV P** 5 ⌘ Resid **SB** £24
DB £48 **HB** £165-£199 **D** £9 **CC** MC Visa Amex

Hillside Awaiting Inspection
Mitchell Avenue, Ventnor PO38 1DR
☎ 01983-852271 **Fax** 01983-852271
11 bedrs, all ensuite, **TCF TV** ✈ **P** 12 No children
under 5 ⌘ Resid **SB** £21-£24 **DB** £42-£48 **HB** £207-£230 **D** £10 **CC** MC Visa Amex

Llynfi Awaiting Inspection
23 Spring Hill, Ventnor PO38 1PF
☎ 01983-852202
Closed Nov-Mar
10 bedrs, 7 ensuite, 2 ↪ **TCF TV P** 6 ⌘ Resid **CC** MC Visa

Esplanade Awaiting Inspection
33 The Esplanade, Shanklin PO37 6BG
☎ 01983-863001 **Fax** 01983-863001
17 bedrs, 6 ensuite, 3 ↪ **TCF TV P** 12 ⌘ ⌘ Rest
SB £19-£24 **DB** £38-£45 **D** £6.50 **CC** MC Visa

LANE HEAD HOUSE
COUNTRY HOTEL

Set in private grounds, formerly 17th Century Manor House. Commanding panoramic views over River Kent Valley to surrounding Fells.

Enter the warmth and ambience of our licensed Country House and just relax, or stroll through our unique Elizabethan Knot garden.

HELSINGTON, KENDAL, CUMBRIA LA9 5RJ
Tel: (Kendal) 01539 731283
Fax: 01539 721023

ISLES OF SCILLY	2A3

Carnwethers Country House
Awaiting Inspection
Pelistry Bay, St Mary's TR21 0NX
☎ 01720-422415 **Fax** 01720-422415
Closed Oct-Apr
9 bedrs, all ensuite, **TCF TV** ☒ ✈ **P** 20 No children
under 8 ⌘ Resid **HB** £315-£350 ⛱ ☒

KENDAL Cumbria	10B2

♦♦♦♦ **Crosthwaite House**
Sparkling Diamond
Crosthwaite, Kendal LA8 8BP
☎ 015395-68264
E-mail crosthwaite.house@kencomp.net
Closed mid Nov-Feb

Home from home Georgian country guest house, with superb views over the Lyth valley. Carefully restored, providing all modern facilities and offering a warm and friendly welcome.
6 bedrs, 6 ⌘ **TCF TV** ✈ **P** 10 ⌘ Resid

♦♦♦♦ **Lane Head House** ⌘
Sparkling Diamond
Helsington, Kendal LA9 5RJ
☎ 01539-731283 **Fax** 01539-721023
6 bedrs, all ensuite, **TCF TV P** 7 ⌘ 10 ⌘ Resid **SB** £41
DB £71-£82 **CC** MC Visa Amex JCB
See advert on this page

♦♦♦ **Garnett House Farm**
Burneside, Kendal LA9 5SF
☎ 01539-724542 **Fax** 01539-724542
Closed Christmas-New Year
5 bedrs, 4 ensuite, 2 ↪ **TCF TV P** 10 **DB** £32-£42 **D** £10

Jolly Anglers Inn Awaiting Inspection
Burneside, Kendal LA9 5QS
☎ 01539-732552
6 bedrs, 1 ensuite, 2 ⌘ 6 ↪ ✈ ⌘ ♿

Keswick 81

Roadchef Lodge Lodge
Killington Lake Motorway Service Area, M6 Southbound, Nr Kendal LA8 0NW
☎ 01539-621666 Fax 01539-621660
Closed 24 Dec-2 Jan
36 bedrs, all ensuite, TCF TV P 150 ⋕ 5 Room £47.95
CC MC Visa Amex DC &

KESWICK Cumbria   10B2

♦♦♦♦ Acorn House
Sparkling Diamond
Ambleside Road, Keswick CA12 4DL
☎ 017687-72553 Fax 017687-75332
E-mail susan@acornhouse.demon.co.uk
Closed Nov-Feb
10 bedrs, all ensuite, TCF TV ⌧ P 10 No children under 8 ⊕ Rest SB £30-£40 DB £50-£65 CC MC Visa

♦♦♦♦ Allerdale House
1 Eskin Street, Keswick CA12 4DH
☎ 017687-73891 Fax 017687-74068

Pleasantly situated, yet convenient for town, theatre, lakes and parks. Comfort and good food a speciality. Perfect base for a relaxing holiday. Non smokers only please.
6 bedrs, all ensuite, TCF TV ⌧ ↑ P 6 No children under 5 ⊕ Resid

♦♦♦♦ Dalegarth House
Sparkling Diamond
Portinscale, Keswick CA12 5RQ
☎ 017687-72817 Fax 017687-72817
E-mail john@dalegarthhousehotel.freeserve.co.uk
10 bedrs, all ensuite, TCF TV ⌧ P 12 No children under 5 ⊕ Rest Resid SB £29-£31 DB £58-£62
HB £275-£285 D £19.95 CC MC Visa JCB

♦♦♦♦ Greenbank Country House
Warm Welcome, Sparkling Diamond
Borrowdale CA12 5UY
☎ 017687-77215
Closed Dec-Jan

10 bedrs, all ensuite, TCF P 15 ⋕ 20 No children under 2 ⊕ Rest Resid SB £28 DB £56-£70 HB £259-£308 D £12 CC MC Visa &

♦♦♦♦ Greystones
Sparkling Diamond
Ambleside Road, Keswick CA12 4DP
☎ 017687-73108
Closed Dec

Traditional Lakeland house, set in a quiet location. Close to town, lake and fells.
8 bedrs, all ensuite, TCF TV ⌧ P 7 No children under 10 ⊕ Resid SB £23.50-£25 DB £47-£50 CC MC Visa

♦♦♦♦ Ravensworth
Sparkling Diamond
29 Station Street, Keswick CA12 5HH
☎ 017687-72476 Fax 017687-75287
E-mail ravensworth@btinternet.com
Closed Dec-Jan

Lovely town house ideally situated for exploring the town and the hills and lakes beyond. Decorated to a high standard. Private parking is available.
8 bedrs, 7 ensuite, TCF TV ⌧ P 5 No children under 6 ⊕ Rest Resid DB £36-£52 CC MC Visa

---

Don't forget to mention the guide

When booking direct, please remember to tell the hotel that you chose it from RAC Inspected Guest Accommodation 2000

Keswick

♦♦♦♦ Rickerby Grange
Sparkling Diamond
Portinscale, Keswick CA12 5RH
☎ 017687-72344

A small and friendly hotel in the pretty village of Portinscale. Walking distance to Keswick and Lake Derwentwater. Easy access to all parts of the Lakes, ample parking, resident proprietor.
12 bedrs, 11 ensuite, 1 ⋒ 1 ⇌ TCF TV ⊁ P 15 No children under 5 ⊕ SB £28-£30 DB £56-£60 HB £265-£280 D £13 CC MC

♦♦♦♦ Sunnyside
Sparkling Diamond
25 Southey Street, Keswick CA12 4EF
☎ 017687-72446 Fax 017687-74347
E-mail raynewton@survey.u-net.com
Closed Christmas
7 bedrs, 5 ensuite, 2 ⇌ TCF TV ⊠ ⊁ P 8 SB £18-£24 DB £36-£48

♦♦♦♦ Tarn Hows
3-5 Eskin Street, Keswick CA12 4DH
☎ 017687-73217 Fax 017687-73217
E-mail david@tarnhows40.freeserve.co.uk

Long established and comfortably appointed guest house. Pleasantly situated in quiet residential area, yet close to lake, parks, fells and town centre. Private parking.

9 bedrs, 6 ensuite, 2 ⇌ TCF TV ⊠ ⊁ P 8 No children under 6 ⊕ Resid SB £24 DB £40-£48 D £11

♦♦♦ Shemara
27 Bank Street, Keswick CA12 5JZ
☎ 017687-73936
Closed Christmas
7 bedrs, all ensuite, TCF TV ⊠ P 5 No children under 3 ⊕ Resid SB £25 DB £34-£50

♦♦♦ Skiddaw Grove
Vicarage Hill, Keswick CA12 5QB
☎ 017687-73324 Fax 017687-73324
Closed Christmas
5 bedrs, all ensuite, TCF TV ⊠ P 5 ⊕ Rest Resid SB £24-£25 DB £48-£50 ⋺

♦♦♦ Swiss Court
Sparkling Diamond
25 Bank Street, Keswick CA12 5JZ
☎ 017687-72637
7 bedrs, all ensuite, ⊕

Parkfield Awaiting Inspection
The Heads, Keswick CA12 5ES
☎ 017687-72328
8 bedrs, 4 ensuite, 1 ⇌

KETTERING Northamptonshire   8C3

♦♦♦ Headlands
Sparkling Diamond
49-51 Headlands, Kettering NN15 7ET
☎ 01536-524624 Fax 01536-483367
14 bedrs, 7 ensuite, 1 ⋒ 3 ⇌ TCF TV P 10 ⋮⋮⋮ 12 SB £25 DB £50 HB £252-£311.85 D £15 CC MC Visa Amex JCB

♦♦♦ Pennels
175 Beatrice Road, Kettering NN16 9QR
☎ 01536-481940 Fax 01536-410798
7 bedrs, 5 ensuite, 1 ⇌ TCF TV ⊁ P 4 SB £20-£22 DB £37-£39 HB £140-£154 D £13 CC MC Visa ⚿

KETTLEWELL North Yorkshire   10C3

♦♦♦♦ Langcliffe Country House ⋒
Warm Welcome, Sparkling Diamond
Kettlewell, Skipton BD23 5RJ
☎ 01756-760243
6 bedrs, 3 ensuite, 3 ⋒ TCF TV ⊠ P 7 ⋮⋮⋮ 20 ⊕ Resid SB £40 DB £60 HB £310 CC MC Visa ⚿

Knaresborough 83

KEYNSHAM Somerset   3E1

♦♦♦♦ Grasmere Court
Sparkling Diamond
22 Bath Road, Keynsham BS18 1SN
☎ 0117-986 2662 Fax 0117-986 2762

Superior family run hotel conveniently situated between Bristol and Bath. The hotel has been recently refurbished to a high standard. All rooms are well appointed with private facilities, fully licensed with free parking for all.
17 bedrs, all ensuite, TCF TV P 18 ⌂ Resid SB £38-£57 DB £54-£65 D £15 CC MC Visa Amex JCB

KING'S LYNN Norfolk   9D3

♦♦ Guanock
South Gates, King's Lynn PE30 5JG
☎ 01553-772959 Fax 01553-772959
17 bedrs, 5 ⇌ TCF TV P 8 ⌂ Rest Resid SB £21-£23 DB £33-£34 CC MC Visa Amex DC JCB

♦♦ Beeches
2 Guannock Terrace, King's Lynn PE30 5QT
☎ 01553-766577 Fax 01553-776664

Established, family run guest house close to the town centre. Bedrooms mostly ensuite, have courtesy tea and coffee, TV and telephone. Evening meals are available on request. Residential and Restaurant licence.
7 bedrs, 4 ensuite, 1 ⇌ TCF TV ⌂ P 3 ⌂ Rest Resid SB £22-£30 DB £38-£44 D £9 CC MC Visa Amex

♦ Twinson Lee
109 Tennyson Road, King's Lynn PE30 5PA
☎ 01553-762900 Fax 01553-769944
Closed Christmas
3 bedrs, 1 ⇌ TCF TV ⌂ ⌂ P 3 SB £17-£20 DB £30-£32 D £7

KINGSBRIDGE Devon   3D4

Crabshell Lodge Lodge
Embankment Road, Kingsbridge TQ7 1JZ
☎ 01548-853301 Fax 01548-856283
24 bedrs, all ensuite, TCF TV ⌂ P 40 ⌘ 15 ⌂ SB £35-£39 DB £52-£58 HB £221-£265 CC MC Visa Amex DC

KINGSTON UPON THAMES Surrey   4C2

♦♦♦ Chase Lodge
10 Park Road, Hampton Wick,
Kingston upon Thames KT1 4AS
☎ 0181-943 1862 Fax 0181-943 9363
13 bedrs, all ensuite, TCF TV ⌂ P 13 ⌘ 55 ⌂ ⌂ Rest SB £48-£62 DB £62-£85 HB £434-£791 D £15 CC MC Visa Amex DC JCB

KNARESBOROUGH North Yorkshire   11D3

♦♦♦♦ Newton House
5-7 York Place, Knaresborough HG5 0AD
☎ 01423-863539 Fax 01423-869748
E-mail newton@hotels.harrogate.com
Closed Feb

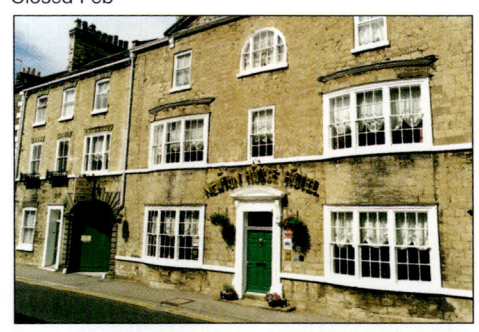

Charming family run 17th century former coaching inn located in picturesque Knaresborough. Two and a half miles from A1. Ideal for York, Harrogate and Dales.
12 bedrs, all ensuite, TCF TV ⌂ P 10 ⌂ Resid SB £35 DB £53-£65 HB £262.50-£297.50 D £17.50 CC MC Visa JCB ♿

84 Knaresborough

♦♦♦ Ebor Mount
18 York Place, Knaresborough HG5 0AA
☎ 01423-863315 Fax 01423-863315
Closed Christmas & New Year
8 bedrs, all ensuite, TCF TV ✉ P 8 SB £20-£21 DB £40-£42 CC MC Visa JCB

♦♦♦ Yorkshire Lass
High Bridge, Harrogate Road, Knaresborough HG5 8DA
☎ 01423-862962 Fax 01423-869091
E-mail yorkshirelass@knaresborough.co.uk
6 bedrs, all ensuite, TCF TV P 32 ♨ SB £30-£40
DB £40-£55 D £10 CC MC Visa Amex

KNOTTINGLEY West Yorkshire 11D4

♦♦♦ Wentvale
Great North Road, Knottingley WF11 8PF
☎ 01977-676714
4 bedrs, all ensuite, TCF TV DB £40

KNUTSFORD Cheshire 7E1

♦♦♦♦ Dog Inn
Well Bank Lane, Over Peover, Knutsford WA16 8UP
☎ 01625-861421 Fax 01625-861421
6 bedrs, all ensuite, TCF TV P 80 ♨ SB £50 DB £60-£70
D £16 CC MC Visa Amex ♿

♦♦♦ Pickmere
Park Lane, Pickmere, Knutsford WA16 0JX
☎ 01565-733433 Fax 01565-733433

Spacious, quiet ensuite rooms. Private parking. Rural location yet swift, easy access to motorways, Airport and major North-West towns and tourist attractions. No smoking. Self-catering cottage also available.
8 bedrs, 7 ensuite, 2 ⇌ TCF TV ✉ ✱ P 12 ⊞ 10
SB £21.50-£32.50 DB £46 CC MC Visa

LAUNCESTON Cornwall 2C3

♦♦♦♦ Hurdon Farm
Launceston PL15 9LS
☎ 01566-772955
Closed Nov-Apr

Elegant, 18th century, stone farmhouse superbly situated in quiet, picturesque countryside. Ideal location for exploring Devon and Cornwall, with delicious, fresh home cooking a speciality.
6 bedrs, all ensuite, TCF TV ✉ P 6 SB £21-£23 DB £42-£46 HB £203-£210 D £11

LEAMINGTON SPA Warwickshire 8A4

♦♦♦♦ Adams
22 Avenue Road, Leamington Spa CV31 3PQ
☎ 01926-450742 Fax 01926-313110
14 bedrs, all ensuite, P 14 ⊞ 24 No children under 12 ♨ SB £48-£56 DB £54.50-£65.50 D £18.75 CC MC Visa Amex DC

LEEDS West Yorkshire 11D3

♦♦♦♦ Pinewood
78 Potternewton Lane, Leeds LS7 3LW
☎ 0800-096 7463 Fax 0113-262 2561

Leominster 85

Attractively decorated and very well furnished hotel, with many extra touches to increase guests' comfort. A warm welcome in a small, comfortable hotel of distinction.
10 bedrs, all ensuite, TCF TV ⌂ Rest Resid ⟨⟨ MC Visa Amex

♦♦ Broomhurst
12 Chapel Lane, Off Cardigan Road,
Leeds LS6 3BW
☎ 0113-278 6836 Fax 0113-230 7099

A small, comfortable, family run hotel in a quiet, pleasantly wooded, conservation area, one and a half miles from the city centre. Convenient for Headingley cricket/rugby grounds and public transport.
18 bedrs, 12 ensuite, 3 ⇌ TCF TV P 10 ⌂ Resid
SB £25 DB £45 HB £245 D £10.50 ⟨⟨ MC Visa ⚒

LEICESTER Leicestershire	8B3

Old Tudor Rectory
Awaiting Inspection
Main Street, Glenfield, Leicester LE3 8DG
☎ 0116-291 5678 Fax 0116-291 1416
Closed 24 Dec-2 Jan

Tudor rectory, a Grade II Listed building with Jacobean and Queen Anne additions. Set in an acre of gardens close to the city centre with easy access to M1(21 and 21A) - two minutes.
15 bedrs, all ensuite, TCF TV ⌂ P 25 ⦙⦙ 25 ⌂ Resid
SB £35-£42 DB £42.40-£60 HB £295-£365 D £10.95
⟨⟨ MC Visa Amex DC

Scotia Awaiting Inspection
10 Westcotes Drive, Leicester LE3 0QR
☎ 0116-254 9200 Fax 0116-254 9200
11 bedrs, 4 ensuite, 3 ⇌ TCF TV ⌂ P 5 ⌂ ⌂ Rest Resid SB £22-£27 DB £42-£45 D £8.45

Stoneycroft Awaiting Inspection
5-7 Elmfield Avenue, Leicester LE2 1RB
☎ 0116-270 7605 Fax 0116-270 6067
E-mail 106731.2644@compuserve.com
44 bedrs, 35 ensuite, 7 ⌂ 2 ⇌ TCF TV P 15 ⦙⦙ 100 ⌂
Rest Resid SB £42 DB £50 HB £320 D £7 ⟨⟨ MC Visa Amex DC ⚒

LENHAM Kent	5E3

Harrow Hill Awaiting Inspection
Warren Street, Lenham ME17 2ED
☎ 01622-858727 Fax 01622-850026
15 bedrs, all ensuite, TCF TV P 75 ⦙⦙ 15 ⌂ SB £40
DB £50 ⟨⟨ MC Visa Amex ⚒

LEOMINSTER Herefordshire	7E3

Wharton Bank Awaiting Inspection
Wharton, Leominster HR6 0NX
☎ 01568-612575 Fax 01568-616089
4 bedrs, 1 ensuite, 1 ⇌ TCF P 8 No children under 6
SB £20-£25 DB £42-£45

ENGLAND

Short Breaks
Many hotels provide special rates for weekend and mid-week breaks – sometimes these are quoted in the hotel's entry, otherwise ring direct for the latest offers.

86 Lewes

LEWES East Sussex   5D4

♦♦♦♦ Berkeley House
Sparkling Diamond
2 Albion Street, Lewes BN7 2ND
☎ 01273-476057 Fax 01273-479575
Closed Christmas

An elegant Georgian townhouse, centrally but quietly located, with a roof terrace giving views across Lewes to the surrounding hills. All rooms have private facilities. Residential licence. Winter breaks available.
5 bedrs, all ensuite, TCF TV P 3 No children under 8 ⌑ Resid SB £40-£50 DB £40-£75 CC MC Visa Amex DC

Millers Awaiting Inspection
134 High Street, Lewes BN7 1XS
☎ 01273-475631 Fax 01273-486226
E-mail millers134@aol.com
Closed 4-5 Nov, 20 Dec-4 Jan
2 bedrs, both ensuite, TCF TV ☒ No children SB £48 DB £54

LICHFIELD Staffordshire   7F2

♦♦♦ Coppers End
Walsall Road, Muckley Corner, Lichfield WS14 0BG
☎ 01543-372910 Fax 01543-360423
Closed Christmas

Charming, detached guest house. Centrally heated, three ensuite, vanity units, hospitality tray, colour TVs, two ground floor rooms, residential licence, lovely conservatory dining room, large attractive garden, parking.
6 bedrs, 3 ensuite, 1 ↩ TCF TV P 8 ⌑ Resid SB £24-£33 DB £38-£46 CC MC Visa Amex DC

LINCOLN Lincolnshire   8C1

♦♦♦♦ D'Isney Place
Sparkling Diamond
Eastgate, Lincoln LN2 4AA
☎ 01522-538881 Fax 01522-511321
E-mail info@disney-place.freespace.co.uk
17 bedrs, all ensuite, TCF TV ↠ P 5 SB £50-£70 DB £76-£96 CC MC Visa Amex DC JCB ♿

♦♦♦ Admiral
16-18 Nelson Street, Lincoln LN1 1PJ
☎ 01522-544467 Fax 01522-544467
E-mail don@admiral63.freeserve.co.uk
9 bedrs, all ensuite, TCF TV ↠ P 12 SB £18-£20 DB £35-£37 HB £160 CC MC Visa ♿

♦♦♦ Halfway Farm
A46 Swinderby, Lincoln LN6 9HN
☎ 01522-868749 Fax 01522-868082
Closed 24 Dec-2 Jan
17 bedrs, 15 ensuite, 1 ↩ TCF TV ↠ P 25 ⋕ 20 SB £30 DB £40 CC MC Visa Amex DC ♿

♦♦♦ Tennyson
Sparkling Diamond
7 South Park Avenue, Lincoln LN5 8EN
☎ 01522-521624 Fax 01522-521624
Closed Christmas & New Year

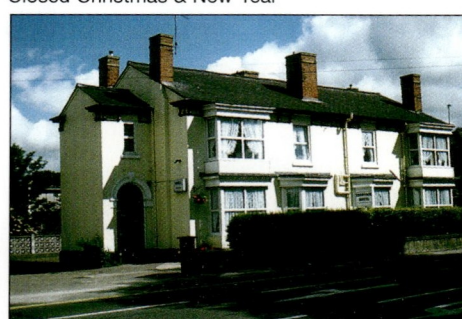

A personally supervised hotel with a comfortable atmosphere, overlooking the South Park, one mile from the city centre. Leisure breaks available.
8 bedrs, all ensuite, TCF TV P 8 ⌑ Resid SB £29-£55 DB £40-£42 CC MC Visa Amex DC

Liverpool 87

THE LONDON INN

Family owned 17th century coaching inn, adjacent to internationally famous parish church, offers the chance to stay in a warm and welcoming village atmosphere on the edge of Bodmin Moor. Local real ales and home prepared food are our speciality.

ST. NEOT, LISKEARD, CORNWALL PL14 6NG
Tel/Fax: 01579-320263

| LISKEARD Cornwall | 2B3 |

London Inn Awaiting Inspection
St. Neots, Liskeard PL14 6NG
☎ 01579-320263 Fax 01579-320263
E-mail jpleisuregroup@compuserve.com
3 bedrs, all ensuite, TCF TV P 14 ⚡ SB £30-£36
DB £40-£48 D £30 CC MC Visa JCB
See advert on this page

| LITTLEHAMPTON West Sussex | 4C4 |

Colbern Awaiting Inspection
South Terrace, Sea Front, Littlehampton BN17 5LQ
☎ 01903-714270 Fax 01903-730955
E-mail colbern.hotel@lineone.net
Closed Christmas

Small, friendly hotel close to the seaside, river and town centre. Ideal base for visiting Arundel, Brighton, Chichester, Portsmouth and the beautiful West Sussex countryside.
9 bedrs, all ensuite, TCF TV ⚡ Rest Resid SB £20-£35
DB £40-£60 HB £224 D £12 CC MC Visa Amex DC JCB

| LIVERPOOL Merseyside | 10B4 |

♦♦♦ **Blenheim**
37 Aigburth Drive, Sefton Park, Liverpool L17 4JE
☎ 0151-727 7380 Fax 0151-727 5833
E-mail blenheimguesthouse@btinternet.com

Beautifully restored Victorian villa, standing in its own grounds overlooking Sefton Park Lake. Licensed residents bar. Tea, coffee and colour TV in all rooms.
17 bedrs, 8 ensuite, 4 ⇌ TCF TV P 17 ⚡ Resid SB £19.50
DB £33 D £6 CC MC Visa

Aachen Awaiting Inspection
89-91 Mount Pleasant, Liverpool L3 5TB
☎ 0151-709 3477 Fax 0151-709 1126
Closed Christmas-New Year
17 bedrs, 10 ensuite, 2 ⇌ TCF TV ⚞ P 4 ⚡ CC MC Visa Amex DC JCB 🏨 ♿

Campanile Liverpool Lodge
Chaloner Street, Queens Dock, Liverpool L3 4AJ
☎ 0151-709 8104 Fax 0151-709 8725
103 bedrs, all ensuite, TCF TV ⚞ P 103 ⏣ 20 ⚡ Rest Resid SB £42.50 DB £47 D £10.55 CC MC Visa Amex DC ♿

| LIZARD Cornwall | 2A4 |

♦♦♦♦ **Parc Brawse House**
Penmenner Road, Lizard TR12 7NR
☎ 01326-290466 Fax 01326-290466
7 bedrs, 4 ensuite, 2 ⇌ TCF TV ⚞ P 7 ⚡ Rest Resid
SB £17.50-£28 DB £31-£45 HB £192-£231 D £12
CC MC Visa

ENGLAND

SPENCER'S

The British Golf Directory

Courses where you can turn up and play

This new Spencer's guide provides full details of golf courses the length and breadth of Britain. All are courses where you can turn up and play, from municipal courses to some of the grandest in the land. You don't need to be members or pay membership fees. Just the rate for the round.

Whether you are an old hand or one of the new wave of golf enthusiasts you will find Spencer's Directory an invaluable companion - for your home, for your car or for your holidays.

With full-colour throughout it's easy-to-use, highly practical and perfect for browsing.

Each entry has a full quarter-page, with a description of the course, and information on yardage, par, standard scratch score, directions and green fees. There's also a full-colour route-planning and map section - a feature of all Spencer's titles.

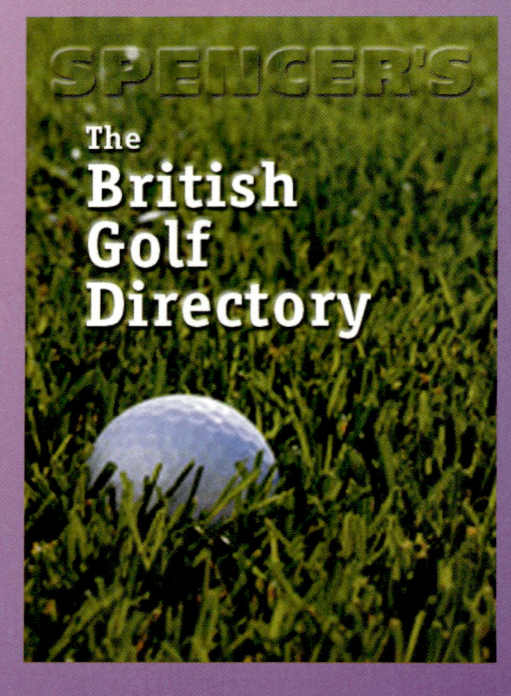

Format:	210x148mm
No. of pages:	112pp
ISBN:	1 900327 51 1
Price:	£4.99
Publication date:	April 2000

West One Publishing
Kestrel House, Duke's PLace
Marlow, Bucks SL7 2QH

tel: 01628 487722

www.WestOneWeb.com

London

Maps

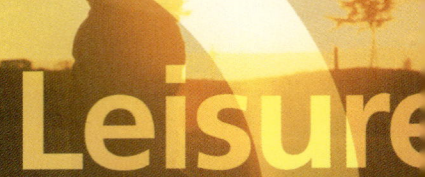

Leisure

Travel

Shoppin

www.WestOneWeb.com

West On

London

Because of the size of London, the Directory has been divided into seven regions for easy reference. These regions equate to groups of postal districts. The postcode map on the next page will allow you to identify the area you wish to stay in and you can then look up the relevant part of the directory to find a hotel.
If you know the name of a hotel or guest house you wish to stay at, but are not sure where it is located, use the list below. This gives its postcode, position on the London Outer or Inner maps (pages 93 to 95) and also the page its entry appears in the directory.

Name	Postcode	Map	Page
Abbey Lodge	W5 3PR	Outer A2	103
Aber	N8 9EG	Outer C1	105
Academy	WC1E 6HG	Inner E2	101
Acton Park	W3 7JT	Outer B2	103
Anchor – Nova	NW11 7QH	Outer B1	102
Ashley	W2 1RU	Inner B2	100
Atlas-Apollo	W8 5JE	Inner B3	99
Averard	W2 3LH	Inner B2	99
Barry House	W2 2TP	Inner C1	100
Barn	HA4 6JB	Outer A2*	106
Blair House	SW3 2SA	Inner C4	101
Caswell	SW1V 2DB	Inner D4	96
Central	NW11 8BS	Inner B1	102
Claverley	SW3 1PS	Inner C3	98
Cranbrook	IG1 4QR	Outer E1	105
Craven Gardens	W2 3ES	Inner B2	99
Crompton	TW3 1JG	Outer A2*	106
Crystal Palace Tower	SE19 2UB	Outer C3	105
Diplomat	SW1X 8DT	Inner C4	96
Dylan	W2 3DW	Inner B2	100
Edward Lear	W1H 5WD	Inner C2	96
Elizabeth	SW1V 1PB	Inner E4	98
Executive	SW1X 0BD	Inner C3	96
Forest View	E7 9HL	Outer E1	105
Four Seasons	NW1 6DX	Inner C2	102
Garden Court	W2 4BG	Inner A2	99
Garth	NW2 2NL	Outer B1	102
Georgian House	W1H 3PG	Inner C2	96
Grange Lodge	W5 5BX	Outer A2	103
Grove Hill	E18 3JG	Outer E1	105
Haddon Hall	WC1B 5JT	Inner F2	102
Hamilton House	SW1V 1SA	Inner D4	96
Hart House	W1H 3PE	Inner C2	97
Heathrow Palace	TW5 9UT	Outer A2*	106
Henley House	SW5 OEN	Inner B4	101
Hotel Orlando	W6 7LR	Outer B2	103
Huttons	SW1V 2BB	Inner D4	98
Kensington Manor	SW7 4HH	Inner B3	101
La Gaffe	NW3 6SS	Outer B1	103
Lakeside	E11 1PQ	Outer E1	105
Langorf	NW3 6AG	Outer B1	103
London Continental	W1H 3HN	Inner C2	97
Merlyn Court	SW5 0EN	Inner B4	101
Mitre House	W2 1TU	Inner B2	99
Park	IG1 4UE	Outer E1	104
Park Lodge	W2 3SU	Inner A3	100
Parkwood	W2 2HB	Inner B2	100
Shepiston Lodge	UB3 1LJ	Outer A2*	106
Sleeping Beauty Motel	E10 7EB	Outer D1	105
Swiss Cottage	NW3 3HP	Outer C1	102
Swiss House	SW5 0AN	Inner B4	101
Trochee	SW19 4AS	Outer B3	105
Trochee	SW19 4SW	Outer B3	105
Victoria Inn	SW1V 2BG	Inner D4	97
Westland	W2 4HP	Inner B3	98
Weston House	SE9 5LB	Outer E3	105
White Lodge	N8	Outer C1	104
Wigmore Court	W1H 3PB	Inner C2	96
Willett	SW1W 8DJ	Inner C4	97
Wimbledon	SW19 4HZ	Outer B3	106
Winchester	SW1 1RB	Inner D4	98
Windermere	SW1V 4JE	Inner D4	96
Woodville	IG1 3BQ	Outer E1	104
Worcester House	SW19 7AE	Outer B3	105

National Code & Number Change

Telephone codes and numbers in London change in April 2000.

0171-XXXXXX becomes 020-7XXX XXXX
0181-XXXXXX becomes 020-8XXX XXXX

GRAND TOUR OF LORD'S

Experience the unique atmosphere of Lord's, the home of cricket.

Tours are normally at Noon and 2pm daily – restrictions on some match days.

TELEPHONE 020-7432 1033

London – Postal Districts

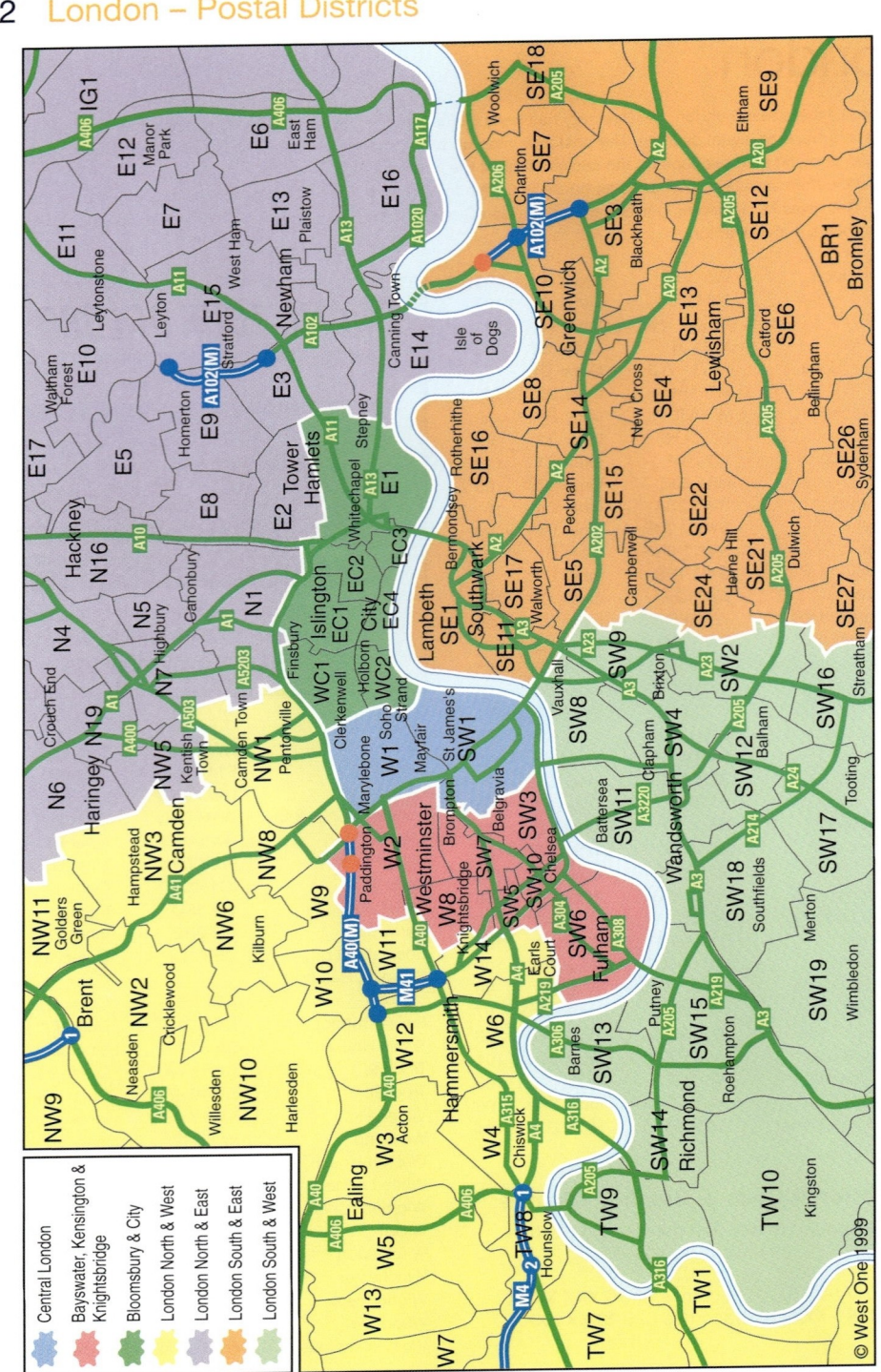

London Outer 93

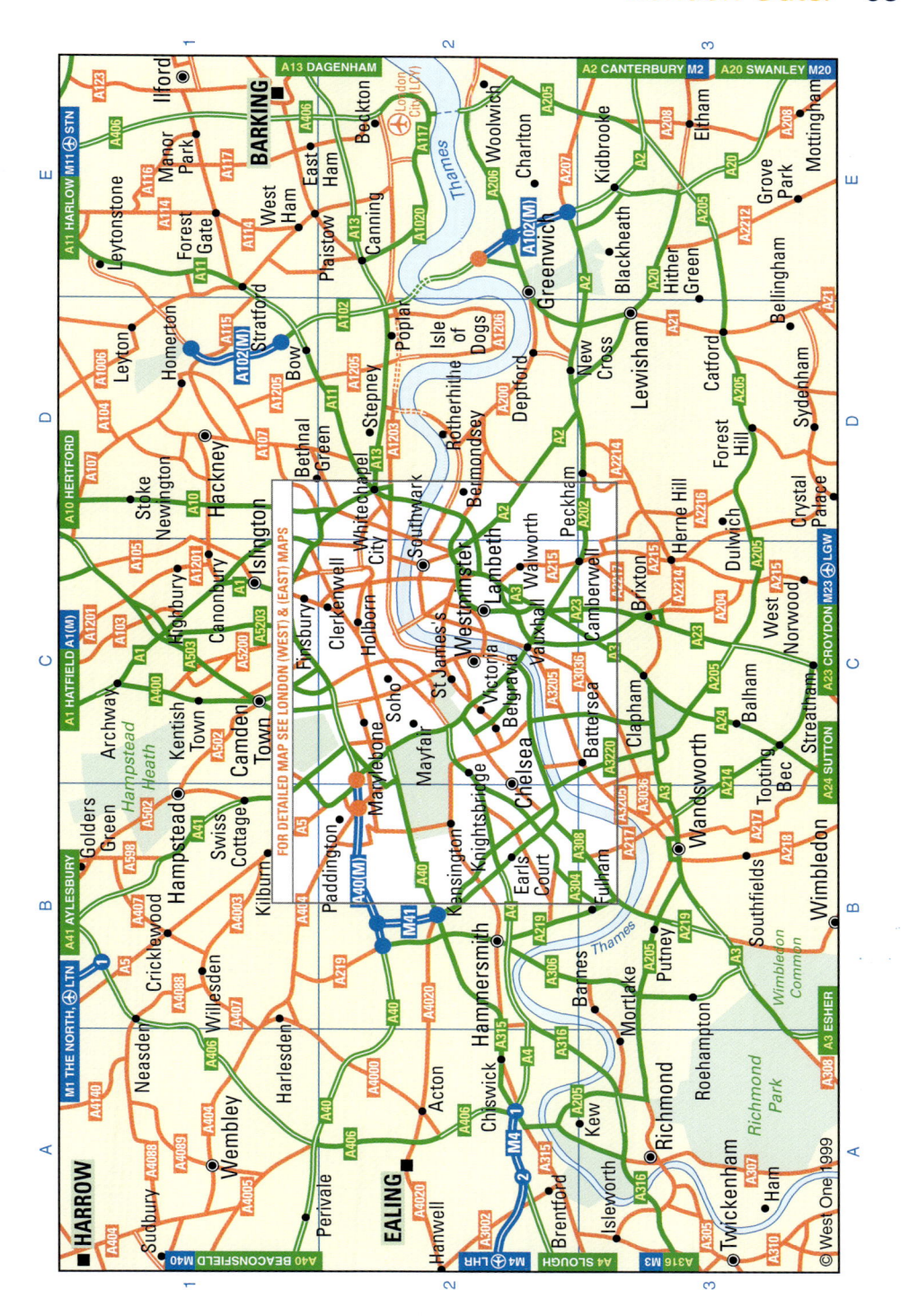

94 London – West

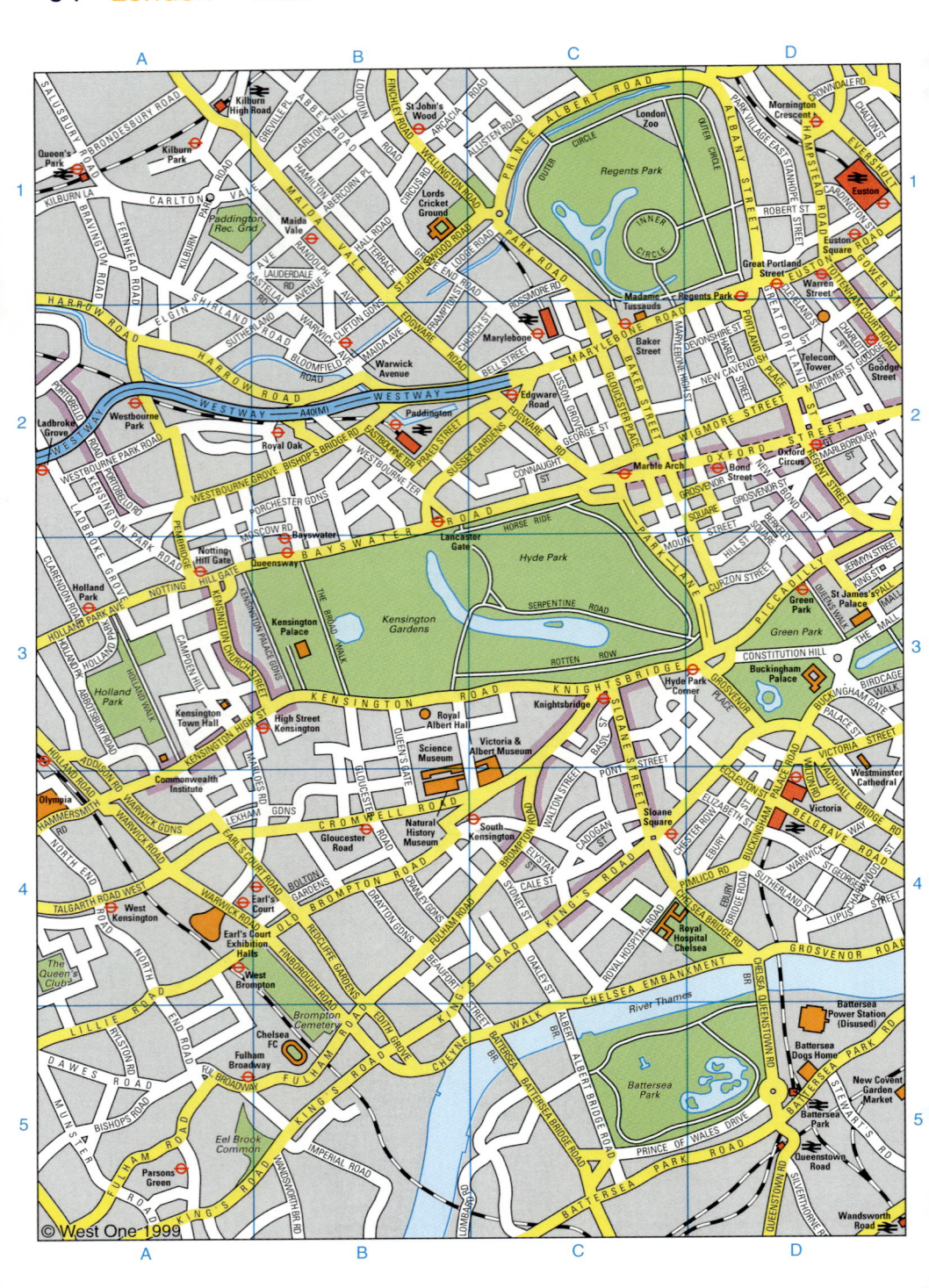

E
F
G
H
1
2
3
4
5
Mornington Crescent
St Pancras
King's Cross
King's Cross Thameslink
Euston
Euston Square
Warren Street
Angel
Old Street
Shoreditch
Russell Square
Coram's Fields
Goodge Street
British Museum
Telecom Tower
Tottenham Court Road
Oxford Circus
Holborn
Farringdon
Barbican
Barbican Centre
Moorgate
Liverpool Street
Aldgate East
Aldgate
St Paul's Cathedral
St Paul's
City Thameslink
Bank
Fenchurch Street
Tower Hill
Mansion House
Cannon Street
Monument
Tower of London
Tower Gateway
Temple
Blackfriars
Thames
River
Piazza
Covent Garden
Leicester Square
Piccadilly Circus
National Gallery
Embankment
Charing Cross
National Theatre
Royal Festival Hall
Waterloo East
Southwark Cathedral
London Bridge
HMS Belfast
Hay's Galleria
St Katharine Docks
Guy's Hospital
Borough
Green Park
St James's Palace
Horse Guards Parade
St James's Park
Government Offices
Westminster
Old County Hall
Waterloo International
Waterloo
Buckingham Palace
Museum
St Thomas Hospital
Houses of Parliament
Westminster Abbey
Lambeth North
Lambeth Palace
RC Cathedral
Imperial War Museum
Crown Court
Elephant & Castle
Westminster Cathedral
Government Offices
Tate Gallery
Victoria
Pimlico
Kennington
Burgess Park
Vauxhall
The Oval Cricket Ground
Oval
Kennington Park
Flower Market
Battersea Power Station (Disused)
Battersea Dogs Home
New Covent Garden Market
Vauxhall College
Town Hall
Stockwell
Maudsley Hospital
King's College Hospital
Denmark Hill
Wandsworth Road
PENTONVILLE ROAD
CITY ROAD
EUSTON ROAD
GRAY'S INN ROAD
CLERKENWELL ROAD
THEOBALD'S ROAD
HIGH HOLBORN
HOLBORN VIADUCT
LONDON WALL
FLEET STREET
STRAND
VICTORIA EMBANKMENT
OXFORD STREET
REGENT STREET
PICCADILLY
THE MALL
WHITEHALL
VICTORIA STREET
BIRDCAGE WALK
LAMBETH BRIDGE
VAUXHALL BRIDGE
GROSVENOR ROAD
KENNINGTON ROAD
KENNINGTON PARK ROAD
KENNINGTON LANE
CAMBERWELL NEW ROAD
CAMBERWELL ROAD
WALWORTH ROAD
OLD KENT ROAD
NEW KENT ROAD
TOWER BRIDGE ROAD
TOWER BRIDGE
JAMAICA ROAD
LONG LANE
BOROUGH HIGH STREET
SOUTHWARK STREET
STAMFORD STREET
BLACKFRIARS ROAD
WATERLOO ROAD
WESTMINSTER BRIDGE ROAD
BRIXTON ROAD
CLAPHAM ROAD
STOCKWELL ROAD
WANDSWORTH ROAD
SOUTH LAMBETH ROAD
PECKHAM ROAD
ALBANY ROAD
COMMERCIAL STREET
BISHOPSGATE
HACKNEY ROAD
KINGSLAND ROAD
BETHNAL GREEN ROAD
GREAT EASTERN ST
BRICK LANE
SHOREDITCH HIGH STREET

96 London

National Code & Number Change
Telephone codes and numbers in London change in April 2000.

0171-XXXXXX becomes 020-7XXX XXXX
0181-XXXXXX becomes 020-8XXX XXXX

LONDON Central London

♦♦♦♦ Windermere
142-144 Warwick Way, Victoria, London SW1V 4JE
0171-834 5163 Fax 0171-630 8831
E-mail windermere@compuserve.com

A small, friendly hotel with well equipped bedrooms. There is a cosy lounge with inviting Chesterfields, while English breakfast and dinner are served in the elegant dining room.
22 bedrs, 20 ensuite, 2 ⇌ TCF TV ⏏ Rest Resid
SB £64-£84 DB £75-£130 D £15.95 CC MC Visa Amex JCB

♦♦♦ Georgian House
87 Gloucester Place, London W1H 3PG
0171-935 2211 Fax 0171-486 7535
E-mail georgian@georgian-hotel.demon.co.uk
19 bedrs, 11 ensuite, 6 ⏏ 2 ⇌ TCF TV ⏏ No children under 5 SB £70-£75 DB £85-£90 CC MC Visa Amex

♦♦♦ Wigmore Court
23 Gloucester Place, London W1H 3PB
0171-935 0928 Fax 0171-487 4254
18 bedrs, 16 ensuite, 2 ⇌ TCF TV SB £57-£62 DB £87-£97 CC MC Visa JCB &

♦♦ Edward Lear
30 Seymour Street, London W1H 5WD
0171-402 5401 Fax 0171-706 3766
31 bedrs, 4 ensuite, 8 ⏏ 6 ⇌ TCF TV SB £43.50 DB £60 CC MC Visa

Caswell Awaiting Inspection
25 Gloucester Street, London SW1V 2DB
0171-834 6345
17 bedrs, 7 ensuite, 5 ⇌ TCF TV No children under 5
SB £35-£65 DB £42-£75 CC MC Visa JCB

Diplomat Awaiting Inspection
2 Chesham Street, Belgrave Square, London SW1X 8DT
0171-235 1544 Fax 0171-259 6153
E-mail diplomathotel@btinternet.co

The Diplomat is situated in Belgravia, the most exclusive and sought after neighbourhood in London. It is within easy walking distance of Harrods and the fashionable Knightsbridge and Chelsea shops.
26 bedrs, all ensuite, TCF TV ⏏ ⏏ Rest Resid SB £85-£90 DB £125-£150 D £10 CC MC Visa Amex DC JCB

Executive Awaiting Inspection
57 Pont Street, London SW1X 0BD
0171-581 2424 Fax 0171-589 9456

Upmarket, quality town-house hotel decorated in elegant English fabrics and prints.
27 bedrs, all ensuite, TCF TV ⏏ P 4 ⏏ Resid SB £81-£86 DB £102-£108 CC MC Visa Amex DC

Hamilton House Awaiting Inspection
60 Warwick Way, London SW1V 1SA
0171-821 7113 Fax 0171-630 0806
40 bedrs, 35 ensuite, 5 ⇌ TCF TV ⏏ Resid CC MC Visa

HUTTONS HOTEL
53-57 BELGRAVE ROAD, LONDON SW1
Tel: 0171-834 3726   Fax: 0171-834 3389

Welcome to Hutton Hotel.

Within a few minutes walk of Victoria railway and coach stations, British Airways, bus stop opposite the hotel.

All rooms en-suite with hot and cold water, shaving points, centrally heated, radio, colour TV and telephone. Elevator. Advanced bookings, open 24 hours, accepted by Mastercard, Visa and American Express.

Enjoy your stay in Central London.

Hart House Awaiting Inspection
51 Gloucester Place, London W1H 3PE
0171-935 2288 Fax 0171-935 8516
E-mail reservations@harthouse.co.uk

Highly recommended by many distinguished guide books and travel organisations. Run by the Bowden family for the last 30 years. In the heart of London's West End.
16 bedrs, 11 ensuite, 1 ➡ TCF TV SB £60-£66 DB £89-£95 CC MC Visa Amex

London Continental Awaiting Inspection
88 Gloucester Place, London W1H 3HN
0171-486 8670 Fax 0171-486 8671
E-mail reservations@london-continental.com
25 bedrs, 22 ensuite, TCF TV CC MC Visa Amex DC &

Victoria Inn Awaiting Inspection
65-67 Belgrave Road, Victoria, London SW1V 2BG
0171-834 6721
41 bedrs, all ensuite,

Willett Awaiting Inspection
32 Sloane Gardens, Sloane Square,
London SW1W 8DJ
0171-824 8415 Fax 0171-730 4830
E-mail willett@eeh.co.uk

19 charming bedrooms, superbly appointed and decorated. Minutes from Harrods. Excellent night life and shopping.
19 bedrs, all ensuite, TCF TV SB £76.37 DB £117 CC MC Visa Amex DC

ELIZABETH HOTEL & APARTMENTS

The Elizabeth Hotel is a beautiful Townhouse overlooking the magnificent gardens of the Famous Eccleston Square, built c1835 by Sir Tomas Cubitt, Queen Elizabeth I's favourite builder. The square has been home to many famous people, including Sir Winston Churchill and Prince Louis of Battenburgh who actually resided at number 37, now the Elizabeth. The hotel is a high quality bed & breakfast hotel in the 2 star market, and is just a few minutes walk from Victoria Coach, Bus, Underground and train stations giving excellent links to the whole of London. For sightseers, it is only a few minutes walk from Buckingham Palace, The Houses of Parliament, Westminster Cathedral and Abbey, Trafalgar Square, Whitehall and Downing Street, and The Tate Gallery is just around the corner. Shoppers have easy access to Harrods and the other famous shops of Knightsbridge, Oxford Street and Regent Street, and for Business Travellers, the links to the City are First Rate. Altogether an excellent package for every customer.

Extremely Reasonable Prices in a fantastic Location
Visa, MasterCard, Switch, Delta & JCB are accepted.

37 ECCLESTON SQUARE, VICTORIA, LONDON, SW1V 1PB
TEL: 020 7 828 6812 FAX: 020 7 828 6814
E-MAIL ELIZABETH@ARGYLLHOTELS.COM

Winchester Awaiting Inspection
17 Belgrave Road, London SW1 1RB
0171-828 2972 Fax 0171-828 5191
22 bedrs, all ensuite, TV No children under 4 SB £70 DB £70

Huttons Awaiting Inspection
55 Belgrave Road, London SW1V 2BB
0171-834 3726 Fax 0171-834 3389
54 bedrs, all ensuite, TV SB £51.50-£54 DB £61-£64
CC MC Visa Amex DC JCB
See advert on previous page

Elizabeth
37 Eccleston Square, London SW1V 1PB
0171-828 6812 Fax 0171-828 6814
40 bedrs, 34 ensuite, 1 3 TV 25
See advert on this page

LONDON Bayswater, Kensington & Knightsbridge

♦♦♦♦ Claverley
13-14 Beaufort Gardens, Knightsbridge, London SW3 1PS
0171-589 8541 Fax 0171-584 3410

Charming town house hotel in a quiet Victorian cul-de-sac. Two minute stroll from Harrods in Knightsbridge. Fourposter beds with designer fabrics available, prices include full English breakfast and VAT.
30 bedrs, 26 ensuite, 1 TV SB £60-£120 DB £110-£195 CC MC Visa Amex DC JCB

♦♦♦♦ Westland
154 Bayswater Road, London W2 4HP
0171-229 9191 Fax 0171-727 1054
E-mail 106411.3060@compuserve.com
31 bedrs, all ensuite, TCF TV P 9 20 Rest Resid SB £89 DB £105-£120 D £10.50 CC MC Visa Amex DC

One of London's best bed and breakfast hotels

All bedrooms with en-suite bathroom, satellite television, six band radio and direct dial telephone • Free car park • Licensed Bar Traditional English Breakfast • Lift • Reasonable rates

Centrally located to all major sights, theatres and shopping areas. One block from Paddington Station and Heathrow Airport Express. RAC Acclaimed, AA Listed LTB Member

MITRE HOUSE HOTEL
178-184 Sussex Gardens, Hyde Park, London W2 1TU
Tel: 020 7723 8040   Fax: 020 7402 0990

Web site: http:\\www.mitrehousehotel.com
e-mail: reservations@mitrehousehotel.com
RAC ♦♦♦

♦♦♦ Atlas-Apollo
18-30 Lexham Gardens, London W8 5JE
☎ 0171-835 1155 Fax 0171-370 4853
91 bedrs, all ensuite, TV 🕭 🍴 SB £70-£75 DB £85-£90
CC MC Visa Amex DC JCB

♦♦♦ Averard
10 Lancaster Gate, London W2 3LH
☎ 0171-723 8877 Fax 0171-706 0860
Closed Christmas

Excellently located, friendly family hotel in an interesting Victorian building with original public rooms and period style painting, sculptures and other features.
60 bedrs, all ensuite, TV 🕭 🍴 Resid SB £55-£70 DB £75-£95 CC MC Visa Amex DC

♦♦♦ Craven Gardens
16 Leinster Terrace, London W2 3ES
☎ 0171-262 3167 Fax 0171-262 2083
E-mail cravengardens@dircon.co.uk
43 bedrs, all ensuite, TCF TV 🕭 🍴 30 🍴 Resid SB £55-£70 DB £70-£85 CC MC Visa Amex DC JCB ♿

♦♦♦ Garden Court
30-31 Kensington Garden Square, London W2 4BG
☎ 0171-229 2553 Fax 0171-727 2749
32 bedrs, 16 ensuite, 6 🛏 TV 🐕 SB £48 DB £78 CC MC Visa

♦♦♦ Mitre House
178-184 Sussex Gardens, Hyde Park, London W2 1TU
☎ 0171-723 8040 Fax 0171-402 0990
E-mail reservations@mitrehousehotel.com
70 bedrs, all ensuite, TV 🕭 P 20 🍴 Resid SB £55-£65 DB £70-£75 CC MC Visa Amex DC JCB ♿
See advert on this page

London

♦♦♦ Park Lodge
73 Queensborough Terrace, Bayswater,
London W2 3SU
📞 0171-229 6424 Fax 0171-221 4772
E-mail smegroup.kfc@mcmail.net

The Park Lodge Hotel is within walking distance of Queensway and Bayswater underground stations, close to Hyde Park and Oxford Street.
29 bedrs, all ensuite, TCF TV 🔲 SB £70 DB £85 CC MC Visa Amex DC JCB

♦♦♦ Parkwood
4 Stanhope Place, London W2 2HB
📞 0171-402 2241 Fax 0171-402 1574
E-mail prkwd@aol.com

An attractive town house situated in a quiet residential street just a two minute walk from Oxford Street, Marble Arch and Hyde Park (Speaker's Corner). Excellently managed with spotlessly clean and airy rooms.
14 bedrs, 12 ensuite, 3 ⇌ TCF TV SB £45-£49
DB £64.50-£88 CC MC Visa

♦♦ Barry House
12 Sussex Place, London W2 2TP
📞 0171-723 7340 Fax 0171-723 9775
E-mail bh-hotel@liaison.demon.co.uk

Providing family-like care, this friendly, comfortable B&B has bedrooms with ensuite facilities. English breakfast included in competitive rates. Very central location close to Paddington Station. Web: www.hotel.uk.com/barryhouse.
18 bedrs, 14 ensuite, 1 🅟 2 ⇌ TCF TV SB £35-£50
DB £72-£75 CC MC Visa Amex DC JCB

♦♦ Dylan
14 Devonshire Terrace, Lancaster Gate,
London W2 3DW
📞 0171-723 3280 Fax 0171-402 2443
18 bedrs, 8 ensuite, 4 🅟 4 ⇌ TCF TV 🔲 SB £32-£38
DB £55-£70 CC MC Visa Amex DC

♦ Ashley
15-17 Norfolk Square, London W2 1RU
📞 0171-723 3375 Fax 0171-723 0173
E-mail ashhot@btinternet.com
Closed 24 Dec-Jan

A very central, quiet hotel, owned and managed by the same Welsh family for 30 years. Quality ensuite rooms with tea/coffee making facilities and excellent English breakfast.
51 bedrs, 40 ensuite, 3 ⇌ TCF TV SB £32.50-£45
DB £69-£71 CC MC Visa

London 101

Blair House Awaiting Inspection
34 Draycott Place, London SW3 2SA
0171-581 2323 Fax 0171-823 7752
17 bedrs, all ensuite, TCF TV SB £85-£87.50
DB £115-£117.50 CC MC Visa Amex DC JCB

Henley House Awaiting Inspection
30 Barkston Gardens, Earls Court,
London SW5 OEN
0171-370 4111 Fax 0171-370 0026
E-mail henleyhse@aol.com

Henley House is a small but very charming 'boutique' style hotel, ideal both for the business traveller and for those looking for that romantic weekend in London. 20 bedrs, all ensuite, TCF TV SB £69-£82 DB £89-£109 CC MC Visa Amex DC JCB

Kensington Manor Awaiting Inspection
8 Emperor's Gate, London SW7 4HH
0171-370 7516 Fax 0171-373 3163
14 bedrs, 12 ensuite, 1 1 TCF TV CC MC Visa Amex DC JCB

Merlyn Court Awaiting Inspection
2 Barkston Gardens, London SW5 0EN
0171-370 1640 Fax 0171-370 4986
Closed 20-26 Dec

Comfortable, good value, family run hotel in a central location off a quiet Edwardian square in Kensington. Family rooms are available. Easy access to Olympia and Earls Court exhibition halls, train stations and motorways.
17 bedrs, 8 ensuite, 1 6 TCF SB £30-£50 DB £55-£65 CC MC Visa JCB

Swiss House Awaiting Inspection
171 Old Brompton Road, South Kensington, London SW5 0AN
0171-373 9383 Fax 0171-373 4983
E-mail recep@swiss-hh.demon.co.uk
15 bedrs, 14 ensuite, 1 1 TCF TV SB £46-£65 DB £80-£90 CC MC Visa Amex DC
See advert on this page

LONDON Bloomsbury & City

Academy Awaiting Inspection
17-21 Gower Street, London WC1E 6HG
0171-631 4115 Fax 0171-636 3442
E-mail academyh@aol.com
48 bedrs, all ensuite, TCF TV 24 Resid Room £100-£125 D £17 CC MC Visa Amex DC JCB

SWISS HOUSE HOTEL

'Excellent value for money' has always been our motto. The hotel knows guests' priorities and aims to meet them all. Cleanliness, service with a smile, value and comfort come as standard. Best value B&B in London. Award Winner. Single rooms from £46. Double rooms from £80.

**171 OLD BROMPTON ROAD, SOUTH KENSINGTON, LONDON SW5 0AN
TEL: 0171-373 9383 FAX: 0171-373 4983**

London

Haddon Hall Awaiting Inspection
39/40 Bedford Place, Russell Square, London WC1B 5JT
☎ 0171-636 2474 Fax 0171-580 4527

Near the British Museum, theatres, shopping (Oxford Street), and tourist attractions. Short walking distances to three tube stations - Russell Square, Holborn and Tottenham Court Road. Euston Station is only a 10-15 minute walk away.
33 bedrs, 12 ensuite, 6 ⇌ SB £44-£57 DB £59-£70
CC MC Visa DC JCB

Swiss Cottage Hotel

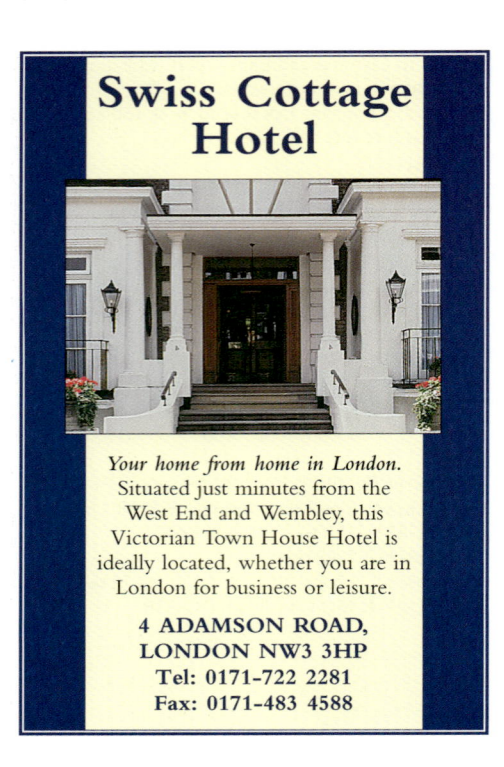

Your home from home in London.
Situated just minutes from the West End and Wembley, this Victorian Town House Hotel is ideally located, whether you are in London for business or leisure.

**4 ADAMSON ROAD,
LONDON NW3 3HP
Tel: 0171-722 2281
Fax: 0171-483 4588**

LONDON North & West

♦♦♦♦ Swiss Cottage
Sparkling Diamond
4 Adamson Road, London NW3 3HP
☎ 0171-722 2281 Fax 0171-483 4588
E-mail reservations@swisscottage2.demon.co.uk
54 bedrs, all ensuite, TCF TV ⊡ P 4 ⋕ 45 ⊕ SB £75-£130 DB £85-£145 CC MC Visa Amex DC
See advert on this page

♦♦♦ Anchor-Nova
10 West Heath Drive, Golders Green, London NW11 7QH
☎ 0181-458 8764 Fax 0181-455 3204

A charming, friendly small hotel, great value, two minutes from Golders Green tube station. One stop from Brent Cross shopping centre, 20 minutes from West End. Mostly ensuite rooms, free parking. Family room £65-£90.
11 bedrs, 8 ensuite, 1 ⇌ TCF TV P 4 SB £33-£44 DB £47-£60 CC MC Visa Amex JCB ♿

♦♦♦ Central
35 Hoop Lane, London NW11 8BS
☎ 0181-458 5636 Fax 0181-455 4792
26 bedrs, all ensuite, TV P 8 SB £45-£50 DB £65-£70 CC MC Visa Amex DC

♦♦♦ Four Seasons
Sparkling Diamond
173 Gloucester Place, London NW1 6DX
☎ 0171-724 3461 Fax 0171-402 5594
227 bedrs, all ensuite, ⊡ P 80 ⋕ 400 ⊕ CC MC Visa Amex DC ⊠

♦♦♦ Garth
64-76 Hendon Way, Cricklewood, London NW2 2NL
☎ 0181-209 1511 Fax 0181-455 4744
50 bedrs, all ensuite, TCF TV P 48 ⋕ 300 ⊕ Rest Resid CC MC Visa Amex DC JCB

London

♦♦♦ Grange Lodge
50 Grange Road, London W5 5BX
☎ 0181-567 1049 Fax 0181-579 5350
E-mail 113146.3004@compuserve.com
14 bedrs, 9 ensuite, 2 ⇌ TCF TV ★ P 8 SB £28-£42
DB £40-£53 CC MC Visa DC

♦♦♦ La Gaffe
107-111 Heath Street, London NW3 6SS
☎ 0171-435 8965 Fax 0171-794 7592
E-mail lagaffe@msn.com
18 bedrs, all ensuite, TCF TV ⊡ P 2 ⊞ SB £60-£95
DB £85-£120 D £12.95 CC MC Visa Amex DC
See advert on this page

♦♦♦ Langorf
20 Frognal, Hampstead, London NW3 6AG
☎ 0171-794 4483 Fax 0171-435 9055
31 bedrs, all ensuite, TCF TV ⊡ ⊞ Resid SB £77-£82
DB £95-£100 CC MC Visa Amex DC
See advert on this page

♦♦ Abbey Lodge
51 Grange Park, Ealing, London W5 3PR
☎ 0181-567 7914 Fax 0181-579 5350
E-mail 113146.3004@compuserve.com

17 bedrs, 16 ensuite, TCF TV ★ SB £37-£42 DB £47-£53
CC MC Visa DC

♦♦ Acton Park
116 The Vale, Acton, London W3 7JT
☎ 0181-743 9417 Fax 0181-743 9417
21 bedrs, all ensuite, TCF TV ★ ⊡ P 20 ⊞ 60 ⊞ Rest
Resid CC MC Visa Amex DC ♿

♦♦ Hotel Orlando
83 Shepherds Bush Road, London W6 7LR
☎ 0171-603 4890 Fax 0171-603 4890
14 bedrs, all ensuite, TCF TV SB £28-£35 DB £46-£52
CC MC Visa

National Code & Number Change

Telephone codes and numbers in London change in April 2000.

0171-XXXXXX becomes 020-7XXX XXXX
0181-XXXXXX becomes 020-8XXX XXXX

La Gaffe

La Gaffe is situated in Hampstead Village, north west London. The hotel is twelve minutes by tube from the city centre and close to both Hampstead Heath and Hampstead tube stations.

The hotel has an excellent Italian restaurant and bar.

**107-111 HEATH STREET,
LONDON NW3 6SS**
Tel: 0171-435 8965 Fax: (0171) 794 7592
Email: LaGaffe@msn.com

The Langorf Hotel and Apartments

Elegant Edwardian Townhouse situated in a quiet residential area just south of the fashionable Hampstead Village, and 4 minutes walk to Finchley Road underground.

All tastefully furnished bedrooms are en-suite and the hotel offers 24hrs room service, bar plus 5 apartments.

The Langorf Hotel
20 Frognal Hampstead
London NW3 6AG
Telephone: 0171-794 4483
Telefax: 0171-435 9055

104 London

PARK HOTEL

Acclaimed.
Situated opposite the beautiful Valentine's Park.
Restaurant Mon-Thurs.
Freshly cooked breakfast.
Fully Licensed.
Most rooms ensuite.
All rooms with Sky TV,
tea/coffee making facilities.
Car Park.
5 mins from town centre/Gants Hill Tube.
Easy access M11, M25 & A406.

**327 CRANBROOK ROAD, ILFORD,
ESSEX IG1 4UE
Tel: 0181-554 9616
Fax: 0181-518 2700**

Woodville Guest House

Very friendly family run business.
Comfortable bedrooms, beamed dining room, garden and terrace make this a delightful stay.

Most rooms en suite. All rooms with sky TV. Families with children particularly welcome. 2 mins from station. 20 mins from city.

Mr & Mrs Murray
**10/12 Argyle Road, Ilford, Essex
Telephone: 0181-478 3779**

LONDON North & East

♦♦♦ **Park**
327 Cranbrook Road, Ilford IG1 4UE
☎ 0181-554 9616 Fax 0181-518 2700

Situated opposite the beautiful Valentine's Park. Easy access to Underground/BR. Ensuite bedrooms with Sky TV. Freshly cooked breakfast, fully licensed.
20 bedrs, 18 ensuite, 2 ⌕ 1 ⇌ TCF TV ⋔ P 20 ⊞ 20
⊕ Resid SB £33.50-£49.50 DB £46.50-£70 D £12
CC MC Visa JCB
See advert on this page

♦♦♦ **White Lodge**
1 Church Lane, Hornsey, London N8
☎ 0181-348 9765 Fax 0181-340 7851
17 bedrs, 8 ensuite, TCF TV CC MC Visa

♦♦♦ **Woodville** Awaiting Inspection
10-12 Argyll Road, Ilford IG1 3BQ
☎ 0181-478 3779 Fax 0181-4783796

A friendly atmosphere pervades this family run business. Bedrooms are bright and comfortable - a beamed dining room, lovely garden and terrace make this a delightful stay. Freshly cooked breakfast. All rooms have Sky TV.
15 bedrs, 7 ensuite, 1 ⌕ 5 ⇌ TCF TV P 12 SB £30-£40 DB £40-£50 ♿
See advert on this page

London

Aber Awaiting Inspection
89 Crouch Hill, Hornsey, London N8 9EG
☎ 0181-340 2847 Fax 0181-340 2847
E-mail 106020.3667@compuserve.com
9 bedrs, 2 ⇌ ⊠ SB £28-£30 DB £38-£42 CC MC Visa JCB

Cranbrook Awaiting Inspection
24 Coventry Road, Ilford IG1 4QR
☎ 0181-554 6544 Fax 0181-518 1463
30 bedrs, 26 ensuite, 1 ⇌ ⋔ P 24 ⋕ 30 ⊞ Resid
CC MC Visa Amex DC ⚲

Forest View Awaiting Inspection
227 Romford Road, Forest Gate, London E7 9HL
☎ 0181-534 4884 Fax 0181-543 8959
20 bedrs, 7 ensuite, 3 ⇌ TCF TV P 15 No children under 2 ⊞ Resid SB £35.85 DB £52.90 HB £250
D £13.80 CC MC Visa JCB ⊞

Grove Hill Awaiting Inspection
38 Grove Hill, South Woodford, London E18 3JG
☎ 0181-989 3344 Fax 0181-530 5286
21 bedrs, all ensuite, TCF TV ⋔ P 12 ⊞ Resid
SB £27.50-£37.50 DB £53 CC MC Visa Amex DC JCB ⚲

Lakeside Awaiting Inspection
51 Snaresbrook Road, Wanstead, London E11 1PQ
☎ 0181-989 6100
Closed Dec-Feb
3 bedrs, all ensuite, TCF TV ⊠ P 3 No children under 10

Sleeping Beauty Motel Lodge Awaiting Inspection
543 Lea Bridge Road, Leyton, London E10 7EB
☎ 0181-556 8080 Fax 0181-556 8080
85 bedrs, all ensuite, TCF ▣ P 75 No children under 4 ⊞ Resid SB £42-£45 DB £47-£50 CC MC Visa Amex DC ⊞ ⚲

LONDON South & East

♦♦♦ Crystal Palace Tower
114 Church Road, Crystal Palace, London SE19 2UB
☎ 0181-653 0176 Fax 0181-653 5167
9 bedrs, all ensuite, TCF TV ⋔ P 10 SB £39-£42
DB £45-£48 CC MC Visa JCB

♦ Weston House
8 Eltham Green, Eltham, London SE9 5LB
☎ 0181-850 5191 Fax 0181-850 0030

A Victorian villa with modern comforts set in quiet Eltham Green conservation area, close to historic Maritime Greenwich and Millennium Dome. 18 minutes from central London, with the A205 in front whilst the A2 and A20 are just a few hundred yards away.
9 bedrs, 7 ensuite, 1 ⇌ TCF TV P 5 ⋕ 16 SB £32-£35
DB £42-£48 CC MC Visa ⚲

LONDON South & West

♦♦♦ Worcester House
38 Alwyne Road, London SW19 7AE
☎ 0181-946 1300 Fax 0181-785 4058
9 bedrs, all ensuite, TCF TV P 2 CC MC Visa Amex DC

Trochee Awaiting Inspection
52 Ridgeway Place, Wimbledon, London SW19 4AS
☎ 0181-946 9425 Fax 0181-785 4058
18 bedrs, 9 ensuite, 4 ⇌ TCF TV P 6 SB £39-£54
DB £55-£66 CC MC Visa Amex
See advert on next page

Trochee Awaiting Inspection
21 Malcolm Road, Wimbledon, London SW19 4SW
☎ 0181-946 3924 Fax 0181-946 1579
18 bedrs, 3 ⇌ TCF TV P 6 SB £40-£44 DB £53-£56
CC MC Visa Amex
See advert on next page

Short Breaks

Many hotels provide special rates for weekend and mid-week breaks – sometimes these are quoted in the hotel's entry, otherwise ring direct for the latest offers.

London

Wimbledon Awaiting Inspection
78 Worple Road, London SW19 4HZ
☎ 0181-946 9265 Fax 0181-946 9265

A small family run hotel offering a warm comfortable atmosphere for both businessmen and tourist, ideally situated for convenient travel to London or Kingston, Richmond and Hampton Court etc.
14 bedrs, 3 ensuite, 8 ⌕ 2 ⇌ TCF TV P 10 SB £55 DB £65 CC MC Visa Amex DC ♿

National Code & Number Change
Telephone codes and numbers in London change in April 2000.

0171-XXXXXX becomes 020-7XXX XXXX
0181-XXXXXX becomes 020-8XXX XXXX

LONDON AIRPORT-HEATHROW 4C2

♦♦ Crompton
49 Lampton Road, Hounslow TW3 1JG
☎ 0181-570 7090 Fax 0181-577 1975
E-mail cromptonguesthouse@btinternet.com
10 bedrs, all ensuite, TCF TV P 12 SB £50-£65 DB £65-£75 CC MC Visa Amex DC JCB ♿
See advert on this page

♦♦ Shepiston Lodge
31 Shepiston Lane, Hayes, London UB3 1LJ
☎ 0181-573 0266 Fax 0181-569 2536
13 bedrs, 7 ⌕ 3 ⇌ TCF TV P 20 ⌇ Resid SB £36.50 DB £49.50-£52.50 CC MC Visa Amex DC JCB ♿

Heathrow Palace Awaiting Inspection
17-19 Haslemere Avenue, Hounslow TW5 9UT
☎ 0181-384 3333 Fax 0181-384 3334
11 bedrs, 9 ensuite, 2 ⇌ TV P 10 CC MC Visa ♿

Barn Awaiting Inspection
West End Road, Ruislip HA4 6JB
☎ 01895-636057 Fax 01895-638379
57 bedrs, all ensuite, TCF TV ⚊ P 60 ⚏ 100 ⌇ SB £60-£84 DB £70-£95 D £15.00 CC MC Visa Amex DC ♿

Trochee Hotel

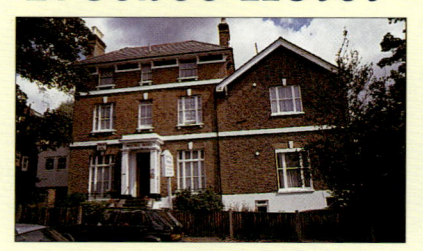

- *Bed and English Breakfast.*
- *All rooms centrally heated with hand basin, colour TV, tea and coffee making facility and hairdryers.*
- *Many rooms have ensuite bathroom and fridge.*
- *Close to town centre and transport facilities.*
- *Parking.*

**21 MALCOLM ROAD and
52 RIDGEWAY PLACE,
WIMBLEDON SW19 4AS
Tel: 0181-946 1579/9425
Fax: 0181-785 4058**

CROMPTON
GUEST HOUSE

"Hotel Facilities at Guest House Prices"

- All rooms ensuite. • Single, double, triple and family rooms. • Colour/Satellite TV. • Full English Breakfast. • Telephones in all rooms. • Disabled facilities available. • Private car park (short/long term). • Major credit cards accepted. • 10 mins Heathrow, M4/M25. • 20 mins Central London. • 50 yards left of Hounslow Central Underground. • Close to town centre.

Family Business with Personal Touch.

**49 LAMPTON ROAD, HOUNSLOW
MIDDLESEX TW3 1JG
Tel: 0181-570 7090 Fax: 0181-577 1975
Email: cromptonguesthouse@btinternet.com**

SPENCER'S

Labels For Less

Famous brands and labels at discount prices

Labels for Less is a revolutionary and colourful new guide to discount shopping.

For keen shoppers everywhere, it offers comprehensive coverage of over 1300 factory shops and factory outlet villages. Wherever you travel you will be able to find a factory shop nearby. It's essential reference for home, car and holiday.

Perfects, slight seconds and clearance lines, all at bargain prices, make Labels For Less the most exciting and rewarding guide to shopping around. For each outlet there's full information on products, labels and discounts. Plus details of locations, transport, parking, opening hours, credit cards and restaurants.

Every entry is in colour, maximising the impact and highlighting the discounts and brands each outlet features. 20 pages of mapping make route-finding easy.

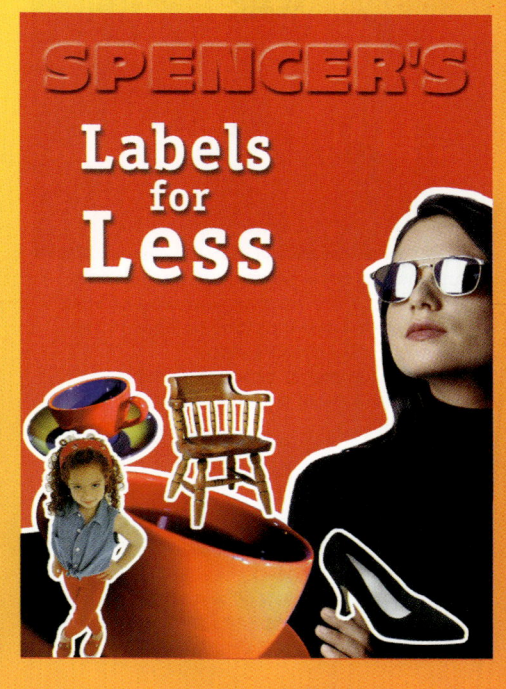

Format:	210x148mm
No. of pages:	480pp
ISBN:	1 900327 35 X
Price:	£13.99
Publication date:	November 1999

West One Publishing
Kestrel House, Duke's PLace
Marlow, Bucks SL7 2QH

tel: 01628 487722

West One PUBLISHING

www.WestOneWeb.com

Looe

LOOE Cornwall — 2B4

♦♦♦♦ Commonwood
Sparkling Diamond
St Martin's Road, Looe PL13 1LP
☎ 01503-262929 Fax 01503-262632
E-mail commonwood@compuserve.com
Closed Christmas

A Victorian villa set in six acres of grounds with spectacular country and river views, yet only five minutes walk to Looe town and harbour. Private parking. Friendly Cornish service.
11 bedrs, all ensuite, TCF TV ⊁ P 20 No children under 8 ⊕ Rest Resid SB £31-£39 DB £62-£78 CC MC Visa Amex JCB ⊰

♦♦♦♦ Coombe Farm
Warm Welcome
Widegates, Looe PL13 1QN
☎ 01503-240223 Fax 01503-240895
Closed Nov-Feb
10 bedrs, all ensuite, TCF TV ⊠ ⊁ P 20 No children under 12 ⊕ Rest Resid SB £28-£33 DB £56-£66 HB £294-£329 D £16 CC MC Visa Amex DC ⊰ ⌺ ⌖

Deganwy Awaiting Inspection
Station Road, Looe PL13 1HL
☎ 01503-262984
Closed Christmas
8 bedrs, 5 ensuite, TCF TV P 9 ⫽ 20 ⊕ Rest Resid SB £16-£20 DB £32-£40

Panorama Awaiting Inspection
Hannafore Road, Looe PL13 2DE
☎ 01503-262123 Fax 01503-265654
E-mail panorama@looe.avel.co.uk
10 bedrs, all ensuite, TCF TV P 7 ⫽ 25 No children under 5 ⊕ Rest Resid SB £23-£27 DB £45-£49 HB £195-£228 D £13.50 CC MC Visa Amex DC

LOSTWITHIEL Cornwall — 2B3

♦♦♦♦ Ship
Sparkling Diamond
Lerryn, Lostwithiel PL22 0PT
☎ 01208-872374
E-mail shiplerryn@aol.com

Cosy 17th century inn offering excellent ale and food, set in an idyllic riverside village, peaceful location, convenient for walking, sailing, riding, golf, coast and moors.
4 bedrs, all ensuite, TCF TV ⊁ ⊕ SB £25 DB £45 D £10 CC MC Visa Amex JCB

LOUGHBOROUGH Leicestershire — 8B3

♦♦♦ De Montfort
88 Leicester Road, Loughborough LE11 2AQ
☎ 01509-216061 Fax 01509-233667

Refurbished Victorian style family run hotel under new ownership.
9 bedrs, 7 ensuite, 2 ⊛ 2 ⇌ TCF TV ⊕ CC MC Visa Amex DC JCB

Garendon Park Awaiting Inspection
92 Leicester Road, Loughborough LE11 2AQ
☎ 01509-236557 Fax 01509-265559
9 bedrs, 7 ensuite, 1 ⇌ TCF TV ⊁ ⫽ 16 ⊕ SB £23-£35 DB £35-£45 D £6 CC MC Visa Amex JCB

LOWESTOFT Suffolk 9F3

♦♦♦ Albany
400 London Road South, Lowestoft NR33 0BQ
☎ 01502-574394 Fax 01502-581198
8 bedrs, 6 ensuite, 1 ⇢ TCF TV ⊁ ⊕ Resid SB £17.50-£25.50 DB £37-£50 HB £165-£189 D £5.95 CC MC Visa Amex

♦♦♦ Hotel Katherine
49 Kirkley Cliff Road, Lowestoft NR33 0DF
☎ 01502-567858 Fax 01502-581341
Closed Jan
10 bedrs, all ensuite, TCF TV ⊁ P 3 ⊕ Rest Resid SB £37 DB £52 HB £232 D £13.50 CC MC Visa Amex

LUDLOW Shropshire 7E3

♦♦♦♦♦ Number Twenty Eight
Little Gem
28 Lower Broad Street, Ludlow SY8 1PQ
☎ 01584-876996 Fax 01584-876860
E-mail ross.no28@btinternet.com.
6 bedrs, all ensuite, TCF TV ⊠ ⊁ ⊕ Resid SB £45-£65 DB £60-£75 CC MC Visa Amex

♦♦♦ Church Inn
Buttercross, Ludlow SY8 1AW
☎ 01584-872174 Fax 01584-877146

There has been an ale house here since the 15th century, though the present inn has a Georgian stucco exterior. Situated in the town centre amidst the old walkways and cobbled streets.
8 bedrs, all ensuite, TCF TV ⊕ SB £30-£50 DB £50 CC MC Visa

Lyme Regis 109

♦♦♦ Crown Inn
Munslow, Ludlow SY7 9ET
☎ 01584-841205 Fax 01584-841205
4 bedrs, all ensuite, TCF TV P 25 ⊕ SB £30 DB £45 CC MC Visa Amex JCB

Moor Hall Awaiting Inspection
Clee Downton, Ludlow SY8 3EG
☎ 01584-823209 Fax 01584-823387
3 bedrs, all ensuite, TCF TV ⊁ P 12 No children under 10 ⊕ ⊠

LYDFORD Devon 2C3

♦♦♦♦♦ Moor View House
Sparkling Diamond
Vale Down, Lydford EX20 4BB
☎ 01822-820220 Fax 01822-820220
4 bedrs, all ensuite, TCF TV ⊠ ⊁ P 15 No children under 12 ⊕ Rest Resid SB £45-£50 DB £60-£80 HB £285-£300 D £20

LYME REGIS Dorset 3E3

♦♦♦♦ Kersbrook
Pound Road, Lyme Regis DT7 3HX
☎ 01297-442596 Fax 01297-442596
Closed Jan-Feb
10 bedrs, all ensuite, TCF TV ⊁ P 16 ⋕ 70 ⊕ Resid SB £50-£65 DB £82.50 HB £300 D £16.50 CC MC Visa Amex

♦♦♦ Tudor House
Church Street, Lyme Regis DT7 3BU
☎ 01297-442472 Fax 01297-442472
Closed Oct-Mar
17 bedrs, 15 ensuite, 3 ⇢ TCF TV P 20 ⋕ ⊕ Rest Resid SB £20 DB £47-£55 CC MC Visa

---

Don't forget to mention the guide

When booking direct, please remember to tell the hotel that you chose it from RAC Inspected Guest Accommodation

110 Lymington

LYMINGTON Hampshire — 4B4

♦♦♦♦♦ Efford Cottage
Warm Welcome, Sparkling Diamond
Everton, Lymington SO41 0JD
☎ 01590-642315 Fax 01590-641030
E-mail effcottage@aol.com

Friendly, spacious, Georgian cottage. Award winning guesthouse, four course multi-choice breakfast with homemade bread and preserves. Traditional country cooking, qualified chef, homegrown produce. Good touring location. Parking.
3 bedrs, all ensuite, TCF TV ✝ P 3 No children under 14 DB £44-£50 HB £252-£376 D £30

♦♦♦♦ Our Bench
9 Lodge Road, Pennington, Lymington SO41 8HH
☎ 01590-673141 Fax 01590-673141
E-mail ourbench@newforest.demon.co.uk.
Closed Christmas & New Year
3 bedrs, all ensuite, TCF TV ⊠ P 5 No children under 14 CC MC Visa JCB 🕭 🖼 ♿

LYNDHURST Hampshire — 4A4

♦♦♦♦ Lyndhurst House
35 Romsey Road, Lyndhurst SO43 7AR
☎ 01703-282230

Refurbished, comfortable guesthouse. All rooms ensuite, some with fourposter beds. Conveniently situated for forest activities. A short stroll from village centre. Excellent breakfast.
5 bedrs, all ensuite, TCF TV ⊠ P 5 No children under 5 DB £40-£50

♦♦♦♦ Penny Farthing
Romsey Road, Lyndhurst SO43 7AA
☎ 01703-284422 Fax 01703-284488
Closed Christmas

A cheerful small hotel, ideally situated in the village of Lyndhurst. Offering licensed bar, bicycle store, comfortable ensuite rooms with colour TV, telephone and tea/coffee making facilities and large private car park. Ideal base for touring New Forest.
15 bedrs, 10 ensuite, 3 ⇌ TCF TV ✝ P 15 ⊕ Resid SB £25-£35 DB £49-£70 CC MC Visa Amex DC JCB

Knightwood Lodge
Awaiting Inspection
Southampton Road, Lyndhurst SO43 7BU
☎ 01703-282502 Fax 01703-283730
Closed 25 Dec
18 bedrs, all ensuite, TCF TV ✝ P 15 ⊕ Resid SB £30-£50 DB £55-£80 D £16.75 CC MC Visa Amex DC JCB
🕭 🖼 ♿

Little Hayes
Awaiting Inspection
43 Romsey Road, Lyndhurst SO43 7AR
☎ 023-8028 3816
5 bedrs, all ensuite, TCF TV ✝ P 7 SB £30 DB £60

LYNMOUTH Devon — 3O2

♦♦ Beacon
Countisbury Hill, Lynmouth EX35 6ND
☎ 01598-753268
Closed winter
5 bedrs, all ensuite, TCF TV P 10 No children under 12 ⊕ Rest Resid SB £22-£23.50 DB £37-£47

Manchester

LYNTON Devon　2C2

♦♦♦♦ Mayfair
The Lynway, Lynton EX35 6AY
📞 01598-753227
9 bedrs, 7 ensuite, 2 ☞ TCF TV P 6 No children under 12 ⊕ Resid SB £18-£25 DB £36-£50 CC MC Visa

LYTHAM ST ANNES Lancashire　10B4

♦♦♦ Strathmore
Sparkling Diamond
305 Clifton Drive South, Lytham St. Annes FY8 1HN
📞 01253-725478
10 bedrs, 5 ensuite, 1 ⇥ TCF TV P 10 No children under 9 ⊕ Resid SB £19-£23 DB £38-£46 HB £154-£189 D £8

Endsleigh Awaiting Inspection
315 Clifton Drive South, Lytham St Annes FY8 1HN
📞 01253-725622
15 bedrs, all ensuite, TCF TV P 9 ⊕ Rest Resid SB £20-£24 DB £40-£48 HB £178-£188

MACCLESFIELD Cheshire　7E1

Moorhayes House Awaiting Inspection
27 Manchester Road, Tytherington, Macclesfield SK10 2JJ
📞 01625-433228 Fax 01625-433228
9 bedrs, 7 ensuite, 1 ⇥ TCF TV ⇤ P 13 SB £38 DB £48

MAIDENHEAD Berkshire　4C2

♦♦♦ Clifton
21 Crauford Rise, Maidenhead SL6 7LR
📞 01628-623572 Fax 01628-623572
18 bedrs, 8 ensuite, 4 ⇥ TCF TV P 18 ⊕ SB £30-£50 DB £55-£60 D £8 CC MC Visa Amex ♿

MAIDSTONE Kent　5E3

Roadchef Lodge Lodge
Maidstone Motorway Service Area, Junction 8 M20, Hollingbourne ME17 1SS
📞 01622-631100 Fax 01622-739535
Closed 25 Dec, 1 Jan
58 bedrs, all ensuite, TCF TV P 100 ⚏ 20 Room £49.95
CC MC Visa Amex DC ♿

MALDON Essex　5E2

Swan Awaiting Inspection
73 High Street, Maldon CM9 7EP
📞 01621-853170 Fax 01621-854490
6 bedrs, 4 ensuite, 1 ⇥ TCF TV P 25 ⚏ 150 ⊕ CC MC Visa Amex DC

MALHAM North Yorkshire　10C3

♦♦♦ Buck Inn
Malham, Skipton BD23 4DA
📞 01729-830317 Fax 01729-830670
10 bedrs, all ensuite, TCF TV P 15 ⚏ 40 ⊕ SB £28.50-£33.50 DB £50-£70 HB £185 D £10 CC MC Visa

MALVERN Worcestershire　7E4

♦♦♦ Sidney House
Sparkling Diamond
40 Worcester Road, Malvern WR14 4AA
📞 01684-574994 Fax 01684-574994
8 bedrs, 5 ensuite, 1 ⇥ TCF TV P 9 ⊕ Rest SB £20-£40 DB £39-£59 CC MC Visa Amex JCB

MANCHESTER Greater Manchester　10C4

Highbury Awaiting Inspection
113 Monton Road, Eccles, Manchester M30 9HQ
📞 0161-787 8545 Fax 0161-787 9023

A small family run hotel, beautifully decorated and restored to modern standards. Ten minutes from city centre, cricket grounds, football grounds and theatres and 20 minutes from airport. One mile from motorway.
15 bedrs, all ensuite, TCF TV P 19 ⊕ Resid CC MC Visa Amex

ENGLAND

112 Manchester

Imperial Awaiting Inspection
157 Hathersage Road, Manchester M13 0HY
☎ 0161-225 6500 Fax 0161-225 6500
27 bedrs, 21 ensuite, 3 ⇌ TCF TV P 30 ⫼ 20 ⊕ Rest Resid SB £31 DB £48 D £13 CC MC Visa Amex DC &

Kempton House Awaiting Inspection
400 Wilbraham Road, Chorlton-cum-Hardy, Manchester M21 0UH
☎ 0161-881 8766 Fax 0161-881 8766
Closed Christmas
12 bedrs, 4 ensuite, 1 ⌂ 2 ⇌ TCF TV P 9 ⊕ Resid SB £25-£31 DB £32-£41 CC MC Visa

New Central Awaiting Inspection
144-146 Heywood Street, Manchester M8 7PD
☎ 0161-205 2169 Fax 0161-205 2169
10 bedrs, 5 ⌂ 2 ⇌ TCF TV ✱ P 5 ⊕ Rest Resid SB £21 DB £33 CC MC Visa

Victoria Park Awaiting Inspection
4-6 Park Crescent, Victoria Park, Manchester M14 5RE
☎ 0161-224 1399 Fax 0161-225 4949
E-mail vph.manchester@claranet.co.uk

Located in a quiet road, close to city centre, university, restaurants, motorways and Manchester Airport. All rooms ensuite with cenral heating, telephone and alarm clock. Free car parking.
19 bedrs, all ensuite, TCF ⌺ P 40 SB £35-£38 DB £48-£52 CC MC Visa ⌘

MARAZION Cornwall	2A4

Chymorvah Awaiting Inspection
Marazion TR17 0DQ
☎ 01736-710497 Fax 01736-710508
Closed Christmas & New Year

Victorian family house built out of granite with access to a private beach. Situated at east end of Marazion overlooking Mount's Bay and St Michael's Mount. Happy atmosphere.
9 bedrs, all ensuite, TCF TV ✱ P 12 CC MC Visa

MARLBOROUGH Wiltshire	4A2

♦♦♦♦ Vines
Sparkling Diamond
High Street, Marlborough SN4 1HJG
☎ 01672-515333 Fax 01672-515338

Six individually appointed ensuite bedrooms in this character property opposite the Ivy House Hotel in the main High Street, Marlborough. Guests enjoy meals and facilities of the hotel.
6 bedrs, all ensuite, TCF TV P 6 ⫼ 30 ⊕ SB £27-£35 DB £53-£55 D £19 CC MC Visa Amex

♦♦♦ Merlin
High Street, Marlborough SN8 1LW
☎ 01672-512151 Fax 01672-514656
15 bedrs, 13 ensuite, 1 ⇌ TCF TV ✱ ⊕ SB £40 DB £60-£65 D £12 CC MC Visa

Minehead

MARLOW Buckinghamshire 4C2

♦♦♦♦ Holly Tree House
Sparkling Diamond
Burford Close, Marlow Bottom, Marlow SL7 3NF
☎ 01628-891110 Fax 01628-481278
5 bedrs, all ensuite, TCF TV ✝ P 8 ⌘ 9 CC MC Visa Amex ⌇

MATLOCK Derbyshire 7F1

♦♦♦♦ Jackson Tor House
76 Jackson Road, Matlock DE4 3JQ
☎ 01629-582348 Fax 01629-582348
Closed Christmas-New Year
29 bedrs, 13 ensuite, 7 ⇌ TCF TV P 20 ⌂ Rest Resid
SB £16-£30 DB £32-£65 CC MC Visa JCB

Coach House Awaiting Inspection
Main Road, Lea, Matlock DE4 5GJ
☎ 01629-534346 Fax 01629-534346
3 bedrs, 1 ensuite, 1 ⇌ TV ✝ P 25 ⌂ Rest SB £19.50
DB £35 D £9.95 CC MC Visa

Hill View Awaiting Inspection
80 New Street, Matlock DE4 3FH
☎ 01246-275736

MELKSHAM Wiltshire 3F1

♦♦♦♦ King's Arms
The Market Place, Melksham SN12 6EX
☎ 01225-707272 Fax 01225-702085
13 bedrs, 10 ensuite, 3 ☍ 2 ⇌ TCF TV ✝ P 50 ⌘ 50 ⌂ CC MC Visa Amex DC

MEVAGISSEY Cornwall 2B4

Fountain Inn Awaiting Inspection
Cliff Street, Mevagissey PL26 6QH
☎ 01726-842320
3 bedrs, 2 ensuite, 1 ⇌ TCF TV ✝ No children ⌂
SB £45 DB £45 D £7.25 CC MC Visa JCB

Ship Inn Awaiting Inspection
Fore Street, Mevagissey PL26 6TU
☎ 01726-843324 Fax 01726-843324
6 bedrs, 1 ⇌ TCF TV ⌂ CC MC Visa Amex DC

MILTON KEYNES Buckinghamshire 4C1

Campanile Milton Keynes Lodge
40 Penn Road (off Watling Street), Fenny Stratford, Bletchley MK2 2AU
☎ 01908-649819 Fax 01908-649818
80 bedrs, all ensuite, TCF TV ⌘ ⌂ CC MC Visa Amex DC

MINEHEAD Somerset 3D2

♦♦♦♦ Gascony
Warm Welcome, Sparkling Diamond
50 The Avenue, Minehead TA24 5BB
☎ 01643-705939
Closed Nov-Mar

Comfortable and well appointed Victorian house hotel, ideally positioned on the level in the lovely tree lined avenue. All bedrooms ensuite, full central heating, cocktail bar, superb home cooked food. Large private car park.
13 bedrs, all ensuite, TCF TV ✝ P 14 ⌂ Rest Resid
SB £23-£24 DB £44-£46 HB £180-£198 D £12 CC MC Visa ♿

♦♦♦♦ Mayfair
Warm Welcome, Sparkling Diamond
The Avenue, Minehead TA24 5AY
☎ 01643-702719 Fax 01643-702719
Closed winter
13 bedrs, all ensuite, TCF TV ☒ P 13 ⌂ Resid SB £25-£28 DB £48-£52 HB £182-£195 D £11 CC MC Visa ♿

♦♦♦ Stockleigh Lodge
Exford, Minehead TA24 7PZ
☎ 01643-831500 Fax 01643-831595
8 bedrs, 7 ensuite, 2 ⇌ TCF ☒ P 10 ⌂ Resid SB £25
DB £40-£50 D £12.50 ⌖

ENGLAND

Morecambe

MORECAMBE Lancashire	10B3

♦♦♦ Beach Mount
Sparkling Diamond
395 Marine Road East, Morecambe LA4 5AN
☎ 01524-420753
Closed winter
22 bedrs, all ensuite, TCF TV ★ P 6 ⌑ SB £23.75
DB £44.50 HB £155-£172.50 D £10 CC MC Visa Amex DC

♦♦♦ Hotel Prospect
Sparkling Diamond
363 Marine Road, Morecambe LA4 5AQ
☎ 01524-417819 Fax 01524-417819
Closed winter
14 bedrs, all ensuite, TCF TV ★ P 10 ⌑ 20 ⌑ SB £17
DB £34 HB £160 D £8 CC MC Visa DC &

♦♦♦ Wimslow
374 Marine Road East, Morecambe LA4 5AH
☎ 01524-421947 Fax 01524-417804
14 bedrs, all ensuite, TCF TV P 10 ⌑ Resid SB £16-£19
DB £32-£38 HB £168 D £9 CC MC Visa Amex

MORETON-IN-MARSH Gloucestershire	4A1

♦♦ Moreton House
High Street, Moreton-in-Marsh GL56 0LQ
☎ 01608-650747 Fax 01608-652747
E-mail moreton_house@msn.com
11 bedrs, 7 ensuite, 2 ⇒ TCF TV ★ P 5 ⌑ Rest Resid
SB £22-£23 DB £42-£60 CC MC Visa

NAILSWORTH Gloucestershire	3F1

Laurels at Inchbrook Awaiting Inspection
Inchbrook, Nailsworth GL5 5HA
☎ 01453-834021 Fax 01453-834021
7 bedrs, all ensuite, TCF TV ⊠ ★ P 8 ⌑ 10 ⌑ Resid
SB £25-£30 DB £38-£45 HB £217-£266 D £15 ⇒ ⊞ &

NEWCASTLE UPON TYNE Tyne & Wear	11D1

♦♦♦ Chirton House
46 Clifton Road, Newcastle upon Tyne NE4 6XH
☎ 0191-273 0407 Fax 0191-273 0407
11 bedrs, 6 ensuite, 2 ⇒ TCF TV ★ P 11 ⌑ 24 ⌑ Rest Resid SB £25-£35 DB £35-£45 HB £210 D £10.50
CC MC Visa

NEWPORT PAGNELL Buckinghamshire	4C1

♦♦♦ Thurston
Sparkling Diamond
90 High Street, Newport Pagnell MK16 8EH
☎ 01908-611377 Fax 01908-611394
8 bedrs, all ensuite, TCF TV P 12 ⌑ 25 ⌑ Resid
SB £42-£44 DB £52-£58 CC MC Visa Amex &

NEWQUAY Cornwall	2B3

♦♦♦ Pendeen
Sparkling Diamond
7 Alexandra Road, Porth, Newquay TR7 3ND
☎ 01637-873521 Fax 01637-873521
E-mail pendeen@cornwall.net
Closed Nov-Dec

Beautifully located two minutes from Porth Beach. Tastefully furnished and a high standard of cuisine assured. Friendly, personal and efficient service is our aim. Mid-week bookings accepted. Ideal for the Cornwall coastal path walks.
15 bedrs, all ensuite, TCF TV P 15 ⌑ Resid SB £18.50-£26.50 DB £37-£48 HB £139-£198 D £9.50 CC MC Visa Amex &

Facilities for the disabled

Hotels do their best to cater for disabled visitors. However, it is advisable to contact the hotel direct to ensure it can provide a particular requirement.

Newquay

♦♦♦♦ Porth Enodoc
Warm Welcome
4 Esplanade Road, Pentire, Newquay TR7 1PY
☎ 01637-872372 Fax 01637-878219
Closed Oct-Mar

Set in its own grounds away from the town, overlooking Fistral beach and Newquay golf course, but within walking distance of the shopping centre.
12 bedrs, all ensuite, TCF TV P 12 ⌂ Rest Resid
SB £18.50-£25.50 DB £37-£51 HB £153-£200 D £9 ♿

♦♦♦♦ Priory Lodge
Sparkling Diamond
30 Mount Wise, Newquay TR7 2BH
☎ 01637-874111 Fax 01637-851803
Closed 3 Jan-6 March

Warm and friendly atmosphere. Set in own grounds with splendid sea views and overlooking town and harbour. Entertainment, sauna, solarium, launderette, swimming pool and games room.
26 bedrs, 24 ensuite, 1 ⇌ TCF TV P 27 ⌂ Rest Resid
SB £25-£30 DB £50-£76 HB £175-£250 D £10 CC MC Visa Amex ⇗ ▦ ♿

♦♦♦♦ Windward
Warm Welcome, Sparkling Diamond
Alexandra Road, Porth, Newquay TR7 3NB
☎ 01637-873185 Fax 01637-852436
E-mail caswind@aol.com

Closed Nov-Easter
14 bedrs, all ensuite, TCF TV P 14 ⌂ Rest Resid
SB £25-£30 DB £50-£60 HB £140-£209 D £15 CC MC Visa Amex

♦♦♦ Carlton
6 Dane Road, Newquay TR7 1HL
☎ 01637-872658

Ideally situated on Towan Headland for exploring spectacular coastlines, sandy coves, wild and wonderful seascapes. Magnificent seaviews. Convenient for all amenities. Friendly atmosphere.
11 bedrs, 8 ensuite, 1 ⌂ 1 ⇌ TCF TV ⇌ ⌂ Resid

♦♦♦ Hotel Trevalsa
Watergate Road, Porth, Newquay TR7 3LX
☎ 01637-873336 Fax 01637-878843
Closed Nov-Mar
24 bedrs, 20 ensuite, 2 ⇌ TCF TV ⇌ P 21 ⌂ Resid
SB £17-£26 DB £34-£52 HB £149-£219 D £12.50
CC MC Visa Amex JCB ♿

♦♦♦ Rolling Waves
Alexandra Road, Porth, Newquay TR7 3NB
☎ 01637-873236
Closed 18 Dec-1 Jan
9 bedrs, 8 ensuite, 1 ⇌ TCF TV P 10 ⌂ Resid SB £20-£26 DB £40-£52 HB £170-£220

♦♦ Arundell
Mount Wise, Newquay TR7 2BS
☎ 01637-872481 Fax 01637-850001
35 bedrs, all ensuite, TCF TV ▦ P 32 ⌂ Resid CC MC Visa Amex DC ⇗ ▦ ▦

Bedruthan House Awaiting Inspection
Bedruthan Steps, St Eval,
Nr Wadebridge PL27 7UW
☎ 01637-860346
Closed Nov
6 bedrs, 5 ensuite, TCF P 12 No children under 3 ⌂
Rest Resid SB £18.50 DB £37 HB £168 D £8.50 CC MC Visa JCB

Newquay

Copper Beach Awaiting Inspection
70 Edgcumbe Avenue, Newquay TR7 2NN
☎ 01637-873376
Closed Oct-Easter
15 bedrs, all ensuite, **TV P** 16 ⋕ 30 ⊕ **SB** £20-£23.50 **DB** £40-£47 **HB** £176-£206.80 ♿

Philema Awaiting Inspection
Esplanade Road, Pentire, TR7 1PY
☎ 01637-872571 Fax 01637-873188
Closed Nov-Mar
33 bedrs, all ensuite, **TCF TV ✱ P** 37 ⋕ 50 ⊕ Resid
SB £20-£35 **DB** £40-£70 **HB** £154-£250 **D** £7.50 **CC** MC Visa

Wheal Treasure Awaiting Inspection
72 Edgcumbe Avenue, Newquay TR7 2NN
☎ 01637-874136
Closed Nov-Feb
12 bedrs, all ensuite, **TCF TV P** 12 ⊕ **SB** £18-£24 **DB** £36-£48 **HB** £168-£196

NEWTON ABBOT Devon 3D3

June Cottage Awaiting Inspection
Dornafield Road, Ipplepen,
Newton Abbot TQ12 5SH
☎ 01803-813081
3 bedrs, 1 ensuite, 2 ✱ **TCF** ☒ No children under 7
SB £17.50 **DB** £35 **HB** £110.25 **D** £10

NORTH NEWNTON Wiltshire 4A3

♦♦♦ Woodbridge Inn
North Newnton SN9 6JZ
☎ 01980-630266 Fax 01980-630266
E-mail woodbridgeinn@btconnect.com
4 bedrs, 3 ensuite, 1 ✱ **TCF TV P** 30 ⊕ **SB** £23 **DB** £40-£46 **HB** £165 **D** £9 **CC** MC Visa Amex

---

Don't forget to mention the guide

When booking direct, please remember to tell the hotel that you chose it from RAC Inspected Guest Accommodation

---

NORTH NIBLEY Gloucestershire 3F1

♦♦♦ Burrows Court
Nibley Green, North Nibley GL11 6AZ
☎ 01453-546230 Fax 01453-546230
E-mail p.f.rackley@tesco.net

18th century Listed former weaving mill in 1 acre garden, peaceful idyllic setting. All rooms ensuite with colour TV. Between junction 13/14 on M5, off A38 at North Nibley.
6 bedrs, all ensuite, **TCF TV ✱ P** 20 ⋕ 20 ⊕ Resid
SB £29-£34 **DB** £42-£50 **CC** MC Visa

NORTH WARNBOROUGH Hampshire 4B3

♦♦♦ Jolly Miller
Hook Road, North Warnborough, Hook RG29 1ET
☎ 01256-702085 Fax 01256-704030
E-mail pubman50@aol.com
9 bedrs, 5 ensuite, 2 ✱ **TCF TV ✱ P** 60 ⋕ 60 ⊕
SB £37-£47 **DB** £47-£57 **CC** MC Visa Amex

NORTHALLERTON North Yorkshire 11D2

Windsor
56 South Parade, Northallerton DL7 8SL
☎ 01609-774100
Closed 29-30 Dec

Nottingham

A comfortable Victorian terraced house, convenient for the station, high street, shops and restaurants. Spacious individually designed bedrooms, some ensuite. Large dining room and comfortable sitting room.
6 bedrs, 2 ensuite, 2 ➡ TCF TV ✠ P 20 CC MC Visa

NORTHAMPTON Northamptonshire 4B1

Poplars Awaiting Inspection
Cross Street, Moulton, Northampton NN3 1RZ
☎ 01604-643983 Fax 01604-790233

Old Northamptonshire stone-built farmhouse converted into a hotel c.1920.
18 bedrs, 14 ensuite, 2 ➡ TCF TV ☒ ✠ P 21 ⌂ Resid SB £43.50-£46.50 DB £51.50-£57.50 D £12 CC MC Visa Amex

NORWICH Norfolk 9F3

♦♦♦♦ Gables
527 Earlham Road, Norwich NR4 7HN
☎ 01603-456666 Fax 01603-250320
Closed 20 Dec-2 Jan
10 bedrs, all ensuite, TCF TV ☒ P 10 SB £35 DB £50-£55 CC MC Visa JCB 🐾 ♿

♦ Belmonte
60-62 Prince Of Wales Road, Norwich NR1 1LT
☎ 01603-622533 Fax 01603-760805
9 bedrs, all ensuite, ⊞ 80 No children under 3 ⌂ SB £34.20 DB £53.50 HB £225 D £10 CC MC Visa Amex DC

Wedgewood
42 St Stephens Road, Norwich NR1 3RE
☎ 01603-625730 Fax 01603-615035
Closed Christmas week

A friendly family run hotel, very close to the bus station and all the city centre places of interest. Car parking. Major credit cards accepted.
13 bedrs, 10 ensuite, 1 ➡ TCF TV P 12 SB £26-£35 DB £42-£48 CC MC Visa Amex DC

NOTTINGHAM Nottinghamshire 8B2

Balmoral Awaiting Inspection
55-57 Loughborough Road, West Bridgford, Nottingham NG2 7LA
☎ 0115-955 2992 Fax 0115-955 2991
Closed Christmas-New Year
31 bedrs, all ensuite, TCF TV P 35 ⌂ Resid CC MC Visa Amex DC

Fairhaven Awaiting Inspection
19 Meadow Road, Beeston Rylands, Nottingham NG9 1JP
☎ 0115-922 7509
E-mail fairhavenb@aol.com
12 bedrs, 4 ensuite, 3 ➡ TCF TV P 12 ⌂ Resid SB £22-£30 DB £32-£40 D £8

Royston Awaiting Inspection
326 Mansfield Road, Nottingham NG5 2EF
☎ 0115-9622947 Fax 0115-956 5018

Pleasant, family run B & B hotel, 1½ miles from city centre. Ample parking. Frequent buses to city. Many rooms ensuite. All have colour tv and tea/coffee making facilities.
14 bedrs, 9 ensuite, 2 🛁 2 ➡ TCF P 10 SB £28.50-£37.50 DB £43.50-£48.50 CC MC Visa Amex DC

ENGLAND

Nottingham

St Andrews Awaiting Inspection
310 Queens Road, Beeston, Nottingham NG9 1JA
☎ 0115-925 4902 Fax 0115-925 4902

All bedrooms have TV, tea/coffee making facilities. Sitting room with TV, books and games for guests use. Near to M1 junction 25. Nottingham city centre 3 miles. Close to University, Boots, Beeston station.
10 bedrs, 3 ensuite, 3 ⇌ TCF TV ✱ P 7 SB £20-£30 DB £32-£40 D £8.50

P & J
277-279 Derby Road, Lenton, Nottingham NG7 2DP
☎ 0115-978 3998 Fax 0115-978 3998

Victorian family run hotel. Half mile from city centre, fully licensed bar lounge, 21 bedrooms, all facilities. Next to Queen's Medical and University. Private car park.
21 bedrs, 9 ensuite, 6 ⇌ TCF TV 🔔 P 15 🍽 Rest Resid SB £28-£38 DB £38-£48 CC MC Visa Amex

---

Short Breaks
Many hotels provide special rates for weekend and mid-week breaks – sometimes these are quoted in the hotel's entry, otherwise ring direct for the latest offers.

OAKAMOOR Staffordshire 7F1

♦♦♦♦ Ribden Farm
Sparkling Diamond
Oakamoor ST10 3BW
☎ 01538-702830 Fax 01538-702830

An 18th century, stone-built farmhouse, tastefully renovated but retaining natural features like oak beams, uneven floor boards and fourposter beds. Ideal for Alton Towers, Peak District and the Potteries.
5 bedrs, all ensuite, TCF TV P 6 DB £40-£44 CC MC Visa

OLD SODBURY Gloucestershire 3F1

♦♦♦♦ Sodbury House
Sparkling Diamond
Badminton Road, Old Sodbury BS17 6LU
☎ 01454-312847 Fax 01454-273105
Closed Christmas-New Year

Former 18th century farmhouse set in extensive grounds on the Cotswold's edge, 12 miles from Bath/Bristol. Ensuite bedrooms with colour TV, radio, hairdryer and trouser press.
17 bedrs, all ensuite, TCF TV ✱ P 30 ⊞ 16 🍽 Resid SB £45-£67.50 DB £65-£88 CC MC Visa Amex

Oxford 119

OSWESTRY Shropshire	7D2

Sebastian's
45 Willow Street, Oswestry SY11 1AQ
☎ 01691-655444 Fax 01691-653452
Closed 25-26 Dec, 1 Jan

A small 16th century hotel and popular restaurant, well known for its innovative French cuisine and the comfort of its ensuite bedrooms. Priced competitively.
4 bedrs, all ensuite, TCF TV P 3 ⋮⋮⋮ 8 ⌇ Rest Resid Room £40-£50 D £22.50 CC MC Visa Amex

OXFORD Oxfordshire	4B2

♦♦♦♦♦ Chestnuts
Sparkling Diamond
45 Davenant Road, Off Woodstock Road, Oxford OX2 8BU
☎ 01865-553375 Fax 01865-553375
Closed Christmas-New Year
5 bedrs, all ensuite, TCF TV ⌇ P 6 No children under 10 SB £39-£43 DB £62-£72

♦♦♦♦ Eltham Villa
148 Woodstock Road, Yarnton, Oxford OX5 1PW
☎ 01865-376037 Fax 01865-376037
Closed Christmas-New Year

An immaculately kept small cottage style guest house, in countryside village area on the main A44 between the city of Oxford and the historic towns of Woodstock and Blenheim Palace.
6 bedrs, all ensuite, TCF TV ⌇ P 10 No children under 5 SB £25-£30 DB £40-£50 CC MC Visa JCB

♦♦♦♦ Gables
Warm Welcome, Sparkling Diamond
6 Cumnor Hill, Oxford OX2 9HA
☎ 01865-862153 Fax 01865-864054
E-mail stay@gables-oxford.co.uk
Closed Christmas-New Year

Award winning establishment situated in excellent location close to city centre. Immaculate ensuite rooms with satellite TV, direct dial telephones, radios, hairdryers and beverage trays.
6 bedrs, all ensuite, TCF TV ⌇ P 6 SB £24-£28 DB £44-£48 CC MC Visa

♦♦♦♦ Marlborough House
Sparkling Diamond
321 Woodstock Road, Oxford OX2 7NY
☎ 01865-311321 Fax 01865-515329
E-mail enquiries@marlbhouse.win-uk.net
Closed Christmas

Located one and a half miles from the city centre off the M40 (jn 9), this modern purpose-built hotel has immaculate ensuite bedrooms with telephone, TV, fridge, tea/coffee making facilities and minibar. Parking.
16 bedrs, all ensuite, TCF TV P 6 No children under 5 ⌇ Resid SB £66.50 DB £77 CC MC Visa Amex DC JCB ♿

Oxford

♦♦♦ Bowood House
238 Oxford Road, Kidlington, OX5 1EB
☎ 01865-842288 Fax 01865-841858
22 bedrs, 20 ensuite, 2 ⇌ TCF TV ✈ P 30 ⫲ 10 ⌂
Rest Resid ℂℂ MC Visa Amex ♿

♦♦♦ Coach and Horses
Stadhampton Road, Chislehampton,
Oxford OX44 7UX
☎ 01865-890255 Fax 01865-891995
Closed 26-30 Dec

A charming 16th century oak beamed inn and free house set in splendid Oxfordshire countryside, within easy reach of Oxford. Excellent reputation for food and service.
9 bedrs, all ensuite, TCF TV ✈ P 30 ⫲ 17 ⌂ SB £48 DB £58 D £14 ℂℂ MC Visa Amex DC ♿

♦♦♦ Conifer
116 The Slade, Headington, Oxford OX3 7DX
☎ 01865-63055 Fax 01865-742232
8 bedrs, all ensuite, TCF TV P 8 SB £30-£35 DB £48
ℂℂ MC Visa ⌇

♦♦♦ Tilbury Lodge
5 Tilbury Lane, Botley, Oxford OX2 9NB
☎ 01865-862138 Fax 01865-863700

Situated in a tranquil spot in a pleasant lane, but only two minutes' walk from buses, pubs, banks and shops, this family run, private hotel has direct dial phones, a jacuzzi and a fourposter, plus ample parking.
9 bedrs, all ensuite, TCF TV ⊡ P 9 SB £43-£47 DB £62-£70 ℂℂ MC Visa

♦♦ Bravalla
242 Iffley Road, Oxford OX4 1SE
☎ 01865-241326 Fax 01865-250511
E-mail bravalla.guesthouse@virgin.net

A late Victorian house, close to the city centre, river and ring road. Most rooms are ensuite, with TV and beverage facilities. Private parking is available.
6 bedrs, all ensuite, TCF TV ✈ P 4 SB £25-£35 DB £40-£48 ℂℂ MC Visa

Acorn Awaiting Inspection
260-26 Iffley Road, Oxford OX4 1SE
☎ 01865-247998
Closed Christmas-New Year
12 bedrs, 1 ensuite, 4 ⇌ TCF TV ⊡ P 11 No children under 9 SB £25-£27 DB £38-£44 ℂℂ MC Visa Amex JCB

Ascot House Awaiting Inspection
283 Iffley Road, Oxford OX4 4AQ
☎ 01865-240259 Fax 01865-727669
6 bedrs, all ensuite, TCF TV ⊡ P 2 No children under 3 ℂℂ MC Visa Amex JCB

Brown's Awaiting Inspection
281 Iffley Road, Oxford OX4 4AQ
☎ 01865-246822 Fax 01865-246822
9 bedrs, 2 ensuite, 3 ⇌ TCF TV ⊡ P 4 ⌂ Resid SB £28 DB £46-£56 ℂℂ MC Visa

---

Don't forget to mention the guide

When booking direct, please remember to tell the hotel that you chose it from RAC Inspected Guest Accommodation

River Awaiting Inspection
17 Botley Road, Oxford OX2 0AA
☎ 01865-243475 Fax 01865-724306
Closed Christmas-New Year
21 bedrs, 17 ensuite, 2 ⌕ TCF TV P 25 No children under 5 ⌂ Rest Resid SB £50-£60 DB £65-£81 CC MC Visa

Galaxie Awaiting Inspection
180 Banbury Road, Oxford OX2 7BT
☎ 01865-515688 Fax 01865-56824
31 bedrs, 25 ensuite, 2 ⌕ 6 ⇌ TCF TV ⚐ ▤ P 31 CC MC Visa

PADSTOW Cornwall	2B3

Green Waves Awaiting Inspection
Trevone Bay, Padstow PL28 8RD
☎ 01841-520114

A friendly, family run hotel, superbly situated with sea views in a residential area near the beach.
19 bedrs, all ensuite, TCF TV P 18 No children under 4 ⌂ Resid SB £26-£30 DB £52-£210 HB £210-£250 D £15 CC MC Visa ⚐

Woodlands Awaiting Inspection
Treator, Padstow PL28 8RU
☎ 01841-532426 Fax 01841-532426
Closed winter
9 bedrs, all ensuite, TCF TV ⚐ P 20 No children under 3 ⌂ Rest Resid SB £25-£30 DB £42-£50 ♿

PAIGNTON Devon	3D3

Paignton

♦♦♦♦♦ **Roundham Lodge**
Warm Welcome, Sparkling Diamond
16 Roundham Road, Paignton TQ4 6DN
☎ 01803-558485 Fax 01803-553090
Closed Christmas, New Year

Family run bed & breakfast. Edwardian house, elegantly furnished, situated in a tranquil area close to Paignton harbour. Most rooms have sea views and/or balconies. 8 bedrooms, all ensuite, with TC, TV, hair dryer, direct dial telephone, clock radio.
8 bedrs, all ensuite, TCF TV ▤ P 9 No children under 2 SB £20-£35 DB £40-£50 CC MC Visa

♦♦♦ **Sea Verge**
Marine Drive, Preston, Paignton TQ3 2NJ
☎ 01803-557795
Closed Mar-Nov
11 bedrs, all ensuite, TCF TV P 14 No children under 9 ⌂ Resid SB £20-£22 DB £32-£38 HB £119-£133 D £8

♦♦♦ **Sealawn**
20 Esplanade Road, Paignton TQ4 6BE
☎ 01803-559031
12 bedrs, all ensuite, TCF TV P 12 ⌂ Rest Resid SB £21-£30 DB £42-£50 HB £182-£210 D £8 CC MC Visa

Redcliffe Lodge Awaiting Inspection
1 Marine Drive, Paignton TQ3 2NJ
☎ 01803-551394

Family run hotel in one of Paignton's finest seafront positions, situated on the seafront opposite the main beach, with its own large free car park. Sole proprietor Paul Davies.
17 bedrs, all ensuite, TCF TV P 17 ⌂ Rest SB £20-£40 DB £40-£80 HB £185-£260 D £12 CC MC Visa

122 Painswick

PAINSWICK Gloucestershire   7E4

♦♦♦ Hambutts Mynd
Edge Road, Painswick GL6 6UP
☎ 01452-812352 Fax 01452-813862

A Cotswold house built in 1700 with old beams, open fires and super views. An ideal centre for the Cotswolds, Bath and Stratford-upon-Avon.
3 bedrs, all ensuite, TCF TV ✱ P 3 No children under 10 SB £27 DB £44

PAR Cornwall   2B4

Elmswood House Hotel Awaiting Inspection
73 Tehidy Road, Tywardreath, Par PL24 2QD
☎ 01726-814221 Fax 01726-814399
7 bedrs, 6 ensuite, 1 ➥ TCF TV P 8 ⋕ 14 ⌘ Resid
SB £20-£27 DB £44-£47 HB £203-£252 D £9

PATELEY BRIDGE North Yorkshire   10C3

♦♦♦ Roslyn
King Street, Pateley Bridge HG3 5AT
☎ 01423-711374 Fax 01423-711374
6 bedrs, all ensuite, TCF TV P 4 ⌘ Rest Resid

PENRITH Cumbria   10B1

♦♦♦♦ Tymparon Hall
Sparkling Diamond
Newbiggin, Stainton, Penrith CA11 0HS
☎ 017684-83236
E-mail margaret@peeearson.freeserve.co.uk
Closed Apr-Nov

A cosy summer garden and glorious views are the backdrop against which to enjoy old-fashioned hospitality, home cooked farmhouse breakfasts and three course dinners as well as a cosy interior.
3 bedrs, 2 ensuite, 1 ➥ TCF ✉ ✱ P 3 SB £25-£30 DB £44-£46 HB £220-£230 D £12

♦♦♦ Limes Country
Redhills, Stainton, Penrith CA11 0DT
☎ 01768-863 343
E-mail jdhanton@aol.com
6 bedrs, all ensuite, TCF TV P 7 ⌘ Resid SB £27-£28 DB £44-£46 HB £215-£235 D £12.50 CC MC Visa

♦♦♦ Woodland House
Wordsworth Street, Penrith CA11 7QY
☎ 01768-864177 Fax 01768-890152
E-mail idaviesa@cix.co.uk
Closed Nov

Elegant and spacious red sandstone house with a library of books and maps for walkers and nature lovers. Ideal base for exploring Eden Valley, the Lakes and Pennines.
8 bedrs, all ensuite, TCF TV ✉ P 6 ⌘ Resid SB £28 DB £45 D £10 CC MC Visa

PENZANCE Cornwall 2A4

♦♦♦ Mount Royal
Chyandour Cliff, Penzance TR18 3LQ
☎ 01736-362233 Fax 01736-362233
Closed winter
7 bedrs, 4 ensuite, 2 ⇌ TCF TV ✝ P 6 SB £25-£30
DB £30-£55

♦♦♦ Penmorvah
Alexandra Road, Penzance TR18 4LZ
☎ 01736-363711 Fax 01736-363711
8 bedrs, all ensuite, TCF TV ✝ 🅰 Resid SB £16-£22.50
DB £32-£45 HB £178-£225 D £15 CC MC Visa Amex

Carlton Awaiting Inspection
Promenade, Penzance TR18 4NW
☎ 01736-362081
Closed Nov-Feb
10 bedrs, 8 ensuite, 2 ⇌ TCF TV No children under 12
SB £18 DB £40-£50

Carnson House Awaiting Inspection
East Terrace, Penzance TR18 2TD
☎ 01736-365589
E-mail rhilder@netcomuk.co.uk
8 bedrs, 2 ensuite, 1 ⇌ TCF TV No children under 12
🅰 Resid CC MC Visa Amex DC JCB

Estoril Awaiting Inspection
46 Morrab Road, Penzance TR18 4EX
☎ 01736-362468 Fax 01736-367471
E-mail jestoril@aol.com
Closed Dec-Jan

Gracious Victorian charm, immaculate surroundings, excellent home cooking and friendly, attentive service provided. A warm welcome at all times.
10 bedrs, all ensuite, TCF TV P 4 🅰 SB £26-£30
DB £52-£60 HB £280-£294 D £16 CC MC Visa ♿

Keigwin Awaiting Inspection
Alexandra Road, Penzance TR18 4LZ
☎ 01736-363930
Closed Christmas
8 bedrs, 5 ensuite, 1 ⇌ TCF TV 🖂 🅰 Resid SB £14-£19
DB £28-£43 D £10.50 CC MC Visa

Kimberley House Awaiting Inspection
10 Morrab Road, Penzance TR18 4EZ
☎ 01736-362727 Fax 01736-362727
Closed Dec-Jan
8 bedrs, 2 ensuite, 3 ⇌ TCF TV P 4 No children under 5 🅰 Resid SB £15-£18 DB £30-£36

Lynwood Awaiting Inspection
41 Morrab Road, Penzance TR18 4EX
☎ 01736-365871 Fax 01736-365871
E-mail lynwood@connexions.co.uk
6 bedrs, 2 ensuite, 3 ⇌ TCF TV ✝ No children under 5
CC MC Visa Amex DC

Woodstock Awaiting Inspection
29 Morrab Road, Penzance TR18 4EL
☎ 01736-369049 Fax 01736-369049
E-mail woodstocp@aol.com
8 bedrs, 4 ensuite, 1 🛏 1 ⇌ TCF TV No children
CC MC Visa Amex DC JCB ♿

PETERBOROUGH Cambridgeshire 8C3

♦♦♦ Aaron Park
109-112 Park Road, Peterborough PE1 2TR
☎ 01733-564849 Fax 01733-564849
14 bedrs, all ensuite, TCF TV ✝ P 11 🅰 Rest Resid
SB £32-£42 DB £42-£56 D £12 CC MC Visa Amex DC JCB

♦♦ Thorpe Lodge
83 Thorpe Road, Peterborough PE3 6JQ
☎ 01733-348759 Fax 01733-891598
18 bedrs, all ensuite, TCF TV P 20 ⚄ 40 🅰 SB £45.83
DB £55.22 D £12.50 CC MC Visa Amex DC JCB

PICKERING North Yorkshire 11E2

Moorlands Awaiting Inspection
Levisham, Pickering YO18 7NL
☎ 01751-460229 Fax 01751-460470
Closed Nov-Feb
7 bedrs, all ensuite, TCF TV 🖂 P 10 No children
SB £30-£35 DB £60-£70 HB £175-£210

124 Plymouth

PLYMOUTH Devon　　　　　　　　　　2C4

♦♦♦ Aaron
Hoe Villa, 11 Sussex Street, Plymouth PL1 2HR
☎ 01752-600022 Fax 01752-600033

Superior quiet Georgian house, minutes from seafront, city centre, Barbican Theatre and station. Ensuite single, double, business and family rooms with TV, video and tea/coffee making facilities.
4 bedrs, 2 ensuite, 1 ➥ TCF TV P 3 SB £25-£35 DB £45-£60

♦♦♦ Georgian House
51 Citadel Road, The Hoe, Plymouth PL1 3AU
☎ 01752-663237 Fax 01752-253953
10 bedrs, all ensuite, TCF TV P 2 ⌑ SB £27-£31 DB £37-£42 D £9 CC MC Visa Amex DC
See advert on this page

Ashgrove Awaiting Inspection
218 Citadel Road, The Hoe, Plymouth PL1 3BB
☎ 01752-664046 Fax 01752-252112

The Ashgrove Hotel is an elegant Victorian town house, 200 yards from the Hoe promenade and within walking distance of the historic Barbican and city centre.

Georgian House Hotel

Ideally situated on The Hoe, within walking distance of the city centre, seafront, historic Barbican ferry port, theatre, Plymouth Pavilions and National Marine Aquarium.

Ten bedrooms all en-suite with TV, direct dial telephone, tea/coffee making facilities and hairdryer.

Special rates for group or long term stay. Fully Licenced bar and restaurant serving a la carte as well as three course meal for £9. Our restaurant serves English and Continental dishes.

Write for brochure to Noel and Virginia Bhadha. All credit cards accepted.

"Restaurant closed on Sunday."

Bristish Hospitality Associate Member　　RAC Highly Acclaimed　　Member of the Plymouth Marketing Bureau
Plymouth and District Hotels, Restaurants and Guest House Association

51 CITADEL ROAD, THE HOE, PLYMOUTH
Telephone: (01752) 663237　Fax: (01752) 253953

10 bedrs, all ensuite, TCF TV SB £20-£25 DB £35-£38
CC MC Visa Amex

Chester Awaiting Inspection
54 Stuart Road, Pennycomequick,
Plymouth PL3 4EE
☎ 01752-663706 Fax 01752-663706
10 bedrs, 3 ensuite, 2 ⇌ TCF TV ⌂ Resid

Cranbourne Awaiting Inspection
278/282 Citadel Road, Plymouth PL1 2PZ
☎ 01752-263858 Fax 01752-263858
36 bedrs, 20 ensuite, 4 ⌂ 4 ⇌ TCF TV ⌂ P 16 ⌂
Resid SB £20 DB £40 CC MC Visa Amex

Devonia Awaiting Inspection
27 Grand Parade, West Hoe, Plymouth PL1 3DQ
☎ 01752-665026 Fax 01752-665026
10 bedrs, 8 ensuite, TCF TV No children under 4
SB £25-£35 DB £40-£50 CC MC Visa

Headland Awaiting Inspection
1a Radford Road, West Hoe, Plymouth PL1 3BY
☎ 01752-660866
Closed Christmas
30 bedrs, 15 ensuite, 3 ⌂ 4 ⇌ TCF TV ⌂ ⌂ CC MC Visa

Oliver's Awaiting Inspection
33 Sutherland Road, Mutley, Plymouth PL4 6BN
☎ 01752-663923

A former Victorian merchant's house situated in a quiet residential part of the town centre. Approved for its hospitality, cuisine and value.
6 bedrs, 4 ensuite, 1 ⇌ TCF TV P 2 ⌘ 12 No children under 11 ⌂ SB £20-£30 DB £45 D £11 CC MC Visa Amex DC

Bowling Green
9-10 Osborne Place, Lockyer Street,
Plymouth PL1 2PU
☎ 01752-209090 Fax 01752-209092
Closed 24-26 Dec

An elegant, family run Georgian hotel, overlooking Hoe Gardens, with superbly appointed bedrooms. Centrally located for the theatre, conference/city centres and ferry port. Enjoy a memorable visit.
12 bedrs, all ensuite, TCF TV ⌂ P 4 CC MC Visa Amex DC

PORT ISAAC Cornwall　　　　　　　　　　2B3

Bay Awaiting Inspection
1 The Terrace, Port Isaac PL29 3SC
☎ 01208-880380
Closed Nov-Easter
10 bedrs, 4 ensuite, 2 ⇌ TCF TV ⌂ P 10 ⌂ Rest
Resid SB £20-£24 DB £40-£48 HB £186.50-£211 D £10

PORTLAND Dorset　　　　　　　　　　3F3

Alessandria Awaiting Inspection
71 Wakeham, Easton, Portland DT5 1HW
☎ 01305-822270 Fax 01305-820561

Quiet location, warm and friendly, 15 bedrooms most ensuite, 2 on the ground floor - new beds. Excellent food, wine and service, reasonable prices. Free parking. Open all year. Chef proprietor Giovanni Bisogno 30 years catering experience.
15 bedrs, 12 ensuite, 1 ⌂ 2 ⇌ TCF TV P 20 ⌘ 20 ⌂
Rest Resid SB £30-£49 DB £50-£60 HB £245-£295
CC MC Visa Amex ♿

Portsmouth & Southsea

PORTSMOUTH & SOUTHSEA Hampshire 4B4

♦♦♦♦ Hamilton House
Warm Welcome, Sparkling Diamond
95 Victoria Road North, Southsea,
Portsmouth PO5 1PS
☎ 02392-823502 Fax 02392-823502
E-mail sandra@hamiltonhouse.co.uk
9 bedrs, 5 ensuite, 2 ⇌ TCF TV DB £38-£48 CC MC Visa

♦♦♦♦ Upper Mount House
Sparkling Diamond
The Vale, Clarendon Road, PO5 2EQ
☎ 01705-820456 Fax 01705-820456

Grade II Listed 19th century hotel standing in its own grounds; close to shops and seafront museums.
11 bedrs, all ensuite, TCF TV P 12 ₤ Rest Resid
SB £25-£28 DB £38-£48 HB £180-£220 D £10 CC MC Visa JCB

♦♦♦ Dolphins
10-11 Western Parade, Portsmouth PO5 3JF
☎ 01705-823823 Fax 01705-820833
33 bedrs, 20 ensuite, 2 ⋒ 5 ⇌ TCF TV ⧖ ⋕ 20 ₤
Rest Resid SB £22-£35 DB £40-£50 HB £210-£252
D £12 CC MC Visa Amex DC

Aquarius Court Awaiting Inspection
34 St Ronan's Road, Southsea PO4 0PT
☎ 01705-822872 Fax 01705-822872
12 bedrs, 4 ensuite, 2 ⇌ TCF TV P 7 ₤ Resid SB £17-£24 DB £33-£44 HB £150-£170 D £8 CC MC Visa Amex DC

PRESTON Lancashire 10B4

♦♦♦♦ Tulketh
209 Tulketh Road, Ashton, Preston PR2 1ES
☎ 01772-726250 Fax 01772-723743
Closed 23 Dec-2 Jan

Impressive detached Edwardian building with modern extension in quiet residential area less than two miles from Preston town centre. Cosy bar. Large private car park.
12 bedrs, 11 ensuite, 1 ⇌ TCF TV P 12 ₤ Resid
SB £36.50 DB £48.50 D £10 CC MC Visa Amex DC JCB

Brook House Awaiting Inspection
662 Preston Road, Clayton-le-Woods,
Preston PR6 7EH
☎ 01772-336403 Fax 01772-336403
E-mail bhhotel@provider.co.uk
20 bedrs, all ensuite, TCF TV P 22 ⋕ 40 ₤ Rest Resid
SB £40 DB £50 HB £350 D £8 CC MC Visa Amex DC

PRINCES RISBOROUGH Buckinghamshire 4C2

♦ George & Dragon
74 High Street, Princes Risborough HP17 0AX
☎ 01844-343087 Fax 01844-343087
8 bedrs, 1 ensuite, 2 ⇌ TV P 20 ⋕ 25 ₤ CC MC Visa ♿

RAMSGATE Kent 5F3

♦♦ Goodwin View
19 Wellington Crescent, Ramsgate CT11 8JD
☎ 01843-591419
13 bedrs, 4 ensuite, 3 ⇌ TCF TV ⋕ 30 ₤ Resid CC MC Visa Amex DC JCB

RAVENGLASS Cumbria 10A2

Muncaster Awaiting Inspection
Muncaster, Ravenglass CA18 1RD
☎ 01229-717693 Fax 01229-717693
Closed 4-31 Jan

Rock 127

A welcoming, comfortable guest house, ideally situated for touring, exploring and walking in the Western Lakes, with castle, gardens, miniature railway, coast, lakes and hills nearby.
8 bedrs, 2 ensuite, 2 ➡ TCF ✱ P 16 ⊟ Resid SB £22 DB £44

REDDITCH Worcestershire	7F3

Campanile Redditch Lodge
Far Moor Lane, Winyates Green, Redditch B98 0SD
☎ 01527-510710 Fax 01527-517269
50 bedrs, all ensuite, TCF TV ✱ P 50 ⊞ 20 No children under 18 ⊟ Rest Resid SB £41.95 DB £46.90 D £10.95 CC MC Visa Amex DC ♿

REDHILL Surrey	5D3

♦♦♦♦ Ashleigh House
Sparkling Diamond
39 Redstone Hill, Redhill RH1 4BG
☎ 01737-764763 Fax 01737-780308
8 bedrs, 6 ensuite, 1 ➡ TCF TV P 8 SB £32-£48 DB £48-£55 CC MC Visa

REDRUTH Cornwall	2A4

♦♦ Lyndhurst
80 Agar Road, Redruth TR15 3NB
☎ 01209-215146 Fax 01209-215146
E-mail sales@lyndhurst-guesthouse.net
6 bedrs, 3 ensuite, 1 ➡ TCF TV P 7 No children under 10 SB £15-£17 DB £34-£40 D £8.50

REIGATE Surrey	5D3

♦♦♦♦ Cranleigh
Sparkling Diamond
41 West Street, Reigate RH2 9BL
☎ 01737-223417 Fax 01737-223734
Closed Christmas
9 bedrs, 8 ensuite, 1 ➡ TCF TV P 6 ⊞ 20 ⊟ Rest Resid SB £52-£70 DB £70-£90 D £15 CC MC Visa Amex DC JCB ♿

RICHMOND North Yorkshire	10C2

♦♦♦ Hartforth Hall
Gilling West, Richmond DL10 5JU
☎ 01748-825715 Fax 01748-825781

A distinguished Grade II Listed Georgian mansion on earlier foundations, set in a beautiful valley near Richmond. Interior decor of great interest: original cornices and fireplaces. Bargain Breaks and Murder Mystery Nights.
20 bedrs, all ensuite, TCF TV ✱ P 100 ⊞ 80 ⊟ SB £45 DB £60-£90 D £18.50 CC MC Visa Amex JCB ♿

ROCK Cornwall	2B3

♦♦♦ Roskarnon House
Rock PL27 6LD
☎ 01208-862785
12 bedrs, 10 ensuite, 1 ➡ TCF TV ✱ P 14 ⊞ 40 ⊟ Rest Resid DB £40 HB £200 D £14 CC Amex

Short Breaks
Many hotels provide special rates for weekend and mid-week breaks – sometimes these are quoted in the hotel's entry, otherwise ring direct for the latest offers.

ENGLAND

Ross-on-Wye

ROSS-ON-WYE Herefordshire	7E4

♦♦♦♦ Arches Hotel
Sparkling Diamond
Walford Road, Ross-on-Wye HR9 5PT
☎ 01989-563348

Lovely Georgian style, family run hotel, in a ½ acre of garden, ideally situated 10 minutes walk from the town centre. All the attractive rooms overlook the lawned garden.
7 bedrs, 5 ensuite, 2 ⇌ TCF TV ⊠ P 10 ⛳ SB £20-£25 DB £46 HB £227 D £7 CC MC Visa ♿

♦♦♦♦ Sunnymount
Ryefield Road, Ross-on-Wye HR9 5LU
☎ 01989-563880
Closed 21-30 Dec
6 bedrs, all ensuite, TCF TV P 7 ⛳ Rest Resid SB £24-£27 DB £44-£50 HB £235-£255 D £12.50 CC MC Visa

♦♦♦ Vaga House
Wye Street, Ross-on-Wye HR9 7BS
☎ 01989-563024
Closed Christmas
7 bedrs, 2 ensuite, 2 ⇌ TCF TV ⊰ P 2 ⛳ Rest Resid SB £19-£23 DB £38-£46 HB £196-£222 D £10.50 CC MC Visa

ROTHERHAM South Yorkshire	11D4

Regis Awaiting Inspection
1 Hall Road, Rotherham S60 2BP
☎ 01709-376666 Fax 01709-513030
Closed Christmas

Large detached property with private car park, close to town centre. You will be sure of a warm welcome and hearty breakfast.
10 bedrs, 4 ensuite, 2 ⇌ TCF TV ⊰ P 8 ⊞ 10 SB £18-£28 DB £25-£31 CC MC Visa Amex

Campanile Rotherham Lodge
Lowton Way, off Denby Way, Hellaby Industrial Estate, Rotherham S66 8RY
☎ 01709-700255 Fax 01709-545169
50 bedrs, all ensuite, TCF TV ⊰ P 50 ⊞ 25 ⛳ Rest Resid SB £41.95 DB £46.90 D £10.85 CC MC Visa Amex DC ♿

RUNCORN Cheshire	7E1

Campanile Runcorn Lodge
Lowlands Road, Runcorn WA7 5TP
☎ 01928-581771 Fax 01928-581730
53 bedrs, all ensuite, TCF TV ⊰ P 53 ⊞ 35 ⛳ Rest Resid SB £41.95 DB £46.90 HB £329 D £10.85 CC MC Visa Amex DC ♿

RUSTINGTON West Sussex	4C4

♦♦♦ Kenmore
Claigmar Road, Rustington BN16 2NL
☎ 01903-784634 Fax 01903-784634
7 bedrs, all ensuite, TCF TV ⊰ P 7 SB £23.50-£26 DB £47-£52 CC MC Visa Amex

RYDAL Cumbria	10B2

♦♦♦ Rydal Lodge
Rydal LA22 9LR
☎ 01539-433208
Closed Jan
8 bedrs, 2 ensuite, 3 ⇌ TCF ⊰ P 12 ⊞ 20 ⛳ SB £30-£31 DB £46-£50 HB £200-£220 D £16.50 CC MC Visa ♿

RYE East Sussex	5E3

♦♦♦♦♦ Benson
Warm Welcome, Sparkling Diamond
15 East Street, Rye TN31 7JY
☎ 01797-225131 Fax 01797-225512
4 bedrs, all ensuite, TCF TV ⛳ Rest Resid CC MC Visa JCB

Rye 129

♦♦♦♦ Jeakes House
Sparkling Diamond
Mermaid Street, Rye TN31 7ET
☎ 01797-222828 Fax 01797-222623
E-mail jeakeshouse@btinternet.com

Stylishly restored bedrooms combine traditional elegance with modern comfort. A roaring fire greets you on cold mornings in the galleried breakfast room, while soft chamber music and attentive service provide the perfect start to the day.
12 bedrs, 10 ensuite, 2 ⇌ TCF TV ↟ ⌂ Resid
SB £26.50 DB £67 CC MC Visa
See advert on this page

JEAKE'S HOUSE

In the heart of the Sussex countryside lies the ancient town of Rye. Its medieval houses and cobbled streets make the perfect base for touring Sussex and Kent. Jeakes House originally built in 1689 has a colourful history of its own having been a wool store and later a baptist school. Today it offers a taste of history together with every modern comfort.
Each bedroom has been individually restored to create its own special atmosphere combining traditional elegance and luxury with all modern amenities.

JEAKE'S HOUSE, MERMAID STREET, RYE TN31 7ET
Tel: 01797 222828 Fax: 01797 222623

♦♦♦♦ Old Borough Arms
Sparkling Diamond
The Strand, Rye TN31 7DB
☎ 01797-222128 Fax 01797-222128
E-mail oldboroughharms@btinternet.com
9 bedrs, all ensuite, TCF TV P 9 No children under 8
⌂ Resid SB £25-£40 DB £45-£60 D £8 CC MC Visa ♿

♦♦♦♦ Strand House
Sparkling Diamond
The Strand, Winchelsea TN36 4JT
☎ 01797-226276 Fax 01797-224806

Fine old 15th century house with lots of oak beams and inglenook fireplaces. Ensuite rooms with TV and drinks tray. Romantic fourposter available. Residents' bar and lounge. Non-smoking establishment.
10 bedrs, 9 ensuite, 1 ⇌ TCF TV 🚭 P 12 ⋮⋮ 12 No children under 2 ⌂ Resid SB £28-£34 DB £50-£62
CC MC Visa JCB

♦♦♦♦ White Vine House
High Street, Rye TN31 7JF
☎ 01797-224748 Fax 01797-223599

Tudor town house in the heart of ancient Rye with comfortable bedrooms, oak beams, stone fireplaces, books and paintings. Excellent breakfasts. Ideal for antique hunting, castles and gardens.
6 bedrs, all ensuite, TCF TV 🚭 ↟ ⋮⋮ 25 ⌂ Rest Resid
SB £35 DB £60 CC MC Visa Amex DC JCB

ENGLAND

130 St Agnes

ST AGNES Cornwall — 2A4

Penkerris Awaiting Inspection
Penwinnick Road (B3277), St Agnes TR5 0PA
☎ 01872-552262 Fax 01872-552262

Enchanting Edwardian residence with garden, on B3277 road just inside the village. Beautiful rooms and excellent food. Dramatic cliff walks and beaches nearby. Licensed.
7 bedrs, 3 ensuite, 3 ⇌ TCF TV ✈ P 9 ⊞ Rest Resid
SB £20–£35 DB £35–£50 HB £150–£199 D £10 CC MC Visa Amex DC

ST ALBANS Hertfordshire — 4C2

♦♦♦♦ Ardmore House
Sparkling Diamond
54 Lemsford Road, St Albans AL1 3PR
☎ 01727-859313 Fax 01727-859313
E-mail 106376.2353@compuserve.com

Large Edwardian house set in the conservation area of St Albans. In close proximity to the main city station for London and easy walking distance of the town centre.
40 bedrs, all ensuite, TCF TV P 40 ⦙⦙⦙ 50 ⊞ SB £45–£49.50 DB £65–£75 D £10 CC MC Visa Amex

---

ST AUSTELL Cornwall — 2B4

♦♦♦♦ Nanscawen Country House
Prideaux Road, St Blazey, Par PL24 2SR
☎ 01726-814488 Fax 01726-814488
E-mail keithmartin@compuserve.com
Closed 25-26 Dec

Nanscawen House stands in 5 acres of grounds and gardens. Three luxury ensuite rooms with spa baths. An ideal base for touring all of Cornwall.
3 bedrs, all ensuite, TCF TV ✉ P 5 No children under 12 ⊞ Resid SB £40–£55.50 DB £74–£78 CC MC Visa JCB ⇨

♦♦♦ Alexandra
52-54 Alexandra Road, St Austell PL25 4QN
☎ 01726-66111 Fax 01726-66111
Closed Christmas
12 bedrs, 4 ensuite, 3 ⇌ TCF TV ✈ P 20 ⦙⦙⦙ 25 ⊞ Resid SB £26–£31 DB £46–£56 HB £151–£183 D £10.75 CC MC Visa Amex DC JCB

ST BRIAVEL'S Gloucestershire — 7E4

♦♦♦ George Inn
High Street, St Briavel's GL15 6TA
☎ 01594-530228 Fax 01594-530260
4 bedrs, all ensuite, TCF TV ✈ P 20 ⊞ SB £35 DB £45 D £6.95 CC MC Visa JCB

ST HELENS Merseyside — 10B4

♦♦ Park View
333/335 Prescot Road, St. Helens WA10 3HP
☎ 01744-20491 Fax 01744-20491
12 bedrs, 10 ensuite, TCF TV P 12 SB £20 DB £35 HB £120 CC MC Visa DC JCB ♿

Salisbury

ST IVES Cornwall   2A4

Dean Court Awaiting Inspection
Trelyon Avenue, St Ives TR26 2AD
☎ 01736-796023 Fax 01736-796233
Closed Nov-Feb

Set in own grounds overlooking Porthminster Beach, St Ives Bay and harbour. Comfortably furnished, all rooms ensuite, excellent cuisine, ample parking. Sorry, no children.
12 bedrs, all ensuite, TCF TV P 12 No children under 14 ⌑ Resid SB £32-£40 DB £60-£78 HB £240-£300 D £10 CC MC Visa JCB

Hollies Awaiting Inspection
Talland Road, St Ives TR26 2DF
☎ 01736-796605
E-mail john@hollieshotel.freeserve.co.uk
Closed Dec-Feb
10 bedrs, all ensuite, TCF TV P 12 ♨ 30 ⌑ Resid SB £15-£20.50 DB £30-£41

Longships Awaiting Inspection
2 Talland Road, St Ives TR26 2DF
☎ 01736-798180 Fax 01736-798180
Closed Nov-Mar
25 bedrs, all ensuite, TCF TV P 18 ⌑ SB £19-£27 DB £38-£54 HB £161-£217 D £8.50 CC MC Visa

Trewinnard Awaiting Inspection
4 Parc Avenue, St Ives TR26 2DN
☎ 01736-794168 Fax 01736-798161
E-mail trewinnard@mcmail.com
Closed Nov-Mar

Trewinnard is a four storey, granite-built Victorian house situated in an elevated position with superb views, yet only a three minute walk into town.
7 bedrs, all ensuite, TCF TV P 6 No children under 6 ⌑ Resid SB £23-£30 DB £42-£60 CC MC Visa JCB

SALCOMBE Devon   2C4

♦♦♦♦ Torre View
Devon Road, Salcombe TQ8 8HJ
☎ 01548-842633 Fax 01548-842633
Closed Nov-Feb
8 bedrs, 5 ensuite, 3 ⇌ TCF TV P 5 No children under 4 ⌑ Rest Resid SB £29-£33 DB £50-£58 HB £247-£272 D £13.50 CC MC Visa

♦♦♦ Penn Torr
Herbert Road, Salcombe TQ8 8HN
☎ 01548-842234
Closed Nov-Easter
7 bedrs, 6 ensuite, 1 ⌂ TCF P 9 No children under 4 SB £28-£30 DB £22-£26

Devon Tor Awaiting Inspection
Devon Road, Salcombe TQ8 8HJ
☎ 01548-843106
6 bedrs, 5 ensuite, 1 ⌂ 1 ⇌ TCF TV P 5 No children under 8 ⌑ Resid

Terrapins Awaiting Inspection
Buckley Street, Salcombe TQ8 8DD
☎ 01548-842861 Fax 01548-842265
E-mail joinus@quayterrapin.demon.co.uk
4 bedrs, all ensuite, TCF TV ⌘ ⌑ SB £35.65-£37.60 DB £51.30-£55.20 HB £172.55-£186.20 D £17.50

SALFORD Gtr Manchester   10C4

♦♦♦ Hazeldean
467 Bury New Road, Kersall, Salford M7 3NE
☎ 0161-792 6667 Fax 0161-792 6668
Closed Christmas
21 bedrs, 20 ensuite, 2 ⇌ TCF TV P 21 ♨ 40 ⌑ Rest Resid SB £42 DB £53 D £12 CC MC Visa Amex DC

SALISBURY Wiltshire   4A3

♦♦♦♦ Rokeby
3 Wain-a-Long Road, Salisbury SP1 1LJ
☎ 01722-329800 Fax 01722-329800
7 bedrs, all ensuite, TCF TV P 7 No children under 10 ⌑ Rest SB £32-£35 DB £42-£45 D £15 ✕

Salisbury

♦♦♦ Byways House
31 Fowler's Road, Salisbury SP1 2QP
☎ 01722-328364 Fax 01722-322146
E-mail bywaybandb@compuserve.com
Closed Christmas-New Year

Attractive family run Victorian guest house situated close to cathedral in quiet area of city centre. From Byways you can walk all around Salisbury. In Salisbury, follow 'Youth Hostel' signs, Fowler's Road is opposite Youth Hostel, we are on the left.
23 bedrs, 19 ensuite, 1 ⇨ TCF TV ★ P 15 ⊞ 43 ⊞
Resid SB £28-£33 DB £45-£55 ℂℂ MC Visa ♿

♦♦♦ Hayburn Wyke
72 Castle Road, Salisbury SP1 3RL
☎ 01722-412627 Fax 01722-412627

A warm welcome awaits you at this attractive Victorian house. Situated by Victoria Park, a ten minute walk by the River Avon to the city centre and cathedral.
7 bedrs, 4 ensuite, 2 ⇨ TCF TV P 7 SB £26-£48 DB £39-£48 ℂℂ MC Visa JCB

♦♦♦ Warren
15 High Street, Downton, SP5 3PG
☎ 01725-510263
Closed 20 Dec-6 Jan
5 bedrs, 2 ensuite, 2 ⇨ TCF ★ P 8 No children under 5 SB £30-£32 DB £44-£48

♦♦ Holmhurst
Downton Road, Salisbury SP2 8AR
☎ 01722-410407 Fax 01722-323164
6 bedrs, 4 ensuite, 1 ⇨ TCF TV P 8 SB £20-£25 DB £36-£42 ℂℂ MC Visa DC JCB

Holly House Awaiting Inspection
Hurdcott Lane, Winterbourne Earls, Salisbury SP4 6HL
☎ 01980-610813 Fax 01980-610813
E-mail sheila@holly-house.co.uk
3 bedrs, 2 ensuite, 2 ⇨ TCF TV ⊠ P 10 No children under 4 SB £25-£35 DB £38-£45 HB £150 ⊠ ⊠

SANDBACH Cheshire   7E1

Poplar Mount Awaiting Inspection
2 Station Road, Elworth, Sandbach CW11 3JG
☎ 01270-761268 Fax 01270-761268
7 bedrs, 4 ensuite, 1 ⇨ TCF TV P 9 SB £20-£28 DB £40 D £8 ℂℂ MC Visa JCB

SAWREY Cumbria   10B2

♦♦♦♦♦ Sawrey House
Warm Welcome, Sparkling Diamond
Sawrey LA22 0LF
☎ 015394-36387 Fax 015394-36010
E-mail enquiries@swarey-house.com
Closed Jan
11 bedrs, all ensuite, TCF TV ★ P 20 ⊞ 30 ⊞ Rest Resid SB £30-£45 DB £60-£84 HB £295-£350 D £15 ℂℂ MC Visa ⊠ ♿

♦♦♦♦ West Vale
Far Sawrey, Ambleside LA22 0LQ
☎ 015394-42817
Closed Nov-Mar

Situated on the edge of the village and offering splendid views, this excellent family run

Scarborough

accommodation provides a warm welcome in a relaxing atmosphere, with home cooking, a log fire and full central heating.
6 bedrs, all ensuite, TCF P 8 No children under 7
Resid SB £28-£29 DB £50-£52 HB £245 D £12

♦♦♦ High Green Gate
Sparkling Diamond
Sawrey, Ambleside LA22 0LF
01539-436296
Closed Nov-Mar
5 bedrs, 3 ensuite, 1 TCF P 7 SB £24-£27 DB £42-£48 HB £190-£210 D £11

SCARBOROUGH North Yorkshire 11E2

♦♦♦ Granby
Queen Street, Scarborough YO11 1HL
01723-373031 Fax 01723-373031
Closed Jan-end Mar
25 bedrs, 17 ensuite, 3 TCF 30 Rest Resid
SB £20-£21 DB £40-£42 HB £189-£196 D £7

♦♦♦ Parade
29 Esplanade, Scarborough YO11 2AQ
01723-361285
Closed Nov-Mar
17 bedrs, all ensuite, TCF TV No children under 2
Resid SB £22-£26 DB £44-£52 HB £196-£210 D £9
MC Visa

♦♦♦ Parmelia
17 West Street, South Cliff, YO11 2QN
01723-361914
E-mail parmeliahotel@btinternet.com
Closed Nov-Feb
15 bedrs, 12 ensuite, 2 TCF TV No children under 3 Resid SB £17.50-£21 DB £36-£39 HB £160-£206.50 D £10

♦♦♦ Phoenix
157 Columbus Ravine, Scarborough YO12 7QZ
01723-368319 Fax 01723-368319
Closed Dec-Feb
8 bedrs, 5 ensuite, 1 TCF TV Resid SB £13-£16
DB £26-£32 HB £133-£154 D £7 MC Visa

♦♦♦ Pickwick Inn
Huntriss Row, Scarborough YO11 2ED
01723-375787 Fax 01723-374284
Closed Christmas
10 bedrs, all ensuite, No children under 13
SB £23-£32 DB £35-£55 MC Visa Amex DC

♦♦♦ Sefton
Sparkling Diamond
18 Prince Of Wales Terrace, South Cliff, Scarborough YO11 2AL
01723-372310
14 bedrs, 10 ensuite, 7 No children under 12 Resid SB £21-£22 DB £42-£44 HB £168-£175 D £6

♦♦♦ Wheatcroft Lodge
156 Filey Road, Scarborough YO11 3AA
01723-374613
Closed Christmas
7 bedrs, all ensuite, TCF TV P 9 No children under 7 SB £21.50 DB £43

Ashcroft Awaiting Inspection
102 Columbus Ravine, Scarborough YO12 7QZ
01723-375092
7 bedrs, all ensuite, TCF TV P 7 Resid SB £18-£20
DB £36-£40 HB £168-£182 D £6 MC Visa

Boundary Awaiting Inspection
124-126 North Marine Road, YO12 7HZ
01723-376737 Fax 01723-376737
12 bedrs, all ensuite, TCF TV No children under 5
Rest Resid SB £17-£19 DB £34-£38 HB £161-£175
D £6 MC Visa

Ramleh Awaiting Inspection
135 Queen's Parade, Scarborough YO12 7HY
01723-365745 Fax 01723-365745
9 bedrs, 8 ensuite, 1 TCF TV P 5 Rest Resid
SB £18 DB £38 HB £168 D £7.50 MC Visa Amex DC JCB

West Lodge Awaiting Inspection
38 West Street, Scarborough YO11 2QP
01723-500754
7 bedrs, 3 ensuite, 1 TCF TV 17 Resid
SB £17-£19 DB £34-£38 HB £168-£182 D £7 MC Visa

Don't forget to mention the guide

When booking direct, please remember to tell the hotel that you chose it from RAC Inspected Guest Accommodation

134 Scotch Corner

SCOTCH CORNER North Yorkshire   11D2

♦♦♦ Vintage
Scotch Corner DL10 6NP
☎ 01748-824424 Fax 01748-826272
Closed Christmas-New Year

Family run roadside hotel overlooking open countryside. Open plan rustic style bar and restaurant. Ideal overnight stop or base for visiting Yorkshire Dales/Moors.
8 bedrs, 5 ensuite, 1 ↦ TCF TV P 50 ⊞ 50 ⊕
SB £29.50-£42.50 DB £36.50-£55 D £15 CC MC Visa Amex DC

SEATON Devon   3E3

♦♦♦♦ Mariners
Sparkling Diamond
The Esplanade, Seaton EX12 2NP
☎ 01297-20560
10 bedrs, all ensuite, TCF TV ↦ P 10 ⊕ Rest Resid
SB £24-£28 DB £40-£44 HB £197-£210 D £10.25
CC MC Visa

SETTLE North Yorkshire   10C3

♦ Golden Lion
Duke Street, Settle BD24 9DU
☎ 01729-822203 Fax 01729-824103
E-mail goldenlion@yorksnet
14 bedrs, 5 ensuite, 2 ↦ TCF TV P 12 ⊕ SB £22.50-£29.50 DB £45-£56 D £7.50 CC MC Visa ♿
See advert on this page

SEVENOAKS Kent   5D3

♦♦♦ Moorings
97 Hitchen Hatch Lane, Sevenoaks TN13 3BE
☎ 01732-452589 Fax 01732-456462
E-mail theryans@mooringshotel.co.uk

We are a small friendly hotel, located opposite Sevenoaks railway station, with 23 bedrooms all ensuite and a large car park at the front.
23 bedrs, all ensuite, TCF TV P 22 ⊞ 15 ⊕ Rest Resid
SB £37-£45 DB £54-£64 D £15 CC MC Visa Amex DC JCB

The Golden Lion Hotel
SETTLE
17c Coaching Inn in the market place

A traditional busy inn with restaurant, offering 14 comfortable bedrooms and log fires. Prime location for Dales, Three Peaks and Settle-Carlisle Railway.

For brochure:
**DUKE STREET, SETTLE,
NORTH YORKSHIRE BD24 9DU**
Tel: 01729 822203   Fax: 01729 824103
www.yorkshirenet.co.uk/stayat/goldenlion

Sheffield 135

SHAFTESBURY Dorset	3F2

♦♦♦♦ Grove House
Sparkling Diamond
Ludwell, Shaftesbury SP7 9ND
☎ 01747-828365 Fax 01747-828365

A small country village with beautiful panoramic views of Cranborne Chase, and overlooking a large delightful garden where badgers are regularly fed at night.
10 bedrs, all ensuite, TCF TV ⊁ P 12 ⊕ Rest Resid
SB £29.50 DB £59 HB £277 D £13.50 CC MC Visa

SHARRINGTON Norfolk	9E2

♦♦♦♦ Daubeney Hall Farm
Warm Welcome
Lower Hall Lane, Sharrington NR24 2PQ
☎ 01263-861412
2 bedrs, both ensuite.

SHEERNESS Kent	5E2

Victoriana Awaiting Inspection
103-109 Alma Road, Sheerness ME12 2PD
☎ 01795-665555 Fax 01795-580633
20 bedrs, 7 ensuite, 3 ⇌ TCF TV ⊁ P 8 ⊕ Resid
CC MC Visa Amex

SHEFFIELD South Yorkshire	11D4

♦♦♦♦♦ Cooke House
Little Gem
Warm Welcome, Sparkling Diamond
78 Brookhouse Hill, Sheffield S10 3TB
☎ 0114-230 8186 Fax 0114-623 0241
Closed 21 Dec-3 Jan
3 bedrs, all ensuite, TCF TV P 3 ⊕ CC MC Visa

♦♦♦♦ Westbourne House
25 Westbourne Road, Broomhill, S10 2QQ
☎ 0114-266 0109 Fax 0114-266 7778
E-mail mike.chris@westbournehotel.co.uk

Country house style hotel near centre, university and hospitals. Rooms are individually furnished with style and character, including Chinese, French, Indian and Venetian themes. Charming terraced garden
11 bedrs, 10 ensuite, 1 ⇌ TCF TV ⊁ P 7 SB £38-£52
DB £70-£78 CC MC Visa Amex

♦♦♦ Etruria House
91 Crookes Road, Broomhill, Sheffield S10 5BD
☎ 0114-266 2241 Fax 0114-267 0853
10 bedrs, 6 ensuite, 2 ⇌ TCF TV ⊁ P 9 SB £28-£38
DB £42-£52 CC MC Visa

♦♦♦ Lindrick
226 Chippinghouse Road, Sheffield S7 1DR
☎ 0114-258 5041 Fax 0114-255 4758
Closed Christmas-New Year

The hotel is a converted Victorian property situated in the quiet, tree-lined residential area of Nether Edge, yet only one and a half miles from the city centre.
23 bedrs, 15 ensuite, 2 ⇌ TCF TV ⊁ P 20 ⊕ Resid
SB £22-£39 DB £46-£50 CC MC Visa Amex

ENGLAND

Sheffield

Hunter House
Awaiting Inspection
Ecclesall Road, Sheffield S11 8TG
0114-266 2709 Fax 0114-268 6370
24 bedrs, 11 ensuite, 4 ⇌ TCF TV ⊀ P 9 ⊞ 30 ⊕ Rest Resid SB £29–£40 DB £40–£52 D £9 CC MC Visa Amex JCB

Millingtons Awaiting Inspection
70 Broomgrove Road, Sheffield S10 2NA
0114-266 9549 Fax 0114-269 2576
6 bedrs, 1 ensuite, 1 ⊹ 2 ⇌ TCF TV P 4 No children under 12 SB £25 DB £39–£42

SHEPTON MALLET Somerset 3E2

♦♦♦ Belfield
Sparkling Diamond
34 Charlton Road, Shepton Mallet BA4 5PA
01749-344353 Fax 01749-344353
6 bedrs, 4 ensuite, 1 ⇌ TCF TV P 6 SB £18 DB £39.50

SHERBORNE Dorset 3E2

Old Vicarage Awaiting Inspection
Sherborne Road, Milborne Port,
Sherborne DT9 5AT
01963-251117 Fax 01963-251515
Closed Jan
7 bedrs, all ensuite, TCF TV P 20 ⊞ No children under 5 ⊕ Rest Resid SB £25–£28 DB £50–£90 D £19 CC MC Visa Amex

---

SHREWSBURY Shropshire 7D2

Abbots Mead Awaiting Inspection
9-10 St Julians Friars, Shrewsbury SY1 1XL
01743-235281 Fax 01743-369133

A Grade II Listed property situated between the river and town walls, a few minutes walk from the town centre, Abbey and Quest.
14 bedrs, all ensuite, TCF TV P 10 ⊕ Rest Resid SB £37–£39 DB £50–£54 D £15 CC MC Visa Amex JCB

SIDMOUTH Devon 3D3

♦♦♦ Canterbury
Salcombe Road, Sidmouth EX10 8PR
01395-513373
Closed Dec
8 bedrs, all ensuite, TCF TV ⊠ ⊀ P 6 ⊕ Resid SB £18–£23.50 DB £36–£47 HB £173–210 D £8.50 CC MC Visa Amex ♿

Groveside Awaiting Inspection
Vicarage Road, Sidmouth EX10 8UQ
01395-513406
E-mail groveside.sidmouth@virgin.net
10 bedrs, 8 ensuite, 1 ⇌ TCF TV ⊠ P 10 ⊕ SB £20–£22 DB £40–£44 HB £130–£144 D £9

Southcombe Awaiting Inspection
Vicarage Road, Sidmouth EX10 8UQ
01395-513861 Fax 01395-512912
7 bedrs, 6 ensuite, 1 ⊹ 1 ⇌ TCF TV P 7 No children under 12 SB £20–£23 DB £40–£46 HB £192–£210 D £9

Hempstead House

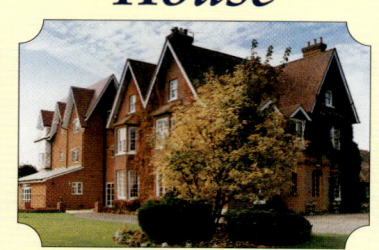

Exclusive private Victorian country house hotel set in three acres of beautifully landscaped gardens. Elegant and spacious reception rooms including new 60 cover restaurant offering fine cuisine. All bedrooms fully en-suite with many extra luxuries.

LONDON ROAD, BAPCHILD, SITTINGBOURNE ME9 9PP
Tel: 01795 428020   Fax: 01795 436362
Email: hemphouse@aol.com

Southampton 137

SITTINGBOURNE Kent	5E3

♦♦♦♦♦ Hempstead House
Sparkling Diamond
London Road, Bapchild, Sittingbourne ME9 9PP
☎ 01795-428020 Fax 01795-436362
E-mail hemphouse@aol.com
13 bedrs, all ensuite, TCF TV ✈ P 25 ⊞ 76 ⊕ Resid
SB £65 DB £75 HB £372 D £19.50 CC MC Visa Amex DC JCB
See advert on opposite page

SKIPTON North Yorkshire	10C3

♦♦♦ Skipton Park Guest'otel
2 Salisbury Street, Skipton BD23 1NQ
☎ 01756-700640 Fax 01756-700641
E-mail derekchurch@skiptonpark.freeserve.co.uk

6 minutes walk from town centre and Norman Castle. Ride the Settle-Carlisle railway, wander the Dales. Ensuite rooms with TV and hospitality tray.
7 bedrs, all ensuite, TCF TV P 2 DB £33-£45

Highfield Awaiting Inspection
58 Keighley Road, Skipton BD23 2NB
☎ 01756-793182 Fax 01756-793182
Closed Christmas
10 bedrs, 9 ensuite, TCF TV ⊕ Resid CC MC Visa Amex

SOLIHULL West Midlands	7F3

♦♦♦ Cedarwood House
347 Lyndon Road, Solihull B92 7QT
☎ 0121-743 5844 Fax 0121-743 5844
5 bedrs, all ensuite, TCF TV P 5 No children under 5
SB £27.50-£42.50 DB £40-£55 CC MC Visa

SOMERTON Somerset	3E2

♦♦♦♦ Lower Farm
Warm Welcome
Kingweston, Somerton TA11 6BA
☎ 01458-223237 Fax 01458-223276
E-mail lowerfarm@kingweston.demon.co.uk
Closed Christmas & New Year

Warm welcome guaranteed in this ancient farmhouse, previously a coaching inn. Relax in peaceful surroundings or explore the Somerset countryside. Comfortable, well equipped rooms.
3 bedrs, all ensuite, TCF TV ✉ P 6 SB £20-£22 DB £40-£44 HB £133-£146 CC MC Visa JCB

SOUTHAMPTON Hampshire	4B4

♦♦♦♦ Hunters Lodge
Sparkling Diamond
25 Landguard Road, Shirley,
Southampton SO1 5DL
☎ 01703-227919 Fax 01703-230913

A friendly, family run hotel. Ensuite bedrooms with colour satellite TV, tea and coffee making facilities and direct dial telephones. Resident's bar. Ample car parking.
16 bedrs, 15 ensuite, 1 ⇌ TCF TV ✈ P 18 ⊕ SB £25-£36 DB £44-£53 HB £125-£167 D £10 CC MC Visa Amex

Southampton

♦♦♦♦ Landguard Lodge
Sparkling Diamond
21 Landguard Road, Southampton SO15 5DL
📞 01703-636904 Fax 01703-632258
E-mail landguard.lodge@mail.com
10 bedrs, all ensuite, TCF TV P 3 No children under 5
SB £25 DB £40 CC MC Visa Amex DC

♦♦ Banister House
11 Brighton Road, Banister Park,
Southampton SO15 2JJ
📞 01703-221279 Fax 01703-221279
Closed Christmas
23 bedrs, 14 ensuite, 3 ⋔ 5 ⇌ TCF TV ⊁ P 14 ⌷ Rest
Resid SB £23.50-£27.50 DB £32-£36 D £7.50 CC MC
Visa Amex

♦♦ Nirvana
386 Winchester Road, Bassett,
Southampton SO16 7DH
📞 01703-790087 Fax 01703-790575
10 bedrs, 7 ensuite, 3 ⇌ TCF TV ⊁ P 18 ∷ 25 No
children under 14 ⌷ Resid CC MC Visa Amex

Roadchef Lodge Lodge
M27 Westbound, Rownhams,
Southampton SO16 8AP
📞 01703-741144 Fax 01703-740204
Closed 24-27 Dec
39 bedrs, all ensuite, TCF TV P 120 ∷ 15 Room £47.95
CC MC Visa Amex DC ♿

SOUTHEND-ON-SEA Essex   5E2

Mayflower Awaiting Inspection
6 Royal Terrace, Southend-on-Sea SS1 1DY
📞 01702-340489
Closed Christmas
23 bedrs, 5 ensuite, 5 ⇌ TCF TV ⊁ SB £23.50-£30
DB £35.25-£42.50

Regency Awaiting Inspection
18 Royal Terrace, Southend-on-Sea SS1 1DU
📞 01702-340747
11 bedrs, 9 ⋔ 3 ⇌ TCF TV ⌷ Rest Resid SB £20-£30
DB £35-£45 CC MC Visa

Terrace Awaiting Inspection
8 Royal Terrace, Southend-on-Sea SS1 1DY
📞 01702-348143 Fax 01702-348143
9 bedrs, 3 ensuite, 2 ⇌ TCF TV ⊁ No children under 3
⌷ Resid SB £20 DB £32

Delightful small licensed hotel with ensuite
bedrooms. 200 yards from Promenade, Conference
Centre and theatre. Adjacent to Lord Street and
Victorian shopping arcades.
8 bedrs, all ensuite, TCF TV ⊁ P 6 ∷ 0 No children
under 3 ⌷ Rest Resid SB £36 DB £50 HB £210 D £10
CC MC Visa

♦♦♦ Rosedale
11 Talbot Street, Southport PR8 1HP
📞 01704-530604 Fax 01704-530604
Closed Christmas
9 bedrs, all ensuite, TCF TV P 7 ⌷ Resid SB £23-£25
DB £44-£48 CC MC Visa

♦♦♦ Whitworth Falls
16 Lathom Road, Southport PR9 0JH
📞 01704-530074 Fax 01704-530074
13 bedrs, 8 ensuite, 3 ⇌ TCF TV P 9 ∷ ⌷ Resid

White Lodge Awaiting Inspection
12 Talbot Street, Southport PR8 1HP
📞 01704-536320 Fax 01704-536320
8 bedrs, 4 ensuite, 1 ⋔ 2 ⇌ TCF TV P 6 ⌷ Resid
SB £23-£28 DB £45-£55 HB £165-£235

SPALDING Lincolnshire   8C2

♦♦ Travel Stop
Cowbit Road, Spalding PE11 2RJ
📞 01775-767290 Fax 01775-767716

Special weekend break for two, £85 for two nights.
On the riverside, half a mile from the centre of

Spalding on B1173. Open fires, bar and breakfast restaurant.
10 bedrs, all ensuite, TCF TV ✝ P 34 ⌂ Rest Resid
SB £25-£35 DB £45-£70 CC MC Visa Amex &

STAFFORD Staffordshire	7E2

Leonards Croft Awaiting Inspection
80 Lichfield Road, Stafford ST17 4LP
☎ 01785-223676
Closed Christmas

Large Victorian house with beautiful gardens, a few minutes walk from the town centre. Ideally situated, with easy access to Shugborough Hall, Alton Towers, County Showground and M6 (jn 13).
10 bedrs, 7 ensuite, 2 ⇌ TCF TV ✝ P 12 ⌂ Resid
SB £20-£28 DB £38-£48 CC MC Visa &

STAINES Surrey	4C2

♦♦♦ **Swan**
The Hythe, Staines TW18 3JB
☎ 01784-452494 Fax 01784-461593
11 bedrs, 5 ensuite, 2 ⇌ TCF TV ⌂ CC MC Visa Amex DC

STAMFORD Lincolnshire	8C3

♦♦ **Candlesticks**
1 Church Lane, Stamford PE9 2JU
☎ 01780-764033 Fax 01780-756071
8 bedrs, all ensuite, TCF TV P 6 ⌂ SB £35 DB £50
D £15.90 CC MC Visa Amex JCB

STAUNTON-ON-WYE Herefordshire	7D4

♦♦♦ **Portway Inn**
Staunton-on-Wye HR4 7NH
☎ 01981-500474 Fax 01981-500151
3 bedrs, all ensuite, TCF TV P 40 ⌗ 50 ⌂ SB £35
DB £50 CC MC Visa JCB

Steyning 139

STEEPLE ASTON Oxfordshire	4B1

♦♦♦♦ **Westfield Farm Motel**
Warm Welcome, Sparkling Diamond
The Fenway, Steeple Aston, Bicester OX6 3SS
☎ 01869-340591 Fax 01869-347594
E-mail info@westfieldmotel.v-net.com
7 bedrs, all ensuite, TCF TV ✝ P 18 ⌂ Resid SB £45-£55 DB £55-£75 D £18 CC MC Visa Amex JCB &

STEYNING West Sussex	4C4

♦♦♦♦ **Penfold Gallery**
30 High Street, Steyning BN44 3GG
☎ 01903-815595

♦♦♦♦ **Springwells**
Sparkling Diamond
High Street, Steyning BN44 3GG
☎ 01903-812446 Fax 01903-879823
Closed Christmas & New Year
10 bedrs, 8 ensuite, 1 ⇌ TCF TV ✝ P 6 ⌗ 12 ⌂ Rest Resid SB £30-£42 DB £52-£85 CC MC Visa Amex DC ⌕ 📶
See advert on this page

SPRINGWELLS

Former Georgian merchants house; all rooms have telephone and TV and most have private facilities. Lovely walled gardens with outdoor swimming pool. Convenient for South Downs Way and Downs Link.

**HIGH STREET,
STEYNING BN4 3GG
Tel: 01903 812446
Fax: 01903 879823**

ENGLAND

Stockbridge

CARBERY

Delightfully situated, two minutes walk to the centre of the attractive old market village of Stockbridge, in one acre of landscaped gardens and lawns overlooking the River Test.

Heated outdoor pool, games room, lounge

**SALISBURY HILL,
STOCKBRIDGE SO20 6EZ
TEL. 01264-810771
FAX. 01264-811022**

STOCKBRIDGE Hampshire 4B3

♦♦♦ Carbery
Salisbury Hill, Stockbridge SO20 6EZ
☎ 01264-810771 Fax 01264-811022
11 bedrs, 8 ensuite, 1 ➥ TCF TV P 12 ♨ Resid SB £26-£33 DB £49-£52 D £13 ⇗
See advert on this page

STOKE-ON-TRENT Staffordshire 7E5

♦♦♦♦ Hanchurch Manor Country House
Hanchurch, Stoke-on-Trent ST4 8SD
☎ 01782-643030 Fax 01782-643035
Closed Christmas-New Year
4 bedrs, all ensuite, TCF TV P 60 ⊞ 10 No children under 14 ♨ CC MC Visa Amex 🖻 &

STONEHOUSE Gloucestershire 7E4

♦♦♦ Beacon Inn
Haresfield, Stonehouse GL10 3DX
☎ 01452-728884
E-mail beaconinn@aol.com
5 bedrs, all ensuite, TCF TV ♨ DB £40-£55 CC MC Visa

MELITA
Private Hotel

37 SHIPSTON ROAD,
STRATFORD-UPON-AVON,
WARWICKSHIRE CV37 7LN
Tel: 01789 292432 Fax: 01789 204867
www.stratford-upon-avon.co.uk/melita.htm

The Melita has over many years established itself as one of the Premier Private Hotels in Stratford-upon-Avon.

Stratford Visitor Satisfaction Business Award Winner.

This beautifully appointed Victorian house offers a friendly welcome, cheerful service and an excellent breakfast menu. Guests can enjoy a drink in the cosy lounge or simply relax in the hotel's beautiful gardens. There is ample car parking and the theatres and town centre are a pleasant seven minutes walk away.
All bedrooms are non smoking, have private facilities, direct dial telephones, TV, tea/coffee. Ground floor rooms are available.
Visa, Mastercard and American Express accepted.

RAC ♦♦♦♦
Sparkling Diamond Award

Stratford-upon-Avon

STOW-ON-THE-WOLD Gloucestershire 4A1

♦♦♦ Limes
Sparkling Diamond
Tewkesbury Road, GL54 1EN
☎ 01451-830034 Fax 01451-830034
Closed Christmas
5 bedrs, 4 ensuite, 1 ☞ TCF TV ⊁ P 4 SB £33-£34
DB £39-£40

STRATFORD-UPON-AVON Warwickshire 4A1

♦♦♦♦ Melita
Sparkling Diamond
37 Shipston Road, Stratford-upon-Avon CV37 7LN
☎ 01789-292432 Fax 01789-204867
E-mail melita37@email.msn.com
Closed Christmas
12 bedrs, all ensuite, TCF TV ☒ ⊁ P 12 ⊞ Resid
SB £35-£56 DB £49-£76 CC MC Visa Amex JCB
See advert on opposite page

♦♦♦♦ Penryn
Sparkling Diamond
126 Alcester Road, Stratford-upon-Avon CV37 9DP
☎ 01789-293718

8 bedrs, 6 ensuite, 2 ⇌ TCF TV P 8 SB £17-£36 DB £17-£50 CC MC Visa Amex DC ♿

♦♦♦♦ Sequoia House
Sparkling Diamond
51-53 Shipston Road,
Stratford-upon-Avon CV57 7LN
☎ 01789-268852 Fax 01789-414559
E-mail info@sequoiahotel.co.uk
Closed 21-27 Dec
23 bedrs, all ensuite, TCF TV ☒ P 28 ⊞ 30 No
children under 5 ⊞ Rest Resid SB £45-£55 DB £65-£85 CC MC Visa Amex DC
See advert on this page

♦♦♦♦ Victoria Spa Lodge
Sparkling Diamond
Bishopton Lane, Bishopton,
Stratford-upon-Avon CV37 9QY
☎ 01789-267985 Fax 01789-204728
7 bedrs, all ensuite, TCF TV ☒ P 12 SB £45-£55
DB £55-£65 CC MC Visa
See advert on next page

♦♦♦ Cymbeline House
24 Evesham Place, CV37 6HT
☎ 01789-292958 Fax 01789-292958
Closed Christmas eve/day
5 bedrs, all ensuite, TCF TV ⊁ P 2

♦♦♦ Hardwick House
1 Avenue Road, CV37 6UY
☎ 01789-204307 Fax 01789-296760

A large Victorian house set in a quiet, mature, tree lined avenue, a few minutes walk from the town centre. Non smoking bedrooms. Large car park.
14 bedrs, 13 ensuite, 1 ⇌ TCF TV P 12 SB £32-£38
DB £44-£60 CC MC Visa Amex JCB

SEQUOIA HOUSE HOTEL

**51-53 Shipston Road,
Stratford-upon-Avon
CV37 7LN**

Superbly situated in prime location just across the Avon for you to park and enjoy the delightful walk through the hotel garden and along the tramway to the Bancroft Gardens, Theatres and town centre. A spacious Victorian house with original period features, decorated and furnished with flair and style, affords excellent facilities and modern comforts. Home cooking and friendly service, all situated in three-quarters of an acre of grounds and gardens.

**Your accommodation arranged with pleasure by resident proprietors:
JEAN and PHILIP EVANS**

Telephone: Reservations (01789) 268852
Fax: (01789) 414559 Guests: (01789) 204805
http://www.stratford-upon-avon.co.uk/sequoia.htm

Victoria Spa Lodge

◆◆◆◆ *Guest House Sparkling Diamond Award*
RAC BEST SMALL HOTEL AWARD FOR MIDLANDS REGION

Paul and Dreen Tozer welcome you to Victoria Spa Lodge. An attractive Victorian 1837 building, originally built as a Spa, the hotel and pump rooms were later divided into three separate residences. Queen Victoria graciously gave her name to the hotel, and her coat-of-arms is built into the gables. Situated in a country setting overlooking Stratford canal. Seven beautifully appointed bedrooms, all en-suite, have colour T.V., radio-alarms, hair dryers, hot beverage makers, central heating and full fire certificate. Queen Victoria stayed as a guest, when she was a Princess and it was a Spa; Captain Bruce Bairnsfather (cartoonist creator of "Old Bill" during the Great War) lived here, also Sir Barry Jackson (founder of the Birmingham Repertory Theatre).

Enjoy a full English breakfast or vegetarian in a most elegant antique furnished dining room. Open all year, approved by RAC, Heart of England Tourist Board, Best B&B, Frommers, and many others.

Tariff

Double Rooms:
- from £27.50 – £30.00 pp per night
(2 persons sharing)

Family Rooms:
- by quotation

Full fire certificate. Open all year. Ample Car Parking.
Bishopton Lane, Bishopton, Stratford upon Avon, Warwickshire CV37 9QY
Tel: 01789 267985 Fax: 01789 204728
www.stratford-upon-avon.co.uk/victoriaspa.htm
Email: ptozer@victoriaspalodge.demon.co.uk

Stroud 143

♦♦♦ Marlyn
3 Chestnut Walk, Stratford-upon-Avon CV37 6HG
☎ 01789-293752 Fax 01789-293752

The Marlyn with Andrew and Rosie welcome you to Stratford, just five minutes away from the centre and theatre. We offer a long, or short, comfortable stay.
8 bedrs, 4 ensuite, 1 ⇌ TCF TV ✈ ⊞ Rest Resid
SB £20 DB £40-£48 D £10 CC MC Visa &

♦♦ Ambleside
41 Grove Road, CV37 6PB
☎ 01789-297239 Fax 01789-295670

Ideal base for exploring the wealth of history and culture both in and around the town, all the Shakespeare properties and the Royal Shakespeare Theatre, etc.
7 bedrs, 4 ensuite, 1 ⇌ TCF TV ✈ P 8 CC MC Visa JCB

♦♦ Dylan
10 Evesham Place, Stratford-upon-Avon CV37 6HT
☎ 01789-204819
5 bedrs, all ensuite, TCF TV ⊠ ✈ P 5 No children under 4

♦♦ Nando's
18 & 19 Evesham Place, Stratford-upon-Avon CV37 6HT
☎ 01789-204907 Fax 01789-204907
20 bedrs, 17 ensuite, 2 ⇌ TCF TV ✈ P 8 SB £21-£30 DB £30-£45 D £8 CC MC Visa Amex DC JCB &

Avon View Awaiting Inspection
121 Shipston Road, Stratford-upon-Avon CV37 9LQ
☎ 01789-297542 Fax 01789-292936
10 bedrs, all ensuite, TCF TV ⊠ P 16 ⊞ Rest Resid
SB £25-£34 DB £46-£64 HB £180-£240 D £12.50

ENGLAND

STROUD Gloucestershire   7E4

♦♦♦ Rose & Crown
Nympsfield, Stonehouse, Stroud GL10 3TU
☎ 01453-860240 Fax 01453-860900
E-mail roseandcrowninn@btinternet.com

A 300 year old Cotswold stone inn of character situated in a peaceful village near the Cotswold edge, within easy reach of the M4 and M5.
4 bedrs, 3 ensuite, 1 ⇌ TCF TV P 30 ⊞ 40 ⊞
SB £37.50 DB £60-£65 D £10 CC MC Visa Amex DC JCB

Short Breaks

Many hotels provide special rates for weekend and mid-week breaks – sometimes these are quoted in the hotel's entry, otherwise ring direct for the latest offers.

Stroud

Downfield Awaiting Inspection
134 Cainscross Road, Stroud GL5 4HN
☎ 01453-764496 Fax 01453-753150
Closed Christmas

This well-known Victorian Cotswolds hotel is now under new ownership. Nigel and Maura promise you excellent personal service and comfort during your stay, while you enjoy the delights of the Cotswolds.
21 bedrs, 11 ensuite, 3 ⇌ TCF TV ✝ P 21 ⊞ Rest
Resid SB £28-£40 DB £38-£50 HB £217-£260 D £9
CC MC Visa Amex DC JCB
See advert on this page

SUDBURY Suffolk 5E1

♦♦ **Old Bull Hotel & Restaurant**
Church Street, Sudbury CO10 6BL
☎ 01787-374120 Fax 01787-379044
10 bedrs, 8 ensuite, 2 ☏ TCF TV ✝ P 16 ⋮⋮ 14 ⊞ Rest
Resid SB £25-£38 DB £40-£49 D £10 CC MC Visa
Amex JCB ♿
See advert on this page

SURBITON Surrey 4C3

♦♦♦ **Pembroke Lodge**
35 Cranes Park, Surbiton KT5 8AB
☎ 0181-390 0731 Fax 0181-390 0731
7 bedrs, 3 ensuite, 3 ☏ 2 ⇌ TCF TV ✝ P 6 SB £34
DB £44

SUTTON Surrey 5D3

♦♦ **Eaton Court**
49 Eaton Road, Sutton SM2 5ED
☎ 0181-643 6766 Fax 0181-642 4580
Closed Christmas

THE DOWNFIELD HOTEL

A favourite for thousands of our guests – comfortable with a friendly atmosphere and quiet. Good fresh food and a cosy bar. Its easy to find - exit 13 from the M5 towards Stroud on the A419 - and you can easily park here. Your pets are very welcome.

134 CAINSCROSS ROAD, STROUD GL5 4HN
Tel: (01453) 764496 Fax: (01453) 753150

The Old Bull Hotel & Restaurant

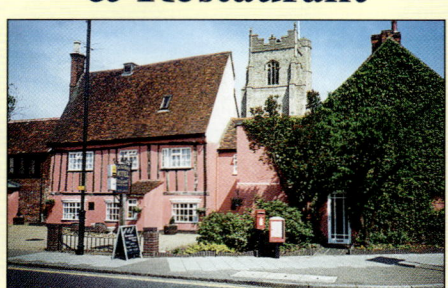

A 16th Century family run 10 bedroom Hotel, offering good food & hospitality in a friendly atmosphere. Just a short walk from the Ancient Water Meadows, Quay Theatre & Town Centre. Central to Constable Country, Colchester, Ipswich and Bury St Edmunds.

**Church Street,
Sudbury, Suffolk. CO10 2BL
Tel: 01787 374120
Fax: 01787 379044**

Sway 145

12 bedrs, 6 ensuite, 2 ⇌ TCF TV ✈ P 6 ⌬ Resid
SB £32-£50 DB £50-£62 CC MC Visa Amex

SUTTON-ON-SEA Lincolnshire 9D1

♦♦♦ Athelstone Lodge
25 Trusthorpe Road, Sutton-on-Sea LN12 2LR
☎ 01507-441521
Closed Nov-Feb
6 bedrs, 5 ensuite, 1 ⌂ 1 ⇌ TCF TV ✈ P 6 ⌬ Rest
Resid SB £18-£21 DB £36-£42 HB £156-£174 D £10
CC MC Visa JCB

SWAFFHAM Norfolk 9E3

Horse & Groom Awaiting Inspection
40 Lynn Street, Swaffham PE37 7AX
☎ 01760-721567 Fax 01760-725542
13 bedrs, 10 ensuite, 2 ⌂ 1 ⇌ TCF TV ✈ P 10 ⌬ ⌬
Rest Resid SB £25-£35 DB £45 HB £285 D £12 CC MC
Visa Amex DC ♿

SWANAGE Dorset 4A4

♦♦♦ Chines
Sparkling Diamond
9 Burlington Road, Swanage BH19 1LR
☎ 01929-422457
Closed Oct-Mar
12 bedrs, 9 ensuite, 2 ⇌ TCF TV P 10 ⌬ Resid SB £18-£22.50 DB £36-£45 ▣

♦♦♦ Sandringham
20 Durlston Road, Swanage BH19 2HX
☎ 01929-423076 Fax 01929-423076
11 bedrs, 9 ensuite, 1 ⇌ TCF P 8 ⌬ Rest Resid
SB £23-£27 DB £46-£54 HB £199-£228 D £11 CC MC
Visa JCB

SWAY Hampshire 4B4

♦♦♦♦♦ The Nurse's Cottage 🏆 🏆
Warm Welcome, Sparkling Diamond
Station Road, Sway, Lymington SO41 6BA
☎ 01590-683402 Fax 01590-683402
E-mail nurses.cottage@lineone.net
Closed mid Nov-mid Dec

RAC Small Hotel of the Year 1998 in Southern England. Booking essential at this cosy cottage on the edge of the New Forest, offering every possible guest comfort.
3 bedrs, all ensuite, TCF TV ✉ ✈ P 4 ⌬ 15 No children under 10 ⌬ Rest Resid SB £52.50-£62.50
DB £90 HB £332.50-£385 D £19.75 CC MC Visa Amex
JCB ♿
See advert on this page

PREPARE TO BE PAMPERED!

- RAC SMALL HOTEL OF THE YEAR 1998 IN SOUTHERN ENGLAND
- "Ideal retreat for a relaxing escape."
  OUTLOOK MAGAZINE
- "The highlight of our visit to England."
  K. & R.C., CALIFORNIA
- "Run with energetic enthusiasm"
  WHICH? HOTEL GUIDE 1999
- ETB England for Excellence Southern Tourist Board B&B of the Year 1998.
- AA Landlady of the Year 1998 & 1999 Top 20 Finalist.

THE NURSE'S COTTAGE
STATION ROAD, SWAY, LYMINGTON,
HANTS. SO41 6BA
Tel/Fax: (01590) 683402
Email: nurses.cottage@lineone.net

146 Swindon

SWINDON Wiltshire 4A2

♦♦♦ Fir Tree Lodge
17 Highworth Road, Stratton St Margaret, Swindon SN3 4QL
☎ 01793-822372 Fax 01793-822372
11 bedrs, all ensuite, TCF TV P 14 SB £25-£30 DB £35-£40

SYMONDS YAT Herefordshire 7E4

♦♦♦♦ Garth Cottage
Warm Welcome, Sparkling Diamond
Symonds Yat East, Ross-on-Wye HR9 6JL
☎ 01600-890364
Closed winter
4 bedrs, all ensuite, TCF P 9 No children under 12
Rest Resid DB £46 HB £248 D £15.50

Saracens Head Inn Awaiting Inspection
Symonds Yat East, Ross-on-Wye HR9 6JL
☎ 01600-890435 Fax 01600-890034
Closed weekdays Dec & Jan
9 bedrs, all ensuite, TCF P 30 ⚑ 30 SB £30-£35 DB £54 D £12.50 CC MC Visa DC
See advert on this page

TAUNTON Somerset 3E2

♦♦♦♦ Meryan House
Sparkling Diamond
Bishops Hull, Taunton TA1 5EG
☎ 01823-337445 Fax 01823-322355

A charming 362-year-old country house set in its own grounds and yet only five minutes from Taunton.
12 bedrs, all ensuite, TCF TV ✱ P 17 ⚑ 25 Rest Resid SB £40-£55 DB £50-£70 D £16 CC MC Visa JCB ♿
See advert on this page

The Saracens Head
16th C. Riverside Inn

Family owned and managed riverside inn situated alongside the River Wye and adjoining the Forest of Dean at Symonds Yat East. Fine bar and restaurant food, real ales, relaxed atmosphere, free fishing for residents. Ideal for activity holidays.

Symonds Yat East, Ross On Wye, Herefordshire HR9 6JL
Tel: (01600) 890435

MERYAN HOUSE HOTEL
RAC *Small Hotel of the Year*
ETB 4 crowns

- Comfortable Country House Hotel.
- En Suite Facilities and Bridal Suite.
- Close to the Town Centre.
- Weddings, Funerals and Conferences.
- Restaurant open to Non-Residents.

BISHOPS HULL, TAUNTON, SOMERSET TA1 5EG
Tel: Taunton (01823) 337445

Torquay 147

Brookfield Awaiting Inspection
16 Wellington Road, Taunton TA1 4EQ
☎ 01823-272786 Fax 01823-326420
8 bedrs, 7 ensuite, 1 ⇌ TCF TV P 8 SB £25 DB £40

Roadchef Lodge Lodge
Taunton Deane Motorway Service Area, M5 Southbound, Trull TA3 7PF
☎ 01823-332228 Fax 01823-338131
Closed 24 Dec-2 Jan
39 bedrs, all ensuite, TCF TV P 150 ⌘ 12 Room £47.95
CC MC Visa Amex DC &

TETBURY Gloucestershire   3F1

♦♦♦♦♦ Tavern House
Warm Welcome, Sparkling Diamond
Willesley, Tetbury GL8 8QU
☎ 01666-880444 Fax 01666-880254
E-mail tavernhousehotel@ukbusiness.com

A 17th century, Cotswold stone, Grade II Listed former staging post with leaded windows. Charming secluded walled gardens. Close to Westonbirt Arboretum. Excellent base from which to explore the Cotswolds.
4 bedrs, all ensuite, TCF TV P 6 No children under 10
SB £45-£57 DB £61-£67 CC MC Visa

TIVERTON Devon   3D2

♦♦♦ Bickleigh Cottage
Bickleigh Bridge, Tiverton EX16 8RJ
☎ 01884-855230
Closed winter
9 bedrs, 7 ensuite, 2 ⇌ TCF P 10 No children under 14 ⊞ Resid SB £29 DB £46 D £12 CC MC Visa

♦♦♦ Lodge Hill
Tiverton EX16 5PA
☎ 01884-252907 Fax 01884-242090
E-mail lodgehill@dial.pipex.com
8 bedrs, all ensuite, TCF TV ⊢ P 12 ⌘ 16 ⊞ Resid
SB £23.50 DB £45 HB £198 D £12.40 CC MC Visa Amex JCB

Bridge Awaiting Inspection
23 Angel Hill, Tiverton EX16 6PE
☎ 01884-252804 Fax 01884-253949
10 bedrs, 6 ensuite, 2 ⇌ TCF TV P 5 ⊞ Rest Resid
SB £20-£24.50 DB £40-£49 HB £210-£240 D £10

TORQUAY Devon   3D3

♦♦♦♦ Colindale
Sparkling Diamond
20 Rathmore Road, Chelston, Torquay TQ2 6NY
☎ 01803-293947
Closed Christmas
8 bedrs, 6 ensuite, 2 ⇌ TCF TV P 6 No children under 6 ⊞ Resid SB £18-£19 DB £38-£40 HB £180-£185
D £10.50 CC MC Visa

♦♦♦♦ Lindens
Sparkling Diamond, Warm Welcome
31 Bampfylde Road, Torquay TQ2 5AY
☎ 01803-212281
7 bedrs, all ensuite, TCF TV ⊢ P 7 ⌘ 14 No children under 5

♦♦♦♦ Seaway
Sparkling Diamond
Chelston Road, Torquay TQ2 6PU
☎ 01803-605320 Fax 01803-605320
13 bedrs, all ensuite, TCF TV ⊢ P 17 ⊞ Resid
SB £18.50-£23.50 DB £37-£47 HB £170-£210 CC MC Visa Amex

♦♦♦ Craig Court
10 Ash Hill Road, Torquay TQ1 3HZ
☎ 01803-294400 Fax 01803-212525
Closed 23-28 Dec
10 bedrs, all ensuite, TCF TV ⊢ P 10 ⊞ Resid
SB £17.50-£23.50 DB £35-£47 HB £182-£220.50 D £10 &

♦♦♦ Cranmore
89 Avenue Road, Torquay TQ2 5LH
☎ 01803-298488
Closed Christmas
8 bedrs, all ensuite, TCF TV P 4 SB £15-£18 DB £30-£36
HB £157.50-£178.50 D £7.50 CC MC Visa

♦♦♦ Glenwood
Rowdens Road, Torquay TQ2 5AZ
☎ 01803-296318 Fax 01803-296318
10 bedrs, 9 ensuite, 1 ⇌ TCF TV ⊢ P 10 No children under 5 ⊞ Resid SB £20-£30 DB £40-£54 HB £196-£231 D £9 CC MC Visa JCB

ENGLAND

Torquay

♦♦♦ Ingoldsby
1 Chelston Road, Torquay TQ2 6PT
☎ 01803-607497 Fax 01803-607497
15 bedrs, 12 ensuite, 1 ⇌ TCF TV ↑ P 12 ⊞ Resid
SB £17-£25 DB £34-£50 HB £185-£227 CC MC Visa
JCB ♿

♦♦♦ Richwood
20 Newton Road, Torquay TQ2 5BZ
☎ 01803-293729 Fax 01803-213632
20 bedrs, all ensuite, TCF TV ↑ P 11 ⊞ SB £18-£26
DB £18-£26 HB £135-£198 D £9 CC Visa ⇌ 🐾

Briarfields Awaiting Inspection
84-86 Avenue Road, Torquay TQ2 5LF
☎ 01803-297844
Closed 15 Nov-13 Jan
12 bedrs, 8 ensuite, 1 🐾 1 ⇌ ↑ P 10 SB £15-£18
DB £24-£34 CC MC Visa Amex

Cranborne Awaiting Inspection
58 Belgrave Road, Torquay TQ2 5HY
☎ 01803-298046 Fax 01803-298046
Closed Christmas-New Year
12 bedrs, 11 ensuite, 1 ⇌ TCF TV P 3 ⊞ Resid CC MC Visa

Elmdene Awaiting Inspection
Rathmore Road, Torquay TQ2 6NZ
☎ 01803-294940 Fax 01803-294940
11 bedrs, 7 ensuite, 1 ⇌ TCF TV ↑ P 10 ⊞ SB £19-£20.50 DB £38-£41 HB £177-£187 D £9.50 CC MC Visa Amex

Haldon Priors Awaiting Inspection
Meadfoot Sea Road, Torquay TQ1 2LQ
☎ 01803-213365 Fax 01803-213365
E-mail eric.grant@btinternet.com
Closed Nov-Feb

Set in its own grounds of three quarters of an acre, with 35ft heated swimming pool. All bedrooms have ensuite facilities. There is a superb dining room overlooking the sea, and a Victorian conservatory. Proprietors provide renowned food and service.
8 bedrs, 7 ensuite, TCF P 7 ⋕ 0 SB £28-£33 DB £28-£33 ⇌

Hotel Patricia Awaiting Inspection
Belgrave Road, Torquay TQ2 5HY
☎ 01803-293339 Fax 01803-293339
E-mail slotties@globalnet.co.uk
11 bedrs, all ensuite, TCF TV P 4 ⋕ 0 ⊞ Resid SB £18-£25 DB £32-£50 HB £180-£200 D £8 CC MC Visa

Kingston House Awaiting Inspection
75 Avenue Road, Torquay TQ2 5LL
☎ 01803-212760
6 bedrs, all ensuite, TCF TV P 6 No children under 8
SB £22.50 DB £35-£45 HB £115-£139 CC MC Visa DC

Morley Awaiting Inspection
16 Bridge Road, Torquay TQ2 5BA
☎ 01803-292955 Fax 01803-290111
E-mail tsaun1000@aol.com
10 bedrs, all ensuite, TCF TV P 4 No children under 5
SB £15-£20 DB £30-£40 HB £149-£179 D £8 CC MC Visa

Newton House Awaiting Inspection
31 Newton Road, Torre, Torquay TQ2 5DB
☎ 01803-297520
Closed 21 Dec-1 Jan
8 bedrs, 6 ensuite, TCF TV P 12 No children under 5

Red Squirrel Lodge Awaiting Inspection
Chelston Road, Torquay TQ2 6PU
☎ 01803-605496 Fax 01803-690170
14 bedrs, 10 ensuite, 4 🐾 TCF TV ↑ P 10 No children under 14 ⊞ Resid SB £20-£25 DB £40-£50 HB £170-£200 CC MC Visa ♿

TORRINGTON Devon	2C2

♦♦♦ Beaford House
Winkleigh, Beaford EX19 8AB
☎ 01805-603305 Fax 01805-603305
9 bedrs, all ensuite, TCF TV ↑ P 50 ⋕ 100 ⊞ SB £28-£32 DB £56-£64 HB £230-£260 D £12 CC MC Visa Amex ⇌ 🐾

Facilities for the disabled
Hotels do their best to cater for disabled visitors. However, it is advisable to contact the hotel direct to ensure it can provide a particular requirement.

Uttoxeter

TRURO Cornwall 2B4

♦♦♦♦ Marcorrie
20 Falmouth Road, Truro TR1 2HX
☎ 01872-277374 Fax 01872-241666
12 bedrs, all ensuite, TCF TV ⚞ P 12 ⚔ Rest Resid
SB £36.50-£40 DB £45-£52 D £10.50 CC MC Visa Amex DC JCB
See advert on this page

Trevispian-Vean Farm Awaiting Inspection
St Erme, Truro TR4 9BL
☎ 01872-279514 Fax 01872-263730
Closed mid Oct-end Mar
9 bedrs, all ensuite, TCF ⚞ P 15 ⚔ Resid ⚞

UCKFIELD East Sussex 5D3

♦♦♦♦♦ Hooke Hall
250 High Street, Uckfield TN22 1EN
☎ 01825-761578 Fax 01825-768025
Closed Christmas
9 bedrs, all ensuite, TCF TV P 8 No children under 12 ⚔ Rest Resid SB £50-£80 DB £70-£130 CC MC Visa Amex

♦♦♦♦♦ Old Oast
Warm Welcome, Sparkling Diamond
Underhill, Maresfield, Uckfield TN22 3AY
☎ 01825-766668 Fax 01825-766669
E-mail stay@oldoast.demon.co.uk
3 bedrs, 1 ensuite, 1 ⚞ TCF TV ⚞ P 5 SB £30-£50
DB £50-£65 ⚞

♦♦♦ The Cottage
Chillies Lane, High Hurstwood, Uckfield TN22 4AA
☎ 01825-732804 Fax 01825-732804

Welcome to our 160 year old stone cottage, with conservatory overlooking pretty garden and view. In a quiet valley of outstanding natural beauty close to Ashdown Forest.
4 bedrs, 2 ensuite, 1 ⚞ TCF TV ⚞ P 5 SB £20-£25
DB £40-£45 HB £126-£140

UPPINGHAM Rutland 8C3

♦♦♦ Old Rectory
Belton-in-Rutland, Oakham LE15 9LE
☎ 01572-717279 Fax 01572-717343
E-mail bb@stablemate.demon.co.uk
6 bedrs, 4 ensuite, 1 ⚞ TCF TV ⚞ ⚞ P 10 ⚔ Rest
Resid SB £27-£29 DB £40-£42 CC MC Visa ♿

UTTOXETER Staffordshire 7F2

♦♦♦ Hillcrest
3 Leighton Road, Uttoxeter ST14 8BL
☎ 01889-564627
Closed 25 Dec
7 bedrs, all ensuite, TCF TV P 12 ⚔ CC MC Visa

MARCORRIE HOTEL

E.T.B. ♕♕♕ Commended
A.A. 4 Diamonds

20 Falmouth Road,
Truro TR1 2AX
Tel: +44 1872 277374
Fax: +44 1872 241666

Victorian family house in city conservation area. Close to cathedral and shops. Comfortable ensuite rooms, parking, central for touring Cornwall.

Bedrooms: Single 4, Double 4, Twin 3, Family 1, Ensuite 12
Prices: Single £36.50, Double £46.50, Family £60
Open: All year

ENGLAND

150 Uttoxeter

Westward Awaiting Inspection
60 Carter Street, Uttoxeter ST14 8EU
☎ 01889-563096 Fax 01889-568039
E-mail westward@telinco.co.uk

6 bedrs, 4 ensuite, 1 ⇌ TCF TV ⊁ P 6 SB £26 DB £38 D £7.50 CC MC Visa Amex

WADEBRIDGE Cornwall 2B3

♦♦♦ Hendra Country House
St Kew Highway, Wadebridge PL30 3EQ
☎ 01208-841343 Fax 01208-841343
Closed Dec-Jan excl Christmas
5 bedrs, all ensuite, TCF TV ⊁ P 8 ⌂ Resid SB £23.50-£29.50 DB £47-£59 HB £276.50-£315 D £17.50 CC MC Visa Amex ▣

WAKEFIELD West Yorkshire 11D4

Campanile Wakefield Lodge
Monkton Road, Wakefield WF2 7AL
☎ 01924-201054 Fax 01924-201055
77 bedrs, all ensuite, TCF TV ⊁ P 77 ♨ 20 ⌂
Room £29.95-£37 D £10.85 CC MC Visa Amex DC &

WALLASEY Merseyside 10B4

♦♦ Sea Level
126 Victoria Road, New Brighton, Wallasey L45 9LD
☎ 0151-639 3408 Fax 0151-639 3408
Closed Christmas-New Year
15 bedrs, 1 ensuite, 2 ⌘ 3 ⇌ TCF TV ⊁ P 10 ⌂ Rest Resid SB £19-£25 DB £35-£50 HB £175-£225 D £8 CC MC Visa JCB

WARWICK Warwickshire 8A4

♦♦♦♦ Croft
Sparkling Diamond
Haseley Knob, Warwick CV35 7NL
☎ 01926-484447 Fax 01926-484447
E-mail croftguesthouse@compuserve.com
Closed Christmas week

Modern, friendly guest house in the picturesque village of Haseley Knob, convenient for the National Exhibition Centre, Birmingham Airport, Stratford and Coventry.
7 bedrs, all ensuite, TCF TV ✉ ⊁ P 8 SB £32-£34 DB £46-£48 CC MC Visa Amex JCB

WASDALE Cumbria 10A2

♦♦♦♦ Wasdale Head Inn ℞
Sparkling Diamond
Wasdale Head CA20 1EX
☎ 01946-726229 Fax 01946-726334
E-mail wasdaleheadinn@msn.com
14 bedrs, all ensuite, TCF ⊁ P 40 ♨ 30 ⌂ SB £35-£45 DB £70-£90 HB £330 D £22 CC MC Visa Amex JCB ▣

WASHINGTON Tyne & Wear 11D1

Campanile Washington Lodge
Emerson Road, Washington NE37 1LE
☎ 0191-416 5010 Fax 0191-416 5023
77 bedrs, all ensuite, TCF TV ⊁ P 77 ♨ 20 ⌂ Rest Resid SB £44.45 DB £49.40 D £10.85 CC MC Visa Amex DC &

WELLS Somerset 3E2

♦♦♦♦ Bekynton
Sparkling Diamond
7 St Thomas Street, Wells BA5 2UU
☎ 01749-672222 Fax 01749-672222
Closed Christmas

Wembley 151

6 bedrs, 4 ensuite, 2 ⇌ TCF TV ⊠ P 5 No children under 5 SB £28-£36 DB £44-£53 CC MC Visa

♦♦♦♦ Double-Gate Farm
Sparkling Diamond
Godney, Wells BA5 1RZ
☎ 01458-832217 Fax 01458-835612
E-mail hilary@doublegate.demon.co.uk
Closed Dec-Jan

Lovely Georgian farmhouse on a working farm. Excellent ensuite accommodation including a fully equipped games room. Pretty garden. Two golden retrievers and a loving moggy. Home from home!
8 bedrs, 7 ensuite, 1 ☞ TCF TV ⊠ P 6 SB £25 DB £40
CC MC Visa ☒ &

♦♦♦♦ Tor House
20 Tor Street, Wells BA5 2US
☎ 01749-672322 Fax 01749-672322
E-mail letitia@torhouse.demon.co.uk

Historic 17th century building set in attractive grounds over looking Wells Cathedral/Bishops Palace. The home is tastefully refurbished throughout and well appointed. Perfect base for touring nearby Glastonbury, Bath, Bristol and the West Country.
8 bedrs, 5 ensuite, 2 ⇌ TCF TV ⊠ P 12 No children under 2 SB £30-£45 DB £45-£60 CC MC Visa ☒

Lana Awaiting Inspection
The Hollow, Westbury Sub Mendip, Wells BA5 1HH
☎ 01749-870635

Old Poor House Awaiting Inspection
7a St. Andrews Street, Wells BA5 2UW
☎ 01749-675052
Closed Christmas week
4 bedrs, 3 ⇌ TCF

WEMBLEY Middlesex	4C2

♦♦♦ Arena
6 Forty Lane, Wembley HA9 9EB
☎ 0181-908 0670 Fax 0181-908 2007

All rooms are ensuite with satellite TV, tea and coffee making facilities and direct dial telephone. Ideally situated with easy access to the Wembley Stadium complex only 1 mile away.
13 bedrs, all ensuite, TCF TV ⚲ P 15 SB £39-£41
DB £49-£51 HB £200-£245 CC MC Visa Amex DC JCB

♦♦♦ Elm
Elm Road, Wembley HA9 7JA
☎ 0181-902 1764 Fax 0181-903 8365
E-mail elmhotel@aol.com
Closed 25 Dec
34 bedrs, 30 ensuite, 5 ⇌ TCF TV ⚲ P 7 ⊕ Resid
CC MC Visa &

Facilities for the disabled

Hotels do their best to cater for disabled visitors. However, it is advisable to contact the hotel direct to ensure it can provide a particular requirement.

ENGLAND

Wembley

♦♦ Adelphi
4 Forty Lane, Wembley HA9 9EB
☎ 0181-904 5629 Fax 0181-908 5314
E-mail adel@dial.pipex.com

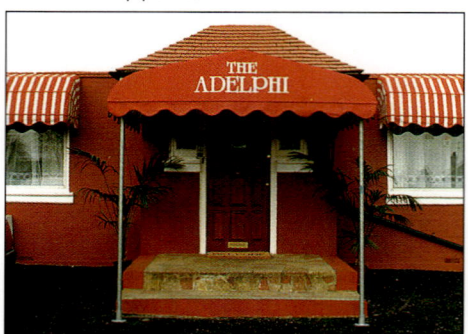

Clean and tidy, pleasant to the eye - noticeable from quite some distance, enjoying a prominent position in Wembley, near major landmarks, yet set back and in a reserved position.
13 bedrs, 9 ensuite, 2 ⇌ TCF TV P 12 SB £35-£42 DB £45-£55 CC MC Visa Amex DC

Brookside Awaiting Inspection
32 Brook Avenue, Wembley HA9 8PH
☎ 0181-904 3333 Fax 0181-908 3333
11 bedrs, 8 ensuite, 2 ⇌ TCF TV P 10 CC MC Visa Amex DC JCB &

Aaron
8 Forty Lane, Wembley HA9 9EB
☎ 0181-904 6329 Fax 0181-385 0472

A family-run bed and breakfast, convenient for the Wembley complex, London's West End and all major routes. All bedrooms ensuite with TV. Free parking.
10 bedrs, all ensuite, TCF TV P 15 CC MC Visa Amex DC &

WEST MALLING Kent	5D3

♦♦♦♦ Scott House
Sparkling Diamond
37 High Street, West Malling ME19 6QH
☎ 01732-841380 Fax 01732-870025
Closed Christmas
3 bedrs, all ensuite, TCF TV ⊠ No children under 10
SB £49 DB £69 CC MC Visa Amex DC JCB

WESTCLIFF-ON-SEA Essex	5E2

♦♦ Rose House
21 Manor Road, Westcliff-on-Sea SS0 7SR
☎ 01702-341959 Fax 01702-390918

Family run Victorian hotel by the sea with 13 ensuite bedrooms. Train to London 200 yards. TV, satellite, hospitality trays in all rooms. Bar, dining hall.
21 bedrs, 13 ensuite, 3 ⇌ TCF TV ✱ P 15 ⊕ Rest Resid SB £20-£25 DB £40-£45 HB £175-£180 D £5.50
CC MC Visa &

WESTERHAM Kent	5D3

Roadchef Lodge Clacket Lane Lodge
M25 Westbound, Westerham TN16 2ER
☎ 01959-565577 Fax 01959-561311
Closed 24-27 Dec
58 bedrs, all ensuite, TCF TV P 100 ⋕ 24 Room £49.95
CC MC Visa Amex DC &

WESTON-SUPER-MARE Somerset	3E1

♦♦♦♦ Braeside
Sparkling Diamond
2 Victoria Park, Weston-super-Mare BS23 2HZ
☎ 01934-626642 Fax 01934-626642
Closed Christmas & New Year

Weymouth 153

Quiet location with fabulous views over Weston Bay. Shops, theatre and park close by. Only a two minute walk from sandy beach. Unrestricted on-street parking.
9 bedrs, all ensuite, TCF TV ✈ ⌂ Resid SB £25 DB £50 D £14

♦♦♦♦ Wychwood
Sparkling Diamond
148 Milton Road, Weston-super-Mare BS23 2UZ
☎ 01934-627793
Closed Christmas
9 bedrs, all ensuite, TCF TV P 12 ⌂ Resid SB £27-£29 DB £44-£46 HB £196-£210 D £11 CC MC Visa ☒ &

♦♦♦ Baymead
19-23 Longton Grove Road, Weston-super-Mare BS23 1LS
☎ 01934-622951 Fax 01934-628110

Central, level, quiet location, 500 yards from seafront and Winter Gardens. Comfortable ensuite rooms with TV, tea/coffee making. Owned by Cutler family since 1965. Lift to all levels.
32 bedrs, 27 ensuite, 3 ⌂ 2 ✈ TCF TV ✈ ▣ P 8 ⌸ 50 ⌂ Resid SB £18-£25 DB £35-£45 HB £170-£210 D £7.50 ⌘

♦♦♦ L'Arrivee
75 Locking Road, BS23 3DW
☎ 01934-625328 Fax 01934-625328
12 bedrs, 10 ensuite, 1 ✈ TCF TV ✈ P 12 ⌂ Rest Resid SB £20-£25 DB £40 HB £199.50 D £8.50 CC MC Visa Amex DC JCB &

♦♦♦ Saxonia
95 Locking Road, Weston-super-Mare BS23 3EW
☎ 01934-633856 Fax 01934-623141
E-mail saxonia@lineone.net
9 bedrs, all ensuite, TCF TV P 4 ⌂ Resid SB £20-£30 DB £36-£40 HB £165-£175 D £10 CC MC Visa Amex DC JCB &

Ashcombe Court Awaiting Inspection
17 Milton Road, Weston-super-Mare
☎ 01934-625104 Fax 01934-625104
6 bedrs, all ensuite, TCF TV P 6 No children DB £30-£38 HB £165-£176 D £9

Oakover Awaiting Inspection
25 Clevedon Road, BS23 1DA
☎ 01934-620125
8 bedrs, 7 ensuite, TCF TV P 8 SB £17-£19 DB £34-£38 CC MC Visa JCB

Vaynor Awaiting Inspection
346 Locking Road, Weston-super-Mare BS22 8PD
☎ 01934-632332
3 bedrs, 1 ✈ TCF TV ✈ P 3

WESTWARD HO! Devon 2C2

Buckleigh Lodge Awaiting Inspection
Bay View Road, Westward Ho! EX39 1BJ
☎ 01237-475988
6 bedrs, 5 ensuite, 1 ✈ TCF TV P 6 ⌂ Resid

WEYMOUTH Dorset 373

♦♦♦ Trelawney
1 Old Castle Road, Weymouth DT4 8QB
☎ 01305-783188 Fax 01305-783181
10 bedrs, all ensuite, TCF TV P 13 ⌂ Resid SB £26-£30 DB £52-£58 HB £200-£248 D £12 CC MC Visa

♦♦♦ Westwey
62 Abbotsbury Road, Weymouth DT4 0BJ
☎ 01305-784564
E-mail dave@westway.demon.co.uk
13 bedrs, all ensuite, TCF TV P 12 No children under 4 ⌂ Resid SB £18.50-£24 DB £37-£48 HB £140-£175 D £7.50

154 Weymouth

Birchfields Awaiting Inspection
22 Abbotsbury Road, Weymouth DT4 0AE
📞 01305-773255 Fax 01305-773255
Closed Oct-1 Mar
9 bedrs, 3 ensuite, 2 ⇌ TCF TV P 3 ⚐ Resid SB £15-£20 DB £30-£40 HB £131-£160 D £7

Greenhill Awaiting Inspection
8 Greenhill, Weymouth DT4 7SQ
📞 01305-786026
17 bedrs, 12 ensuite, 2 ⇌ TCF TV P 14 ⌘ 40 ⚐ Rest Resid CC MC Visa

Hotel Concorde Awaiting Inspection
131 The Esplanade, Weymouth DT4 7EY
📞 01305-776900 Fax 01305-776900
14 bedrs, all ensuite, TCF TV ⤳ P 4 ⚐ Resid
SB £22.50-£25 DB £45-£50 HB £175-£205 D £8

Kenora Awaiting Inspection
5 Stavordale Road, Westham, Weymouth DT4 0AD
📞 01305-771215
E-mail kenora.hotel@wdi.co.uk
Closed Oct-Easter
15 bedrs, 13 ensuite, 1 ⇌ TCF TV P 15 ⚐ Resid
SB £26-£35 DB £52-£58 HB £195-£220 D £10.50
CC MC Visa

Sou West Lodge Awaiting Inspection
Rodwell Road, Weymouth DT4 8QT
📞 01305-783749
Closed Christmas
8 bedrs, all ensuite, TCF TV ⤳ P 10 ⚐ Resid CC MC Visa ♿

Sunningdale Awaiting Inspection
52 Preston Road, Weymouth DT3 6QD
📞 01305-832179 Fax 01305-832179
Closed Nov-Mar
18 bedrs, 12 ensuite, 2 ❦ 3 ⇌ TCF TV ⤳ P 18 ⌘ 40 ⚐ Rest Resid SB £22-£28 DB £44-£58 HB £175-£217 D £7.50 CC MC Visa ⏳ 🖼

WHEDDON CROSS Somerset	3D2

♦♦♦♦ **Rest & Be Thankful Inn**
Wheddon Cross, Minehead TA24 7DR
📞 01643-841222 Fax 01643-841222
E-mail enquiries@restandbethankful.co.uk
5 bedrs, all ensuite, TCF TV P 30 ⌘ 40 No children under 11 ⚐ SB £24-£27 DB £48-£54 HB £249 D £12
CC MC Visa Amex DC JCB

WHITBY North Yorkshire	11E2

♦♦♦♦ **Glendale**
16 Crescent Avenue, Whitby YO21 3ED
📞 01947-604242
Closed Nov
6 bedrs, 5 ensuite, 2 ⇌ TCF TV ⤳ P 6 ⚐ Resid

♦♦♦ **Sandbeck**
2 Crescent Terrace, West Cliff, YO21 3EL
📞 01947-604012 Fax 01947-606402
E-mail dysonsandbeck@tesco.net
Closed Christmas & New Year
15 bedrs, all ensuite, TCF TV ⚐ Resid DB £40-£55
CC MC Visa Amex JCB

♦♦♦ **Seacliffe**
West Cliff, Whitby YO21 3JX
📞 01947-603139 Fax 01947-603139
20 bedrs, all ensuite, TCF TV ⤳ P 8 ⌘ 40 ⚐ Rest Resid SB £37-£45 DB £59-£65 D £17 CC MC Visa Amex DC

Fairfield House Hotel

A cosy 17th century hotel, in the West Somerset village of Williton, between the Quantock and Brendon Hills, is personally run by owners Judy and Fred Mellor. Fairfield House aims to provide first class, friendly service, excellent food and wine combined with comfortable accommodation.

The hotel rooms are well appointed, combining 17th century charm (the oak panelled lounge with its huge fireplace dates back 300 years) with 20th century comfort; all bedrooms have private bath or shower rooms with W.C.'s, comfortable furnishings, clock radios and tea/coffee making facilities. The hotel is centrally heated. Ample off-street parking is also available.

51 Long Street, Williton, Somerset TA4 4QY
Tel: (01984) 632636

Windermere 155

WHITLEY BAY Tyne & Wear 11D1

♦♦♦♦ York House
30 Park Parade, Whitley Bay NE26 1DX
☎ 0191-252 8313 Fax 0191-251 3953
E-mail reservations@yorkhousehotel.com
16 bedrs, 15 ensuite, 1 ⋒ TCF TV ✈ P 6 ∰ 30 ⚑
Resid SB £30-£40 DB £45-£60 HB £275-£350 D £12.50
CC MC Visa Amex ⚑

WILLITON Somerset 3D2

♦♦♦ Fairfield House
51 Long Street, Williton TA4 4QY
☎ 01984-632636
5 bedrs, all ensuite, TCF P 8 No children under 11 ⚑
Resid SB £23.50 DB £47 D £13.50 CC MC Visa
See advert on opposite page

WINCHESTER Hampshire 4B3

♦♦♦♦ Shawlands
46 Kilham Lane, Winchester SO22 5QD
☎ 01962-861166 Fax 01962-861166
Closed Christmas-New Year

An attractive house and large garden in a peaceful area overlooking farmland with ample parking. Excellent breakfast with home made bread and preserves. Some of the accommodation consists of ground floor suite with private bathroom and sitting room.
5 bedrs, 1 ensuite, 3 ⇌ TCF TV 🖻 ✈ P 4 SB £26-£30
DB £38-£44 CC MC Visa JCB ⚑

♦♦♦♦ Wykeham Arms
75 Kingsgate Street, Winchester SO23 9PE
☎ 01962-853834 Fax 01962-854411
Closed 25 Dec

An 18th century coaching inn/hostelry tucked away in the quiet backstreets of historic Winchester.
13 bedrs, all ensuite, TCF TV ✈ P 12 ∰ 10 No children under 14 ⚑ SB £45-£99 DB £79.50-£117.50
D £18 CC MC Visa Amex DC 🖻

WINDERMERE Cumbria 10B2

♦♦♦♦♦ Beaumont
Warm Welcome, Sparkling Diamond
Holly Road, Windermere LA23 2AF
☎ 015394-47075 Fax 015394-47075
E-mail thebeaumonthotel@btinternet.com

Elegant Victorian villa where the highest standards prevail. Immaculate ensuite bedrooms designed for maximum guest comfort. Superb breakfasts. Private car park. Exceptional value.
10 bedrs, all ensuite, TCF TV 🖻 P 10 No children under 10 ⚑ Resid CC MC Visa JCB
See advert on next page

♦♦♦♦♦ Newstead
Warm Welcome, Sparkling Diamond
New Road, Windermere LA23 2EE
☎ 015394-44485
7 bedrs, all ensuite, TCF TV 🖻 P 10 No children under 7 DB £43-£52

156 Windermere

The Beaumont

The Beaumont is an elegant Victorian Villa occupying an enviably tranquil location yet is only a few minutes walk to Windermere village centre making it the ideal base from which to explore Lakeland. The highest standards of accommodation, food and hospitality are assured.
Excellent Private Car Park • Children over 10 years • Non Smoking

Holly Road, Windermere, Cumbria LA23 2AF.
Tel: (015394) 47075 Fax: (015394) 47075
E-mail: thebeaumonthotel@btinternet.com
www.lakesbeaumont.co.uk

♦♦♦♦ **Blenheim Lodge**
Sparkling Diamond
Brantfell Road, Bowness on Windermere, Windermere LA23 3AE
📞 015394-43440 Fax 015394-43440
E-mail blenheim@dedicate.co.uk

Overlooking Lake Windermere, set amid idyllic countryside yet close to local attractions. This beautiful hotel makes a perfect base for exploring the lakes.
10 bedrs, all ensuite, TCF TV P 14 10 No children under 6 Rest Resid SB £27-£40 DB £48-£80 HB £175-£350 D £20 CC MC Visa Amex DC JCB
See advert on this page

BLENHEIM LODGE HOTEL

Set amongst idyllic countryside yet close to local attractions and shops, our Country Guest House gives unsurpassed lake views and peace and quiet, and makes a perfect base for the Lakes.

Highly Acclaimed Restaurant Award

**BRANTFELL ROAD,
BOWNESS ON WINDERMERE,
WINDERMERE LA23 3AE
Tel/Fax: 015394 43440**
Email: blenheim@dedicate.co.uk
(Answered by Fax)

Windermere 157

♦♦♦♦ Fairfield
Sparkling Diamond
Brantfell Road, Windermere LA23 3AE
☏ 015394-46565 Fax 015394-46565
E-mail ray&barb@the-fairfield.co.uk
Closed Dec-Jan excl New Year

An attractive 200 year old house set in a quiet, secluded, well matured garden, close to the village, lake, fells and Dales Way. Superb value
9 bedrs, all ensuite, TCF TV ☒ P 14 ⌖ Rest Resid
SB £25-£32 DB £50-£64 CC MC Visa

♦♦♦♦ Hawksmoor
Lake Road, Windermere LA23 2EQ
☏ 015394-42110
Closed 25 Nov-26 Dec
10 bedrs, all ensuite, TCF TV P 12 No children under 6 ⌖ Resid SB £25-£35 DB £44-£62 HB £243-£278
D £12.50 CC MC Visa JCB ♿

♦♦♦♦ Kirkwood
Warm Welcome, Sparkling Diamond
Princes Road, Windermere LA23 2DD
☏ 015394-43907 Fax 015394-43907
7 bedrs, all ensuite, TCF TV ☒ ⌖ P 2 DB £46-£60
CC MC Visa JCB

♦♦♦ Brook House
Sparkling Diamond
30 Ellerthwaite Road, Windermere LA23 2AH
☏ 015394-44932

Located in a quiet part of Windermere, Winbrook House offers immaculate accommodation and excellent breakfasts. All bedrooms have TV and tea/coffee, some with ensuite. Private car park.
6 bedrs, 3 ensuite, 3 ⌖ 1 ⌖ TCF TV P 6 No children under 8 SB £18-£25 DB £33-£44 D £8.95

♦♦♦ Green Gables
37 Broad Street, Windermere LA23 2AB
☏ 015394-43886
Closed Christmas-New Year
8 bedrs, 3 ensuite, 2 ⌖ TCF TV P 2

♦♦♦ Holly-Wood
Holly Road, Windermere LA23 2AF
☏ 015394-42219
Closed Jan

Beautiful Victorian house in quiet position, yet only 3 minutes walk from village centre and amenities. Comfortable accommodation, traditional breakfasts, high standards at affordable rates.
6 bedrs, 4 ensuite, 1 ⌖ TCF TV ☒ P 4 SB £16-£22
DB £30-£44

♦♦♦ Orrest Close
3 The Terrace, Windermere LA23 1AJ
☏ 015394-43325 Fax 015394-43325
E-mail orrest.close@btinternet.com
6 bedrs, 4 ensuite, 2 ⌖ TCF TV ☒ P 6 No children under 6 DB £40-£52 HB £220-£240 D £12 CC MC Visa JCB

Don't forget to mention the guide

When booking direct, please remember to tell the hotel that you chose it from RAC Inspected Guest Accommodation

158 Windermere

♦♦♦ Royal
Queen's Square, Bowness-on-Windermere, Windermere LA23 3DB
☎ 015394-43045 Fax 015394-44990

Standing in the centre of Bowness village, only two minutes walk to Lake Windermere. All rooms are ensuite, most with spectacular fell or lake views.
29 bedrs, all ensuite, TCF TV ✈ P 20 ⌑ SB £31
DB £59.50 CC MC Visa Amex DC JCB

♦♦♦ Westbourne
Biskey Howe Road, Bowness-on-Windermere LA23 2JR
☎ 015394-43625 Fax 015394-43625
E-mail westbourne@btinternet.com
Closed 24-25, 31 Dec, 1 Jan
9 bedrs, all ensuite, TCF TV ✈ P 11 No children under 5 ⌑ Resid SB £26-£42 DB £40-£56 CC MC Visa Amex DC

Fir Trees Awaiting Inspection
Lake Road, Windermere LA23 2EQ
☎ 015394-42272 Fax 015394-42272
E-mail firtreeshotel@email.msn.com
8 bedrs, all ensuite, TCF TV ⌑ P 8 SB £35-£40 DB £44-£64 HB £155-£185 CC MC Visa Amex JCB

Oakthorpe Awaiting Inspection
High Street, Windermere LA23 1AF
☎ 015394-43547
Closed 25 Dec-24 Jan
16 bedrs, 7 ensuite, TCF TV P 18 CC MC Visa Amex

Rockside Awaiting Inspection
Ambleside Road, Windermere LA23 1AQ
☎ 015394-45343 Fax 015394-45343
Closed Christmas

Superb accommodation 100 yards from Windermere village, train and bus station. Most rooms ensuite with remote TV, telephone, clock, radio, hair dryer, etc. Parking for 12 cars. Tours arranged if required.
13 bedrs, 9 ensuite, 2 ↙ TCF TV P 9 SB £19.50-£23.50
DB £39-£55 HB £122.50-£171.50 CC MC Visa JCB

WINDSOR Berkshire   4C2

♦♦♦ Clarence
9 Clarence Road, Windsor SL4 5AE
☎ 01753-864436 Fax 01753-857060

A comfortable hotel close to the town centre, Windsor Castle, Eton College and the Thames. Convenient for Heathrow Airport and Legoland.
20 bedrs, all ensuite, TCF TV ✈ 4 ⌑ Resid SB £33-£47 DB £42-£58 CC MC Visa Amex DC JCB

♦♦♦ Melrose House
53 Frances Road, Windsor SL4 3AQ
☎ 01753-865328 Fax 01753-865328
9 bedrs, all ensuite, TCF TV ⌑ ✈ P 9 SB £45-£50
DB £55-£65 CC MC Visa JCB

Worthing 159

♦♦♦ Netherton
96-98 St Leonards Road, Windsor SL4 3DA
📞 01753-855508 Fax 01753-621267
E-mail netherton@btconnect.com

A three storey, red-brick hotel, five minutes from the centre of Windsor. Private parking facilities.
19 bedrs, all ensuite, TCF TV P 13 ⋕ 20 SB £50-£60 DB £60-£85 CC MC Visa &

♦♦♦ Park Farm
Sparkling Diamond
St Leonards Road, Windsor SL4 3EA
📞 01753-866823
3 bedrs, 1 ensuite, 1 ➡ TCF TV DB £40-£49

WOODSTOCK Oxfordshire 4B2

♦♦ Gorselands
Gorselands, Boddington Lane, Woodstock OX8 6PU
📞 01993-881895 Fax 01993-882799

An old Cotswold stone house, with oak beams and flagstone floors, in a rural location. Licensed, with meals available. Near to Oxford, Blenheim Palace and the Cotswolds.
6 bedrs, all ensuite, TCF TV ⊠ ➡ P 8 ⋕ 20 ⊕ Rest SB £29-£40 DB £40-£50 HB £198-£260 D £14 CC MC Visa Amex JCB 🈯

WOOLACOMBE Devon 2C2

♦♦♦♦ Sunnycliffe
Sparkling Diamond
Mortehoe, Woolacombe EX34 7EB
📞 01271-870597 Fax 01271-870597
Closed Nov-Jan

The Sunnycliffe is a family-run hotel, with a quiet, luxurious ambience, in an idyllic setting overlooking Woolacombe Bay and Lundy Island, adjacent to the Heritage coastal path.
8 bedrs, all ensuite, TCF TV P 8 No children under 12 ⊕ Resid SB £25-£34 DB £50-£68 HB £255-£285 D £16 CC MC Visa JCB

Caertref Awaiting Inspection
Beach Road, Woolacombe EX34 7BT
📞 01271-870361
Closed Dec-Feb
11 bedrs, all ensuite, TCF TV P 13 ⊕ SB £19-£23 DB £38-£46 HB £179-£205 D £8

WORCESTER Worcestershire 7E3

♦♦♦ Park House
12 Droitwich Road, Worcester WR3 7LJ
📞 01905-21816 Fax 01905-612178
7 bedrs, 4 ensuite, 2 ➡ TCF TV 🐾 P 8 ⊕ Resid SB £26-£30 DB £36-£42 HB £248-£276 D £10 CC MC Visa

---

WORTHING West Sussex 4C4

♦♦♦ Bonchurch House
1 Winchester Road, Worthing BN11 4DJ
📞 01903-202492 Fax 01903-202492
7 bedrs, 6 ensuite, 1 ☂ TCF TV P 6 No children under 4 ⊕ Rest SB £21-£23 DB £42-£46 CC MC Visa JCB

160 Yelverton

YELVERTON Devon   2C3

♦♦♦♦ Harrabeer Country House
Harrowbeer Lane, Yelverton PL20 6EA
📞 01822-853302 Fax 01822-853302
Closed 25-26 Dec
7 bedrs, 5 ensuite, 1 ⇌ TCF TV ✈ P 7 ⏣ 12 ⏣ Rest Resid CC MC Visa

YORK North Yorkshire   11D3

♦♦♦♦ Arndale
Sparkling Diamond
290 Tadcaster Road, York YO2 2ET
📞 01904-702424 Fax 01904-709800

A rare gem of Victorian elegance, close to city centre, overlooking the racecourse. Antiques, fresh flowers, paintings, fourposter and half-tester beds. Extensive walled gardens with gated car park.
12 bedrs, all ensuite, TCF TV P 14 ⏣ Resid SB £50-£65 DB £65-£78 CC MC Visa

♦♦♦♦ Ashbourne House
139 Fulford Road, York YO1 4HG
📞 01904-639912 Fax 01904-631332
Closed Christmas & New Year

A most charming and comfortable family run hotel situated on the A19 southern approach to York, but within walking distance of the city. Licensed.
6 bedrs, all ensuite, TCF TV ⏣ P 6 ⏣ Resid SB £34-£40 DB £40-£50 HB £262.50-£297.75 D £17.50 CC MC Visa Amex DC

♦♦♦♦ Curzon Lodge & Stable Cottages
23 Tadcaster Road, Dringhouses,
York YO24 1QG
📞 01904-703157
Closed Christmas

A delightful 17th century former farmhouse and stables within historic city overlooking the racecourse. Country antiques, cottage style bedrooms, fourposter and brass beds. Cosy and informal. Parking in grounds. Restaurants nearby.
10 bedrs, all ensuite, TCF TV ⏣ P 16 No children under 7 SB £45-£55 DB £59-£79 CC MC Visa JCB

♦♦♦♦ Eastons
90 Bishopthorpe Road, York YO23 1JS
📞 01904-626646 Fax 01904-626165

Award-winning residence 300 yards from the city walls. Decorated in the style of William Morris, with period furnishings and original paintings. Extensive Victorian sideboard breakfasts - kedgeree, kidneys and more. Private car park.
10 bedrs, all ensuite, TCF TV ⏣ P 8 No children under 5 SB £36-£62 DB £41-£69

York

♦♦♦♦ Hazelwood
Sparkling Diamond
24-25 Portland Street, York YO3 7EH
📞 01904-626548 Fax 01904-628032
E-mail hazwdyork@aol.com

Situated in the very centre of York, only 400 yards from Minster yet in an extremely quiet location. Elegant Victorian town house with private car park. Non smoking.
14 bedrs, all ensuite, TCF TV ☒ P 11 No children under 8 ⊕ Resid SB £35-£55 DB £55-£80 CC MC Visa JCB
See advert on this page

♦♦♦♦ Holmwood House
114 Holgate Road, York YO2 4BB
📞 01904-626183 Fax 01904-670899
E-mail holmwood.house@dial.pipex.com

Elegant Victorian house
14 bedrs, all ensuite, TCF TV ☒ P 10 ⊞ 12 No children under 8 ⊕ Resid SB £45-£60 DB £55-£80 CC MC Visa Amex

♦♦♦ Acorn
Sparkling Diamond
1 Southlands Road, York YO2 1NP
📞 01904-620081 Fax 01904-613331
E-mail acorn.guesthouse@btinternet.com
5 bedrs, all ensuite, TCF TV ☒ DB £36-£46 CC MC Visa

♦♦♦♦♦ The Hazelwood ♦♦♦♦♦

24-25 Portland Street, York YO31 7EH
Telephone (01904) 626548 Fax (01904) 628032
e-mail hazwdyork@aol.com

In the very heart of York only 400 yards from York Minster yet in an extremely quiet location and with private car park. Enjoy the relaxed atmosphere of our elegant Victorian townhouse providing high quality accommodation in individually designed en-suite bedrooms. Wide choice of delicious breakfasts including vegetarian. Completely non-smoking.

162 York

♦♦♦ Ascot House
80 East Parade, York YO31 7YH
☎ 01904-426826 Fax 01904-431077
E-mail j&k@ascot-house-york.demon.co.uk

An attractive, family run Victorian villa with rooms of character, some with fourposter or canopy beds. Within easy walking distance of the city centre.
15 bedrs, 12 ensuite, 2 ⇌ TCF TV ⚞ P 12 ⌂ Resid
SB £19-£24 DB £38-£48 CC MC Visa DC 🖥
See advert on this page

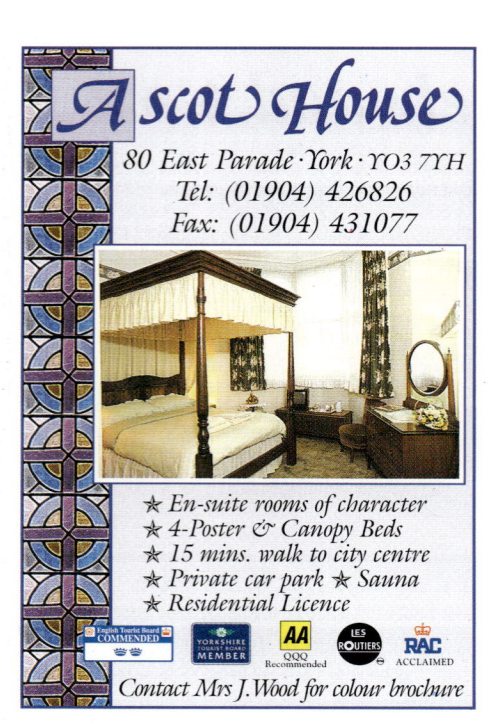

♦♦♦ Beech House
6-7 Longfield Terrace, York YO3 7DJ
☎ 01904-634581
Closed Dec-Jan

An attractive Victorian ensuite guest house in a quiet tree lined street. Only 5 minutes from York Minster and city centre via museum gardens or riverside walk.
10 bedrs, all ensuite, TCF TV P 3 No children under 10 SB £28-£34 DB £50-£56

♦♦♦ Carlton House
134 The Mount, York YO24 1AS
☎ 01904-622265 Fax 01904-637157
E-mail rac@carltonhouse.co.uk
Closed Christmas-New Year

Georgian terraced home on the Royal entry to the historic city of York. Run by the same family for more than 45 years and retains a real sense of the 'Upstairs, Downstairs' lifestyle.
13 bedrs, all ensuite, TCF TV P 6 ⌂ Rest Resid
SB £28-£29 DB £50-£52

Ascot House
80 East Parade · York · YO3 7YH
Tel: (01904) 426826
Fax: (01904) 431077

★ En-suite rooms of character
★ 4-Poster & Canopy Beds
★ 15 mins. walk to city centre
★ Private car park ★ Sauna
★ Residential Licence

ENGLISH TOURIST BOARD COMMENDED
YORKSHIRE TOURIST BOARD MEMBER
AA QQQ Recommended
LES ROUTIERS
RAC ACCLAIMED

Contact Mrs J. Wood for colour brochure

York 163

♦♦♦ Ivy House Farm
Sparkling Diamond
Hull Road, Kexby YO4 5LQ
☎ 01904-489368

Situated on the A1079 east of York, with easy access to the Yorkshire wolds, dales, moors and east coast. Comfortable accommodation with lounge, dining room and gardens, with TV and hot and cold water in all rooms.
4 bedrs, 1 ensuite, 1 ⇌ TCF TV P 10 SB £17-£19
DB £30-£32

♦♦♦ Priory
126 Fulford Road, York YO1 4BE
☎ 01904-625280 Fax 01904-637330
Closed Christmas

Established by the Jackson family in the 1930s, this elegant Victorian hotel stands in secluded gardens and boasts a superb licensed bar, restaurant and large car park.
16 bedrs, all ensuite, TCF TV P 26 ⌁ Rest Resid
SB £35-£45 DB £45-£55 D £8 CC MC Visa Amex DC

♦♦♦ St Denys
St Denys Road, York YO1 9QD
☎ 01904-622207 Fax 01904-624800
E-mail comeryork@aol.com

New for the Millennium; Next generation ownership; New larger Keith's Bar; New reception, refurbished bedrooms, stairs and hallways; and host of additional services.
13 bedrs, all ensuite, TCF TV ⚲ P 9 ⋕ 25 ⌁ Resid
SB £30-£39 DB £45-£55 CC MC Visa JCB
See advert on this page

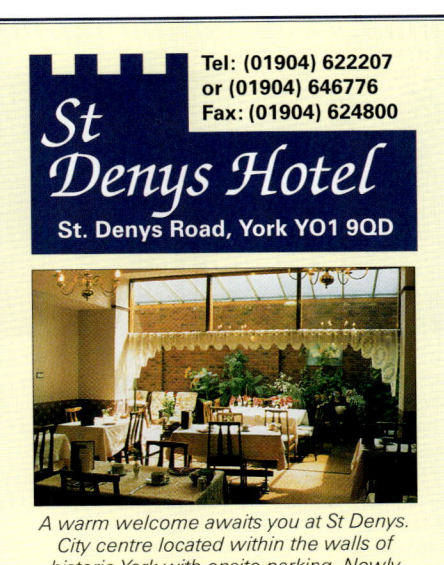

**Tel: (01904) 622207
or (01904) 646776
Fax: (01904) 624800**

St Denys Hotel
St. Denys Road, York YO1 9QD

A warm welcome awaits you at St Denys. City centre located within the walls of historic York with onsite parking. Newly refurbished, licensed bar. Corporate accounts and group bookings welcome. With the Jorvik Viking Centre two minutes walk away, we offer the ideal base from which to explore this beautiful city.

164 York

♦♦♦ St Georges
6 St Georges Place, York YO2 2DR
☎ 01904-625056 Fax 01904-625009
E-mail sixstgeorg@aol.com

Small Victorian hotel, situated in a quiet cul-de-sac. Select area, ten minutes walk from the city walls. High standard rooms, including family and fourposters. Car park.
10 bedrs, all ensuite, TCF TV ♨ P 7 ⏏ SB £30-£35 DB £45-£55 D £6.50 ₵₵ MC Visa Amex DC ♿

Bank House Awaiting Inspection
9 Southland Road, York YO23 1NP
☎ 01904-627803
7 bedrs, 1 ensuite, 7 ➥ TCF TV ✉ ♨ SB £16-£25 DB £32-£40 HB £105-£140 ♿

Bloomsbury Awaiting Inspection
127 Clifton, York YO3 6BL
☎ 01904-634031 Fax 01904-676789

An elegantly appointed large Victorian town house, recently refurbished, centrally situated with large private car park. Completely non-smoking.
9 bedrs, all ensuite, TCF TV ✉ P 9 ⛔ 9 No children under 7 ₵₵ MC Visa JCB

Georgian Awaiting Inspection
35 Bootham, York YO3 7BT
☎ 01904-622874 Fax 01904-635379
13 bedrs, 10 ensuite, 1 ☎ 1 ➥ TCF TV ✉ P 8 No children SB £18-£35 DB £36-£50 ₵₵ MC Visa

Holly Lodge Awaiting Inspection
204-206 Fulford Road, York YO1 4DD
☎ 01904-646005

Beautifully appointed Grade II Listed building, a pleasant 10 minute riverside stroll from the centre, convenient for all of York's attractions. On site parking with all rooms ensuite overlooking garden or terrace. 1½ miles from A64/A19 entrance.
5 bedrs, all ensuite, TCF TV P 5 SB £40-£50 DB £40-£60 ₵₵ MC Visa

Linden Lodge Awaiting Inspection
6 Nunthorpe Avenue, Scarcroft Road, York YO23 1PF
☎ 01904-620107 Fax 01904-620985
12 bedrs, 9 ensuite, 1 ➥ TCF TV ✉ ♨ Resid ₵₵ MC Visa Amex JCB
See advert on this page

Midway House Awaiting Inspection
145 Fulford Road, York YO1 4HG
☎ 01904-659272 Fax 01904-659272
12 bedrs, 11 ensuite, 1 ➥ TCF TV ✉ P 14 ♨ Resid ₵₵ MC Visa Amex

---

Linden Lodge Hotel

A small friendly non-smoking hotel with licensed bar and lounge, providing comfortable quality accommodation with welcome trays, hairdryers and TVs in all rooms. Unrestricted car parking, only 10 minutes walk to the railway station, city centre and race course

6 Nunthorpe Avenue, York YO23 1PF
Tel: 01904 620107 Fax: 01904 620985

Scotland

SPENCER'S

Labels For Less

Famous brands and labels at discount prices

Labels for Less is a revolutionary and colourful new guide to discount shopping.

For keen shoppers everywhere, it offers comprehensive coverage of over 1300 factory shops and factory outlet villages. Wherever you travel you will be able to find a factory shop nearby. It's essential reference for home, car and holiday.

Perfects, slight seconds and clearance lines, all at bargain prices, make Labels For Less the most exciting and rewarding guide to shopping around. For each outlet there's full information on products, labels and discounts. Plus details of locations, transport, parking, opening hours, credit cards and restaurants.

Every entry is in colour, maximising the impact and highlighting the discounts and brands each outlet features. 20 pages of mapping make route-finding easy.

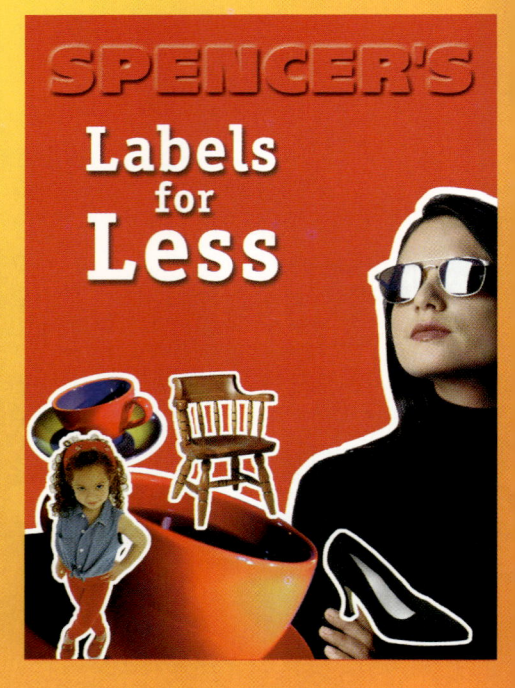

Format:	210x148mm
No. of pages:	480pp
ISBN:	1 900327 35 X
Price:	£13.99
Publication date:	November 1999

West One Publishing
Kestrel House, Duke's PLace
Marlow, Bucks SL7 2QH

tel: 01628 487722

West One PUBLISHING

www.WestOneWeb.com

Aberdeen

ABERDEEN Aberdeenshire   15F3

♦♦♦♦ Craiglynn
Sparkling Diamond
36 Fonthill Road, Aberdeen AB11 6UJ
☎ 01224-584050 Fax 01224-212225
E-mail craiglynn@compuserve.com
Closed 25-26 Dec

Craiglynn provides modern comforts whilst retaining Victorian elegance. All bedrooms are non-smoking. There are two comfortable lounges where smoking is permitted. 'Taste of Scotland' featured.
8 bedrs, all ensuite, TCF TV P 8 ⌑ Restricted SB £39-£65 DB £55-£78 D £15.95 CC MC Visa Amex DC JCB

♦♦♦♦ Jays
Warm Welcome, Sparkling Diamond
422 King Street, Aberdeen AB24 3BR
☎ 01224-638295 Fax 01224-638295
E-mail jaysguesthouse@clara.net
Closed Aug & Dec-Jan
10 bedrs, all ensuite, TCF TV ⌑ P 8 No children under 16 SB £33-£40 DB £56-£70 CC MC Visa Amex JCB

♦♦♦ Arkaig Guest House
43 Powts Terrace, Aberdeen AB25 3PP
☎ 01224-638872 Fax 01224-622189
E-mail arkaig@netcomuk.co.uk
9 bedrs, 7 ensuite, 1 ⇌ TCF TV ⇌ P 10 SB £22-£34 DB £42-£44 D £9 CC MC Visa

---

Don't forget to mention the guide

When booking direct, please remember to tell the hotel that you chose it from RAC Inspected Guest Accommodation

---

♦♦♦ Bimini
69 Constitution Street, Aberdeen AB2 IET
☎ 01224-646912 Fax 01224-646912
E-mail biminiabz@aol.com

Genuine Scottish hospitality. With the emphasis on quality and only minutes walking distance from city centre and beachfront, we are an excellent choice for business or leisure. Private parking.
8 bedrs, 3 ensuite, 2 ⇌ TV ⌑ P 6 SB £20-£35 DB £40-£50 CC MC Visa

♦♦♦ Cedars
339 Great Western Road, Aberdeen AB10 6NW
☎ 01224-583225 Fax 01224-585050
13 bedrs, 10 ensuite, 3 ⌑ 1 ⇌ TCF TV P 13 SB £38-£45 DB £52-£54 CC MC Visa Amex

♦♦♦ Strathboyne
26 Abergeldie Terrace, Aberdeen AB1 6EE
☎ 01224-593400
Closed 24 Dec-1 Jan

A friendly, family-run guest house in a quiet residential area, close to the city centre. All rooms are ensuite or have private facilities. Cable TV available.
5 bedrs, 4 ensuite, 1 ⇌ TCF TV No children under 10

SCOTLAND

Aberdeen

Kildonan
410 Great Western Road, Aberdeen AB10 6NR
☎ 01224-316115 Fax 01224-316115
Closed Christmas-New Year

A comfortable homely guest house serving a hearty Scottish breakfast. Ensuite rooms and private parking available. Colour TV in all rooms. Ideally located for Deeside and Donside.
6 bedrs, 5 ensuite, 2 ⇌ TCF TV ✉ P 3 SB £20-£30 DB £36-£45 CC MC Visa

---

LYN-LEVEN

A friendly, family run, modern guest house situated near the shores of Loch Leven, and one mile from lovely Glencoe. With all home cooking and private parking. Awarded small hotel of the year for Scotland 1996.

WEST LAROCH, BALLACHULISH, ARGYLE PA39 4JP
Tel: 01855-811392 Fax: 01855-811600

ABOYNE Aberdeenshire   15E4

♦♦♦♦♦ Arbor Lodge
Warm Welcome, Sparkling Diamond
Ballater Road, Aboyne AB34 5HY
☎ 013398-86951 Fax 013398-86951
E-mail arborlodge@aol.com
Closed Nov-Feb
3 bedrs, all ensuite, TCF TV P 4 No children under 12
SB £30 DB £52 CC MC Visa

ANSTRUTHER Fife   13E2

♦♦♦♦ Spindrift
Sparkling Diamond
Pittenweem Road, Anstruther KY10 3DT
☎ 01333-310573 Fax 01333-310573
Closed 20 Nov-10 Dec

A Victorian tea clipper's captain's home, with high standards of hospitality and service. Delicious home cooking. Table licence. Non-smoking. St Andrews - 10 minutes, Edinburgh - 1 hour.
8 bedrs, all ensuite, TCF TV ✉ P 10 No children under 10 ⊕ Restricted Resid SB £35-£50 DB £53-£63 HB £238-£350 D £13.50 CC MC Visa Amex

---

ARBROATH Angus   13E1

♦♦ Kingsley House
29/31 Market Gate, Arbroath DD11 1AU
☎ 01241-873933 Fax 01241-873933
15 bedrs, 9 ensuite, 4 ⇌ TV ✝ P 4 ⊕ Resid SB £17-£22 DB £30-£37 CC MC Visa JCB

Scurdy Awaiting Inspection
33 Marketgate, Arbroath DD11 1AU
☎ 01241-872417 Fax 01241-874603
10 bedrs, 3 ensuite, 3 ⇌ TCF TV ✝ P 2 ⊕ Restricted CC MC Visa Amex ♿

Callander 169

AVIEMORE Inverness-shire 15D3

♦♦♦ Ravenscraig
141 Grampian Road, Aviemore PH22 1RP
☎ 01479-810278 Fax 01479-812472
E-mail ravenscrg@aol.com

Feel at home in informal and comfortable surroundings. A full Highland breakfast served.
12 bedrs, all ensuite, TCF TV ✝ P 15 SB £18-£25 DB £36-£50 CC MC Visa

BALLACHULISH Argyll 14C4

♦♦♦♦ Lyn-Leven
Sparkling Diamond
West Laroch, Ballachulish PA39 4JP
☎ 01855-811392 Fax 01855-811600
Closed Christmas
12 bedrs, all ensuite, TCF TV ✝ P 14 ⊞ Rest SB £23-£27 DB £40-£46 HB £200-£210 D £9 CC MC Visa
See advert on opposite page

BEAULY Inverness-shire 15D3

♦♦♦ Heathmount
Station Road, Beauly IV4 7EQ
☎ 01463-782411
5 bedrs, 2 ⇌ TCF TV ✝ P 6 SB £18-£20 DB £36-£40 HB £126

BLAIRGOWRIE Perthshire 13D1

♦♦♦ Rosebank House ⓡ
Sparkling Diamond
Balmoral Road, Blairgowrie PH10 7AF
☎ 01250-872912
Closed Nov-Dec
7 bedrs, 6 ensuite, 1 ⇌ TCF P 12 No children under 10 ⊞ Restricted Resid SB £22-£24 DB £44-£48 HB £208.50-£218.50 D £11.50

BOAT OF GARTEN Inverness-shire 15D3

♦♦♦♦♦ Glenavon House ⓡ
Little Gem
Warm Welcome, Sparkling Diamond
Kinchurdy Road, Boat of Garten PH24 3BP
☎ 01479-831213 Fax 01479-831213
E-mail strain@glenavonhouse.freeserve.co.uk
Closed Nov-Mar
5 bedrs, all ensuite, TCF TV ✝ P 10 ⊞ 14 ⊞ Resid SB £27.50-£30 DB £55-£60 HB £316-£332 D £22.50 CC MC Visa

BONAR BRIDGE Sutherland 15D2

♦♦♦ Kyle House
Dornoch Road, Bonar Bridge IV24 3EB
☎ 01863-766360 Fax 01863-766360
Closed Nov-Dec

Comfortable old established Scottish house with views over Kyle of Sutherland to Ross-shire hills offering quiet, comfortable accommodation. Ideal Highland touring base. Off street parking.
6 bedrs, 3 ensuite, 1 ⇌ TCF TV P 6 No children under 4 ⊞ Resid SB £18 DB £35-£40 HB £125

CALLANDER Perthshire 12C1

♦♦♦♦ Arden House
Warm Welcome, Sparkling Diamond
Bracklinn Road, Callander FK17 8EQ
☎ 01877-330235 Fax 01877-330235
Closed Nov-Mar
6 bedrs, all ensuite, TCF TV ☒ P 10 No children under 14 SB £27.50 DB £50-£70 CC MC Visa

Annfield House Awaiting Inspection
18 North Church Street, Callander FK17 8EG
☎ 01877-330204
7 bedrs, 4 ensuite, 2 ⇌ TCF ✝ P 9

SCOTLAND

Campbeltown

CAMPBELTOWN Argyll   12B3

♦♦♦ Westbank
Dell Road, Campbeltown PA28 6JG
☎ 01586-553660 Fax 01586-553660
Closed Nov-Feb
8 bedrs, 2 ensuite, 2 ⇨ TCF TV No children under 3 ♿
Resid ££ MC Visa

CONNEL Argyll   12B1

♦♦♦♦ Loch Etive House
Connel, Oban PA37 1PH
☎ 01631-710400 Fax 01631-710680
Closed Nov-Mar
6 bedrs, 4 ensuite, 1 ⇨ TCF TV ✈ P 7 ♿ Resid
SB £25-£28 DB £40-£50 HB £227-£246 D £13.50
££ MC Visa

♦♦♦♦ Ronebhal
Sparkling Diamond
Connel PA37 1PJ
☎ 01631-710310 Fax 01631-710310
E-mail ronebhal@argyllinternet.co.uk
Closed Oct-Mar
5 bedrs, all ensuite, TCF TV 🅿 P 6 ⛔ 12 No children under 7 SB £18-£23 DB £36-£56 HB £126-£196 ££ MC Visa ♿

CRIEFF Perthshire   12C1

Gwydyr House Awaiting Inspection
Comrie Road, Crieff PH7 4BP
☎ 01764-653277 Fax 01764-653277
E-mail george.blackie@iclweb.com

Delightful eight bedroom Victorian house hotel in own quiet grounds. Colour TV, hairdryer, heating and tea/coffee tray in all rooms. Five minutes walk to town centre. Superb views. Residents licence.
8 bedrs, all ensuite, TCF TV ✈ P 8 ♿ Rest Resid
SB £28 DB £64 D £15 ££ MC Visa

CUPAR Fife   13D1

Rathcluan Awaiting Inspection
Carslogie Road, Cupar KY15 4HY
☎ 01334-650000 Fax 01334-650000
E-mail reservations@rathcluan.co.uk
Closed Jan
12 bedrs, 6 ensuite, 1 ☏ 1 ⇨ TCF TV ✈ P 20 ⛔ ♿
Resid SB £22-£28 DB £44-£56 D £10 ££ MC Visa Amex ♿

DALMALLY Argyll   12B1

♦♦♦ Rockhill Farm
Rockhill, Ardbrecknish, Dalmally PA33 1BH
☎ 01866-833218 Fax 01866-833218

Secluded lochside setting with magnificent mountain views, on a 120 acre horse breeding estate. Real peace and quiet, yet accessible. Family run since 1954. 1 mile free trout fishing.
5 bedrs, all ensuite, TCF TV ✈ P 8 ♿ Resid SB £25 DB £40 HB £225-£245 D £15 📧

DENNY Stirlingshire   12C2

♦♦♦ Topps
Fintry Road, Denny, Falkirk FK6 5JF
☎ 01324-822471 Fax 01324-823099

A chalet farmhouse in a beautiful hillside location with stunning, panoramic views. Family double or

Edinburgh

twin-bedded rooms available, all ensuite, tea/coffee, shortbread and TV. Food a speciality (Taste of Scotland listed).
8 bedrs, all ensuite, TCF TV ⌧ ✝ P 12 ⌑ Rest Resid
SB £25-£32 DB £38-£44 CC MC Visa ♿

DORNOCH Sutherland 15D2

♦♦ Achandean
The Meadows, Dornoch IV25 3SF
☎ 01862-810413 Fax 01862-810413
E-mail bhellier@lineone.net
Closed mid Oct-Feb

Central spacious comfortable bungalow with large ensuite rooms. Suit disabled. Special rates OAP's. Ideal for touring beautiful northern Highlands, walks, golf, car drives, Orkneys. Short breaks welcome. Quiet location. Off road parking. Pets accepted.
3 bedrs, all ensuite, TCF TV ✝ P 4 DB £38-£44 HB £180 D £10 ♿

DUMFRIES Dumfriesshire 10A1

♦♦♦ Franklea
Castle Douglas Road, Dumfries DG2 8PP
☎ 01387-253255 Fax 01387-259301
Closed 1 Nov-1 Apr
3 bedrs, 2 ensuite, 2 ➡ TCF TV ✝ P 8 No children under 6 SB £20-£22 DB £35-£40 HB £175-£210

DUNDEE Angus 13D1

♦♦♦♦ Beach House
Sparkling Diamond
22 Esplanade, Broughty Ferry, Dundee DD5 2EN
☎ 01382-776614 Fax 01382-480241
5 bedrs, all ensuite, TCF TV ✝ ⌑ Restricted Resid
SB £32-£38 DB £45-£50 D £12.50 CC MC Visa

---

for road maps...
www.WestOneWeb.com
...great offers

SCOTLAND

DUNOON Argyll 12B2

♦♦♦♦♦ Anchorage Hotel & Restaurant
Warm Welcome, Sparkling Diamond
Shore Road, Ardnadam, Sandbank, PA23 8QG
☎ 01369-705108 Fax 01369-705108
E-mail info@anchorage.co.uk
Closed Nov
5 bedrs, all ensuite, TCF TV ⌧ P 14 ⌗ 18 ⌑ Resid
DB £55-£70 HB £241-£252 D £13 CC MC Visa ♿

♦♦♦ Ardtully
297 Marine Parade, Hunters Quay, PA23 8HN
☎ 01369-702478 Fax 01369-702478
E-mail ardtully@fsbdial.co.uk
3 bedrs, all ensuite, TCF TV ✝ P 6 No children under 12 ⌑ Resid SB £15-£20 DB £30-£40 D £10

EDINBURGH 13D2

♦♦♦♦ Ashlyn
Sparkling Diamond
42 Inverleith Row, Edinburgh EH3 5PY
☎ 0131-552 2954 Fax 0131-552 2954
8 bedrs, 5 ensuite, 3 ➡ TCF TV ⌧ No children under 12 SB £25-£30 DB £50-£70

172 Edinburgh

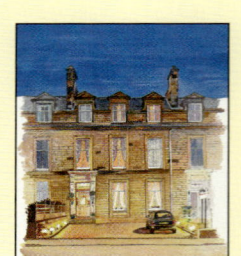

Ben Doran Guest House

RAC ♦♦♦♦

11 Mayfield Gardens, Edinburgh EH9 2AX
Telephone: 0131 667-8488
Fax: 0131 667-0076
Email: bendoran.guesthouse@virgin.net
www.asper.co.uk/bendoran.html

Ben Doran is centrally located, yet with private off-street parking. Edinburgh castle and city centre are less than one mile. Ben Doran offers an excellent accommodation where comfort and elegance are combined. The property is a listed Georgian townhouse, close to all historical attractions. If you have no car, transportation is not a problem, as we are on bus routes.

Most rooms ensuite; all rooms have colour television, clock/radios, central heat, complimentary coffee/tea and full Scottish breakfast cooked to your liking. Ben Doran is popular, family run, and proud of its cleanliness and service.

♦♦♦♦ Ben Doran
Sparkling Diamond
11 Mayfield Gardens, Edinburgh EH9 2AX
☎ 0131-667 8488 Fax 0131-667 0076
E-mail bendoran.guesthouse@virgin.net
10 bedrs, 6 ensuite, 3 ⇌ TCF TV ☒ P 11 ⋕ SB £30-£50
DB £40-£80 CC MC Visa
See advert on this page

♦♦♦♦ Corstorphine Guest House
Warm Welcome
188 St John's Road, Edinburgh EH12 8SG
☎ 0131-539 4237 Fax 0131-539 4945
E-mail corsthouse@aol.com

A warm and welcoming Victorian house, tastefully decorated and furnished to the highest standard and providing excellent facilities. Conveniently located midway between airport and city centre with private parking and large gardens.
4 bedrs, all ensuite, TCF TV ☒ P 7 SB £20-£50 DB £36-£80 CC MC Visa ♿

♦♦♦♦ Dorstan
Warm Welcome, Sparkling Diamond
7 Priestfield Road, Edinburgh EH16 5HJ
☎ 0131-667 5138 Fax 0131-668 4644
E-mail reservations@dorstan-hotel.demon.co.uk

Located close to the city centre's many attractions, this tastefully decorated Victorian house exudes the warm hospitality of its proprietor Mairae Campbell.
14 bedrs, 9 ensuite, 3 ℝ 2 ⇌ TCF TV P 6 SB £36-£41
DB £72-£82 D £16 CC MC Visa Amex

Edinburgh 173

♦♦♦♦ Duthus Lodge
5 West Coates, Edinburgh EH12 5JG
☎ 0131-337 6876 Fax 0131-313 2264
8 bedrs, all ensuite, TCF TV DB £50-£70 CC MC Visa

♦♦♦♦ Eglinton
29 Eglinton Road, Edinburgh EH12 5BY
☎ 0131-337 2641
12 bedrs, all ensuite, TCF TV DB £50-£120 CC MC Visa Amex

♦♦♦♦ Grosvenor Gardens
1 Grosvenor Gardens, Edinburgh EH12 5JU
☎ 0131-313 3415 Fax 0131-340 8732
E-mail hotel@grosvenor-gardens.com
8 bedrs, all ensuite, TCF TV ✠ No children under 5
SB £35-£55 DB £55-£120 CC MC Visa Amex

♦♦♦♦ Ivy House
Sparkling Diamond
7 Mayfield Gardens, Edinburgh EH9 2AX
☎ 0131-667 3411 Fax 0131-620 1422
E-mail ivy.guesthouse@cableinet.co.uk
8 bedrs, 6 ensuite, 2 ➥ TCF TV ✠ P 9 SB £20-£50
DB £32-£70

♦♦♦♦ Kew
Sparkling Diamond
1 Kew Terrace, Murrayfield, Edinburgh EH12 5JE
☎ 0131-313 0700 Fax 0131-313 0747
E-mail kewhouse@worldsites.net

Victorian terraced house on main A8. Luxuriously refurbished. Within easy walking distance of city centre, conference centre and Murrayfield. Secure car park. Apartments also available.
6 bedrs, all ensuite, TCF TV ✉ ✠ P 6 ⊞ Rest Resid
SB £44-£55 DB £62-£90 D £14 CC MC Visa Amex DC JCB ♿

♦♦♦♦ Roselea House
Sparkling Diamond
11 Mayfield Road, Edinburgh EH9 2NG
☎ 0131-667 6115 Fax 0131-667 3556
E-mail roseleall@aol.com

Tasteful decor and elegant fabrics enhance the period style, while the luxurious bathrooms would grace a top hotel. Each of the bedrooms without ensuites has its own bathroom, and bathrobes are thoughtfully provided. There is a lounge and dining room.
5 bedrs, 4 ensuite, 1 ➥ TCF TV ✉ P 3 No children
SB £30-£45 DB £50-£80 CC MC Visa

♦♦♦ Abbotts Head
40 Minto Street, Edinburgh EH9 2BR
☎ 0131-668 1658 Fax 0131-668 1658
8 bedrs

♦♦♦ Averon
44 Gilmore Place, Edinburgh EH3 9NQ
☎ 0131-229 9932

A comfortable, fully restored townhouse, built in 1770, in central Edinburgh, with the advantage of a private car park and just ten minutes walk to Princes Street and castle. B&B from £14.
10 bedrs, 3 ➥ TCF TV P 10 ⊞ SB £14-£25 DB £28-£46
CC MC Visa Amex DC JCB ♿

SCOTLAND

Facilities for the disabled

Hotels do their best to cater for disabled visitors. However, it is advisable to contact the hotel direct to ensure it can provide a particular requirement.

Edinburgh

♦♦♦ Boisdale
9 Coates Gardens, Edinburgh EH12 5LG
📞 0131-337 1134 Fax 0131-313 0048

The Boisdale Hotel is situated 5 minutes from Edinburgh city centre and 2 minutes from Haymarket Station. All rooms ensuite with tea/coffee making failities and TV. Full Scottish breakfast a speciality.
10 bedrs, all ensuite, TCF TV 🐾 ⚐ Resid SB £25-£45 DB £50-£90 D £10 CC MC Visa

♦♦♦ Cumberland
1 West Coates, Edinburgh EH12 5JQ
📞 0131-337 1198 Fax 0131-337 1022
E-mail cumblhotel@aol.com

Within 5 minutes walk from the city centre, a warm welcome awaits you at this elegant family run hotel. Excellent facilities in spacious ensuite bedrooms. An attractive cocktail bar, residents lounge and sunny garden offer comfort in a relaxed atmosphere.
10 bedrs, all ensuite, TCF TV P 17 ⚐ SB £35-£80 DB £50-£100 CC MC Visa ♿

♦♦♦ Galloway
22 Dean Park Crescent, Edinburgh EH4 7PH
📞 0131-332 3672 Fax 0131-332 3672
10 bedrs, 6 ensuite, 4 🍴 TCF TV 🐾 SB £30-£45 DB £36-£54

♦♦♦ Hotel Ceilidh-Donia
14-16 Marchhall Crescent, Edinburgh EH16 5HL
📞 0131-667 2743 Fax 0131-668 2181
E-mail reservations@hotelceilidh-donia.freeserve.co.uk

Family run terraced Victorian townhouse hotel in a quiet residential area south of centre. Close to university, Holyrood Park Palace and Parliament buildings. Excellent bus service.
15 bedrs, 13 ensuite, 1 🍴 TCF TV ♨ 30 ⚐ SB £22-£35 DB £44-£70 HB £182-£280 D £5.50 CC MC Visa JCB

♦♦♦ Newington
18 Newington Road, Edinburgh EH9 1QS
📞 0131-667 3356 Fax 0131-667 8307
E-mail newington.guesthouse@dial.pipex.com
9 bedrs, 5 ensuite, 3 🛏 1 🍴 TCF TV 🖂 🐾 P 3 ⚐
Restricted SB £30-£40 DB £50-£70 CC MC Visa JCB

♦♦♦ Quaich
87 St Johns Road, Edinburgh EH12 6NN
📞 0131-334 4440 Fax 0131-476 9002
6 bedrs, 4 ensuite, 1 🍴 TCF TV 🖂 P 6 SB £20-£26 DB £40-£52

♦♦♦ Rutland
3 Rutland Street, Edinburgh EH1 2AE
📞 0131-229 3402 Fax 0131-228 5322
15 bedrs, 10 ensuite, 4 🍴 TCF TV 📺 No children under 16 ⚐ Room £39.50-£59.50 CC MC Visa Amex DC

♦♦♦ Stra'ven
3 Brunstane Road North, Edinburgh EH15 2DL
📞 0131-669 5580 Fax 0131-657 2517
E-mail m&m@straven.force9.co.uk
8 bedrs, all ensuite, TCF TV 🖂 SB £22-£35 DB £40-£70 CC MC Visa

♦♦ Kariba
10 Granville Terrace, Edinburgh EH10 4PQ
📞 0131-229 3773
9 bedrs, all ensuite, TCF TV P 6 ♨ 0 No children under 4 SB £22-£28 DB £40-£56 ♿

Gatehouse of Fleet   175

Adam Awaiting Inspection
19 Lansdowne Crescent, Edinburgh EH12 5EH
☎ 0131-337 1148 Fax 0131-337 1729
E-mail welcome@adam-hotel.co.uk
13 bedrs, all ensuite, TCF TV ☒ ⊕ Resid SB £25-£60
DB £50-£120 HB £210-£315 D £10 CC MC Visa Amex

Brunswick
7 Brunswick Street, Edinburgh EH7 5JB
☎ 0131-556 1238 Fax 0131-557 1404
Closed Christmas

Georgian town house refurbished to a high standard, centrally located, close to bus and rail stations. Two fourposter bedrooms for honeymooners or romantics. Personal welcome and attention from resident owners.
11 bedrs, all ensuite, TCF TV ☒ No children under 2
CC MC Visa Amex

FALKLAND Fife   13D1

♦♦♦ Covenanter 🍴
The Square, Falkland KY15 7BU
☎ 01337-857224 Fax 01337-857163

Relax in the warm, friendly atmosphere of this family run hotel in this historic village, only 20 minutes from St Andrews. Excellent restaurant and bistro.
7 bedrs, all ensuite, TCF TV P 6 ⋕ 16 ⊕ SB £39 DB £48
HB £280 D £15 CC MC Visa Amex DC

FORT WILLIAM Inverness-shire   14C4

♦♦♦♦ Distillery House
Sparkling Diamond
Nevis Bridge, North Road, Fort William PH33 6LH
☎ 01397-700103 Fax 01397-702980
E-mail disthouse@aol.com

This friendly guest house is an ideal base for enjoying a comfortable stay at the end of Glen Nevis, but only five minutes from the town centre.
7 bedrs, all ensuite, TCF TV ☒ ⊁ P 12 SB £20-£35
DB £40-£70 CC MC Visa Amex JCB

GATEHOUSE OF FLEET Kirkcudbrightshire   12C4

♦♦ Bank O'Fleet
47 High Street, Gatehouse of Fleet DG7 2HR
☎ 01557-814302 Fax 01557-814302
E-mail bankhotel@gatehouseoffleet.ndirect.co.uk

An attractive hotel, resting in the heart of picturesque and historic Galloway town, Gatehouse of Fleet. The hotel has earned reputation for good food. Ideal for golf, hillwalking and fishing.
6 bedrs, 5 ensuite, 1 ⇌ TCF TV ⊁ ⋕ 80 ⊕ SB £25
DB £47 D £10 CC MC Visa Amex ♿

SCOTLAND

Glasgow

GLASGOW   12C2

♦♦♦♦ Theatre
Sparkling Diamond
25-27 Elmbank Street, Glasgow G2 4PB
☎ 0141-227 2772 Fax 0141-227 2774
E-mail theatrehotel@clara.net

Set in the heart of Scotland, the Theatre Hotel is a stylish B-listed building, providing elegant accommodation combined with the warmth of traditional Scottish hospitality.
59 bedrs, 53 ensuite, 3 ⇌ TCF TV ⚲ SB £35-£45
DB £45-£55 CC MC Visa ♿

♦♦♦ Angus
970 Sauchiehall Street, Glasgow G3 7TH
☎ 0141-357 5155 Fax 0141-339 9469
E-mail argyll_angus.hotel@virgin.net

Ideally located ½ mile west of city centre. Excellent value B&B close to all amenities. Recently refurbished, family run with a warm Scottish welcome. Free parking
18 bedrs, all ensuite, TCF TV SB £34-£42 DB £48-£52
CC MC Visa Amex DC

♦♦ McLays
264-276 Renfrew Street, Charing Cross, Glasgow G3 6TT
☎ 0141-332 4796 Fax 0141-353 0422
E-mail mclaysguesthouse@compuserve.com

Pleasant hotel in the city centre, with Sauchiehall street only a minute away. 62 modern rooms, 39 with ensuite facilities. Colour TV (satellite), tea/coffee, telephone in each room.
62 bedrs, 39 ensuite, 11 ⇌ TCF TV ▣ SB £23-£27
DB £40-£48 CC MC Visa Amex

♦♦ Smith's
963 Sauchiehall Street, Glasgow G3 7TQ
☎ 0141-339 6363 Fax 0141-334 1892

Terraced house on three floors.
33 bedrs, 9 ensuite, 8 ⇌ TCF TV SB £25 DB £36

Rennie Mackintosh Awaiting Inspection
218-220 Renfrew Street, Glasgow G3 6TX
☎ 0141-333 9992 Fax 0141-333 9995
24 bedrs, all ensuite, TCF TV SB £30 DB £48 HB £50
CC MC Visa Amex JCB

GRANTOWN-ON-SPEY Morayshire   15E3

♦♦♦♦ Garden Park
Warm Welcome, Sparkling Diamond
Woodside Avenue, Grantown-on-Spey PH26 3JN
☎ 01479-873235

Innellan 177

Closed Nov-Feb
5 bedrs, all ensuite, TCF TV P 8 No children under 12
Resid SB £21.50-£24 DB £43-£48 HB £207-£233
D £12.50

GRETNA Dumfriesshire 10B1

♦♦♦ Surrone House
Annan Road, Gretna DG16 5DL
01461-338341 Fax 01461-338341
E-mail surrone@aol.com

This beautifully maintained and quiet establishment offers modern and spacious accommodation with ensuite facilities in the centre of Gretna, but off the main road.
7 bedrs, 6 ensuite, TCF TV P 10 Restricted SB £32-£40 DB £46 D £9.50 CC MC Visa Amex

HADDINGTON East Lothian 13E2

♦♦♦♦ Brown's
Warm Welcome, Sparkling Diamond
1 West Road, Haddington EH41 3RD
01620-822254 Fax 01620-822254
5 bedrs, all ensuite, TCF TV P 10 ▦ 30 CC MC Visa Amex DC

HAMILTON Lanarkshire 12C2

Roadchef Lodge Lodge
M74 Northbound, Hamilton ML3 6JW
01698-891904 Fax 01698-891682
Closed 25-27 Dec
36 bedrs, all ensuite, TCF TV P 120 ▦ 25 Room £47.95
CC MC Visa Amex DC &

HELENSBURGH Dunbartonshire 12C2

♦♦♦♦♦ Kirkton House
Warm Welcome, Sparkling Diamond
Darleith Road, Cardross G82 5EZ
01389-841951 Fax 01389-841868
E-mail kirktonhouse@compuserve.com
Closed Dec-Jan

Set in a tranquil country setting with panoramic views of the Clyde and easy access to Glasgow Airport (14 miles), Kirkton House offers a relaxed atmosphere with home cooked dinners lit by oil lamp.
6 bedrs, all ensuite, TCF TV ✈ P 12 Restricted
SB £42.50 DB £65 HB £291-£304 D £19 CC MC Visa Amex DC JCB

INNELLAN Argyll 12B2

♦♦♦ Osborne
Shore Road, Innellan, Dunoon PA23 7TJ
01369-830445 Fax 01369-830445

Relax and enjoy our excellent food and hospitality in this long established family operated hotel with superb views of the Clyde Estuary. Great golfing nearby, special rates arranged. Pony trekking, tennis, outdoor bowls and forestry walks nearby.
4 bedrs, all ensuite, TCF TV ✈ SB £25 DB £42 D £15
CC MC Visa

SCOTLAND

Invergarry

INVERGARRY Inverness-shire	14C4

♦♦♦ Craigard House
Warm Welcome
Invergarry PH35 4HG
☎ 01809-501258
Closed Christmas & New Year
7 bedrs, 3 ensuite, 3 ⇌ TCF TV ✉ P 10 No children under 12 ⏚ Resid SB £18-£20 DB £36-£40 D £15

INVERNESS Inverness-shire	15D3

♦♦♦♦ Culduthel Lodge
Sparkling Diamond
14 Culduthel Road, Inverness IV2 4AG
☎ 01463-240089 Fax 01463-240089
E-mail culduth@globalnet.co.uk

Georgian residence set in attractive gardens in a quiet location near the town centre. Ample parking. All rooms individually furnished to a high standard.
12 bedrs, all ensuite, TCF TV ✈ P 12 No children under 10 ⏚ Resid SB £45 DB £85-£99 HB £410-£450 D £19 CC MC Visa

♦♦♦ St Ann's House
37 Harrowden Road, Inverness IV3 5QN
☎ 01463-236157 Fax 01463-236157
E-mail stannshous@aol.com
Closed Nov-Feb

Quiet family run hotel a few minutes walk from the town centre. All rooms ensuite with private facilities. Restricted licence. Brochure available.
6 bedrs, all ensuite, TCF TV P 4 ⏚ Resid SB £20-£28 DB £44-£48

♦♦♦ Sunnyholm
12 Mayfield Road, Inverness IV2 4AE
☎ 01463-231336

Large sandstone bungalow set in a mature, secluded garden, five minutes walk from the town centre.
4 bedrs, all ensuite, TCF TV ✉ P 6 No children under 3 SB £25-£28 DB £35-£40

INVERURIE Aberdeenshire	15F3

♦♦ Grant Arms
Monymusk, Inverurie AB51 7HJ
☎ 01467-651226 Fax 01467-651494
17 bedrs, 8 ensuite, TCF ✈ ⌘ 40 ⏚ CC MC Visa Amex ◨ ♿

JEDBURGH Roxburghshire	13E3

♦♦♦ Ferniehirst Mill Lodge
Jedburgh TD8 6PQ
☎ 01835-863279 Fax 01835-863279

Situated two and a half miles south of Jedburgh on the A68, this modern purpose-built guest house is

St Andrews

set in 25 acres overlooking the River Jed.
9 bedrs, all ensuite, TCF ✱ P 10 ⌂ Restricted SB £23 DB £46 HB £238 D £14 CC MC Visa ▧ ▨

| KYLESKU Sutherland | 14C1 |

♦♦♦♦ Newton Lodge
Kylesku IV27 4HW
☎ 01971-502070 Fax 01971-502070
E-mail newtonlge@aol.com
Closed mid Oct-mid Mar
7 bedrs, all ensuite, TCF TV ▧ ✱ P 10 No children ⌂ Resid DB £56-£60 D £15 CC MC Visa

| LADYBANK Fife | 13E1 |

♦♦♦♦ Redlands Country Lodge
Warm Welcome, Sparkling Diamond
By Ladybank, Cupar KY15 7SH
☎ 01337-831091 Fax 01337-831091
Closed Dec-Feb
4 bedrs, all ensuite, TCF TV ▧ ✱ P 6 SB £25-£35 DB £23-£25 HB £210-£220 D £12 CC MC Visa

| OBAN Argyll | 12B1 |

♦♦♦ Corriemar
6 Corran, Esplanade, Oban PA34 5AQ
☎ 01631-562476 Fax 01631-564339
13 bedrs, all ensuite, TCF TV ▧ P 10 SB £20-£35 DB £36-£70 CC MC Visa

♦♦♦ Sgeir-mhaol
Soroba Road, Oban PA34 4JF
☎ 01631-562650 Fax 01631-562650
7 bedrs, 5 ensuite, 1 ⇌ TCF TV P 11 SB £18-£26 DB £36-£42 ♿

Glenbervie Awaiting Inspection
Dalriach Road, Oban PA34 5JD
☎ 01631-564770
8 bedrs, 5 ensuite, 2 ⌂ TCF TV P 6 No children under 5 ♿

| PERTH Perthshire | 13D1 |

♦♦♦ Clunie
Sparkling Diamond
12 Pitcullen Crescent, Perth PH2 7HT
☎ 01738-623625 Fax 01738-623625
7 bedrs, all ensuite, TCF TV ✱ P 8 SB £18-£25 DB £18-£25 HB £195-£230 D £10 CC MC Visa Amex DC

Achnacarry Awaiting Inspection
3 Pitcullen Crescent, Perth PH2 7HT
☎ 01738-621421 Fax 01738-444110
E-mail achnacarry@yahoo.co.uk

A Victorian house, tastefully decorated, offering a warm friendly atmosphere. All rooms are ensuite and the breakfast menu has a Scottish flavour. Ten minutes walk from the city centre.
4 bedrs, all ensuite, TCF TV ✱ P 7 No children under 5 SB £25-£40 DB £40-£44 CC MC Visa Amex

| PITLOCHRY Perthshire | 13D1 |

♦♦ Dalnasgadh House
Killiecrankie, Pitlochry PH16 5LN
☎ 01796-473237
Closed Oct-Easter
3 bedrs, 2 ⇌ TCF ▧ P 10 No children under 12 SB £20 DB £38-£40

| ST ANDREWS Fife | 13E1 |

Cleveden House Awaiting Inspection
3 Murray Place, St Andrews KY16 9AP
☎ 01334-474212 Fax 01334-474212
6 bedrs, 4 ensuite, 1 ⇌ TV

West Park House Awaiting Inspection
5 St Mary's Place, St Andrews KY16 9UY
☎ 01334-475933
Closed Dec-Jan
4 bedrs, 3 ensuite, 2 ⇌ TCF TV ▧ SB £20-£35 DB £40-£50 CC MC Visa

SCOTLAND

180 Shetland Islands

SHETLAND ISLANDS　　　　　　　　13F1

♦♦♦♦ Glen Orchy House
Sparkling Diamond
20 Knab Road, Lerwick ZE1 0AX
☎ 01595-692031 Fax 01595-692031

Family run guest house. Bedrooms with ensuite facilities, underfloor heating, air-conditioning, 21 inch digital and teletext TV. The non-smoking wing consists of 7 bedrooms, lounge and dining room. 22 bedrs, all ensuite, TCF TV ★ P 10 ⊕ Resid
SB £37.50 DB £64 HB £322-£360.50 D £14 &

STRATHPEFFER Ross-shire　　　　　15D3

♦♦♦♦ White Lodge
Warm Welcome, Sparkling Diamond
Strathpeffer IV14 9AL
☎ 01997-421730 Fax 01997-421730
E-mail whitelodge@vacations-scotland.co.uk
Closed Apr, Nov
3 bedrs, all ensuite, TCF TV ✉ P 3 No children under 10 SB £25-£30 DB £40-£50

THURSO Caithness　　　　　　　　15E1

St Clair Awaiting Inspection
Sinclair Street, Thurso KW14 7AJ
☎ 01847-896481 Fax 01847-896481
36 bedrs, 29 ensuite, 4 ➥ TCF TV ★ ⫙ 90 ⊕ CC MC Visa Amex JCB &

---

for leisure...

www.WestOneWeb.com

...great
expectations

CULZEAN CASTLE & COUNTRY PARK

Spectacular Robert Adam Castle set in coastal woodland, garden and parkland. A great day out for families. **The Eisenhower Apartment** *in the top of the castle offers charming country house accommodation in six double bedrooms and the best of Scottish food.*

**Maybole, Ayrshire, KA19 8LE
Tel: 01655 884455   Fax: 884503
web site: www.nts.org.uk**

Wales

Abercraf

ABERCRAF Powys 6C4

Maes-y-Gwernen Awaiting Inspection
School Road, Abercraf SA9 1XD
☎ 01639-730218 Fax 01639-730765

Country house hotel in private grounds. All rooms ensuite plus satellite TV. Noted restaurant serving local produce. Spa, sauna, solarium off fitness room. B & B from £26.
10 bedrs, all ensuite, TCF TV ✈ P 12 ⋮⋮⋮ 30 ⚑ Rest
Resid SB £33–£39 DB £52–£66 HB £250–£330 D £12.50
cc MC Visa

ABERYSTWYTH Ceredigion 6C3

♦♦♦♦ Glyn Garth
South Road, Aberystwyth SY23 1JS
☎ 01970-615050 Fax 01970-636835
10 bedrs, 6 ensuite, 1 ✈ TCF TV ⌧ P 2 No children under 7 SB £19–£20 DB £42–£48

♦♦♦ Southgate
Anatron Avenue, Penparcau,
Aberystwyth SY23 1SF
☎ 01970-611550

Family run licensed hotel, one mile from the town centre, with ensuite double, twin and family rooms offering TV and tea and coffee facilities. Cot and high chair available. Dinner optional. Pool table. Parking in own grounds.
10 bedrs, 9 ensuite, 3 ✈ TCF TV ✈ P 30 ⚑ Resid
cc MC Visa

Queensbridge Awaiting Inspection
Promenade, Aberystwyth SY23 2DH
☎ 01970-612343 Fax 01970-617452
E-mail queensbrij@aol.com
Closed Jan

Situated on the promenade, the Queensbridge boasts a passenger lift and offers superior comfort in 15 spacious ensuite bedrooms, with TV, hospitality tray and telephone.
15 bedrs, all ensuite, TCF TV ▤ SB £32–£36 DB £52–£55
cc MC Visa Amex DC

---

for hotels...

www.WestOneWeb.com

...great locations

Brecon 183

BANGOR Gwynedd 6C1

♦♦♦ Goetre Isaf Farmhouse
Caernarfon Road, Bangor LL57 4DB
☎ 01248-364541 Fax 01248-364541
E-mail fred@whowell.enterprise-plc.com

Superb country situation, Bangor 3km. Ideal touring centre for Snowdonia. Imaginative farmhouse cooking, vegetarians welcome. Bedrooms with dial-phone facilities, Stabling by arrangement. O/S ref: SH562699.
3 bedrs, 1 ensuite, 2 ⇌ ↑ P 10 SB £16.50-£39 DB £29-£39 D £9.50

BETWS-Y-COED Conwy 6C1

♦♦♦♦ Penmachno Hall
Little Gem
Warm Welcome, Sparkling Diamond
Penmachno, Betws-y-Coed LL24 0PU
☎ 01690-760207 Fax 01690-760207
Closed Christmas & New Year
4 bedrs, all ensuite, No children under 5 ⊕ Rest Resid SB £30 DB £50 HB £255 D £15 CC MC Visa

Llanmerch Goch Awaiting Inspection
Capel Garmon, Betws-y-Coed LL26 0RL
☎ 01690-710261
Closed Dec-Feb
3 bedrs, all ensuite, TCF TV P 4 No children under 8
SB £25 DB £38-£50

BONTDDU Gwynedd 6C2

♦♦♦♦ Borthwnog Hall
Sparkling Diamond
Bontddu, Dolgellau LL40 2TT
☎ 01341-430271 Fax 01341-430682
Closed Christmas
3 bedrs, all ensuite, TCF TV ↑ P 8 ⊕ Rest Resid
CC MC Visa Amex

BORTH Ceredigion 6C3

♦♦ Glanmor
High Street, Borth SY24 5JP
☎ 01970-871689
7 bedrs, 2 ensuite, 2 ⇌ TCF TV ↑ P 6 ⊕ Resid SB £21 DB £42 HB £220.50 D £10.50

BRECON Powys 7D4

♦♦♦♦ Usk Inn
Station Road, Talybont-on-Usk, Brecon
☎ 01874-676251 Fax 01874-676392
E-mail uskinn@aol.com
10 bedrs, all ensuite, TCF TV P 30 ⋮⋮ 12 ⊕ SB £30-£45 DB £40-£65 D £11.95 CC MC Visa

for travel books...

www.WestOneWeb.com

...great value

Brecon

♦♦♦ Beacons
Sparkling Diamond
16 Bridge Street, Brecon LD3 8AH
☎ 01874-623339 Fax 01874-623339
E-mail beacons@brecon.co.uk

Georgian town house, Grade II Listed, close to the River Usk and town centre. Cosy bar.
12 bedrs, 9 ensuite, 2 ⇌ TCF TV ⚞ P 16 ⊞ Rest Resid SB £20-£25 DB £36-£59 D £10 CC MC Visa

♦♦♦ Maeswalter
Heol Senni, Brecon LD3 8SU
☎ 01874-636629
3 bedrs, 1 ensuite, 2 ⇌ TCF TV ⚞ No children SB £20-£25 DB £36-£39 HB £252

BURRY PORT Carmarthenshire   2C1

♦♦♦♦ George
Stepney Road, Burry Port SA16 0BH
☎ 01554-832211
Closed Christmas
9 bedrs, 5 ensuite, 4 ⇌ TCF TV No children under 8 ⊞
SB £18.50-£35 DB £35-£45 D £8

CAERNARFON Gwynedd   6B1

♦♦♦ Menai View
North Road, Caernarfon LL55 1BD
☎ 01286-674602 Fax 01492-876661
9 bedrs, 8 ensuite, 1 ⇌ TCF TV ⚞ ⁂ ⊞ Rest Resid
SB £16-£26 DB £30-£45 D £9.95 ♿

CARDIFF   3D1

♦♦♦♦ Marlborough
Sparkling Diamond
98 Newport Road, Cardiff CF24 1DG
☎ 01222-492385 Fax 01222-492385

A smart family run Victorian guest house, well sited just 5 minutes walk from the city centre, theatre, castle, St Davids Hall, Cardiff International Arena, cinema and shops.
9 bedrs, 6 ensuite, 1 ⇌ TCF TV P 8 ⊞ Resid

♦♦♦ Albany
191/193 Albany Road, Roath, Cardiff CF2 3NU
☎ 01222-494121
Closed Christmas
11 bedrs, 7 ensuite, 2 ⚞ 1 ⇌ TCF TV SB £25 DB £35

♦♦♦ Clare Court
46-48 Clare Road, Cardiff CF1 7QP
☎ 01222-344839 Fax 01222-251511

Small family run hotel, 10-15 minute walk to bus/railway station, town centre, castle, CIA Millennium Stadium. Bus stops outside Cardiff Bay and motorway access road 5 minutes away.
8 bedrs, all ensuite, TCF TV ⊞ Resid SB £25-£28
DB £36-£44 CC MC Visa

Campanile Cardiff Lodge Awaiting Inspection
Caxton Place, Pentwynn, Cardiff CF2 7HA
☎ 01222-549044 Fax 01222-549900
50 bedrs, all ensuite, TCF TV ⚞ P 50 ⁂ 20 ⊞ Rest
Resid SB £34.90-£41.95 DB £39.85-£46.90 HB £343
D £10.85 CC MC Visa Amex DC ♿

Criccieth 185

CARDIGAN Ceredigion 6B4

♦♦♦ Brynhyfryd
Gwbert Road, Cardigan SA43 1AE
☎ 01239-612861 Fax 01239-612861
7 bedrs, 3 ensuite, 2 ⇌ TCF TV No children under 4
SB £17 DB £34-£38 D £9

CARMARTHEN Carmarthenshire 6B4

♦♦♦♦ Four Seasons
Sparkling Diamond
Cwmtwrch Farm, Nantgaredig, Carmarthen
☎ 01267-290238 Fax 01267-290808
5 bedrs, all ensuite, TCF TV ⇌ P 40 ⌘ 12 ⌘ Rest
SB £40 DB £54 D £20 CC MC Visa JCB ⌘ ⌘ &

Capel Dewi Uchaf Country House Awaiting Inspection
Capel Dewi, Carmarthen SA32 8AY
☎ 01267-290799 Fax 01267-290003
E-mail uchaffarm.aol.com
Closed Christmas

A beautiful country house tucked away along the Towy River. Peace and comfort prevail. Lovely food, guests own drawing room. Private fishing. Lots to do and see.

5 bedrs, 4 ensuite, 1 ⌘ TCF TV ⌘ P 10 ⌘ 8 ⌘ Resid
SB £37 DB £50 HB £157.50 D £25 CC MC Visa JCB ⌘

COLWYN BAY Conwy 6C1

♦♦♦♦ Whitehall
Sparkling Diamond
Cayley Promenade, Rhos-on-Sea, Colwyn Bay LL28 4EP
☎ 01492-547296
Closed Nov-Mar
14 bedrs, 7 ensuite, 3 ⇌ ⌘ P 5 ⌘ CC MC Visa

♦♦♦ Northwood
47 Rhos Road, Rhos-on-Sea, Colwyn Bay LL28 4RS
☎ 01492-549931
Closed Nov-Feb
12 bedrs, 11 ensuite, 1 ⇌ TCF TV ⌘ P 12 ⌘ Rest Resid CC MC Visa &

♦♦ Cabin Hill
College Avenue, Rhos-on-Sea, Colwyn Bay LL28 4NT
☎ 01492-544568
10 bedrs, 7 ensuite, 2 ⇌ TCF TV ⌘ ⌘ Resid

CRICCIETH Gwynedd 6B2

♦♦♦♦ Glyn-y-Coed
Portmadoc Road, Criccieth LL52 OHL
☎ 01766-522870 Fax 01766-523341
Closed Christmas-New Year
11 bedrs, all ensuite, TCF TV ⌘ P 14 ⌘ 40 ⌘ Rest Resid SB £20-£25 DB £40-£50 HB £190-£230 D £10
CC MC Visa Amex &

♦♦♦♦ Min y Gaer
Porthmadog Road, Criccieth LL52 0HP
☎ 01766-522151 Fax 01766-523540
E-mail minygaer.hotel@virgin.net
Closed Nov-Feb

A substantial Victorian building in a convenient position overlooking Criccieth Castle and the Cardigan Bay coastline, 200 yards from the beach. An ideal base for touring Snowdonia and the Lleyn Peninsula.

10 bedrs, all ensuite, TCF TV ⌘ P 12 ⌘ Resid
SB £20.50-£23.50 DB £41-£47 HB £213.50-£220.50 D £10.50 CC MC Visa Amex

WALES

Crickhowell

| CRICKHOWELL Powys | 7D4 |

♦♦♦ Stables
Llangattock, Crickhowell NP8 1LE
☎ 01873-810244
14 bedrs, all ensuite, TCF TV ✱ P 50 ⋕ 30 ⌂ SB £35
DB £55 HB £350 D £15 CC MC Visa

| DOLGELLAU Gwynedd | 6C2 |

♦♦♦ Clifton House
Smithfield Square, Dolgellau LL40 1ES
☎ 01341-422554 Fax 01341-423580
Closed Jan
6 bedrs, 4 ensuite, 1 ⇌ TCF TV ✱ P 2 ⌂ Rest Resid
SB £33-£35 DB £41-£45 D £14.50 CC MC Visa ⚭

Fronolau Farm Awaiting Inspection
Tabor, Dolgellau LL40 2PS
☎ 01341-422361 Fax 01341-422023
11 bedrs, all ensuite, TCF TV ✱ P 30 ⋕ 150 ⌂ SB £36
DB £54 D £10 CC MC Visa ⚭

The Valley Hotel

Situated on A5 only 4 miles from ferries to Ireland. Ideal Base for touring North Wales Excellent Island, Golf, Bird watching, Water sports. 19 en-suite bedrooms with TV, coffee/tea makers, telephone etc.
Bars open and food served all day.

London Road, Valley, Holyhead LL65 3DU
Tel 01407 740203 Fax: 01407 740686

| FISHGUARD Pembrokeshire | 6A4 |

♦♦♦ St James
76b Walter Road, Swansea SA1 4QA
☎ 01792-649984
Closed first two weeks Jan
4 bedrs, all ensuite, TCF TV ✱ P 6 ⌂ SB £30-£38
DB £45-£52 D £16.50 CC MC Visa Amex ⚭

| HARLECH Gwynedd | 6C2 |

♦♦♦♦ Castle Cottage
Pen Llech, Harlech LL46 2YL
☎ 01766-780479 Fax 01766-780479
Closed Feb
6 bedrs, 4 ensuite, 1 ⇌ TCF ✱ ⌂ Rest Resid SB £27
DB £58 D £22.50 CC MC Visa

Byrdir
High Street, Harlech LL46 2YA
☎ 01766-780316 Fax 01766-780316

Byrdir, renowned for its homely atmosphere, is situated in the centre of Harlech within easy reach of Harlech Castle, the four mile long sandy beach, indoor swimming pool, tennis courts and the famous Royal St David's Golf Course.
15 bedrs, 7 ensuite, 3 ⇌ TCF TV ✱ P 12 ⌂ Resid

| HAY-ON-WYE Powys | 7D4 |

York House Awaiting Inspection
Hardwicke Road, Cusop, Hay-on-Wye HR3 5QX
☎ 01497-820705
4 bedrs, all ensuite, TCF TV ☐ ✱ P 6 No children under 8 CC MC Visa Amex

| HOLYHEAD Anglesey | 6B1 |

♦♦♦ Valley
London Road, Valley, Holyhead LL65 3DU
☎ 01407-740203 Fax 01407-740686

Llandudno 187

On A5, three and a half miles from ferry and some of the best beaches in the UK. Recently refurbished, ensuite bedrooms, excellent bar meals served from noon, sheltered garden.
19 bedrs, 16 ensuite, 1 ⇌ TCF TV ✝ P 100 ⁝⁝⁝ 100 ⌑ SB £20-£33.75 DB £28-£44.75 D £11 CC MC Visa Amex ⊞
See advert on opposite page

LLANDOVERY Carmarthenshire 6C4

♦♦ Llwyncelyn ⓡ
Llandovery SA20 0EP
☎ 01550-720566
Closed Christmas
5 bedrs, 2 ⇌ TCF P 12 ⌑ Rest Resid SB £20-£24 DB £35 HB £185.50-£227.50 D £12.50 ▣

LLANDRINDOD WELLS Powys 7D3

♦♦♦♦ Three Wells Farm ⓡ
Warm Welcome
Chapel Road, Howey, LD1 5PB
☎ 01597-824427 Fax 01597-822484
15 bedrs, all ensuite, TCF TV ✝ P 20 ⁝⁝⁝ 30 No children under 8 ⌑ Rest Resid SB £25-£30 DB £40-£56 HB £190-£220 D £10 ▣

♦♦♦ Griffin Lodge
Temple Street, Llandrindod Wells LD1 5HF
☎ 01597-822432 Fax 01597-825196
8 bedrs, 5 ensuite, 2 ⇌ TCF TV P 8 ⁝⁝⁝ 12 ⌑ Rest Resid SB £21-£28 DB £42-£49.50 HB £205-£235 D £11.85 CC MC Visa Amex DC

♦♦ Kincoed
Temple Street, Llandrindod Wells LD1 5HF
☎ 01597-822656 Fax 01597-824660
10 bedrs, 5 ensuite, 2 ⇌ TCF TV ✝ P 12 ⌑ Rest Resid CC MC Visa

LLANDUDNO Conwy 6C1

♦♦♦ Cedar Lodge
7 Degawny Lodge, Llandudno LL30 2YB
☎ 01492-877730
Closed Dec-Jan
7 bedrs, 6 ensuite, 1 ⇌ TCF TV P 5 SB £20-£25 DB £37-£40 HB £159-£165 D £7.50 CC MC Visa

♦♦♦ Hollybank
9 St Davids Place, Llandudno LL30 2UG
☎ 01492-878521 Fax 0870 054 9854
E-mail mike@hollybank-gh.demon.co.uk
Closed Nov-Feb
6 bedrs, all ensuite, TCF TV P 4 ⌑ Resid SB £21.50 DB £43 HB £210 D £10

♦♦♦ Minion
21-23 Carmen Sylva Road, Craig-Y-Don, Llandudno LL30 1EQ
☎ 01492-877740
Closed 24 Oct-Easter

The family run Minion Hotel is ideally situated on a pleasant corner site, in a quiet residential area. Close to promenade, conference centre, theatre, public swimming pool, indoor 10pin-bowling, paddling pool.
12 bedrs, all ensuite, TCF ✝ P 8 No children under 2 ⌑ Resid SB £16-£17.50 DB £32-£35 HB £161-£185.50

♦♦♦ Orotava
105 Glan-y-Mor Road, Llandudno LL30 3PH
☎ 01492-549780
6 bedrs, all ensuite, TCF TV ▣ P 10 No children under 15 ⌑ Rest Resid SB £19.50 DB £39 HB £185 D £7 CC MC Visa

♦♦ Montclare
4 North Parade, Llandudno LL30 2LP
☎ 01492-877061
15 bedrs, 13 ensuite, 2 ⌂ TCF TV ⌑ Rest Resid SB £19 DB £38 HB £170 D £9

WALES

Llandudno

♦♦ Rosedene
Sparkling Diamond
10 Arvon Avenue, Llandudno LL30 2DY
☎ 01492-876491 Fax 01492-872150
Closed Jan-Mar

"Janet and Bill welcome you." We are situated on a pleasant tree-lined avenue. Central for Promenade and shopping. Home cooking and choice of menu. Please ring or write for brochure, to Janet and Bill (proprietors) Hodgett.
11 bedrs, all ensuite, TCF TV ✈ ⌂ Resid SB £17 DB £34 HB £182 D £9

♦♦ Seaclyffe
11 Church Walks, Llandudno LL30 2HG
☎ 01492-876803 Fax 01492-876803
Closed Jan-Feb
27 bedrs, all ensuite, TCF TV ⌂ Resid SB £17.50-£18.50 DB £35-£37 HB £180-£190

♦ Karden House
16 Charlton Street, Llandudno LL30 2AN
☎ 01492-879347
10 bedrs, 4 ensuite, 2 ↔ TCF TV ⌂ Resid SB £14-£15 DB £32-£34 HB £126-£137

♦ Westdale
37 Abbey Road, Llandudno LL30 2EH
☎ 01492-877996
Closed Dec-Jan
12 bedrs, 3 ensuite, 2 ↔ TCF ✈ P 5 ⌂ Resid SB £16.50-£17.50 DB £33-£35 HB £154-£161 D £6

Short Breaks

Many hotels provide special rates for weekend and mid-week breaks – sometimes these are quoted in the hotel's entry, otherwise ring direct for the latest offers.

Carmel Awaiting Inspection
17 Craig-y-Don Parade, Llandudno LL30 1BG
☎ 01492-877643

Situated in a prime position on the main promenade, with uninterrupted sea views and overlooking the famous Great and Little Ormes.
9 bedrs, 6 ensuite, 2 ↔ TCF TV ☒ P 6 No children under 4 SB £15.50-£18.50 DB £31-£37 HB £150.50-£168

Concord Awaiting Inspection
35 Abbey Road, Llandudno LL30 2EH
☎ 01492-875504 Fax 01492-875504
Closed Oct-Easter
11 bedrs, all ensuite, TCF P 11 No children under 5 ⌂ Resid

Cornerways Awaiting Inspection
2 St Davids Place, Llandudno LL30 2UG
☎ 01492-877334 Fax 01492-873324
E-mail cornerwayshotel@btinternet.com
Closed Nov-Feb
7 bedrs, all ensuite, TCF TV ☒ P 5 No children ⌂ Resid SB £24-£26 DB £48-£52 HB £238-£252 D £10

Rosaire Awaiting Inspection
2 St Seiriols Road, Llandudno LL30 2YY
☎ 01492-877677
Closed Nov-Feb
10 bedrs, 9 ensuite, 1 ↔ TCF TV ☒ ✈ P 7 ⌂ Resid

St Hilary Awaiting Inspection
16 Craig-y-don Parade, Promenade, Llandudno LL30 1BG
☎ 01492-875551 Fax 01492-877538
E-mail sjprobert@compuserve.com
Closed Dec-Jan

Mumbles 189

Situated on the seafront affording magnificent views of Llandudno Bay and Great Orme. Ideal for touring North Wales and Snowdonia. Excellent accommodation and value for money. Special breaks.
11 bedrs, 9 ensuite, 1 ➥ TCF TV SB £15.95-£40 DB £31.95-£45 CC MC Visa Amex JCB

LLANELLI Carmarthenshire 2C1

♦♦ Southmead
72 Queen Victoria Road, Llanelli SA15 2TH
☎ 01544-758588
7 bedrs, 4 ensuite, 1 ➥ TCF TV ✈ P 5 SB £17 DB £30

MENAI BRIDGE Anglesey 6B1

Gazelle Awaiting Inspection
Glyn Garth, Menai Bridge LL59 5PD
☎ 01248-713364 Fax 01248-713167
9 bedrs, 5 ensuite, 3 ➥ TCF TV P 50 ⅲ 20 ⅎ CC MC Visa DC

MERTHYR TYDFIL Merthyr Tydfil 7D4

Travellers Lodge
Dowlais Top, Merthyr Tydfil CF48 2YE
☎ 01685-723362 Fax 01685-377467
Closed 25 Dec

Travellers Lodge situated on the edge of the Brecon Beacons National Park. All rooms ensuite, very friendly atmosphere, great food. All welcome. Open all year. Singles from £29.95. Doubles from £39.95.
6 bedrs, all ensuite, TCF TV ✈ P 38 ⅎ Resid CC MC Visa Amex DC

MILFORD HAVEN Pembrokeshire 6A4

♦♦ Belhaven House
29 Hamilton Terrace, Milford Haven SA73 3JJ
☎ 01646-695983 Fax 01646-690787
E-mail hbruceh@aol.com

The Belhaven hotel, which includes the Tallships restaurant (Highly commended - 1998 Good Food Guide), has rooms overlooking the marina. An ideal centre for touring all Pembrokeshire.
11 bedrs, 3 ensuite, 5 ↑ 4 ➥ TCF TV ✈ P 8 ⅎ Rest Resid CC MC Visa Amex DC

MUMBLES Swansea 2C1

♦♦♦ Shoreline
648 Mumbles Road, Southend, Mumbles SA3 4EA
☎ 01792-366233
14 bedrs, 9 ensuite, 2 ↑ 2 ➥ TCF TV ✈ ⅎ Rest Resid
SB £20-£29.50 DB £36-£50 HB £190-£200 D £9.95
CC MC Visa

St Anne's Awaiting Inspection
Western Lane, Mumbles SA3 4EY
☎ 01792-369147 Fax 01792-360537
33 bedrs, all ensuite, TCF TV ✈ P 50 ⅲ 100 ⅎ
SB £37.50-£45 DB £50-£64.50 HB £235-£245 D £13.75
CC MC Visa Amex ♿

WALES

New Quay

NEW QUAY Ceredigion	6B3

♦♦♦ Brynarfor
New Road, New Quay SA45 9SB
☎ 01545-560358 Fax 01545-561204
Closed Nov-Feb

A well run comfortable hotel, situated in beautiful gardens with panoramic sea views over Cardigan Bay. Superb area for beaches, cliff walks, bird watching and dolphin spotting.
7 bedrs, all ensuite, TCF TV P 10 ⊞ 12 ⏣ Rest Resid
SB £30-£35 DB £50-£64 HB £220-£260 CC MC Visa

NEWPORT	3E1

Comfort Inn Awaiting Inspection
Junc 23a (M4), Magor, Newport NP6 3YL
☎ 01633-881887 Fax 01633-881896
43 bedrs, all ensuite, TCF TV ⊬ P 100 Room £44.95
CC MC Visa Amex ⛑

PORTHCAWL Bridgend	3D1

♦♦♦ Penoyre
Sparkling Diamond
29 Mary Street, Porthcawl CF36 3YN
☎ 01656-784550
Closed Christmas
7 bedrs, 4 ensuite, 1 ⊬ TCF TV ⊬ ⏣ Resid SB £16-£25
DB £30-£36 HB £150-£175 D £8

RHYL Denbighshire	6C1

♦♦♦ Pier
23 East Parade, Rhyl LL18 3AL
☎ 01745-350280
Closed Christmas
8 bedrs, TCF TV ⊬ P 3 ⏣ Resid SB £16-£19 DB £32-£38 HB £130-£160 D £7 CC MC Visa

ST DAVID'S Pembrokeshire	6A4

♦♦♦♦ Ramsey House
Warm Welcome, Sparkling Diamond
Lower Moor, St David's SA62 6RP
☎ 01437-720321 Fax 01437-720025

Exclusively for non-smoking adults seeking quiet relaxation, with award winning Welsh food and wines. Convenient for the cathedral, coast path, beaches and attractions. Pleasant garden. Easy parking.
7 bedrs, all ensuite, TCF TV ✉ ⊬ P 10 No children under 16 ⏣ Rest Resid SB £27-£62 DB £54-£62
HB £246-£276 D £14 CC MC Visa JCB

♦♦♦ Y Glennydd
Sparkling Diamond
51 Nun Street, St David's SA62 6NU
☎ 01437-720576 Fax 01437-720184
Closed Nov-Jan
10 bedrs, 8 ensuite, 2 ⊬ TCF TV ⏣ Rest Resid SB £19-£25 DB £36-£42 D £13.95 CC MC Visa

SAUNDERSFOOT Pembrokeshire	6B4

♦♦♦ Woodlands
Sparkling Diamond
St Brides Hill, Saundersfoot SA69 9NP
☎ 01834-813338
Closed Nov-Mar
10 bedrs, all ensuite, TCF TV P 10 ⏣ Rest Resid
SB £24-£28 DB £42-£50 HB £180-£205 D £9.50 CC MC Visa

♦♦ Bay View
Pleasant Valley, Stepaside, Saundersfoot SA67 8LR
☎ 01834-813417
Closed Oct-Mar
11 bedrs, 8 ensuite, 3 ⊬ TCF P 15 ⏣ Resid SB £15-£19 DB £30-£37 HB £140-£165 ⛑

Tenby

SOLVA Pembrokeshire 6A4

♦♦♦♦♦ Lochmeyler Farm
Sparkling Diamond
Pen-y-cwm, Solva, Haverfordwest SA62 6LL
☎ 01348-837724 Fax 01348-837622
16 bedrs, all ensuite, TCF TV ⚲ P 16 ⋕ 40 ⊕ Resid
SB £20-£30 DB £40-£60 D £12.50 CC MC Visa ♿

SWANSEA 2C1

♦♦♦♦ Woodside
Sparkling Diamond
Oxwich, Swansea SA3 1LS
☎ 01792-390791
5 bedrs, all ensuite, TCF TV P 6 ⊕ Rest SB £30-£36
DB £40-£52

♦♦♦ Alexander
Sparkling Diamond
3 Sketty Road, Uplands, Swansea SA2 0EU
☎ 01792-470045 Fax 01792-476012
Closed 24 Dec-2 Jan
7 bedrs, 6 ensuite, 1 ⚲ TCF TV ⚲ No children under 2
⊕ Resid SB £30-£33 DB £44-£45 HB £200 CC MC Visa
Amex DC 🅿 🅿

♦♦♦ Coast House
708 Mumbles Road, Mumbles, Swansea SA3 4EH
☎ 01792-368702
Closed Christmas
6 bedrs, 4 ensuite, 1 ⚲ TCF TV ⚲ SB £20-£22 DB £38-£40

♦♦♦ Coynant & Ganol Farm
Warm Welcome
Felindre, Swansea SA5 7PU
☎ 01269-595640
5 bedrs, 3 ensuite, 1 🏠 TCF TV P 10 ⊕ Resid 🅿

♦♦♦ Crescent
Sparkling Diamond
132 Eaton Crescent, Uplands, Swansea SA1 4QR
☎ 01792-466814 Fax 01792-466814
E-mail conveyatthecrescent@compuserve.com
Closed Christmas & New Year
6 bedrs, all ensuite, TCF TV ⚲ P 6 SB £25-£30 DB £40-£48 CC MC Visa

♦♦♦ Grosvenor House
Sparkling Diamond
Mirador Crescent, Uplands, Swansea SA2 0QX
☎ 01792-461522 Fax 01792-461522
E-mail grosvenor@ct6.com

Grosvenor House warmly welcomes businessmen and holiday visitors. Quietly situated providing quality comfort. Convenient for Swansea and Gower.
7 bedrs, all ensuite, TCF TV P 3 SB £26-£29 DB £42-£48
CC MC Visa DC JCB

♦♦♦ Rock Villa
1 George Bank, Southend, Mumbles SA3 4EQ
☎ 01792-366794
6 bedrs, 3 ensuite, 2 ⚲ TCF TV ⚲ No children under 3
SB £17-£20 DB £38-£42

♦♦♦ St James
76b Walter Road, Swansea SA1 4QA
☎ 01792-649984
Closed first two weeks Jan
4 bedrs, all ensuite, TCF TV ⚲ P 6 ⊕ SB £30-£38
DB £45-£52 D £16.50 CC MC Visa Amex ♿

TENBY Pembrokeshire 2B1

♦♦♦♦ Broadmead 🍴
Warm Welcome, Sparkling Diamond
Heywood Lane, Tenby SA70 8DA
☎ 01834-842641 Fax 01834-845757
20 bedrs, all ensuite, TCF TV P 20 ⊕ Rest Resid
SB £30-£36 DB £46-£58 HB £238-£280 D £13 CC MC Visa JCB

♦♦♦♦ Kinloch Court
Queens Parade, Tenby SA70 7EG
☎ 01834-842777 Fax 01834-843097
Closed Oct-Mar
12 bedrs, all ensuite, TCF TV P 25 No children under
3 ⊕ Resid SB £29-£30 DB £58-£60 D £13 CC MC Visa 🅿

♦♦♦ Ashby House
Sparkling Diamond
24 Victoria Street, Tenby SA70 7DY
☎ 01834-842867 Fax 01834-842867
9 bedrs, 8 ensuite, 1 ⚲ TCF TV No children under 3
SB £18-£26 DB £30-£44 CC MC Visa

WALES

Tenby

♦♦♦ Hildebrand
29 Victoria Street, Tenby SA70 7DY
☎ 01834-842403 Fax 01834-844748
E-mail hotel@hildebrand-hotel.co.uk
Closed Nov-Feb
7 bedrs, all ensuite, TCF TV No children under 3
Resid SB £25-£35 DB £34-£50 D £11 CC MC Visa
Amex DC

♦♦♦ Pen Mar
New Hedges, Tenby SA70 8TL
☎ 01834-842435 Fax 01834-842435

A modern, detached hotel in Pembrokeshire National Park situated between Tenby and Saundersfoot with fine sea views. 'A Touch of Italy' awaits in the restaurant's Anglo/Continental cuisine.
10 bedrs, 2 ensuite, 4 ☎ 2 ⇥ TCF TV P 10 ⋕ 25
Rest Resid SB £18.50-£23 DB £37-£46 HB £116-£143 D £11.50 CC MC Visa Amex DC JCB

♦♦♦ Ripley St Mary's
St Mary's Street, Tenby SA70 7HN
☎ 01834-842837 Fax 01834-842837
Closed Oct-Easter

A Tenby In Bloom award hotel, situated in a quiet street in the centre of Tenby and only 75 yards from the seafront and the Paragon Gardens. Free car parking in private garage.
12 bedrs, 8 ensuite, 3 ⇥ TCF TV ⇥ P 12 No children
Resid SB £21-£25 DB £42-£50 CC MC Visa

♦♦ Castle View
The Norton, Tenby SA70 8AA
☎ 01834-842666
10 bedrs, all ensuite, TCF TV P 10 Resid SB £20-£25
DB £40-£50 D £8.50

Heywood Mount Awaiting Inspection
Heywood Lane, Tenby SA70 8BN
☎ 01834-842087 Fax 01834-842087
20 bedrs, all ensuite, P 20 ⋕ 60 Rest Resid
SB £21-£28 DB £42-£56 HB £185-£250 D £9 CC MC Visa Amex DC ♿

TINTERN Monmouthshire	3E1

Valley House Awaiting Inspection
Raglan Road, Tintern NP6 6TH
☎ 01291-689652 Fax 01291-689805
E-mail 106323.3017@compuserve.com
Closed Christmas
3 bedrs, all ensuite, TCF TV ✉ ⇥ P 7 CC Amex

TREARDDUR BAY Anglesey	6B1

♦♦♦ Moranedd
Sparkling Diamond
Trearddur Road, Trearddur Bay LL65 2UE
☎ 01407-860324
Closed Christmas
6 bedrs, 2 ⇥ TCF P 10 SB £16-£17 DB £32.50-£34

SPENCER'S

The British Golf Directory

Courses where you can turn up and play

This new Spencer's guide provides full details of golf courses the length and breadth of Britain. All are courses where you can turn up and play, from municipal courses to some of the grandest in the land. You don't need to be members or pay membership fees. Just the rate for the round.

Whether you are an old hand or one of the new wave of golf enthusiasts you will find Spencer's Directory an invaluable companion - for your home, for your car or for your holidays.

With full-colour throughout it's easy-to-use, highly practical and perfect for browsing.

Each entry has a full quarter-page, with a description of the course, and information on yardage, par, standard scratch score, directions and green fees. There's also a full-colour route-planning and map section - a feature of all Spencer's titles.

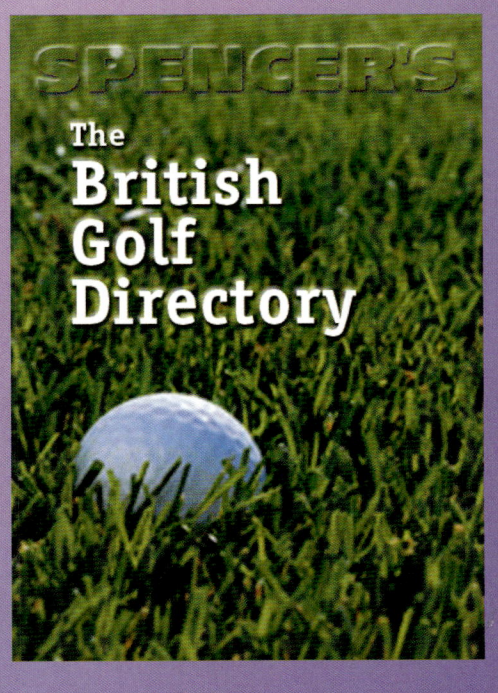

Format:	210x148mm
No. of pages:	112pp
ISBN:	1 900327 51 1
Price:	£4.99
Publication date:	April 2000

West One PUBLISHING

West One Publishing
Kestrel House, Duke's PLace
Marlow, Bucks SL7 2QH

tel: 01628 487722

www.WestOneWeb.com

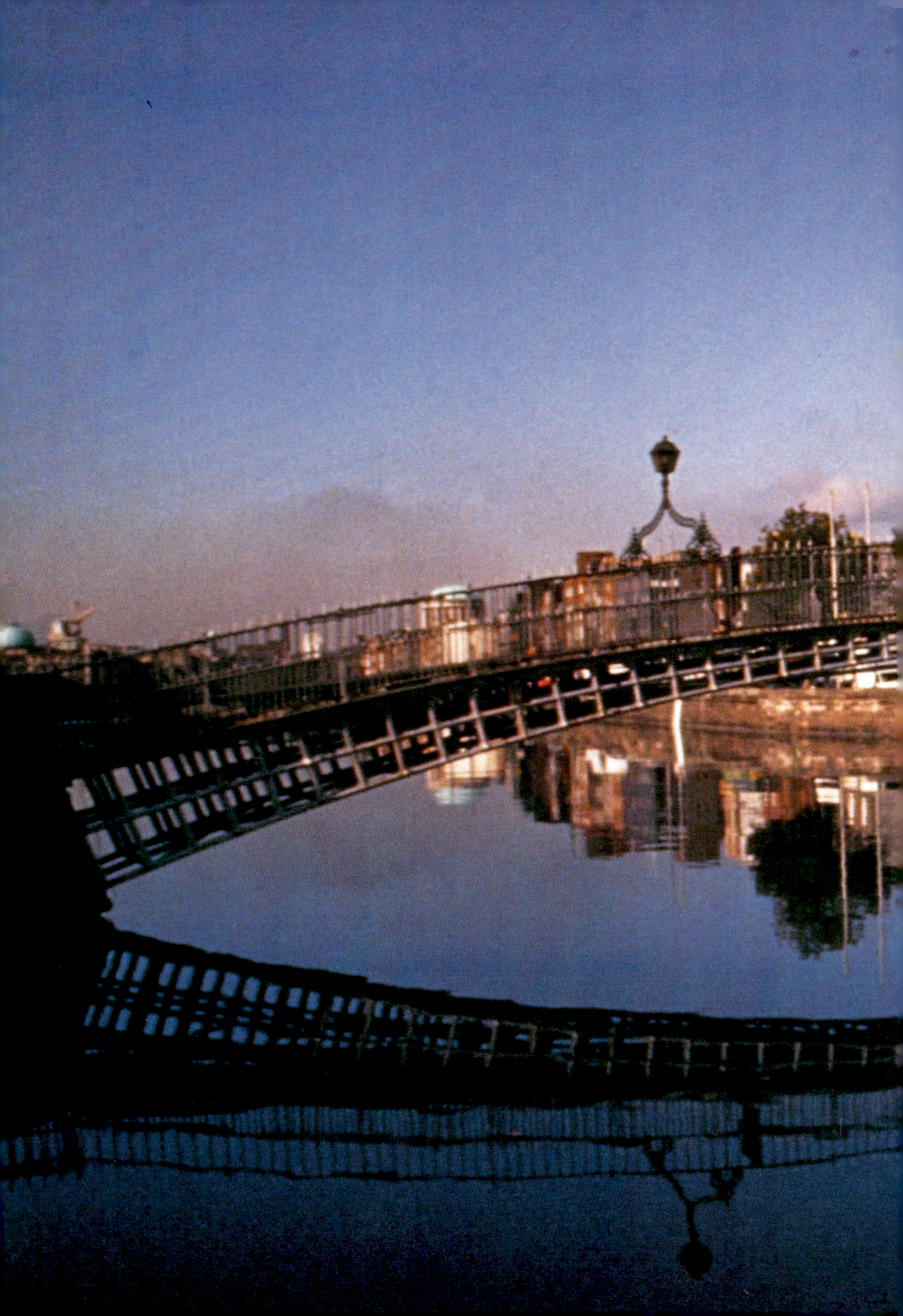

Ireland

Achill Island

Republic of Ireland
Please not that due to the constraints of inspections for Harmonised Quality Standards and for ease of comparison, we have shown both the new rating and existing rating where applicable.

ACHILL ISLAND Co. Mayo   16A3

♦♦♦♦ **Achill Cliff House** Highly Acclaimed
Sparkling Diamond
Keel, Achill Island
📞 098-43400 Fax 098-43007
E-mail achwch@anu.ie
Closed 15 Jan-10 Feb

New purpose built guesthouse in superb location. Non-smoking, spacious ensuite bedrooms, luxuriously furnished with baths, D.D phone, TV, tea/coffee, hairdryers, trouser press. In house sauna and restaurant. Panoramic views.
11 bedrs, all ensuite, TCF TV P 30 No children under 8 ⌑ Rest DB £44-£70 HB £249-£299 D £15 CC MC Visa Amex 🖻 &

♦♦♦ **Finncorry House** Highly Acclaimed
Sparkling Diamond
Bleanaskill Bay, Atlantic Drive, Achill Island
📞 098-45755 Fax 098-45755
E-mail achill_island@hotmail.com
Closed Nov-Feb
6 bedrs, all ensuite, TV P 8 SB £20-£24.50 DB £34-£38 HB £180-£195 D £14 CC MC Visa Amex &

Lavelle's Sea Side House Awaiting Inspection
Dooega, Achill Island
📞 098-45116 Fax 098-45116
9 bedrs, all ensuite, TCF ⚞ P 20 ⌑ SB £18-£22 DB £28-£36 HB £170-£190 D £12 CC MC Visa Amex DC

ADARE Co. Limerick   18C2

Berkeley Lodge Awaiting Inspection
Station Road, Adare
📞 061-396857
6 bedrs, 5 ensuite, 1 ⚞

Coatesland House Awaiting Inspection
Killarney Road, Graigue, Adare
📞 061-396372

ASHFORD Co. Wicklow   19F1

Chester Beatty Inn Awaiting Inspection
Ashford
📞 0404-40206
Closed 24-25 Dec
12 bedrs, all ensuite

ATHY Co. Kildare   19E1

♦♦♦♦♦ **Coursetown Country House** Highly Acclaimed
Warm Welcome, Sparkling Diamond
Stradbally Road, Athy
📞 0507-31101 Fax 0507-32740

This old country house is set on a 250 acre arable farm, surrounded by secluded gardens.
4 bedrs, all ensuite, TCF TV ⊠ ⚞ P 20 No children under 8 SB £35 DB £60 CC MC Visa Amex &

BALLINAMORE Co. Leitrim   17D3

♦♦♦ **Riversdale Farm Guesthouse** Acclaimed
Ballinamore
📞 078-44122 Fax 078-44813

Carlow 197

Spacious, beautiully situated, family run guesthouse overlooking Shannon-Erne waterway. With heated indoor swimming pool, sauna, squash, fitness suite. Local golf, horse-riding, boating. Brochures available.
12 bedrs, all ensuite, **TCF TV P** 20 **Rest SB** £30-£35 **DB** £52 **HB** £195-£200 **D** £12 **CC** MC Visa

---

BALLYVAUGHAN Co. Clare   18B1

♦♦♦♦ Rusheen Lodge Highly Acclaimed
Knocknagrough, Ballyvaughan
065-707 7092 Fax 065-707 7152
E-mail jmcgann@iol.ie
Closed Nov-Feb
8 bedrs, all ensuite, **TCF TV P** 12 **SB** £35-£40 **DB** £50-£60 **CC** MC Visa Amex

---

BANTRY Co. Cork   18B4

♦♦♦ Mill Highly Acclaimed
Glengariff Road, New Town, Bantry
027-50278 Fax 027-50278
Closed Nov-Mar
6 bedrs, all ensuite, **TV P** 10 **SB** £25 **DB** £40 **CC** Visa

---

CAPPAGH Co. Waterford   19D3

♦♦♦♦ Castle Farm Acclaimed
Millstreet, Cappagh
058-68049 Fax 058-68099
Closed mid Nov-Feb

Award winning restored wing of 15th century castle on large dairy farm. Excellent cuisine and elegant decor. Breakfast menu.
5 bedrs, all ensuite, **TCF TV P** 10 **Rest SB** £27 **DB** £42-£50 **HB** £222-£260 **D** £17 **CC** MC Visa DC

CAPPOQUIN Co. Waterford   19D3

Richmond House Highly Acclaimed
Cappoquin
058-54278 Fax 058-54988
Closed 23 Dec-Jan

An 18th century country house in extensive private grounds with lovely garden. Relax in total tranquillity in front of log fires or treat yourself to a gourmet meal in our award winning restaurant.
9 bedrs, all ensuite, **TCF TV P** 15 **Rest SB** £40-£60 **DB** £80-£110 **HB** £440-£550 **D** £29 **CC** MC Visa Amex DC

CARLOW Co. Carlow   19E2

Barrowville Town House Highly Acclaimed
Kilkenny Road, Carlow Town
0503-43324 Fax 0503-41953

Regency house in own grounds. Antique furnishing. Four minutes walk to town centre, pubs and restaurants. Ideal location for golf and touring south east and midlands, Kilkenny, Glendalough.
7 bedrs, all ensuite, **TCF TV P** 11 No children under 12 **SB** £25-£30 **DB** £45-£55 **CC** MC Visa Amex

IRELAND

Carrigans

CARRIGANS Co. Donegal — 17D1

Mount Royd Country Home Acclaimed
Carrigans, Nr Londonderry
📞 074-40163

Perfectly situated for visiting historic treasures. Old fashioned Irish hospitality and 'far from the maddening crowd'. Giants Causeway, 1 hour away, Londonderry, 5 miles on R236. A40 off N13, N14.
4 bedrs, all ensuite, TCF TV P 8 SB £20 DB £32
HB £252-£266 D £12

CLIFDEN Co. Galway — 16A4

Buttermilk Lodge Highly Acclaimed
Westport Road, Clifden
📞 095-21951 Fax 095-21953
E-mail buttermilk@connemara.net

A warm friendly, home from home, 400m from town centre. Spacious bedrooms with satellite TV, DD telephone, hairdryer, radio. Mountain views, turf fires, tea/coffee facilities, breakfast menu.
11 bedrs, all ensuite, TV P 14 No children under 3
SB £25-£40 DB £40-£60 CC MC Visa

Mal Dua Highly Acclaimed
Galway Road, Clifden
📞 095-21171 Fax 095-21739
E-mail maldua@iol.ie
Closed Dec

A family run guest house, about a mile from Clifden in the heart of Connemara. Spacious bedrooms all individually designed, with TV, radio, telephone, and tea/coffee facilities.
14 bedrs, all ensuite, TCF TV P 40 SB £30-£66 DB £50-£66 CC MC Visa Amex

O' Grady's Sunnybank Highly Acclaimed
Church Hill, Clifden
📞 095-21437 Fax 095-21976
Closed 3 Nov-1 Mar

A period house of character, situated in its own grounds and surrounded by gardens with many interesting features. The house overlooks the picturesque town of Clifton. A warm Irish welcome awaits our guests from the O'Gradys.
11 bedrs, all ensuite, TV P 12 No children under 8
Resid DB £50-£60 CC MC Visa

Dun Ri Acclaimed
Clifden
📞 095-21625 Fax 095-21635
E-mail dunri@anu.ie
Closed Nov-Mar
10 bedrs, all ensuite, TV P 10 No children under 3
SB £20-£35 DB £40-£50 CC MC Visa

Ben View House Listed
Bridge Street, Clifden
📞 095-21256 Fax 095-21226
Closed 24-26 Dec
10 bedrs, 9 ensuite, TV CC MC Visa

Cork

Kingstown House **Listed**
Bridge Street, Clifden
📞 095-21470 **Fax** 095-21530
Closed 23-27 Dec
8 bedrs, 6 ensuite, 2 🛏 TCF TV No children under 3
SB £18-£25 **DB** £32-£36 **CC** MC Visa

CORK Co. Cork   18C3

Garnish House **Acclaimed**
Western Road, Cork
📞 021-275111 **Fax** 021-273872
E-mail garnish@iol.ie

A stay in Garnish House is a memorable one. Our tastefully appointed rooms with an optional ensuite jacuzzi and extensive gourmet breakfast is certain to please. Opposite UCC and convenient to ferry, airport and bus terminal. Ideal base for touring South.
14 bedrs, all ensuite, TCF TV 🛏 P 12 **SB** £30-£40 **DB** £50-£60 **CC** MC Visa Amex DC ♿

Killarney House **Acclaimed**
Western Road (opp U.C.C.), Cork
📞 021-270290 **Fax** 021-271010
E-mail killarneyhouse@iol.ie
Closed 25-26 Dec
19 bedrs, all ensuite, TCF TV P 20 ⊞ 10 **CC** MC Visa Amex

Roserie Villa **Acclaimed**
Mardyke Walk, Off Western Road, Cork
📞 021-272958 **Fax** 021-274087
16 bedrs, all ensuite, TCF TV P 8 No children under 5
SB £23-£40 **DB** £40-£60 **CC** MC Visa Amex DC

St Kilda **Acclaimed**
Western Road, Cork
📞 021-273095 **Fax** 021-275015
E-mail stkilda@cork-guide.ie
Closed 22 Dec-11 Jan

Directly opposite the main University gate on the main Cork to Killarney road, with off street floodlight parking. A ten minute stroll to the city centre.
21 bedrs, all ensuite, TCF TV P 16 **SB** £25-£35 **DB** £38-£60 **CC** MC Visa
See advert on this page

Antoine **Listed**
Antoine House, Western Road, Cork
📞 021-273494 **Fax** 021-273092
10 bedrs, all ensuite, TCF TV P 12 **SB** £25-£35 **DB** £40-£50 **HB** £60-£80 **CC** MC Visa

---

ST KILDA
GUEST HOUSE

Imposing three storey establishment built in 1896. Just 20 minutes drive to airport and Blarney Castle. 30 minutes to ferryport and Kinsale, Ireland's gourmet capital. Numerous superb golf courses within easy reach. 10 minute stroll to city centre. Opposite University.

WESTERN ROAD, CORK
Tel: 353 (21) 273095
Fax: 353 (21) 275015

IRELAND

Crusheen

CRUSHEEN Co. Clare　　　　　　　　18C1

Lahardan House Listed
Crusheen
📞 065-682 7128 Fax 065-682 7319

Family residence 9½ miles north of Ennis, 1½ miles off N18 Ennis/Galway road at Crusheen. Rooms ensuite, direct dial telephones, hairdryers, central heating. Fishing, golf, pitch and putt available locally. Relax in the peace and quiet of Lahardan.
8 bedrs, all ensuite, TV ⚹ P 15 CC MC Visa

DINGLE Co. Kerry　　　　　　　　18A3

♦♦♦♦ Greenmount House Highly Acclaimed
Sparkling Diamond
Upper John Street, Dingle
📞 066-915 1414 Fax 066-915 1974
E-mail greenmounthouse@tinet.ie

Luxury guest house, set on a hillside in a peaceful, tranquil location with panoramic views over Dingle town and harbour.
12 bedrs, all ensuite, TCF TV P 15 No children under 8 SB £28-£65 DB £50-£75 CC MC Visa ♿

Alpine House Highly Acclaimed
Mail Road, Dingle
📞 066-915 1250 Fax 066-915 1966

Elegant house with beautiful bedrooms and spacious bathrooms, all individually furnished to a high standard. Wide choice of breakfasts offered. 2 minutes walk to town centre. Car park.
12 bedrs, all ensuite, TCF TV P 20 No children under 5 SB £17.50-£37 DB £30-£50 CC MC Visa

Ard-Na-Greine Highly Acclaimed
Spa Road, Dingle
📞 066-915 1113 Fax 066-915 1898
E-mail maryhoul@iol.ie
4 bedrs, all ensuite, TCF TV ✉ P 4 No children under 7 DB £34-£40 CC MC Visa

Cleevaun House Highly Acclaimed
Ladys Cross, Milltown, Dingle
📞 066-915 1108 Fax 066-915 1108
E-mail cleevaun@iol.ie
Closed Dec-Feb
9 bedrs, all ensuite, TV P 9 No children under 8 SB £40-£50 DB £50-£65 CC MC Visa

Doyles Town House Highly Acclaimed
John Street, Dingle
📞 066-915 1816 Fax 066-915 1816
Closed mid Nov-mid Mar
8 bedrs, all ensuite, TV No children under 10 ⌨
SB £70 DB £80 D £15 CC MC Visa Amex DC

Milltown House Highly Acclaimed
Dingle
📞 066-915 1372 Fax 066-915 1095
E-mail milltown@indigo.ie
Closed 24-27 Dec
10 bedrs, all ensuite, TCF TV P 10 No children under 10 SB £25-£55 DB £45-£75 CC MC Visa Amex ♿

Pax House Highly Acclaimed
Upper John Street, Dingle
📞 066-915 1518 Fax 066-915 1518
E-mail paxhouse@iol.ie
Closed 5 Nov-1 Mar
7 bedrs, all ensuite, TCF TV P 10 CC MC Visa

Dublin 201

Bamburys Guesthouse Listed
Mail Road, Dingle
📞 066-51244 Fax 066-51780
E-mail berniebb@tinet.ie

A charming ITB 3 star guest house, just 1 minutes walk from Dingle town. 12 bedrooms, all ensuite with DD phone and TV. Hotel has own car park.
12 bedrs, all ensuite, TCF TV P 12 No children under 4 SB £20-£40 DB £36-£55 CC MC Visa ♿

Bolands Listed
Goat Street, Dingle
📞 066-915 1426
Closed 25 Dec

House with view of Dingle Bay offering Sky TV, hairdryers, clock radio, tea/coffee making facilities and orthopedic beds. Walking distance to all amenities.
6 bedrs, all ensuite, TCF TV SB £18-£20 DB £38-£40 CC MC Visa ♿

DONEGAL Co. Donegal   16C2

Ardeevin Highly Acclaimed
Lough Eske, Barnesmore, Donegal
📞 073-21790 Fax 073-21790
E-mail seanmcginty@tinet.ie
Closed Mid nov - 1st Mar

Award winning country residence nestled beneath the Bluestack Mountains. Bedrooms overlooking Lough Eske. Lake and sea fishing locally. Web site: http:// members.tripod.com/~Ardeevin
6 bedrs, all ensuite, TCF TV ✉ P 10 SB £27.50 DB £40

DUBLIN Co. Dublin   19F1

Aberdeen Lodge Highly Acclaimed
53-55 Park Avenue, Ballsbridge, Dublin
📞 01-283 8155 Fax 01-283 7877
E-mail aberdeen@iol.ie

Luxurious combination of early Edwardian grace an modern comfort, including suites with jacuzzi and executive facilities. Private parking. Superb location, premier service and elegant surroundings - the tasteful option on Dublin's Park Avenue.
18 bedrs, all ensuite, TCF TV P 16 ⛲ DB £117-£143
CC MC Visa Amex DC

Don't forget to mention the guide

When booking direct, please remember to tell the hotel that you chose it from RAC Inspected Guest Accommodation

IRELAND

Dublin

♦♦♦♦♦ Butlers Highly Acclaimed
Sparkling Diamond
44 Lansdowne Road, Ballsbridge, Dublin
☎ 01-667 4022 Fax 01-667 3960
E-mail info@butlers-hotel.com
Closed 25-28 Dec

Award winning house is a must for the discerning traveller in the heart of Dublin's embassy belt - minutes walk from all of the city's top attractions.
19 bedrs, all ensuite, TV P 8 ⊕ Resid SB £84-£96 DB £117-£143 CC MC Visa Amex DC &

66 Town House Highly Acclaimed
66 Northumberland Road, Ballsbridge, Dublin 4
☎ 01-660 0333 Fax 01-660 1051
9 bedrs, all ensuite, TCF TV P 6 SB £40-£55 DB £55-£70
CC MC Visa

Ariel House Highly Acclaimed
50-52 Lansdowne Road, Ballsbridge
☎ 01-668 5512 Fax 01-668 5845
28 bedrs, all ensuite, TCF TV P 24 No children under 9 ⊕ Rest SB £58-£88 DB £96-£129 CC MC Visa

Charleville Lodge Highly Acclaimed
268-272 North Circular Road, Phisboro, Dublin
☎ 01-838 6633 Fax 01-838 5854
E-mail charleville@indigo.ie.
Closed Christmas

Completely refurbished to combine old charm and character with all modern facilities, the luxurious premises are located 15 minutes walk from O'Connell Street and are on main bus routes. Large car park.
30 bedrs, 28 ensuite, 1 ⇌ TV P 15 ⋕ 20 SB £35-£60
DB £60-£100 CC MC Visa Amex DC &

Glenogra Highly Acclaimed
64 Merrion Road, Ballsbridge, Dublin
☎ 01-668 3661 Fax 01-668 3698
E-mail glenogra@indigo.ie
Closed 20 Dec-12 Jan

A beautifully appointed Edwardian residence opposite RDS, close to the city centre.
9 bedrs, all ensuite, TCF TV ⊠ P 9 SB £45-£60 DB £60-£90 CC MC Visa Amex DC

Hedigans Highly Acclaimed
14 Hollybrook Park, Clontarf
☎ 01-853 1663 Fax 01-833 3337
Closed 15 Dec-10 Jan

Hedigans is a refurbished Victorian house situated 3 km from the city centre, on the main bus and train routes, 15 minutes from the airport and 5 minutes from the port of Dublin. ITB 3 Star.
9 bedrs, all ensuite, TCF TV P 10 SB £35-£45 DB £56-£70 CC MC Visa

Trinity Lodge Highly Acclaimed
12 South Frederick Street, Dublin 2
☎ 01-679 5044 Fax 01-679 5223
E-mail trinitylodge@tinet.ie
13 bedrs, all ensuite, TCF TV ⋕ 12 SB £60-£87.50
DB £95-£160 CC MC Visa Amex DC

Dublin 203

Tara Hall
RAC LISTED

This refurbished Regency style house once the former residence of 'William Monk Gibbon' poet & writer is ideally situated in Sandycove. A short walk to the 'Joyce Tower' & Dun Laoghaire Harbour. All rooms have TV and tea/coffee facilities. FREE off road parking. Smoking & non-smoking rooms available

RATES FROM £18.00 P.P.S.
24 Sandycove Road, DUN LAOGHAIRE,
CO DUBLIN. TEL/FAX 2805120
EMAIL: tarahall@indigo.ie

BAGGOT COURT

RAC ♦♦♦♦

Luxurious accommodation in refurbished Georgian House. All rooms en-suite with modern facilities. Only a 5 min walk to city centre Rate includes Full Irish Breakfast FREE car parking
Non-smoking establishment

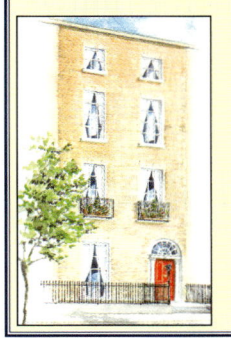

RATES FROM £35.00 P.P.S.

Ph: 661 2819
Fax: 661 0253
Email
baggot@indigo.ie

92 Lwr Baggot st
Dublin 2

HARCOURT INN

RAC ACCLAIMED

This Georgian House is only a 5 minute walk to Grafton St. and St. Stephens Green. All rooms are en-suite and have modern facilities. Rate includes Full Irish Breakfast. We are a Non-smoking establishment.

RATES FROM £35.00 P.P.S.
PH: 478 3927   FAX: 478 2550
27 Harcourt Street Dublin 2
EMAIL: harcourt@indigo.ie

HERBERT LODGE
65 Morehampton Rd, Donnybrook, D4
PH: 660 3403   FAX: 668 8794
EMAIL: herbertl@indigo.ie
RAC LISTED

Situated in Dublin 4, close to the RDS, Lansdowne Rugby Stadium and several pubs and restaurants. A short walk to St. Stephens Green and Grafton St. All rooms are en-suite with modern facilities.
FREE off road car parking
Smoking & non-smoking rooms
Full Irish Breakfast included

RATES FROM £25.00 P.P.S

IRELAND

Dublin

Baggot Court Acclaimed
92 Lower Baggot Street, Dublin
01-661 2819 Fax 01-661 0253
E-mail baggot@indigo.ie
11 bedrs, all ensuite, TCF TV ⊠ P 8 No children under 5 ⊕ Rest Club SB £45-£60 DB £70-£140 CC MC Visa Amex
See advert on previous page

Fitzwilliam Acclaimed
41 Upper Fitzwilliam Street, Dublin 2
01-662 5155 Fax 01-676 7488
Closed 21 Dec-1 Jan
12 bedrs, all ensuite, TV ⊁ ⊕ Rest SB £45 DB £60-£80 D £23 CC MC Visa Amex DC

Glenveagh Town House Acclaimed
31 Northumberland Road, Ballsbridge, Dublin 4
01-668 4612 Fax 01-668 4559
E-mail glenveagh@tinet.ie
Closed 22-28 Dec
13 bedrs, all ensuite, TCF TV P 10 ⊞ 10 SB £45-£90 DB £65-£80 CC MC Visa Amex &

Harcourt Inn Acclaimed
27 Harcourt Street, Dublin 2
01-478 3927 Fax 01-478 2550
E-mail harcourt@indigo.ie
15 bedrs, all ensuite, TCF TV ⊠ No children under 5
SB £50-£55 DB £70-£90 CC MC Visa
See advert on previous page

Kingswood Country House Acclaimed
Naas Road, Clondalkin
01-459 2428 Fax 01-459 2428
E-mail kingswoodcountryhse@tinet.ie
Closed Christmas & Good Friday
7 bedrs, all ensuite, TV P 70 ⊞ 20 ⊕ Rest SB £65-£75 DB £90-£120 D £27.95 CC MC Visa Amex DC

Lyndon Guest House Acclaimed
26 Gardiner Place, Dublin 1
01-878 6950 Fax 01-878 7420

Luxurious Georgian period guesthouse. Superbly located in the city centre, next to all tourist attractions: Croke Park, Point Depot. All rooms ensuite, TVs, coffee/tea. Secure parking.
9 bedrs, all ensuite, TCF TV P 9 SB £50-£70 DB £50-£70
CC MC Visa Amex

Mount Herbert Acclaimed
Herbert Road, Lansdowne Road, Dublin 4
01-668 4321 Fax 01-660 7077
E-mail info@mountherberthotel.ie

Good value accommodation, 5 minutes from city centre in the exclusive Embassy district. Easy access from the ferry port. Secure car park, restaurant, bar, sauna and sunbed.
200 bedrs, all ensuite, TCF TV ⊡ P 90 ⊞ 100 ⊕
SB £54.50-£64.50 DB £79-£89 D £16.50 CC MC Visa Amex DC ⊠ &

Uppercross House Acclaimed
26-30 Upper Rathmines Road, Dublin
01-497 5486 Fax 01-497 5486
E-mail mahond@indigo.ie
25 bedrs, all ensuite, TCF TV ⊁ P 24 ⊕ SB £30-£49.50
DB £60-£85 D £15 CC MC Visa Amex DC

Clifden House Listed
32 Gardner Place, Dublin 1
01-874 6364 Fax 01-874 6122
10 bedrs, all ensuite, TCF TV CC MC Visa

Herbert Lodge Listed
65 Morehampton Road, Donnybrook, Dublin 4
01-660 3403 Fax 01-668 8794
E-mail herbertl @ indigo.ie
Closed 24-27 Dec
6 bedrs, all ensuite, TCF TV P 4 No children under 10
SB £30-£45 DB £50-£100 CC MC Visa
See advert on previous page

Merrion Hall Listed
54/56 Merrion Road, Ballsbridge
01-668 1426 Fax 01-668 4280
23 bedrs, all ensuite, TCF TV P 10 SB £50-£100 DB £55-£100 CC MC Visa
See advert on opposite page

Ennistymon 205

Merrion Hall

Award-winning elegant Victorian red brick house situated in Ballsbridge, Dublin's most exclusive suburb and centre of Dublin's Embassy belt.

Beautifully refurbished, the dining room looks out onto gardens. Drawing room and library are available. An enclosed car park is encompassed within the grounds. Close to the city centre, airport and car ferry - beside DART link station.

National Breakfast of the Year 1989.
RAC Best Small Hotel/Guesthouse 1994.

54 Merrion Road, Ballsbridge, Dublin 4.
Tel: 01 668 1426 • Fax: 01 668 4280
Email: merrionhall@iol.ie

Othello House Listed
74 Lower Gardiner Street, Dublin
01-855 4271 Fax 01-855 7460

Two hundred year old house situated in the city centre. Central bus station 50 metres, direct bus from the airport (number 41) stops outside. O'Connell Street 100 metres. Abbey 100 metres, train station 150 metres.
26 bedrs, all ensuite, TCF TV P 12 CC MC Visa Amex DC JCB

Raglan Lodge
10 Raglan Road, Ballsbridge, Dublin
01-660 6697 Fax 01-660 6781

A large Victorian residence dating from 1861, carefully restored to its former splendour.
7 bedrs, all ensuite, TCF ✱ P 20 CC MC Visa Amex

DUN LAOGHAIRE Co. Dublin 19F1

♦♦ Tara Hall Listed
24 Sandycove Road, Dun Laoghaire
01-280 5120 Fax 01-280 5120
6 bedrs, 5 ensuite, 1 ➡ TCF TV ⊠ P 6 SB £22-£25 DB £44-£50 CC MC Visa
See advert on previous page

Ferry House Listed
15 Clarinda Park North, Dun Laoghaire
01-280 8301 Fax 01-284 6530
Closed Christmas
4 bedrs, all ensuite, TCF TV SB £30-£40 DB £45-£55
CC MC Visa

ENNISTYMON Co. Clare 18B1

Grovemount House Highly Acclaimed
Lahinch Road, Ennistymon
065-707 1431 Fax 065-707 1823
Closed Oct-Apr

Situated on the outskirts of Ennistymon and offering east access to the Burren and Cliffs of Moher. Golfing, fishing and traditional music sessions can be arranged.
8 bedrs, all ensuite, TCF TV P 20 SB £28-£32 DB £36-£45 CC MC Visa ♿

Fanore

FANORE Co. Clare	18B1

Admirals Rest Listed
Coast Road, Fanore
☎ 065-707 6105 Fax 065-707 6161

GALWAY & SALTHILL Co. Galway	18C1

Imperial Awaiting Inspection
Eyre Square, Galway
☎ 091-563033 Fax 091-568410
85 bedrs, all ensuite, TCF TV ⊞ SB £40-£110 DB £70-£110

GLENDALOUGH Co. Wicklow	19F1

Carmel's Acclaimed
Annamoe, Glendalough
☎ 0404-45297 Fax 0404-45297
Closed Nov-Feb
4 bedrs, 4 ↾ 1 ➡ TCF P 5 DB £34-£36 ♿

GOREY Co. Wexford	19F2

Woodlands House Awaiting Inspection
Killierin, Gorey
☎ 0402-37125 Fax 0402-37133
Closed 1 Nov-1 Apr
6 bedrs, all ensuite, TV P 10 ⊞ Rest SB £35-£40 DB £50 D £22.50 CC MC Visa ✉

HOWTH Co. Dublin	19F1

Inisradharc Awaiting Inspection
Balkill Road, Howth
☎ 01-832 2306 Fax 01-832 2306
Closed 22 Dec-2 Jan
3 bedrs, all ensuite, TCF TV ⊞ P 3 No children under 4 DB £22-£24 CC MC Visa

Short Breaks

Many hotels provide special rates for weekend and mid-week breaks – sometimes these are quoted in the hotel's entry, otherwise ring direct for the latest offers.

KENMARE Co. Kerry	18B3

Ardmore House Acclaimed
Killarney Road, Kenmare
☎ 064-41406 Fax 064-41406
Closed Dec-Feb
6 bedrs, all ensuite, TCF P 10 SB £25-£27 DB £36-£40
CC MC Visa ♿

KILKEE Co. Clare	18B1

Halpins Highly Acclaimed
Kilkee
☎ 065-905 6032 Fax 065-905 317
E-mail halpins@iol.ie

Highly acclaimed hotel and award winning Vittles restaurant, combines old world charm, fine food, vintage wine and modern comforts - overlooking old Victorian Kilkee. Close to Shannon airport, Killimer car ferry, Cliffs of Moher, The Burren and Loop Drive.
12 bedrs, all ensuite, TCF TV P 20 ⊞ DB £36-£45
CC MC Visa Amex DC

KILKENNY Co. Kilkenny	19E2

Chaplins Acclaimed
Castlecomer Road, Kilkenny
☎ 056-52236
Closed 23-29 Dec
6 bedrs, all ensuite, TCF TV P 7 SB £22 CC Visa

KILLARNEY Co. Kerry	18B3

Ashville Guest House Highly Acclaimed
Rock Road, Killarney
☎ 064-36405 Fax 064-36778
E-mail ashvillhouse@tinet.ie
Closed Dec-Jan

Killarney 207

Spacious, family-run guesthouse, 2 minutes walk from the town centre, situated on the main Tralee road (N22). Private car park. Comfortably furnished ensuite bedrooms. Your ideal touring base.
10 bedrs, all ensuite, TCF TV P 12 SB £25-£35 DB £36-£50 CC MC Visa

Earls Court House Highly Acclaimed
Woodlawn Junction, Muckross Road, Killarney
☎ 064-34009 Fax 064-34366
E-mail earls@tinet.ie
Closed Nov-10 Mar

Awarded RAC Small Hotel of the Year for Ireland 1998. 5 minutes walk to town centre. Country house ambience, antique furnishings. Individually themed bedrooms, full bathrooms, TV, phone. Private parking.
11 bedrs, all ensuite, TV P 15 Resid SB £38-£65 DB £57-£90 CC MC Visa

Foley's Townhouse Highly Acclaimed
23 High Street, Killarney
☎ 064-31217 Fax 064-34683
Closed Nov-5 Mar
28 bedrs, all ensuite, TCF TV P 60 ⋮⋮ 25 No children under 3 SB £49.50 DB £82.50 D £23 CC MC Visa Amex

Gleann Fia Country House Highly Acclaimed
Old Deer Park, Killarney
☎ 064-35035 Fax 064-35000
E-mail gleanfia@iol.ie
Closed 1 Dec-1 Mar

Idyllic secluded setting in 30 acres of mature woodlands. Private river walks, open peat fires, extensive breakfast menu. Gleann Fia - 'out on its own'.
17 bedrs, all ensuite, TCF TV P 25 SB £30-£40 DB £46-£60 CC MC Visa Amex

Kathleens Country House Highly Acclaimed
Tralee Road, Killarney
☎ 064-32810 Fax 064-32340
Closed 14 Nov-7 Mar
17 bedrs, all ensuite, TV P 20 No children under 5 Resid CC MC Visa Amex
See advert on this page

Kathleen's Country House

Kathleen's is a family run Irish Tourist Board 4 star registered guest house where traditional hospitality, combined with courteous personal attention, is a way of life. 17 rooms furnished in antique pine with private bathrooms, direct dial telephones, TV, radio, tea/coffee facilities. Your ideal golfing base or for touring Killarney Lake and Mountains, the Ring of Kerry, Dingle Bay, and Blarney.

Easy to get to... Hard to leave!
RAC "Guest House of Year" 1993.
Highly Acclaimed.

Tralee Road, Killarney, Co. Kerry
Tel: 353 64 32810 Fax: 353 64 32340

IRELAND

Killarney

Lohans Lodge Highly Acclaimed
Tralee Road, Killarney
064-33871 Fax 064-33871
Closed 10 Nov-10 Feb

Modern bungalow situated about three and a half miles from Killarney. All bedrooms are ensuite with colour TV and tea/coffee making facilities. Convenient centre for golfing and touring lakes and gardens. Golf and bus tours arranged.
5 bedrs, all ensuite, TCF TV P 10 No children under 6 DB £36-£37

Killarney Villa Acclaimed
Waterford Road (N72), Killarney
064-31878 Fax 064-31878
E-mail killarneyvilla@tinet.ie
Closed Nov-Easter
6 bedrs, all ensuite, TCF TV P 8 No children under 6 SB £20-£25 DB £35-£39 CC MC Visa

Purple Heather Listed
Gap of Dunloe, Beaufort, Killarney
064-44266 Fax 064-44266
E-mail purpleheather@tinet.ie
Closed 30 Oct-Mar

Set in a scenic area and offering electric blankets, hairdryers, tea/coffee, TV in bedrooms, pool room. Tennis, pony riding, golf, and fishing arranged, restaurant, Irish music only 1 km.
6 bedrs, 5 ensuite, 1 TCF TV P 6 SB £18-£23 DB £31-£36 HB £177-£187 D £12 CC MC Visa DC

Sliabh Lauchra House Listed
Loreto Road, Killarney
064-32012 Fax 064-32012
Closed Sep

A beautiful, award-winning house set in landscaped gardens one mile from the town centre, and adjacent to the National Park and lakes. All rooms are ensuite, with hair dryer and tea and coffee-making facilities. No children under 12.
6 bedrs, all ensuite, TCF P 6 No children under 12 SB £28 DB £36-£38

Park Lodge Awaiting Inspection
Cork Road, Killarney
064-31539 Fax 064-34892
20 bedrs, all ensuite, TCF TV P 22 CC MC Visa

Ross Castle Lodge Awaiting Inspection
Ross Road, Killarney
064-36942 Fax 064-36942
E-mail rosslodge@inkerry.com

Situated on the edge of Killarney town in a magical woodland setting bordering the lakes, National Park, and golf course. Large gardens, a walkers paradise.
4 bedrs, all ensuite, TCF TV P 8 No children DB £36-£50

Victoria House
Muckross Road, Killarney
064-35430 Fax 064-35439

Kinsale 209

Located in a scenic area at the gateway to the National Park (N71). Spacious bedrooms, all ensuite with TV and telephone. Varied breakfast menu. Ample parking
15 bedrs, all ensuite, TV P 15 CC MC Visa Amex DC

KILLINICK Co. Wexford 19F3

♦♦♦♦ Danby Lodge Highly Acclaimed
Sparkling Diamond
Rosslare Road, Killinick
053-58191 Fax 053-58191

Nestling in the heart of South County Wexford, Danby Lodge has rightfully earned for itself a reputation for excellence in cuisine and accommodation. Once the home of the painter Francis Danby, it bears all the hallmarks of a charming country residence
14 bedrs, all ensuite, TCF TV CC MC Visa Amex DC

KILLORGLIN Co. Kerry 18A3

Grove Lodge Highly Acclaimed
Killarney Road, Killorglin
066-976 1157 Fax 066-976 2330
10 bedrs, all ensuite, TCF TV P 14 SB £25-£40 DB £50-£72 CC MC Visa DC

KINSALE Co. Cork 18C4

♦♦♦ Deasys Highly Acclaimed
Long Quay House, Long Quay, Kinsale
021-774563 Fax 021-773201
Closed 1-27 Dec

A Georgian residence, which is ideally situated overlooking the inner harbour and yacht marina. Within walking distance of all Kinsale's gourmet restaurants and many tourist attractions.
7 bedrs, all ensuite, TCF TV P 3 SB £35-£45 DB £50-£60
CC MC Visa

Old Bank House Highly Acclaimed
11 Pearse Street, Kinsale
021-774075 Fax 021-774296
Closed Christmas

The Old Bank House is a Georgian residence with classic period furniture, orthopaedic beds and ultra modern bathrooms. Consistently voted one of the top 100 places to stay in Ireland.
17 bedrs, all ensuite, TV Resid SB £55-£95 DB £95-£120 CC MC Visa Amex

Rivermount House Highly Acclaimed
Knocknabinny, Kinsale
021-778033 Fax 021-778225
Closed 5 Nov-1 Feb
6 bedrs, all ensuite, TCF TV P 10 SB £20-£28 DB £38-£45

IRELAND

Knock

KNOCK Co. Mayo	16B4

Belmont Acclaimed
Knock
☎ 094-88122 Fax 094-88532
E-mail belmonthotel@tinet.ie
64 bedrs, all ensuite, TCF TV ♈ ▣ P 120 ⚙ 300 ⚐
SB £42-£57 DB £60-£90 HB £265-£315 D £20 CC MC Visa Amex DC 🌳 🎨 ♿

LARNE Co. Antrim	17F2

♦♦♦ **Derrin**
2 Prince's Gardens, Larne BT40 1RQ
☎ 01574-273269 Fax 01574-273269
Closed Christmas
6 bedrs, 4 ensuite, 1 ⇌ TCF TV ♈ P 3 CC MC Visa Amex

LETTERKENNY Co. Donegal	17D1

Hillcrest House Acclaimed
Lurgy Brack, Sligo Road, Letterkenny
☎ 074-22300 Fax 074-25137
Closed Christmas

Modern bungalow on N13 to Sligo, overlooking town and river. Rooms ensuite with TV and tea-making facilities. Private car park. Ideal touring base for Donegal and Northern Ireland.
6 bedrs, 5 ensuite, 1 ⇌ TCF TV P 10 SB £20-£30 DB £34-£36 CC MC Visa Amex

LIMERICK Co. Limerick	18C2

Clifton House Acclaimed
Ennis Road, Limerick
☎ 061-451166 Fax 061-451224
Closed 24 Dec-6 Jan
16 bedrs, all ensuite, TV P 22 CC MC Visa

NEW ROSS Co. Wexford	19E3

Woodlands House Highly Acclaimed
Carrigbyrne, Newbawn, New Ross
☎ 051-428287 Fax 051-428287
Closed 1 Dec-1 Feb

On Rosslare/Waterford road (N25), 35 minutes Rosslare ferry. Ideal base for Wexford, Waterford and Kilkenny. Recently refurbished, ensuite bedrooms with electric blankets, TV, complimentary tray. Snacks/light meals available. Parking.
5 bedrs, 4 ensuite, 1 ⇌ TCF TV P 7 No children under 5 SB £20 DB £36 CC MC Visa

Oakwood House Awaiting Inspection
Ring Road, Mountgarrett, New Ross
☎ 051-425494 Fax 051-425494
4 bedrs, all ensuite, TCF TV ⊠ P 6 No children under 6 SB £25 DB £38 CC MC Visa Amex

ORANMORE Co. Galway	18C1

Moorings Acclaimed
Main Street, Oranmore
☎ 091-790462 Fax 091-790462

The Moorings is an ideal base when on business or touring the Burren and Connemara. Amenities close by include golf, sailing, wind surfing, Renville Park and a language centre.
6 bedrs, all ensuite, TCF TV P 30 ⚙ 20 ⚐ Rest Resid SB £25-£35 DB £45-£50 D £19 CC MC Visa Amex ♿

Tramore 211

| PORTLAOISE Co. Laois | 19E1 |

♦♦♦♦♦ Ivyleigh House Highly Acclaimed
Little Gem
Warm Welcome, Sparkling Diamond
Bank Place, Portlaoise
☎ 0502-22081 Fax 0502-63343
E-mail ivyleigh@oceanfree.net

Ivyleigh, luxurious listed Georgian accommodation, excellent service and superb breakfast cuisine. Golf, Slieve Blooms, equestrian centre, fishing, and 100 yards from the train station. Art centre and theatre. Excellent base for touring Ireland.
4 bedrs, all ensuite, TCF TV ✍ P 6 No children under 8 SB £36-£45 DB £65-£70 CC Visa

♦♦♦♦ Chez Nous Highly Acclaimed
Kilminchy, Portlaiose
☎ 0502-21251
Closed 20 Dec-3 Jan
5 bedrs, all ensuite, ✍ P 8 No children under 8
SB £25-£35 DB £44-£50

| SNEEM Co. Kerry | 18A3 |

Tahilla Cove Country House Highly Acclaimed
Tahilla, Sneem
☎ 064-45204 Fax 064-45104
Closed mid Oct-Easter
9 bedrs, all ensuite, TV ⚁ P 20 ⚂ CC MC Visa Amex DC

| THOMASTOWN Co. Kilkenny | 19E2 |

♦♦♦ Belmore Country Home Acclaimed
Jerpoint Church, Thomastown
☎ 056-24228
E-mail teesdale@trailblazer.ie

Charming country home on family farm featuring a warm welcome, spacious ensuite rooms and own fishing for guests. Golf and many other activities and attractions locally, all year.
3 bedrs, all ensuite, ⚁ P 12 SB £25 DB £40 ☑ ⚂

| TRALEE Co. Kerry | 18B3 |

Barnagh Bridge Awaiting Inspection
Cappalogh, Camp, Tralee
☎ 066-713 0145 Fax 066-713 0299
E-mail mwarch@iol.ie
Closed 1 Nov-17 Mar
5 bedrs, all ensuite, TCF TV P 8 No children under 10
SB £28-£35 DB £36-£50 CC MC Visa Amex

Glenduff House Awaiting Inspection
Kielduff, Tralee
☎ 066-713 7105 Fax 066-713 7099
Closed 23-27 Dec
5 bedrs, all ensuite, TCF TV CC MC Visa

| TRAMORE Co. Waterford | 19E3 |

Glenorney Highly Acclaimed
Newrown, Tramore
☎ 051-381056 Fax 051-381103
6 bedrs, all ensuite, TCF TV ✍ P 8 CC MC Visa

Telephoning the Republic of Ireland

When telephoning the Republic of Ireland from the United Kingdom dial 00 353 and omit the initial 0 of the Irish code.

Prices are shown in Punts (£IR)

Waterford

WATERFORD Co. Waterford — 19E3

Diamond Hill Acclaimed
Milepost, Slieverue, Waterford
051-832855 Fax 051-832254
Closed 24-25 Dec

Country guest house set in national award winning gardens. All rooms ensuite with TV, phones, tea/coffee facilities. Recommended by Frommes, Foders, Michelin, RAC. Member of Premier Guest House and Les Routiers. Single supplement £5.
10 bedrs, all ensuite, TCF TV P 14 SB £27-£30 DB £44-£54 CC MC Visa

Villa Eildon Awaiting Inspection
Belmont Road, Rosslare Road, Ferrybank, Waterford
051-832174
Closed Nov-Apr
4 bedrs, 3 ensuite, 1 P 6 No children under 7
SB £26.50-£28.50 DB £37

WATERVILLE Co. Kerry — 18A3

Brookhaven Awaiting Inspection
New Line Road, Waterville
066-947 4431

WEXFORD Co. Wexford — 19F2

Darral House Highly Acclaimed
Spawell Road, Wexford
053-24264

Luxury accommodation close to town centre. Beautiful period house renovated to the highest standards in 1995. All rooms ensuite with tea/coffee facilities and television.
4 bedrs, all ensuite, TCF TV P 6 SB £25-£30 DB £40-£55
CC MC Visa

WICKLOW Co. Wicklow — 19F1

Old Coach House Awaiting Inspection
Vale of Avoca, Wicklow
0402-35408 Fax 0402-35720
E-mail coach_house@e-mail.com
6 bedrs, all ensuite, TCF TV P 10 Rest Resid
SB £32-£35 DB £25 HB £245-£250 D £16.50 CC MC Visa

---

for shopping guides...
www.WestOneWeb.com
...great bargains

Channel Islands & Isle of Man

Channel Islands

GUERNSEY 2A2

♦♦♦ Le Galaad
Warm Welcome, Sparkling Diamond
Rue Des Francais, Castel GY5 7FH
☎ 01481-57233 Fax 01481-53028
12 bedrs, all ensuite, TCF TV P 12 ⌑ Resid SB £22-£28 DB £44-£56 HB £189-£238 CC MC Visa 🏠

La Michele Awaiting Inspection
Les Hubits de Bas, St Martins GY4 6NB
☎ 01481-38065 Fax 01481-39492
Closed Nov-Mar
16 bedrs, all ensuite, TCF TV P 17 No children under 8 ⌑ Resid SB £25-£38 DB £50-£76 HB £210-£301 D £9 CC MC Visa Amex ⚡ ♿

Marine Awaiting Inspection
Well Road, St Peter Port GY1 1WS
☎ 01481-724978 Fax 01481-711729

An old granite-built Guernsey house with a sun-trap patio with sea views.
11 bedrs, all ensuite, TCF TV SB £16-£26.50 DB £32-£49 CC MC Visa JCB

JERSEY 2A2

♦♦♦♦ Bon Air
Warm Welcome, Sparkling Diamond
Coast Road, Pontac, St Clements JE2 6SE
☎ 01534-855324 Fax 01534-857801
Closed Nov-Feb
18 bedrs, all ensuite, TCF TV P 20 ⌑ Resid DB £48-£70 D £8.95 🎬

♦♦♦ Bryn-y-Mor
Route de la Haule, St Aubin's Bay JE3 8BA
☎ 01534-720295 Fax 01534-24262

Situated in St Aubin's Bay, 25 yards from miles of golden sand. Ensuite rooms, many with sea views. Pleasant gardens, sun terrace, cocktail bar. B&B from £20-£35. Dinner available from £18.50 table d'hote. Ample car parking.
14 bedrs, 12 ensuite, 2 ⇌ TCF TV 🐕 P 6 ⋮⋮ 20 ⌑ Rest Resid SB £20-£35 DB £40-£70 HB £180-£304 D £10.50 CC MC Visa Amex DC JCB

♦♦♦ Domino Central
6 Vauxhall Street, St Helier JE2 4TJ
☎ 01534-30360 Fax 01534-31546
E-mail domino@localdial.com
13 bedrs, 11 ensuite, 2 ⇌ TCF TV No children under 12 ⌑ Resid CC MC Visa Amex

Hotel Des Pierres Awaiting Inspection
Greve de Lecq Bay, St Ouen JE3 2DT
☎ 01534-481858 Fax 01534-485273
Closed 15 Dec-15 Jan

Small family run hotel delightfully situated in woodland, yet only a few yards from the beach.
16 bedrs, all ensuite, TCF TV P 15 ⌑ Resid SB £29-£34 DB £48-£58 HB £224-£245 D £9.85 CC MC Visa 🏠

Isle of Man 215

Millbrook House Awaiting Inspection
Rue De Trachy, Millbrook, St Helier JE2 3JN
☎ 01534-733036 Fax 01534-724317
Closed 5 Oct-19 Apr

Traditional house of character in 10 acres of own grounds, 1½ miles west of St Helier. Most rooms with views to sea offering peace and quiet.
27 bedrs, all ensuite, TCF TV ⏹ P 20 ⏣ Resid SB £28-£36 DB £56-£72 HB £228-£287 D £9 CC MC Visa Amex JCB ⏵

DOUGLAS 10A4

Modwena Awaiting Inspection
39-40 Loch Promenade, Douglas
☎ 01624-675728 Fax 01624-670954
Closed 1 May-30 Sep
32 bedrs, 17 ensuite, 2 ⏣ 3 ⏩ TCF TV ⏵ ⏹ ⏣ Resid
CC MC Visa DC ⏵

Rio Awaiting Inspection
Loch Promenade, Douglas IM1 2LY
☎ 01624-623491 Fax 01624-670966
14 bedrs, 12 ensuite, 1 ⏩ TCF TV ⏣ Resid SB £25-£26 DB £44-£46 HB £210-£220 D £12 CC MC Visa

ISLE OF MAN   CHANNEL ISLANDS

Distance Chart

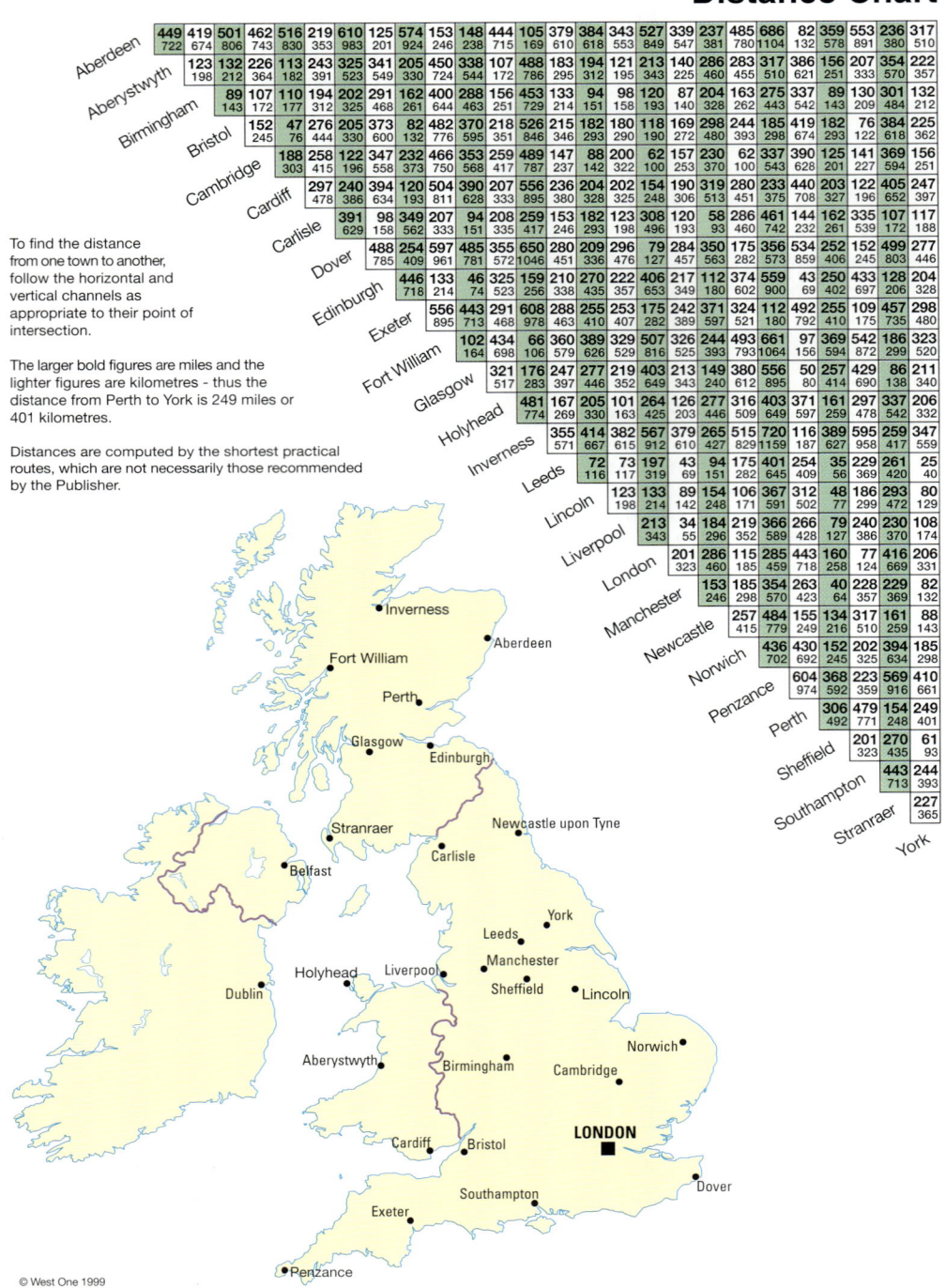

To find the distance from one town to another, follow the horizontal and vertical channels as appropriate to their point of intersection.

The larger bold figures are miles and the lighter figures are kilometres - thus the distance from Perth to York is 249 miles or 401 kilometres.

Distances are computed by the shortest practical routes, which are not necessarily those recommended by the Publisher.

	Aberdeen	Aberystwyth	Birmingham	Bristol	Cambridge	Cardiff	Carlisle	Dover	Edinburgh	Exeter	Fort William	Glasgow	Holyhead	Inverness	Leeds	Lincoln	Liverpool	London	Manchester	Newcastle	Norwich	Penzance	Perth	Sheffield	Southampton	Stranraer	York
Aberdeen		449/722	419/674	501/806	462/743	516/830	219/353	610/983	125/201	574/924	153/246	148/238	444/715	105/169	379/610	384/618	343/553	527/849	339/547	237/381	485/780	686/1104	82/132	359/578	553/891	236/380	317/510
Aberystwyth			123/198	132/212	226/364	113/182	243/391	325/523	341/549	205/330	450/724	107/172	488/786	183/295	194/312	121/195	213/343	140/225	286/460	283/455	317/510	386/621	156/251	207/333	354/570	132/357	
Birmingham				89/143	107/172	110/177	194/312	202/325	291/468	162/261	400/644	288/463	156/251	453/729	133/214	94/151	98/158	120/193	87/140	204/328	163/262	275/443	337/542	89/143	130/209	301/484	132/212
Bristol					152/245	47/76	276/444	205/330	373/600	82/132	482/776	370/595	218/351	526/846	215/346	182/293	180/290	118/190	169/272	298/480	244/393	185/298	419/674	182/293	76/122	384/618	225/362
Cambridge						188/303	258/415	122/196	347/558	232/373	466/750	353/568	259/417	489/787	147/237	88/142	200/322	62/100	157/253	230/370	62/100	337/543	390/628	125/201	141/227	369/594	156/251
Cardiff							297/478	240/386	394/634	120/193	504/811	390/628	207/333	556/895	236/380	204/328	202/325	154/248	190/306	319/513	280/451	233/375	440/708	203/327	122/196	405/652	247/397
Carlisle								391/629	98/158	349/562	207/333	94/151	208/335	259/417	153/246	182/293	123/198	308/496	120/193	58/93	286/460	461/742	144/232	162/261	335/539	107/172	117/188
Dover									488/785	254/409	597/961	485/781	355/572	650/1046	280/451	209/336	296/476	79/127	284/457	350/563	171/282	356/573	534/859	252/406	152/245	499/803	277/446
Edinburgh										446/718	133/214	46/74	325/523	159/256	210/338	270/435	222/357	406/653	217/349	112/180	374/602	559/900	43/69	250/402	433/697	128/206	204/328
Exeter											556/895	443/713	291/468	608/978	288/463	255/410	253/407	175/282	242/389	371/597	324/521	112/180	492/792	255/410	109/175	457/735	298/480
Fort William												102/164	434/698	66/106	360/579	389/626	329/529	507/816	326/525	244/393	493/793	661/1064	97/156	369/594	542/872	186/299	323/520
Glasgow													321/517	176/283	247/397	277/446	219/352	403/649	213/343	149/240	380/612	556/895	50/80	257/414	429/690	86/138	211/340
Holyhead														481/774	167/269	205/330	101/163	264/425	126/203	277/446	316/509	403/649	371/597	161/259	297/478	337/542	206/332
Inverness															355/571	414/667	382/615	567/912	379/610	265/427	515/829	720/1159	116/187	389/627	595/958	259/417	347/559
Leeds																72/116	73/117	197/319	43/69	94/151	175/282	401/645	254/409	35/56	229/369	261/420	25/40
Lincoln																	123/198	133/214	89/142	154/248	106/171	367/591	312/502	48/77	186/299	293/472	80/129
Liverpool																		213/343	34/55	184/296	219/352	366/589	266/428	79/127	240/386	230/370	108/174
London																			201/323	286/460	115/185	285/459	443/718	160/258	77/124	416/669	206/331
Manchester																				153/246	185/298	354/570	263/423	40/64	228/357	229/369	82/132
Newcastle																					257/415	484/779	155/249	134/216	317/510	161/259	88/143
Norwich																						436/702	430/692	152/245	202/325	394/634	185/298
Penzance																							604/974	368/592	223/359	569/916	410/661
Perth																								306/492	479/771	154/248	249/401
Sheffield																									201/323	270/435	61/93
Southampton																										443/713	244/393
Stranraer																											227/365

© West One 1999

Key to Maps

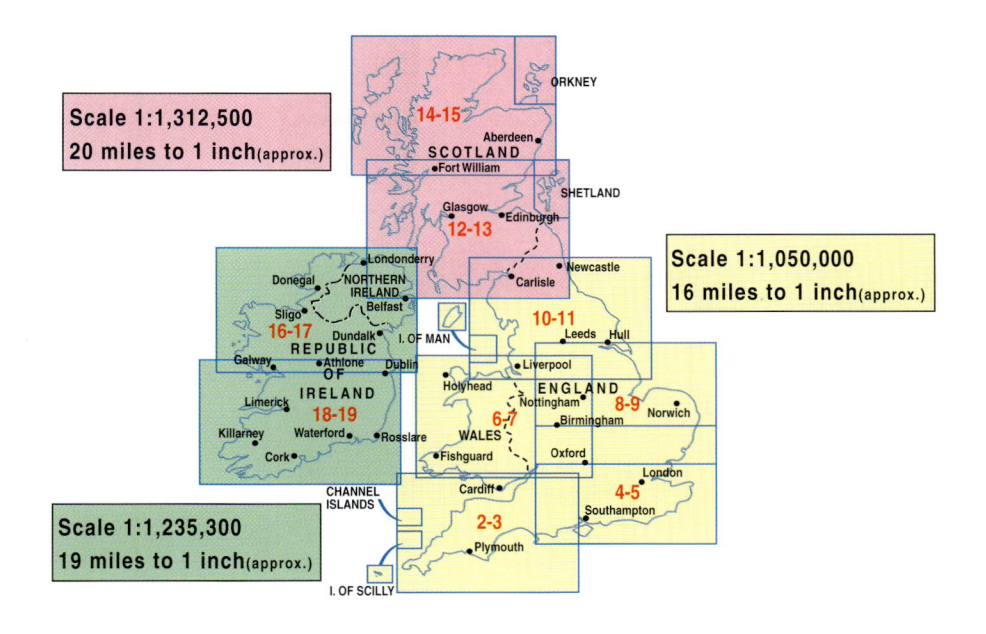

Scale 1:1,312,500
20 miles to 1 inch (approx.)

ORKNEY
14-15
SCOTLAND
Aberdeen
Fort William
SHETLAND
Glasgow
Edinburgh
12-13
Londonderry
Newcastle
Donegal
NORTHERN IRELAND
Carlisle
Sligo
Belfast
16-17
Dundalk
I. OF MAN
10-11
REPUBLIC
Leeds
Hull
Galway
Athlone
Dublin
OF
Liverpool
IRELAND
Holyhead
ENGLAND
18-19
Limerick
6-7
Nottingham
8-9
Norwich
Killarney
Waterford
Rosslare
WALES
Birmingham
Cork
Fishguard
Oxford
London
CHANNEL
Cardiff
4-5
ISLANDS
2-3
Southampton
Plymouth
I. OF SCILLY

Scale 1:1,050,000
16 miles to 1 inch (approx.)

Scale 1:1,235,300
19 miles to 1 inch (approx.)

Legend

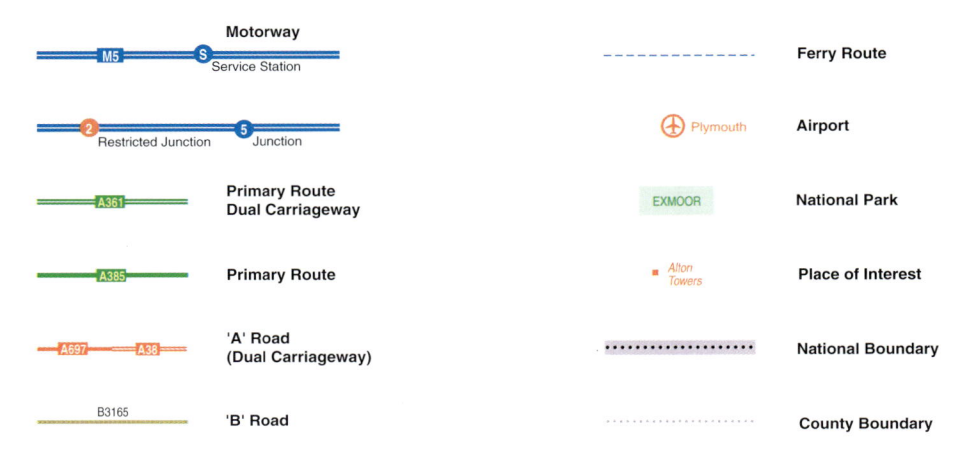

M5 S	Motorway / Service Station	- - - - - -	Ferry Route
2 5	Restricted Junction / Junction	⊕ Plymouth	Airport
A361	Primary Route Dual Carriageway	EXMOOR	National Park
A385	Primary Route	■ Alton Towers	Place of Interest
A697 A38	'A' Road (Dual Carriageway)	■■■■■■■■■■	National Boundary
B3165	'B' Road	....	County Boundary

© West One 1999

2
6
A
B
C
1
2
3
4
Broad Haven
Haverfordwest
Narberth
Ammanford
Skomer I.
Milford Haven
PEMBROKESHIRE
Pendine
Kidwelly
Kidwelly Castle
Pontardu
Dale
Neyland
Saundersfoot
St. Ann's Head
Pembroke Dock
Pembroke
Tenby
Carmarthen Bay
Burry Port
Llanelli
SWANSEA
Monastery
Caldey I.
The Mumbles
PEMBROKESHIRE COAST
NATIONAL PARK
St. Govan Head
Port Eynon
Oxwich Castle
St. Anne
Alderney
To Cork
L'Ancresse
St. Sampson
Herm
Catel
St. Saviour
St. Peter Port
St. Martin
Guernsey
Sark
Lundy
Ilfracombe
Woolacombe
Braunton
Barnstaple or Bideford Bay
Barnstaple
Channel Islands
Jersey
Rozel
St. Ouen
St. Lawrence
St. Peter
St. Saviour
Gorey
St. Brelade
St. Aubin
St. Helier
St. Clement
Hartland Point
Westward Ho!
Northam
Bideford
Hartland
Clovelly
Great Torrington
Torridge
Stratton
Bude
Holsworthy
Hatherleigh
Tamar
Okehampton
Boscastle
Tintagel
Launceston
Moretonhampstead
Camelford
Isles of Scilly
St. Mary's
Hugh Town
To Penzance
Port Isaac
BODMIN MOOR
DARTMOOR
Trevose Head
Padstow
Wadebridge
Two Bridges
Tavistock
Callington
Bodmin
Liskeard
Newquay
St. Columb Major
Restormel Castle
Lostwithiel
Plymouth
Trerice
CORNWALL
Saltash
Torpoint
Saltram
Mount Edgcumbe
PLYMOUTH
Perranporth
St. Agnes
Par
St. Austell
Fowey
Looe
Polperro
Mevagissey
Mevagissey Bay
Bigbury-on-Sea
St. Ives Bay
St. Ives
Redruth
Truro
Camborne
Chysauster Ancient Village
Hayle
Penryn
St. Mawes
St. Just
Penzance
Marazion
Falmouth
St. Michael's Mount
Helston
Falmouth Bay
Land's End
Mount's Bay
St. Keverne
Mullion
To St. Mary's
Lizard
Lizard Point
To Santander and Roscoff
To St Malo

3
Tredegar
Merthyr Tydfil
Hirwaun
Rhymney
Ebbw Vale
Blaenavon
Abertillery
Monmouthshire
Chepstow
Usk
Pontypool
Cwmbran
Caerleon
Newbridge
Bargoed
Gelligaer
Mountain Ash
Ystrad
Abercarn
Pontypridd
Caerphilly
Llantrisant
NEWPORT
Bridgend
Cowbridge
CARDIFF
Penarth
Barry
Vale of Glamorgan
Cardiff
Cinderford
Coleford
Newnham
Blakeney
Stonehouse
Painswick
Northleach
Burford
Cirencester
Fairford
Lechlade
Faringdon
Stroud
Nailsworth
Tetbury
Dursley
Cricklade
Highworth
Thornbury
Wotton-under-Edge
Malmesbury
SWINDON
Yate
Chipping Sodbury
Wootton Bassett
Wroughton
Avonmouth
Filton
Portishead
Mangotsfield
Kingswood
BRISTOL
Chippenham
Corsham
Avebury
Calne
Marlborough
Clevedon
Keynsham
Bath
Bradford-on-Avon
Melksham
Devizes
Trowbridge
Upavon
Weston-super-Mare
Bristol Channel
Mouth of the Severn
Severn
Mendip Hills
Cheddar
Midsomer Norton
Radstock
Frome
Westbury
Warminster
Salisbury Plain
Stonehenge
Amesbury
Bridgwater Bay
Burnham-on-Sea
Minehead
Dunster
Watchet
Williton
Exmoor National Park
Wells
Shepton Mallet
Glastonbury
Street
Somerset
Bridgwater
Bruton
Mere
Wilton
Salisbury
Gillingham
Wiveliscombe
Othery
Langport
Somerton
Castle Cary
Wincanton
Milverton
Taunton
Wellington
Bampton
Ilchester
Henstridge
Shaftesbury
Fordingbridge
Yeovil
Sherborne
Stalbridge
Ilminster
Crewkerne
Sturminster Newton
Tiverton
Hemyock
Chard
Blandford Forum
New Forest
Cullompton
Uffculme
Wimborne Minster
Ferndown
Ringwood
Beaminster
Dorset
Honiton
Axminster
Bridport
Puddletown
Bere Regis
Christchurch
New Milton
Exeter
Ottery St. Mary
Lyme Regis
Burton Bradstock
Dorchester
Wareham
POOLE
BOURNEMOUTH
Topsham
Seaton
Sidmouth
Budleigh Salterton
Exmouth
Chudleigh
Dawlish
Teignmouth
Weymouth
Swanage
Durlston Head
Corfe Castle
Lyme Bay
Isle of Portland
Fortuneswell
Bill of Portland
Newton Abbot
Torquay
Tor Bay
Paignton
Brixham
Kingswear
Start Point
To Guernsey, Jersey and St Malo
To Cherbourg
20 Miles
30 Kilometres
D
E
F
1
2
3
4

4
A
B
C
8
3
Coventry
Rugby
Kenilworth
Royal Leamington Spa
Henley-in-Arden
Warwick
Daventry
Wellingborough
Rushden
Irthlingborough
Higham Ferrers
Raunds
Northampton
Droitwich
Alcester
Southam
Weedon Bec
St. Neots
Worcester
Stratford-upon-Avon
Kineton
Ettington
Olney
Bedford
Newport Pagnell
Great Malvern
Pershore
Evesham
Towcester
Silverstone
Kempston
Middleton Cheney
Wolverton
Stony Stratford
Ampthill
Clophill
Upton-upon-Severn
Broadway
Chipping Campden
Shipston-on-Stour
Banbury
Adderbury
Brackley
Milton Keynes
Woburn
Moreton-in-Marsh
Deddington
Aynho
Buckingham
Letchworth
Hitchin
Tewkesbury
Winchcombe
Stow-on-the-Wold
Chipping Norton
Leighton Buzzard
Winslow
Luton
Cheltenham
Bicester
Whitchurch
Linslade
Dunstable
Bourton-on-the-Water
Charlbury
Whipsnade
Gloucester
Woodstock
Kidlington
Northleach
Aylesbury
Tring
Painswick
Burford
Witney
Thame
Wendover
Berkhamsted
Stonehouse
Oxford
Wheatley
Princes Risborough
Chesham
Hemel Hempstead
Stroud
Cirencester
Fairford
Amersham
Nailsworth
Abingdon
High Wycombe
Tetbury
Lechlade
Faringdon
Dorchester
Stokenchurch
Bushey
Rickmansworth
Cricklade
Wantage
Wallingford
Beaconsfield
Wotton-under-Edge
Malmesbury
Highworth
Harwell
Didcot
Marlow
Harrow
Chipping Sodbury
Swindon
Goring
Henley-on-Thames
Maidenhead
Slough
Ealing
Wootton Bassett
Wroughton
Lambourn
Pangbourne
Reading
Windsor
Eton
Chippenham
Corsham
Avebury
Marlborough
Egham
Bracknell
Staines
Calne
Hungerford
Newbury
Aldermaston
Wokingham
Sandhurst
Chertsey
Bradford-on-Avon
Melksham
Devizes
Burbage
Kingsclere
Hartley Wintney
Camberley
Weybridge
Woking
Farnborough
Leatherhead
Trowbridge
Upavon
Basingstoke
Hook
Fleet
Aldershot
Westbury
Salisbury Plain
Andover
Whitchurch
Farnham
Guildford
Warminster
Alton
Godalming
Milford
Cranleigh
Amesbury
Stockbridge
Hindhead
Haslemere
Mere
Wilton
Salisbury
Winchester
New Alresford
Liphook
Gillingham
Wincanton
Shaftesbury
Romsey
Chandler's Ford
Eastleigh
Petersfield
Billingshurst
Fordingbridge
Bishop's Waltham
Midhurst
Petworth
Pulborough
Stalbridge
Southampton
Horndean
Havant
Totton
Lyndhurst
Sturminster Newton
New Forest
Chichester
Arundel
Blandford Forum
Wimborne Minster
Ferndown
Ringwood
Fareham
Emsworth
Portsmouth
Fawley
Beaulieu
Gosport
South Hayling
Littlehampton
Bognor Regis
Lymington
New Milton
Cowes
East Cowes
East Wittering
Selsey
Bere Regis
Christchurch
Ryde
Wareham
Poole
Bournemouth
Yarmouth
Newport
Selsey Bill
The Needles
Sandown
Shanklin
Swanage
Ventnor
Weymouth
Durlston Head
St. Catherine's Point
Isle of Wight
The Solent
Southampton Water
To Guernsey, Jersey and St Malo
To Cherbourg
To Santander and Bilbao
To St Malo
To Caen
To Le Havre
Wiltshire
Hampshire
Oxfordshire
Northamptonshire
Buckinghamshire
Bedfordshire
Cotswolds
Chiltern Hills
Thames
Avon

5
9
D
E
F
1
2
3
4
SUFFOLK
ESSEX
KENT
NORTH DOWNS
THE WEALD
EAST SUSSEX
Ives
Soham
Mildenhall
Cottenham
Burwell
Histon
Newmarket
Bury St. Edmunds
Ixworth
Eye
Framlingham
Leiston
Saxmundham
Aldeburgh
Cambridge
Stowmarket
Needham Market
Wickham Market
Ickworth House
Great Shelford
Kentwell Hall
Lavenham
IPSWICH
Woodbridge
Orford
Orford Ness
Melbourn
Haverhill
Royston
Saffron Walden
Audley End
Sudbury
Hadleigh
Bawdsey
East Bergholt
Flatford Mill
Shotley Gate
Felixstowe
Manningtree
Harwich
Buntingford
Halstead
Stansted
Great Dunmow
Braintree
Colchester
Bishop's Stortford
Coggeshall
Marks Tey
Wivenhoe
The Naze
Walton on the Naze
Frinton-on-Sea
Holland-on-Sea
Clacton-on-Sea
Kelvedon
Witham
Brightlingsea
Tiptree
West Mersea
Mersea I.
Ware
Harlow
Hoddesdon
Waltham Abbey
Epping
Chipping Ongar
Chelmsford
Maldon
Loughton
Billericay
Brentwood
Wickford
Burnham-on-Crouch
Foulness I.
Rayleigh
Southend
SOUTHEND-ON-SEA
Shoeburyness
BARKING
Basildon
Coryton
Canvey Island
Thames Estuary
Grays
Tilbury
BEXLEY
Dartford
Gravesend
Grain
Sheerness
Isle of Sheppey
Leysdown on Sea
Whitstable
Herne Bay
Margate
Cliftonville
North Foreland
Broadstairs
Ramsgate
Rochester
Chatham
Rainham
Gillingham
Sittingbourne
Faversham
Canterbury
Kent International
Richborough Castle
Sandwich
Deal
Walmer
BROMLEY
Caterham
Sevenoaks
Wrotham
Maidstone
Leeds Castle
Charing
Chartwell
Ightham Mote
Godstone
Edenbridge
Tonbridge
Southborough
Penshurst Place
East Grinstead
Royal Tunbridge Wells
Ashford
Eurotunnel Terminal
South Foreland
Dover
Folkestone
Hythe
Calais
Strait of Dover
To Oostende
Channel Tunnel
Crowborough
Cranbrook
Sissinghurst
Tenterden
Hawkhurst
Rother
Haywards Heath
Uckfield
Heathfield
Burgess Hill
New Romney
Lydd
Rye
Battle
Dungeness
Baldslow
Lewes
Hailsham
Hastings
Bexhill
BRIGHTON
Newhaven
Pevensey
Polegate
Seaford
Eastbourne
Beachy Head
Boulogne
To Dieppe
To Göteborg
To Esbjerg
To Hamburg
To Hoek van Holland
0 20 Miles
0 30 Kilometres
M11
M25
M20
M26
M2
A12
A14
A120
A13
A2
A20
A21
A28
A259

A
B
C
1
2
3
4
2
20 Miles
30 Kilometres
To Dublin & Dun Laoghaire
To Rosslare
Carmel Head
Anglesey
Amlwch
Moelfre
Holyhead (Caergybi)
Holy I.
Dyffryn
Rhosneigr
Llangefni
Beaumaris
Beaumaris Castle
Menai Bridge
Bangor
Bethesda
Menai Strait
Caernarfon
Dinorwic Slate Quarry
Great Ormes Head
Llandudno
Rhos-on-Sea
Colwyn Bay
Conwy Bay
Conwy
Penmaenmawr
Bodnant Gdns.
CONWY
Capel Curig
Gwydir Castle
Llanrwst
Betws-y-coed
Caernarfon Bay
Blaenau Ffestiniog
Ffestiniog
Penrhyndeudraeth
Porthmadog
Criccieth
Nefyn
Pwllheli
Aberdaron
Abersoch
Bardsey I.
Tremadog Bay
Harlech Castle
Harlech
Bala
SNOWDONIA NATIONAL PARK
L. Vyrnwy
GWYNEDD
Dolgellau
Barmouth
Dinas-Mawddwy
Mallwyd
Llwyngwril
Tywyn
Machynlleth
Aberdyfi
Borth
MOUNTAINS
Cardigan Bay
Aberystwyth
Llywernog Silver-Lead Mine
Ponterwyd
Devil's Bridge
WALES
Rhayader
CAMBRIAN
Aberaeron
New Quay
Tregaron
CEREDIGION
Llangranog
Aberporth
Cemaes Head
Lampeter
PEMBROKESHIRE COAST NATIONAL PARK
Strumble Head
Cardigan
Newport
Goodwick
Fishguard
MYNYDD PRESELI
Cenarth Fishing Museum
Newcastle Emlyn
Teifi
Dolaucothi Roman Gold Mine
Llandovery
Llanwrda
St. David's Head
St. David's
Ramsey I.
PEMBROKESHIRE
CARMARTHENSHIRE
Scolton Manor
Haverfordwest
St. Bride's Bay
Broad Haven
Carmarthen
Dynevor Castle
Llandeilo
Carreg Cennen Castle
BRECON BEACONS NATIONAL PARK
Towy
St. Clears
Narberth
Ammanford
Skomer I.
Milford Haven
Neyland
Dale
Pendine
Kidwelly
Kidwelly Castle
Pontardulais
Pontardawe
Saundersfoot
St. Ann's Head
Pembroke Dock
Pembroke
Tenby
Monastery
Caldey I.
Carmarthen Bay
Burry Port
Llanelli
SWANSEA
The Mumbles
Port Talbot
NEATH PORT TALBOT
Neath
Maesteg
St. Govan Head
A5
A55
A487
A470
A499
A497
A40
A48
A4076
A477
A4075
A4139
A478
A485
A482
A484
A486
A475
A4120
A44
A493
A494
A496
A498
A4085
A4086
A4212
A5025
A4080
A547
A548
A483
A474
A4069
A4068
A4067
A4109
A465
A4066
A4107
A4118
A4063
A476
M4
B5109
B5111
B5112
B5110
B4222
B4419
B4366
B4418
B4417
B4354
B4411
B4413
B4391
B4407
B4573
B4405
B4403
B4518
B4577
B4343
B4337
B4342
B4333
B4570
B4571
B4299
B4310
B4302
B4337
B4331
B4313
B4330
B4329
B4327
B4314
B4328
B4312
B4306
B4317
B4320
B5106
B5381
B5384
© West One 1999

7
MANCHESTER
Crosby
Kirkby
ST. HELENS
Atherton
Leigh
Newton-le-Willows
Salford
Ashton-under-Lyne
Stocksbridge
Mexborough
Rotherham
SHEFFIELD
Maltby
Hoylake
BIRKENHEAD
LIVERPOOL
WARRINGTON
Widnes
Runcorn
Mersey
Altrincham
Lymm
STOCKPORT
Cheadle
Hyde
Glossop
Marple
New Mills
Whaley Bridge
Bramhall
Wilmslow
Knutsford
Alderley Edge
Macclesfield
Buxton
PEAK DISTRICT
NATIONAL PARK
Dronfield
Eckington
Staveley
Chesterfield
Bolsover
Neston
Ellesmere Port
Frodsham
Northwich
Holywell
Flint
Queensferry
Mold
Hawarden
Chester
Buckley
Tarporley
Winsford
Middlewich
Sandbach
Alsager
Congleton
Biddulph
Leek
Bakewell
Matlock
Clay Cross
Alfreton
Sutton
Kirkby
Ripley
Wirksworth
Belper
Heanor
Ruthin
Hope
Moss
Wrexham
Overton
Nantwich
Crewe
Kidsgrove
Tunstall
Burslem
Hanley
Newcastle-under-Lyme
Keele
STOKE-ON-TRENT
Longton
Cheadle
Alton Towers
Ashbourne
Ilkeston
Beeston
DERBY
Llangollen
Chirk
Whitchurch
Woore
Market Drayton
Stone
Uttoxeter
Sudbury
Burton upon Trent
Castle Donington
Melbourne
Long
Oswestry
Ellesmere
Whittington
Wem
Hodnet
Eccleshall
Stafford
Llanfyllin
ENGLAND
Newport
Penkridge
Rugeley
Swadlincote
Ashby-de-la-Zouch
Coalville
Shrewsbury
Wellington
TELFORD
Shifnal
Cannock
Lichfield
Welshpool (Y Trallwng)
Ironbridge
Brownhills
Aldridge
Tamworth
Much Wenlock
WOLVERHAMPTON
WALSALL
SUTTON COLDFIELD
Atherstone
Hinckley
Montgomery (Trefaldwyn)
WEST BROMWICH
DUDLEY
Nuneaton
Bedworth
Newtown (Y Drenewydd)
Lydham
Bishop's Castle
Church Stretton
Bridgnorth
Halesowen
BIRMINGHAM
Stourbridge
Hagley
Craven Arms
Clun
Cleobury Mortimer
Kidderminster
Bewdley
Solihull
COVENTRY
Rugby
Bromfield
Ludlow
Tenbury Wells
Stourport-on-Severn
Bromsgrove
Redditch
Kenilworth
Knighton
Royal Leamington Spa
Henley-in-Arden
WARWICK
Presteigne
Woofferton
Droitwich
New Radnor
Leominster
Alcester
Southam
Kington
Bromyard
Worcester
STRATFORD-UPON-AVON
Eardisley
Great Malvern
Pershore
Kineton
Ettington
Evesham
Hay-on-Wye
Hereford
Ledbury
Upton-upon-Severn
Broadway
Chipping Campden
Shipston-on-Stour
Banbury
Llyswen
Moreton-in-Marsh
Adderbury
Deddington
Tewkesbury
BLACK MOUNTAINS
Portrilas
Ross-on-Wye
Newent
Winchcombe
Cheltenham
Stow-on-the-Wold
Chipping Norton
Charlbury
Huntley
Mitcheldean
GLOUCESTER
Bourton-on-the-Water
Woodstock
Abergavenny
Monmouth (Trefynwy)
Cinderford
Northleach
Blaenavon
Newnham
Painswick
Burford
Witney
Ebbw Vale
Abertillery
Coleford
Blakeney
Stonehouse
Cirencester
OXFORD
Usk
Lydney
Stroud
Fairford
Pontypool
Cwmbran
Chepstow
Nailsworth
Tetbury
Cricklade
Faringdon
Abercarn
Caerleon
Thornbury
Highworth
Wantage
NEWPORT
Wotton-under-Edge
Malmesbury
SWINDON
COTSWOLDS

8
11
BRADFORD
Halifax
Brighouse
Elland
HUDDERSFIELD
Dewsbury
Wakefield
Castleford
Knottingley
Pontefract
Goole
Barton-upon-Humberside
New Holland
Winterton
Scunthorpe
Thorne
Crowle
Hatfield
Adwick le Street
Bentley
Doncaster
Belton
Brigg
Caistor
Kirton in Lindsey
Accrington
Todmorden
Rochdale
Holmfirth
BARNSLEY
Middleton
OLDHAM
MANCHESTER
Salford
Ashton-under-Lyne
Stocksbridge
Mexborough
Rawmarsh
Rotherham
Conisbrough
Tickhill
Bawtry
Maltby
Hyde
Glossop
Marple
PEAK DISTRICT NATIONAL PARK
SHEFFIELD
Sale
Cheadle
STOCKPORT
New Mills
Bramhall
Whaley Bridge
Wilmslow
Knutsford
Alderley Edge
Dinnington
Eckington
Dronfield
Staveley
Worksop
East Retford
Gainsborough
Market Rasen
Lincoln
Wragby
Buxton
Macclesfield
Bakewell
Chesterfield
Bolsover
Ollerton
Boughton
Mansfield
Mansfield Woodhouse
MANSFIELD
Sutton in Ashfield
Kirkby in Ashfield
Clay Cross
Alfreton
Matlock
Wirksworth
Congleton
Alsager
Biddulph
Leek
Tunstall
Burslem
Hanley
STOKE-ON-TRENT
Longton
Cheadle
Swinderby
Newark-on-Trent
Southwell
Woodhall Spa
Cranwell
Sleaford
Ripley
Hucknall
Belper
Heanor
Arnold
Carlton
Bingham
NOTTINGHAM
West Bridgford
Ilkeston
Beeston
Long Eaton
Ashbourne
DERBY
Castle Donington
Melbourne
Uttoxeter
Sudbury
Stone
Eccleshall
Stafford
Burton upon Trent
Swadlincote
Grantham
Croxton Kerrial
Corby Glen
Bourne
Shepshed
Loughborough
Melton Mowbray
Cottesmore
Market Deeping
ENGLAND
Penkridge
Rugeley
Ashby-de-la-Zouch
Coalville
Mountsorrel
Syston
Thurmaston
Oakham
Stamford
Cannock
Lichfield
Shifnal
Brownhills
Aldridge
Tamworth
LEICESTER
Oadby
Wigston
Duddington
Uppingham
Wansford
WALSALL
SUTTON COLDFIELD
Atherstone
Hinckley
WEST BROMWICH
DUDLEY
Nuneaton
Bedworth
Market Harborough
Corby
Desborough
Oundle
Stilton
Halesowen
Stourbridge
Hagley
BIRMINGHAM
Lutterworth
COVENTRY
Rugby
Husband's Bosworth
Rothwell
Kettering
Thrapston
Kidderminster
Solihull
Naseby
Burton Latimer
Raunds
Irthlingborough
Higham Ferrers
Rushden
Godmanchester
Bromsgrove
Redditch
Kenilworth
Royal Leamington Spa
Wellingborough
Henley-in-Arden
WARWICK
Daventry
Droitwich
Alcester
Southam
Weedon Bec
NORTHAMPTON
St. Neots
Worcester
STRATFORD-UPON-AVON
Roade
Olney
Bedford
Kineton
Ettington
Towcester
Newport Pagnell
Kempston
Great Malvern
Pershore
Evesham
Middleton Cheney
Silverstone
Stony Stratford
Wolverton
Ampthill
Clophill
Shipston-on-Stour
Banbury
Brackley
MILTON KEYNES
Woburn
Letchworth
Upton-upon-Severn
Broadway
Chipping Campden
Adderbury
Deddington
Aynho
Buckingham
Leighton Buzzard
Hitchin
Tewkesbury
Moreton-in-Marsh
Winchcombe
Stow-on-the-Wold
Chipping Norton
Bicester
Winslow
Whitchurch
Linslade
Dunstable
LUTON
Cheltenham
GLOUCESTER
Bourton-on-the-Water
Charlbury
Woodstock
Kidlington
Whipsnade
Harpenden
Northleach
Aylesbury
Tring
St. Albans
A
B
C
4
7
1
2
3

D
E
F
1
2
3
4
0
20 Miles
0
30 Kilometres
Easington
Spurn Head
Estuary
North
Somercotes
Mablethorpe
Sutton on Sea
Alford
Spilsby
Skegness
Wainfleet
All Saints
Gibraltar Point
To Rotterdam and Zeebrugge
The
Wash
Hunstanton
Wells-next-the-Sea
Blakeney
Sheringham
Cromer
Holt
Burnham
Market
Walsingham
Abbey
North Walsham
Sandringham
House
Sandringham
Fakenham
Blickling Hall
Aylsham
Reepham
Stalham
NORFOLK
BROADS
Holbeach
Long Sutton
King's Lynn
Wroxham
Winterton-on-Sea
Norwich
Caister-on-Sea
East Dereham
Swaffham
Acle
Wisbech
NORWICH
Great Yarmouth
Downham
Market
NORFOLK
Oxborough Hall
Guyhirn
Stoke Ferry
Watton
Wymondham
Hopton
Corton
March
Methwold
Attleborough
Mundford
Beccles
Lowestoft
Great Ouse
Bungay
Grime's
Graves
Brandon
Harleston
Littleport
Thetford
Waveney
Diss
Ely
Halesworth
Southwold
Soham
Mildenhall
Eye
Ixworth
Cottenham
Burwell
Histon
Newmarket
Bury St. Edmunds
Saxtead Green Post Mill
Framlingham
Castle
Framlingham
Saxmundham
Leiston
Cambridge
Ickworth
House
Stowmarket
SUFFOLK
Aldeburgh
Wickham
Market
Needham
Market
Cambridge
Great Shelford
Kentwell Hall
Lavenham
Orford
Woodbridge
Orford Ness
To Göteborg
To Esbjerg
IPSWICH
Melbourn
Haverhill
Royston
Saffron Walden
Audley
End
Sudbury
Hadleigh
Bawdsey
To Hamburg
East
Bergholt
Shotley
Gate
Felixstowe
Flatford Mill
Manningtree
Harwich
To Hoek van Holland
Buntingford
Halstead
Stansted
Colchester
The Naze
Great
Dunmow
Braintree
5
Stansted
Wivenhoe
Walton on the Naze
Bishop's
Stortford
Frinton-on-Sea
Kelvedon
Brightlingsea
Holland-on-Sea
Ware
Witham
Tiptree
West Mersea
Clacton-on-Sea
ESSEX
THE FENS
M11
A149
A148
A1065
A47
A140
A11
A12
A14
A134
A143
A1101
A10
A142
A120
A131
A133
A1067
A146
A1151
A1062
A1064
A1075
A1066
A1088
A1122
A1092
A1071
A1124
A1017
A137
A1094
A1120
A1152
A144
A145
A52
A158
A1104
A1028
A157
A1123
A1307
A505
A1184
A130
B1145
B1135
B1077
B1078
B1159
B1149
B1145
B1150
B1140
B1332
B1134
B1113
B1114
B1111
B1123
B1117
B1116
B1118
B1122
B1083
B1063
B1061
B1053
B1054
B1038
B1051
B1057
B1508
B1068
B1080
B1456
B1414
B1025
B1022
B1058
B1115
B1102
B1104
B1382
B1112
B1386
B1106
B1108
B1160
B1098
B1454
B1155
B1153
B1105
B1355
B1388
B1354
B1110
B1146
B1147
B1200
B1196
B1195
B1359

Parts of the M62, M63 & M66 are forming the new M60 Manchester Outer Ring Road with renumbered junctions. Work is in progress.

11
To Esbjerg
D
E
F
1
2
3
4
0
20 Miles
30 Kilometres
Newbiggin-by-the-Sea
Ashington
Blyth
Whitley Bay
Tynemouth
NEWCASTLE UPON TYNE
South Shields
Jarrow
Boldon
TYNE AND WEAR
SUNDERLAND
Washington
Houghton le Spring
Seaham
Hetton-le-Hole
Easington
Horden
Peterlee
Hartlepool
Spennymoor
Sedgefield
TEESSIDE
Billingham
Redcar
Saltburn-by-the-Sea
Stockton-on-Tees
MIDDLESBROUGH
Eston
Loftus
Darlington
Guisborough
Thornaby-on-Tees
Whitby
Teesside
Stokesley
Robin Hood's Bay
NORTH YORK MOORS
NORTH YORK MOORS NATIONAL PARK
Northallerton
NORTH
Scalby
Scarborough
Kirkbymoorside
Thirsk
Rievaulx Abbey
Helmsley
Pickering
Filey
YORKSHIRE
Hunmanby
Flamborough Head
Easingwold
Castle Howard
Malton
Norton
Boroughbridge
Aldborough Roman Town
Kirkham Priory
Burton Agnes Hall
Bridlington
Bridlington Bay
YORKSHIRE WOLDS
Fridaythorpe
Great Driffield
Knaresborough
YORK
Stamford Bridge
Hornsea
Wetherby
Harewood House
Tadcaster
Pocklington
EAST RIDING OF YORKSHIRE
Market Weighton
Beverley
Leeds/Bradford
LEEDS
Selby
North Cave
KINGSTON UPON HULL
Howden
South Cave
Hedon
Withernsea
Rothwell
Castleford
Knottingley
Goole
Barton-upon-Humberside
New Holland
Patrington
Humber
Easington
WEST YORKSHIRE
Wakefield
Pontefract
Normanby Hall
Winterton
Immingham
Spurn Head
Adwick le Street
Thorne
Crowle
Scunthorpe
NORTH LINCOLNSHIRE
Grimsby
Cleethorpes
BARNSLEY
Hatfield
Humberside
Estuary
Bentley
Brigg
Mexborough
Doncaster
Belton
Caistor
To Rotterdam and Zeebrugge
Rawmarsh
Conisbrough
Kirton in Lindsey
Trent
North Somercotes
Rotherham
Bawtry
Maltby
Tickhill
Old Hall
LINCOLNSHIRE
SHEFFIELD
Gainsborough
Louth
Market Rasen
Mablethorpe
Dinnington
Sutton on Sea
Eckington
East Retford
Wragby
Alford
Dronfield
Worksop
Staveley
Bolsover Castle
NOTTINGHAMSHIRE
Lincoln
Horncastle
LINCOLNSHIRE WOLDS
8
© West One 1999

Muck
Point of Ardnamurchan
Glenfinnan
Corpach
Bridge
Fort William
Ben Nevis
Caledonian Canal
14
Acharacle
Corran
Onich
Kinlochleven
Kinloch Rannoch
Loch Rannoch
Coll
Tobermory
Glencoe
GRAMPIAN
Tiree
Sound of Mull
Loch Linnhe
Portnacroish
Lochaline
Salen
Ulva
Mull
Craignure
Lismore
Connel
Bridge of Orchy
Loch Etive
Oban
Taynuilt
Lochawe
Clifton
Killin
Loch Tay
Iona
Fionnphort
Bunessan
Ardanaiseig Gardens
Crianlarich
Lochearnhead
Comrie
Kilninver
ARGYLL AND BUTE
Firth of Lorn
Seil
Luing
Loch Awe
Kilmelford
Ardlui
L. Katrine
Callander
Inveraray
Scarba
Colonsay
Scalasaig
Craignish Castle
Kilmartin
Furnace
Arrochar
Tarbet
Inchmahome Priory
Doune
Loch Lomond
Aberfoyle
STIRLING
Kippen
Luss
Drymen
Balfron
Ardlussa
Lochgilphead
Loch Fyne
Younger Botanic Gardens
Coulport
Garelochhead
Helensburgh
Alexandria
Dumbarton
Milngavie
Kilsyth
Kirkintilloch
Jura
Sound of Jura
Castle Sween
Dunoon
Gourock
Greenock
Port Glasgow
Clydebank
Bishopbriggs
Port Askaig
Feolin Ferry
Craighouse
Tighnabruaich
Tarbert
Portavadie
Wemyss Bay
Rothesay
Johnstone
Paisley
GLASGOW
Islay
Bridgend
Kennacraig
Largs
Kilbirnie
Barrhead
East Kilbride
Hamilton
Portnahaven
Claonaig
Bute
Millport
Beith
Dalry
Clachan
Lochranza
West Kilbride
Stewarton
Strathaven
Port Ellen
Arminish
Gigha
Tayinloan
KINTYRE
Kilbrannan Sound
Arran
Ardrossan
Saltcoats
Kilwinning
Stevenston
Irvine
Kilmarnock
Darvel
Galston
Mull of Oa
Brodick Castle
Brodick
Glenbarr
Lamlash
Troon
Prestwick
Mauchline
Blackwaterfoot
Holy I.
Firth of Clyde
Ayr
Muirkirk
0
20 Miles
0
30 Kilometres
Campbeltown
Holmhead
Cumnock
New Cumnock
Rathlin
Culzean Castle
Southend
Fair Head
Mull of Kintyre
Sanda
Maybole
Crossraguel Abbey
Dalmellington
Ballycastle
Ailsa Craig
Girvan
SOUTH AYRSHIRE
Carsphairn
Moniaive
Carleton Castle
Ballymoney
Glenariff
Garron Point
North Channel
Ballantrae
Barrhill
Bargrennan
Carnlough
Milleur Point
Kilrea
New Galloway
Kirkcolm
Cairnryan
Newton Stewart
Ballymena
ANTRIM
Larne
Island Magee
Stranraer
Glenluce Abbey
Glenluce
Gatehouse of Fleet
Threave Castle
Portpatrick
Sandhead
Wigtown
Kirkcudbright
Randalstown
Ballyclare
Carrickfergus
Whitehead
Luce Bay
Antrim
Belfast Lough
Port William
Wigtown Bay
Lough Neagh
Belfast International
Newtownabbey
Bangor
Logan Gardens
Drummore
Whithorn
Isle of Whithorn
Holywood
Donaghadee
BELFAST
Belfast City
Newtownards
Mount Stewart
Mull of Galloway
Burrow Head
16
Lisburn
Dundonald
Comber
Craigavon
Lurgan
Portadown
Saintfield
Strangford Lough

13
15
10
D
E
F
1
2
3
4
0
20 Miles
0
30 Kilometres
SHETLAND
Shetland
Islands
Mainland
Haroldswick
Unst
Gutcher
Fetlar
Mid Yell
Yell
Isbister
Ulsta
Out Skerries
Hillswick
Toft
Sullom
St. Magnus Bay
Papa Stour
Muckle Roe
Voe
Whalasay
Sandness
Lerwick
Scalloway
Bressay
To Bergen & Torshavn
Easter Quarff
Sumburgh
Sumburgh Head
To Stromness
To Fair Isle
Clova
Edzell Castle
Brechin
Kirriemuir
ANGUS
Montrose
Lunan Bay
Kirkmichael
Bridge of Cally
Alyth
Forfar
Blairgowrie
Rattray
Glamis
Glamis Castle
Dunkeld
Meigle
Coupar Angus
Arbroath
DUNDEE
Carnoustie
Buddon Ness
Perth
Newport-on-Tay
Firth of Tay
Newburgh
Cupar
St. Andrews
Auchtermuchty
Ladybank
Fife Ness
Crail
Kilrenny
Anstruther
Pittenweem
Upper Largo
Leslie
Markinch
Kinross
Glenrothes
Leven
Methil
Buckhaven
L. Leven
Cowdenbeath
Dunfermline
Kirkcaldy
Burntisland
Inverkeithing
S. Queensferry
Firth of Forth
North Berwick
Tantallon Castle
Dunbar
Bo'ness
EDINBURGH
Linlithgow
Musselburgh
Tranent
Haddington
East Linton
Livingston
Dalkeith
Lasswade
Loanhead
Cockburnspath
Penicuik
Ayton
Eyemouth
Duns
Berwick-upon-Tweed
Lauder
Carnwath
Stow
Greenlaw
Lindisfarne Castle
Holy I.
Peebles
Galashiels
Coldstream
Tweed
Biggar
Broughton
Melrose
Dryburgh Abbey
Kelso
Belford
Bamburgh
Bamburgh Castle
Traquair House
Innerleithen
Melrose Abbey
Selkirk
St. Boswells
Kelso Abbey
Wooler
UPLANDS
BORDERS
Teviot
Jedburgh
Hawick
CHEVIOT HILLS
Alnwick
NORTHUMBERLAND
Amble
Moffat
Rothbury
Beattock
Felton
NATIONAL
PARK
Hermitage Castle
Kielder Water
Otterburn
Morpeth
Newbiggin-by-the-Sea
Ashington
Lockerbie
Langholm
Bedlington
Blyth
Lochmaben
Lochmaben Castle
Canonbie
Whitley Bay
Tynemouth
Ponteland
Housesteads
Newcastle
Gosforth
NEWCASTLE UPON TYNE
South Shields
Longtown
Haltwhistle
Lanercost Priory
Irthing
Caerlaverock Castle
Annan
Gretna
Carlisle
Brampton
Haydon Bridge
Hexham
Corbridge
Tyne
Prudhoe
Blaydon
Gateshead
Jarrow
Boldon
TYNE AND WEAR
SUNDERLAND
Allendale Town
Consett
Stanley
Washington
Houghton le Spring
Silloth
Wigton
Thursby
Eden
Chester-le-Street
Seaham
Easington
Hetton-le-Hole
Alston
DURHAM
Horden
Aspatria
Peterlee
Stanhope
Tow Law
Crook
Maryport
Bothel
Hartlepool
Spennymoor
Wear
Derwent
Cockermouth
Penrith
Sedgefield
Bishop Auckland
TEESSIDE
CUMBRIAN
Newton Aycliffe
Redcar
Middleton in Teesdale
Billingham
Stockton-on-Tees
MIDDLESBROUGH
Saltburn-by-the-Sea
Keswick
Castlerigg Stone Circle
Ullswater
Appleby-in-Westmorland
Barnard Castle
Darlington
Eston
Guisborough
Cleator Moor
MOUNTAINS
Shap
Shap Abbey
Brough
Thornaby-on-Tees
Teesside
Egremont
Stockesley
M90
M9
M6
A1(M)
A194(M)
A66(M)
A74(M)

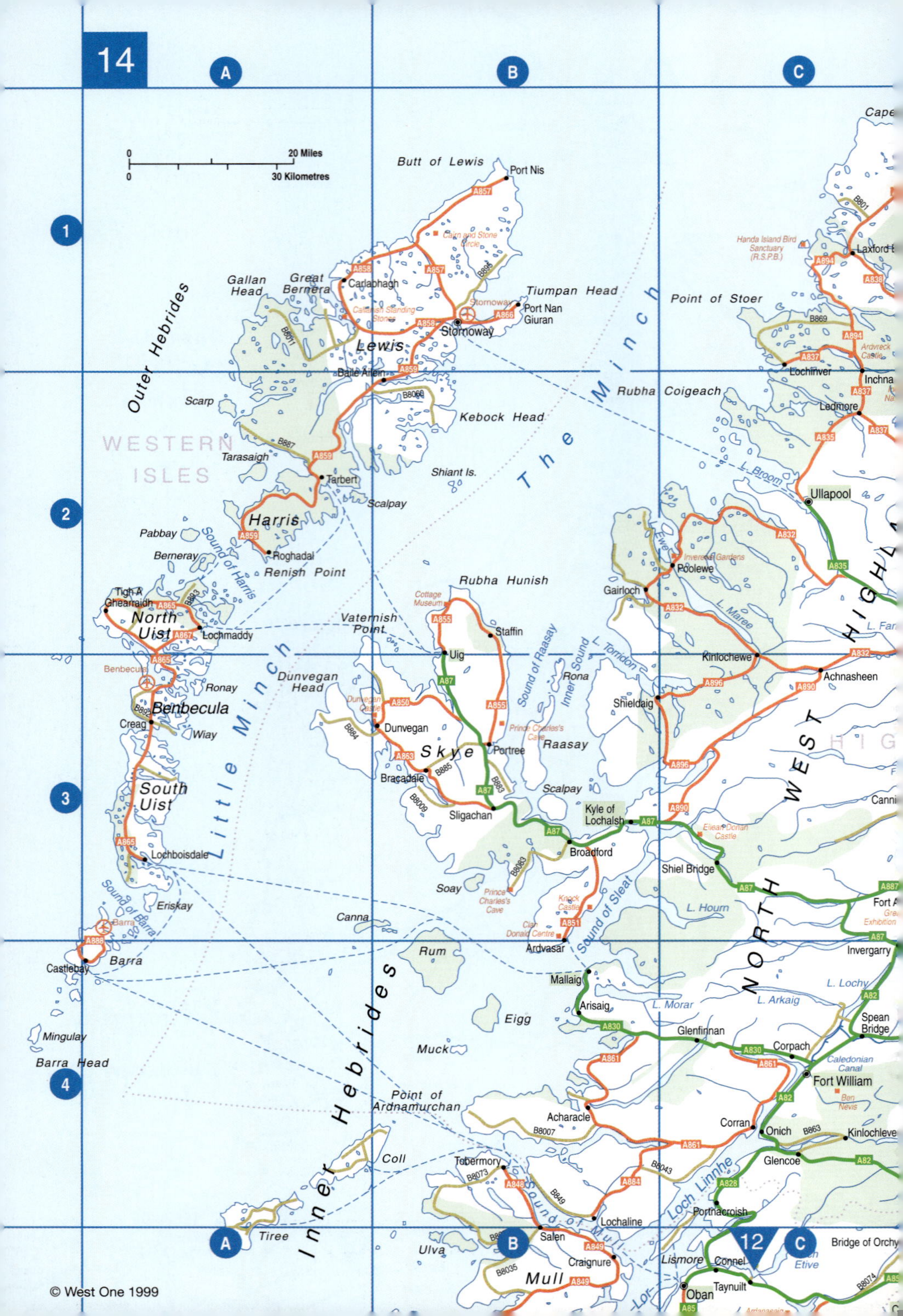
A
B
C
1
2
3
4
0
20 Miles
30 Kilometres
Butt of Lewis
Port Nis
Cairn and Stone Circle
Gallan Head
Great Bernera
Carlabhagh
Tiumpan Head
Port Nan Giuran
Callanish Standing Stones
Stornoway
Lewis
Baile Ailein
Outer Hebrides
WESTERN ISLES
Scarp
Kebock Head
Tarasaigh
Shiant Is.
Tarbert
Scalpay
Harris
Pabbay
Berneray
Sound of Harris
Roghadal
Renish Point
Rubha Hunish
Tigh A Ghearraidh
North Uist
Lochmaddy
Vaternish Point
Cottage Museum
Staffin
Uig
Benbecula
Ronay
Dunvegan Head
Dunvegan Castle
Dunvegan
Creag
Wiay
Skye
Portree
Prince Charles's Cave
Raasay
Sound of Raasay
Rona
Inner Sound
L. Torridon
Bracadale
Sligachan
South Uist
Little Minch
Lochboisdale
Sound of Barra
Eriskay
Barra
Castlebay
Mingulay
Barra Head
Canna
Rum
Eigg
Muck
Soay
Prince Charles's Cave
Knock Castle
Clan Donald Centre
Ardvasar
Sound of Sleat
Broadford
Kyle of Lochalsh
Scalpay
Mallaig
Arisaig
L. Morar
Inner Hebrides
Point of Ardnamurchan
Acharacle
Coll
Tiree
Tobermory
Sound of Mull
Lochaline
Salen
Ulva
Craignure
Mull
Lismore
The Minch
Rubha Coigeach
Point of Stoer
Cape
Handa Island Bird Sanctuary (R.S.P.B.)
Laxford
Ardvreck Castle
Lochinver
Inchna
Ledmore
L. Broom
Ullapool
L. Ewe
Inverewe Gardens
Poolewe
Gairloch
L. Maree
L. Fan
Kinlochewe
Achnasheen
Shieldaig
NORTH WEST HIGHLANDS
Eilean Donan Castle
Shiel Bridge
L. Hourn
Canni
Fort A
Invergarry
L. Lochy
L. Arkaig
Spean Bridge
Glenfinnan
Corpach
Caledonian Canal
Fort William
Ben Nevis
Corran
Onich
Kinlochleve
Glencoe
Loch Linnhe
Portnacroish
Connel
Taynuilt
Oban
Bridge of Orchy
Etive
12
A857
A858
A866
A859
A865
A867
A855
A850
A87
A863
A851
A830
A861
A848
A849
A884
A828
A82
A835
A837
A894
A838
A832
A896
A890
A887
A85
A888
B801
B869
B8011
B895
B8060
B887
B893
B882
B884
B885
B883
B8009
B8083
B8007
B8043
B8073
B849
B8035
B863
B8074

Pentland Firth
Stroma
Castle of Mey
John 'o' Groats
Duncansby Head
Strathy Point
Scrabster
Castletown
Thurso
Golval
Reay
Bettyhill
Tongue
Noss Head
Wick
Grey Cairns
Syre
Latheron
Altnaharra
Kinbrace
To Kirkwall
Suisgill Burn
Ord of Caithness
Helmsdale
Helmsdale Castle
Dalchork
Shin
Lairg
Brora
Dunrobin Castle
Golspie
Shin Falls
Bonar Bridge
Dornoch
Dornoch Firth
Tarbat Ness
Tain
Moray Firth
Alness
Invergordon
Cromarty
Branderburgh
Lossiemouth
Burghead
Elgin
Lhanbryde
Buckie
Portknockie
Cullen
Findochty
Portsoy
Banff
Macduff
Rosehearty
Kinnairds Head
Fraserburgh
Fochabers
Nairn
Forres
Fortrose
Fort George
Avoch
Pluscarden Priory
Inverness
Cawdor Castle
Beauly Priory
Findhorn
Rothes
Keith
Aberchirder
Turriff
Deveron
Mintlaw
Peterhead
Buchan Ness
MORAY
Dufftown
Balvenie Castle
Huntly
ABERDEENSHIRE
Haddo House
Ellon
Drumnadrochit
Urquhart Castle
Tomatin
Lochindorb Castle
Grantown-on-Spey
Spey
Carrbridge
Rhynie
Oldmeldrum
Inverurie
Aberdeen
Kintore
Don
Dyce
To Stromness, Lerwick
Tomintoul
Kildrummy Castle
Alford
Haughton House
Aviemore
Highland Wildlife Park
Craigievar Castle
ABERDEEN
Girdle Ness
Kingussie
Newtonmore
Aboyne
Peterculter
Crathes Castle
Balmoral Castle
Ballater
Dee
Banchory
Braemar Castle
Braemar
Cairngorms Nature Reserve
MOUNTAINS
Stonehaven
Dalwhinnie
COTLAND
Clova
Inverbervie
Edzell Castle
Laurencekirk
Blair Castle
Blair Atholl
Pass of Killiecrankie
ANGUS
Brechin
Queen's View
Kinloch Rannoch
Pitlochry
Kirkmichael
Kirriemuir
South Esk
Montrose
Loch Rannoch
Bridge of Cally
Alyth
Forfar
Lunan Bay
Aberfeldy
Tay
Blairgowrie
Rattray
Glamis Castle
Glamis
Kenmore
Meigle
Dunkeld
Coupar Angus
Arbroath
PERTH AND KINROSS
Loch Tay
Amulree
Carnoustie
Buddon Ness
DUNDEE
Killin
Scone Palace
Perth
Firth of Tay
Newport-on-Tay
Lochearnhead
Comrie
Crieff
Inverness
Dingwall
0 20 Miles
0 30 Kilometres
Mull Head
North Ronaldsay
Papa Westray
Westray
Orkney Islands
Sanday
Westray Firth
Rousay
Eday
Brough Head
Birsay
Stronsay
Stronsay Sound
ORKNEY
Shapinsay
Finstown
Kirkwall
Stromness
Mainland
St. Mary's
Rora Head
Hoy
Scapa Flow
Rose Ness
South Ronaldsay
Burwick
Old Head
To Lerwick
D
E
F
1
2
3
4
13

A
B
C
1
2
3
4
0
20 Miles
0
15 Kilometres
Tory
Tory
Bloody Foreland
Falcar
R257
Bunbeg
Gweedore
Aran
R259
N56
Dungloe
DERRYVEAG
R254
R252
Mass
R250
R261
Glenties
Rossan Point
Glencolumbkille
Ardara
R262
Carrick
R263
N56
Do
Donegal Bay
Ballyshannon
Bundoran
Belleek
R230
N15
Lissadell House
R280
R282
Erris Head
Downpatrick Head
Killala Bay
Sligo Bay
N16
Manorhamilton
Belmullet
The Mullet
R314
R315
R297
Sligo
R286
L. Gill
R313
R314
Mayne Abbey
Dromore West
N59
R292
N4
R286
R287
R280
Bangor Erris
SLIEVE GAMPH MTS
Ballisodare
SLIGO
Blacksod Bay
N59
Ballina
Crossmolina
R294
R312
N17
R293
L. Arrow
R284
R280
Lough Allen
Achill Head
Ballycroy
Lough Conn
N26
Moy
Tubbercurry
R207
R316
R294
Dru
Foxford
R315
Charlestown
R293
R294
R280
Mulrany
R317
N26
Swinford
Newport
R310
N58
N5
Boyle
Carrick-on-Shannon
Drum
Clew Bay
Clare Bay
R311
Castlebar
R321
Ballaghaderreen
R322
R325
R361
R368
N5
N59
N5
N60
R324
R323
Frenchpark
R370
N61
Louisburgh
R335
Westport
Balla
R320
Knock
N83
R293
R325
R369
R368
R371
Inishturk
R330
N84
N17
R327
Ballyhaunis
MAYO
ROSCOMMON
Castlerea
Tulsk
Inishbofin
Partry
Claremorris
N60
N60
N5
Killary Harbour
Lough Mask
Lough Carra
R331
R327
R327
R367
Ballymoe
R366
R371
Kylemore Abbey
N59
R328
R360
Aasleagh
Ballinrobe
R360
N60
Letterfrack
CONNEMARA NATIONAL PARK
R332
N17
R362
Roscommon
R392
CONNEMARA
R336
Dunmore
Clifden
R345
R362
R366
N59
Lough Corrib
R334
N83
R328
R364
Athleague
Slyne Head
Recess
Maam Cross
Tuam
R332
R357
R362
Lough Ree
R341
R340
R336
Headford
R
R340
Oughterard
R347
N63
Mount Bellew
R363
N59
N17
N84
N61
R350
R358
R357
R362
A
18
Moycullen
B
R339
C
Athlone
Claregalway
GALWAY
R348
N6
N64
Gorumna Is.
R336
Galway
N6
Athenry
R348
Ballinasloe
R357
Oranmore
R347
R350
I

D
E
F
1
2
3
4
NORTHERN IRELAND
LONDONDERRY
TYRONE
ANTRIM
ARMAGH
DOWN
MONAGHAN
CAVAN
LOUTH
MEATH
UBLIC OF
LAND
North Channel
IRISH SEA
Malin Head
Ballyhillin
Rathlin
Fair Head
Dunagree Point
Portrush
Portstewart
Coleraine
Ballycastle
Lough Swilly
Ballyliffen
Carndonagh
Moville
Buncanra
Fahan
Milford
Lough Foyle
Quigley's Point
Muff
Bridge End
Londonderry
Limavady
Ballymoney
Glenariff
Garron Point
Carnlough
Dungiven
Garvagh
Kilrea
Strabane
Sion Mills
Stranorlar
Maghera
Ballymena
Larne
Island Magee
Whitehead
Newtownstewart
Castlederg
Magherafelt
Randalstown
Moneymore
Springhill
Antrim
Ballyclare
Carrickfergus
Carrickfergus Castle
Newtownabbey
Belfast Lough
Bangor
Donaghadee
Holywood
BELFAST
Belfast City
Belfast International
Ulster American Folk Park
Wellbrook Beetling Mill
Cookstown
Omagh
Lough Neagh
Newtownards
Mount Stewart
Kesh
Dromore
Fintona
Irvinestown
Coalisland
Dungannon
Lisburn
Dundonald
Comber
Ballygawley
Clogher
Aughnacloy
The Argory
Ardress House
Portadown
Lurgan
Craigavon
Saintfield
Strangford Lough
Rowallane Garden
Killyleagh
Portaferry
Strangford
Castle Ward
Enniskillen
Armagh
Tandragee
Banbridge
Ballynahinch
Maguiresbridge
Lisnaskea
Florence Court
Upper Lough Erne
Markethill
Monaghan
Downpatrick
Clough
Castlewellan
Ballyquintin Point
Ardglass
Keady
Rathfriland
Newcastle
St. John's Point
Clones
Newbliss
Belleek
Bessbrook
Newtownhamilton
Newry
Ballybay
Belturbet
Castleblayney
Warrenpoint
Butler's Bridge
Cootehill
Crossmaglen
Kilkeel
Cavan
Shercock
Carrickmacross
Dundalk
Ballinagh
Bailieborough
Dundalk Bay
Kingscourt
Castlebellingham
Ballyjamesduff
Virginia
Ardee
Dunany Point
Granard
L. Sheelin
Carrigglas Manor
Oldcastle
Dunleer
Collon
Edgeworthstown
Castlepollard
Ceanannus Mór
Slane Castle
Slane
Drogheda
Boyne
Navan
Athboy
L. Owel
Delvin
Balbriggan
Trim
Hill of Tara
Skerries
Mullingar
Dunshaughlin
Ashbourne
Swords
Newbridge House
Dublin
Malahide Castle
Lambay I.
Howth Castle
Howth Head
Kinnegad
Enfield
Kilcock
Clonee
Lucan
Leixlie
Castletown
Kilbeggan
Edenderry
DUBLIN
19
To Cairnryan
To Stranraer
To Douglas
To Liverpool & Holyhead

18
16
A
B
C
1
2
3
4
Slyne Head
Maam Cross
Corrib
Headford
Tuam
Oughterard
Mount Bellew
Moycullen
Claregalway
GALWAY
Galway
Oranmore
Athenry
Gorumna Is.
Galway Bay
Aran Islands
Inishmore
Inishmaan
Inisheer
Kilcolgan
Loughrea
Ballyvaughan
Kinvara
Thoor Ballylee
SLIEVE AUGHTY MTS
Gort
Haggs Head
Ennistymon
Milltown Malbay
CLARE
Tuamgraney
Ennis
Craggaunowen Project
Knappogue Castle
Killaloe
Shannon
Cratloe Woods House
Bunratty Castle
Birdhill
Newport
Kilkee
Kilrush
LIMERICK
Loop Head
Mouth of the Shannon
Askeaton
Tarbert
Foynes
Ballylongford
Glin Castle
Adare Manor
Patrickswell
Rathkeale
Croom
Listowel
Newcastle West
Tralee Bay
Abbeyfeale
Kilmallock Castle
Kilmallock
Knocklong
Brandon Head
Tralee
Drumcollogher
Rathluirc
SLIEVE MISH MTS
Castleisland
Dingle
Anascaul
Castlemaine
Buttevant
Kildorrey
Farranfore
Annes Grove Gardens
Castletownroche
Dingle Bay
Killorglin
KERRY
Glenbeigh
Killarney
Rathmore
Mallow
Blackwater
Fermoy
Lough Leane
Valentia Is.
Rathcormac
Cahirciveen
KILLARNEY NATIONAL PARK
CORK
Waterville
Lough Currane
Kenmare
Ballymakeery
Blarney Castle
Macroom
Sneem
Bolus Head
CORK
Midleton
DERRYNANE NATIONAL HISTORY PARK
Lee
Douglas
Cobh
Glengarriff
Dunmanway
Bandon
Bantry
Dursey Head
Bear Is.
Bantry Bay
Drimoleague
Kinsale
Bantry House
Ballydehob
Clonakilty
Timoleague Castle Gardens
Schull
Skibbereen
Old Head of Kinsale
Galley Head
Mizen Head
Clear Is.
Cape Clear
N6
N17
N18
N59
N84
N65
N66
N67
N85
N68
N7
N20
N69
N21
N22
N23
N69
N70
N71
N72
N73
N8
N25
R336
R340
R341
R347
R348
R349
R350
R351
R353
R332
R339
R477
R476
R478
R480
R460
R462
R461
R352
R474
R452
R465
R470
R463
R473
R483
R487
R551
R553
R524
R518
R523
R520
R522
R519
R515
R505
R512
R513
R516
R555
R576
R578
R579
R559
R561
R563
R562
R577
R582
R583
R580
R581
R517
R565
R566
R568
R569
R571
R584
R587
R585
R590
R589
R618
R614
R572
R575
R586
R591
R599
R588
R602
R603
R605
R607
R600
R611
R612
R592
R593

REPUBLIC OF
IRELAND
19
17
D
E
F
1
2
3
4
WEST MEATH
MEATH
OFFALY
KILDARE
LAOIS
WICKLOW
CARLOW
KILKENNY
TIPPERARY
WEXFORD
WATERFORD
Ballymahon
L. Owel
Delvin
Trim
Hill of Tara
Balbriggan
Skerries
Lambay I.
Mullingar
Dunshaughlin
Ashbourne
Athlone
Moate
Rochfortbridge
Kinnegad
Enfield
Kilcock
Swords
Newbridge House
Malahide Castle
Howth Castle
Howth Head
Kilbeggan
Edenderry
Clonee
Lucan
Leixlip
Castletown House
DUBLIN
Dublin Bay
To Douglas
To Holyhead
Tullamore
Daingean
Clogham
Rathcoole
Dun Laoghaire
James Joyce Tower
Ballybrack
Rathangan
Brittas
Powerscourt House
Bray
Naas
Kildare
Greystones
The Curragh
Kilcullen
Birr
Birr Castle Demesne
Mountmellick
Emo Court
Monasterevan
Pollaphuca Lakes
Port Laoise
Dunlavin
Roundwood
Stradbally
Mountrath
Roscrea
Athy
Glendalough
Mount Usher Gardens
Ashford
Rathnew
Wicklow
Wicklow Head
Borris-in-Ossory
Abbeyleix
Baltinglass
Rathdrum
WICKLOW MOUNTAINS
Durrow
Castledermot
Templemore
Carlow
Ballyragget
Castlecomer
Tullow
Arklow
Leighlinbridge
Slaney
Thurles
Urlingford
Kilkenny
Bunclody
Gorey
Killenaule
Callan
Cashel
Rock of Cashel
Thomastown
Kells Priory
Cahore Point
Knocktopher
Jerpoint Abbey
Barrow
Fethard
Enniscorthy
Cahir
Clonmel
New Ross
Carrick-on-Suir
Wexford Bay
John F. Kennedy Arboretum
Wexford
Suir
Waterford
Rosslare
Rosslare Harbour
To Fishguard
Lismore Castle
Lismore
Tramore
Carnsore Point
Dungarvan
Hook Head
Saltee Is.
Youghal Bay
Knockadoon Head
St. George's Channel
To Pembroke Dock
To Roscoff & Cherbourg
0
20 Miles
0
15 Kilometres

INDEX TO GREAT BRITAIN

Abbreviations of County and new Unitary Authority names used in this index.

Aber	= Aberdeenshire	Guer	= Guernsey	Oxon	= Oxfordshire
Arg	= Argyll & Bute	Hants	= Hampshire	Pemb	= Pembrokeshire
Brid	= Bridgend	Herts	= Hertfordshire	S Lan	= South Lanarkshire
Bucks	= Buckinghamshire	High	= Highland	S York	= South Yorkshire
Camb	= Cambridgeshire	IoM	= Isle of Man	Shrop	= Shropshire
Corn	= Cornwall	IoW	= Isle of Wight	Som	= Somerset
Derb	= Derbyshire	Jer	= Jersey	Staf	= Staffordshire
Dor	= Dorset	Linc	= Lincolnshire	Suff	= Suffolk
Dur	= Durham	Med	= Medway Towns	W Isl	= Western Isles
E York	= East Riding of Yorkshire	New	= Newport	W York	= West Yorkshire
G Man	= Greater Manchester	Norf	= Norfolk	Wrek	= The Wrekin
Glos	= Gloucestershire	North	= Northamptonshire		

A

Aberaeron 6 B3
Abercarn 3 E1
Aberchirder 15 F3
Aberdare 6 C4
Aberdaron 6 B2
Aberdeen 15 F3
Aberdyfi 6 C3
Aberfeldy 12 C1
Aberfoyle 12 C2
Abergavenny 7 D4
Abergele 6 C1
Aberporth 6 B3
Abersoch 6 B2
Abertillery 7 D4
Aberystwyth 6 C3
Abingdon 4 B2
Abington 13 D3
Aboyne 15 E4
Accrington 10 C4
Acharacle 12 A1
Achnasheen 14 C3
Acle 9 F3
Adderbury 4 B1
Adwick le Street 11 D4
Airdrie 12 C2
Alcester 4 A1
Aldeburgh 5 F1
Alderley Edge 7 E1
Aldermaston 4 B3
Aldershot 4 C3
Aldridge 7 F2
Alexandria 12 C2
Alford *(Aber)* 15 F3
Alford *(Linc)* 9 D1
Alfreton 8 B2
Allendale Town 10 C1
Alloa 13 D2
Alness 15 D2
Alnwick 13 F3
Alsager 7 E1
Alston 10 B1
Altnaharra 15 D1
Alton 4 B3
Altrincham 10 C4
Alyth 13 D1
Amble 13 F3
Ambleside 10 B2
Amersham 4 C2
Amesbury 4 A3
Amlwch 6 B1

Ammanford 6 C4
Ampthill 4 C1
Amulree 13 D1
Andover 4 B3
Annan 10 A1
Anstruther 13 E2
Appleby in Westmorland 10 B2
Arbroath 13 E1
Ardlui 12 C1
Ardlussa 12 A2
Ardrossan 12 B3
Ardvasar 14 B4
Arisaig 14 B4
Armadale 13 D2
Arminish 12 A2
Arnold 8 B2
Arrochar 12 B2
Arundel 4 C4
Ashbourne 7 F1
Ashburton 3 D3
Ashby-de-la-Zouch 7 F2
Ashford 5 E3
Ashington 13 F3
Ashton-under-Lyne 10 C4
Askrigg 10 C2
Aspatria 10 A1
Atherstone 7 F2
Atherton 10 B4
Attleborough 9 E3
Auchterarder 13 D1
Auchtermuchty 13 D1
Avebury 4 A2
Aviemore 15 D3
Avoch 15 D3
Avonmouth 3 E1
Axminster 3 E3
Aycliffe 11 D2
Aylesbury 4 C2
Aylsham 9 E2
Aynho 4 B1
Ayr 12 C3
Ayton 13 E2

B

Bacup 10 C4
Baile Ailein 14 B2
Bakewell 7 F1
Bala 6 C2
Baldock 4 C1
Baldslow 5 E4
Balfron 12 C2

Ballantrae 12 B4
Ballater 15 E4
Bamburgh 13 F3
Bampton 3 D2
Banbury 4 B1
Banchory 15 F4
Banff 15 F2
Bangor 6 C1
Banstead 5 D3
Bargoed 3 D1
Bargrennan 12 C4
Barking 5 D2
Barmouth 6 C2
Barnard Castle 10 C2
Barnet 5 D2
Barnoldswick 10 C3
Barnsley 11 D4
Barnstaple 2 C2
Barrhead 12 C2
Barrhill 12 B4
Barrow-in-Furness 10 A3
Barry 3 D1
Barton-upon-Humberside 11 E4
Basildon 5 D2
Basingstoke 4 B3
Bath 3 F1
Bathgate 13 D2
Battle 5 E4
Bawdsey 5 F1
Bawtry 11 E4
Beaconsfield 4 C2
Beaminster 3 E3
Beattock 13 D3
Beaulieu 4 B4
Beauly 15 D3
Beaumaris 6 C1
Beccles 9 F3
Bedale 11 D2
Bedford 4 C1
Bedlington 13 F4
Bedworth 8 B3
Beeston 8 B2
Beith 12 C2
Belford 13 F3
Belper 7 F1
Belton 11 E4
Bentley 11 D4
Bere Regis 3 F3
Berkhamsted 4 C2
Berwick-upon-Tweed 13 E2

Bethesda 6 C1
Bettyhill 15 D1
Betws-y-coed 6 C1
Beverley 11 E3
Bewdley 7 E3
Bexhill 5 E4
Bexley 5 D2
Bicester 4 B1
Biddulph 7 E1
Bideford 2 C2
Bigbury-on-Sea 2 C4
Biggar 13 D3
Biggleswade 4 C1
Billericay 5 D2
Billingham 11 D2
Billingshurst 4 C3
Bingham 8 B2
Bingley 10 C3
Birkenhead 10 B4
Birmingham 7 F3
Birsay 15 F1
Bishop Auckland 11 D1
Bishop's Castle 7 D3
Bishop's Stortford 5 D1
Bishop's Waltham 4 B4
Bishopbriggs 12 C2
Blackburn 10 B4
Blackford 12 C1
Blackpool 10 B3
Blackwaterfoot 12 B3
Blaenau Ffestiniog 6 C1
Blaenavon 7 D4
Blair Atholl 15 D4
Blairgowrie 13 D1
Blakeney *(Glos)* 7 E4
Blakeney *(Norf)* 9 E2
Blandford Forum 3 F2
Blaydon 10 C1
Blyth 13 F4
Bo'ness 13 D2
Bodmin 2 B3
Bognor Regis 4 C4
Boldon 11 D1
Bolsover 8 B2
Bolton 10 B4
Bonar Bridge 15 D2
Bootle 10 B4
Boroughbridge 11 D3
Borth 6 C3
Boscastle 2 B3
Boston 9 D2
Bothel 10 A1

Boughton 8 B2
Bourne 8 C3
Bournemouth 4 A4
Bourton-on-the-Water 4 A1
Bovey Tracey 3 D3
Bracadale 14 B3
Brackley 4 B1
Bracknell 4 C2
Bradford 10 C3
Bradford-on-Avon 3 F1
Braemar 15 E4
Braintree 5 E1
Bramhall 7 E1
Brampton 10 B1
Branderburgh 15 E2
Brandon 9 E3
Braunton 2 C2
Brechin 13 E1
Brecon 7 D4
Brentwood 5 D2
Bridge of Allan 12 C2
Bridge of Cally 13 D1
Bridge of Earn 13 D1
Bridge of Orchy 12 B1
Bridgend *(Arg)* 12 A2
Bridgend *(Brid)* 3 D1
Bridgnorth 7 E3
Bridgwater 3 E2
Bridlington 11 F3
Bridport 3 E3
Brigg 11 E4
Brighouse 10 C4
Brightlingsea 5 E1
Brighton 5 D4
Bristol 3 E1
Brixham 3 D4
Broad Haven 6 A4
Broadford 14 B3
Broadstairs 5 F2
Broadway 4 A1
Brodick 12 B3
Bromfield 7 D3
Bromley 5 D2
Bromsgrove 7 E3
Bromyard 7 E3
Brora 15 D2
Brough 10 C2
Broughton in Furness 10 A2
Broughton 13 D3
Brownhills 7 F2

Bruton 3 F2
Brynmawr 7 D4
Buckfastleigh 2 C3
Buckhaven 13 D2
Buckie 15 E2
Buckingham 4 B1
Buckley 7 D1
Bude 2 B2
Budleigh Salterton 3 D3
Builth Wells 7 D3
Bunessan 12 A1
Bungay 9 F3
Buntingford 5 D1
Burbage 4 A3
Burford 4 A2
Burgess Hill 5 D3
Burghead 15 E2
Burnham Market 9 E2
Burnham-on-Crouch 5 E2
Burnham-on-Sea 3 E2
Burnley 10 C3
Burntisland 13 D2
Burry Port 2 C1
Burslem 7 E1
Burton Bradstock 3 E3
Burton Latimer 8 C3
Burton upon Trent 7 F2
Burwell 9 D4
Burwick 15 F2
Bury St Edmunds 9 E4
Bury 10 C4
Bushey 4 C2
Buxton 7 F1

C

Caerleon 3 E1
Caernarfon 6 B1
Caerphilly 3 D1
Cairnryan 12 B4
Caister-on-Sea 9 F3
Caistor 11 F4
Callander 12 C1
Callington 2 C3
Calne 4 A2
Camberley 4 C3
Camborne 2 A4
Cambridge 5 D1
Camelford 2 B3
Campbeltown 12 B3
Cannich 14 C3
Cannock 7 F2
Canonbie 10 B1

Canterbury 5 E3	Coldstream 13 E3	Darvel 12 C3	Edinburgh 13 D2	Gelligaer 3 D1	Hatfield *(Herts)* 4 C2
Canvey Island 5 E2	Coleford 7 E4	Darwen 10 B4	Egham 4 C2	Gillingham *(Dor)* 3 F2	Hatfield *(S York)* 11 E4
Capel Curig 6 C1	Colne 10 C3	Daventry 4 B1	Egremont 10 A2	Gillingham *(Med)* 5 E2	Hatherleigh 2 C3
Cardiff 3 D1	Colwyn Bay 6 C1	Dawlish 3 D3	Elgin 15 E2	Girvan 12 B3	Havant 4 B4
Cardigan 6 B4	Combe Martin 2 C2	Deal 5 F3	Elland 10 C4	Gisburn 10 C3	Haverfordwest 6 A4
Carlabhagh 14 A1	Comrie 12 C1	Deddington 4 B1	Ellesmere Port 7 D1	Glamis 13 D1	Haverhill 5 D1
Carlisle 10 B1	Congleton 7 E1	Denbigh 7 D1	Ellesmere 7 D2	Glasgow 12 C2	Hawarden 7 D1
Carlton 8 B2	Conisbrough 11 D4	Denny 12 C2	Ellon 15 F3	Glastonbury 3 E2	Hawes 10 C2
Carluke 12 C2	Coniston 10 B2	Derby 7 F1	Ely 9 D3	Glenbarr 12 A3	Hawick 13 E3
Carmarthen 6 B4	Connel 12 B1	Desborough 8 B3	Emsworth 4 B4	Glencoe 12 B1	Hawkhurst 5 E3
Carnforth 10 B3	Consett 10 C1	Devizes 4 A3	Epping 5 D2	Glenfinnan 14 C4	Hawkshead 10 B2
Carnoustie 13 E1	Contin 15 D3	Dewsbury 11 D4	Epsom 4 C3	Glenluce 12 B4	Haworth 10 C3
Carnwath 13 D3	Conwy 6 C1	Didcot 4 B2	Eribol 14 C1	Glenrothes 13 D2	Haydon Bridge 10 C1
Carrbridge 15 D3	Corbridge 10 C1	Dinas-Mawddwy 6 C2	Esher 4 C3	Glossop 10 C4	Hayle 2 A4
Carsphairn 12 C3	Corby Glen 8 C2	Dingwall 15 D3	Eston 11 D2	Gloucester 7 E4	Hay-on-Wye 7 D4
Castle Cary 3 E2	Corby 8 C3	Dinnington 11 D4	Eton 4 C2	Godalming 4 C3	Haywards Heath 5 D3
Castle Donington 8 B2	Corpach 14 C4	Diss 9 E3	Ettington 4 A1	Godmanchester 8 C4	Heanor 8 B2
Castle Douglas 12 C4	Corran 12 B1	Dolgellau 6 C2	Evesham 4 A1	Godstone 5 D3	Heathfield 5 D3
Castlebay 14 A4	Corsham 3 F1	Dollar 13 D2	Exeter 3 D3	Golspie 15 D2	Hebden Bridge 10 C4
Castleford 11 D	Corton 9 F3	Doncaster 11 D4	Exford 3 D2	Golval 15 D1	Hedon 11 F4
Castletown *(High)* 15 E1	Corwen 7 D2	Donington 8 C2	Exmouth 3 D3	Goodwick 6 A4	Helensburgh 12 C2
Castletown *(IoM)* 10 A4	Coryton 5 E2	Dorchester *(Dor)* 3 F3	Eye 9 E3	Goole 11 E4	Helmsdale 15 E2
Catel 2 A2	Cottenham 9 D4	Dorchester *(Oxon)* 4 B2	Eyemouth 13 E2	Gorey 2 B2	Helmsley 11 D2
Caterham 5 D3	Cottesmore 8 C3	Dorking 4 C3		Goring 4 B2	Helston 2 A4
Catterick Camp 10 C2	Coulport 12 B2	Dornoch 15 D2	**F**	Gorstan 14 C2	Hemel Hempstead 4 C2
Chandler's Ford 4 B3	Coupar Angus 13 D1	Douglas *(IoM)* 10 A4	Fairford 4 A2	Gosforth 11 D1	Hemyock 3 D2
Chard 3 E2	Coventry 7 F3	Douglas *(S Lan)* 12 C3	Fakenham 9 E2	Gosport 4 B4	Henley-in-Arden 7 F3
Charing 5 E3	Cowbridge 3 D1	Doune 12 C2	Falkirk 13 D2	Gourock 12 B2	Henley-on-Thames 4 B2
Charlbury 4 B1	Cowdenbeath 13 D2	Dover 5 F3	Falmouth 2 B4	Grain 5 E2	Henstridge 3 F2
Chatham 5 E2	Cowes 4 B4	Downham Market 9 D3	Fareham 4 B4	Grangemouth 13 D2	Hereford 7 E4
Chatteris 9 D3	Craighouse 12 A2	Droitwich 7 E3	Faringdon 4 A2	Grange-over-Sands 10 B3	Herne Bay 5 E2
Cheadle *(G Man)* 10 C4	Craignure 12 A1	Dronfield 8 B1	Farnborough 4 C3	Grantham 8 C2	Hertford 5 D2
Cheadle *(Staf)* 7 F2	Crail 13 E1	Drummore 12 B4	Farnham 4 C3	Grantown-on-Spey 15 E3	Hetton-le-Hole 11 D1
Cheddar 3 E1	Cranbrook 5 E3	Drumnadrochit 15 D3	Farnworth 10 C4	Grasmere 10 B2	Hexham 10 C1
Chelmsford 5 D2	Cranleigh 4 C3	Drymen 12 C2	Faversham 5 E3	Gravesend 5 D2	Heysham 10 B3
Cheltenham 7 E4	Cranwell 8 C2	Duddington 8 C3	Fawley 4 B4	Grays 5 D2	High Wycombe 4 C2
Chepstow 3 E1	Craven Arms 7 D3	Dudley 7 E3	Felixstowe 5 F1	Great Driffield 11 E3	Higham Ferrers 8 C4
Chertsey 4 C3	Crawley 5 D3	Dufftown 15 E3	Felton 13 F3	Great Dunmow 5 D1	Highworth 4 A2
Chesham 4 C2	Cray Cross 8 B2	Dulverton 3 D2	Feolin Ferry 12 A2	Great Malvern 7 E4	Hillswick 13 F1
Cheshunt 5 D2	Creag 14 A3	Dumbarton 12 C2	Ferndown 4 A4	Great Shelford 5 D1	Hinckley 8 B3
Chester 7 D1	Crediton 3 D3	Dumfries 10 A1	Ffestiniog 6 C2	Great Torrington 2 C2	Hindhead 4 C3
Chesterfield 8 B1	Crewe 7 E1	Dunbar 13 E2	Filey 11 F2	Great Yarmouth 9 F3	Hirwaun 6 C4
Chester-le Street 11 D1	Crewkerne 3 E2	Dunblane 12 C2	Filton 3 E1	Greenlaw 13 E3	Histon 9 D4
Chichester 4 C4	Crianlarich 12 C1	Dundee 13 D1	Findochty 15 E2	Greenock 12 B2	Hitchin 4 C1
Chippenham 3 F1	Criccieth 6 B2	Dunfermline 13 D2	Finstown 15 F1	Greenod 10 B2	Hoddesdon 5 D2
Chipping Campden 4 A1	Cricklade 4 A2	Dunkeld 13 D1	Fionnphort 12 A1	Gretna 10 B1	Hodnet 7 E2
Chipping Norton 4 A1	Crieff 12 C1	Dunoon 12 B2	Fishguard 6 A4	Grimsby 11 F4	Holbeach 9 D2
Chipping Ongar 5 D2	Crocketford 12 C4	Duns 13 E2	Fleet 4 C3	Guildford 4 C3	Holland-on-Sea 5 F1
Chipping Sodbury 3 F1	Cromarty 15 D2	Dunstable 4 C1	Fleetwood 10 B3	Guisborough 11 D2	Holmfirth 10 C4
Chirk 7 D2	Cromer 9 F2	Dunster 3 D2	Flint 7 D1	Gutcher 13 F1	Holmhead 12 C3
Chorley 10 B4	Crook 10 C1	Dunvegan 14 B3	Fochabers 15 E3	Guyhirn 9 D3	Holsworthy 2 C3
Christchurch 4 A4	Crosby 10 B4	Durham 11 D1	Folkestone 5 F3		Holt 9 E2
Chudleigh 3 D3	Crowborough 5 D3	Durness 14 C1	Fordingbridge 4 A4	**H**	Holyhead (Caergybi) 6 B1
Chumleigh 2 C2	Crowland 8 C3	Dursley 3 F1	Forfar 13 D1	Haddington 13 E2	Holywell 7 D1
Church Stretton 7 D3	Crowle 11 E4	Dyce 15 F3	Formby 10 B4	Hadleigh 5 E1	Honiton 3 D3
Cinderford 7 E4	Croxton Kerrial 8 B2	Dyffryn 6 B1	Forres 15 E3	Hagley 7 E3	Hook 4 B3
Cirencester A2	Croydon 5 D3		Fort Augustus 14 C3	Hailsham 5 D4	Hope 7 D1
Clachan 12 B2	Cuckfield 5 D3	**E**	Fort William 14 C4	Halesowen 7 F3	Hopton 9 F3
Clacton-on-Sea 5 E1	Cullen 15 E2	Ealing 4 C2	Fortrose 15 D3	Halesworth 9 F3	Horden 11 D1
Claonaig 12 B2	Cullompton 3 D2	Eardisley 7 D3	Fortuneswell 3 F3	Halifax 10 C4	Horley 5 D3
Cleator Moor 10 A2	Cumbernauld 12 C2	Easington *(Dur)* 11 D1	Fowey 2 B4	Halstead 5 E1	Horncastle 8 C1
Cleethorpes 11 F4	Cumnock 12 C3	Easington *(E York)* 11 F4	Framlingham 4 A1	Haltwhistle 10 B1	Horndean 4 B4
Cleobury Mortimer 7 E3	Cupar 13 D1	Easingwold 11 D3	Fraserburgh 15 F2	Hamilton 12 C2	Hornsea 11 F3
Clevedon 3 E1	Cwmbran 3 E1	East Bergholt 5 E1	Fridaythorpe 11 E3	Hanley 7 E1	Horsham 4 C3
Cleveleys 10 B3		East Cowes 4 B4	Frinton-on-Sea 5 F1	Harlech 6 C2	Houghton le Spring 11 D1
Clifton 12 C1	**D**	East Dereham 9 E3	Frodsham 7 E1	Harleston 9 F3	Hounslow 4 C2
Cliftonville 5 F2	Dalbeattie 12 C4	East Grinstead 5 D3	Frome 3 F2	Harlow 5 D2	Hove 5 D4
Clitheroe 10 C3	Dalchork 15 D2	East Kilbride 12 C2	Furnace 12 B2	Haroldswick 13 F1	Howden 11 E4
Clophill 4 C1	Dale 6 A4	East Linton 13 E2		Harpenden 4 C2	Hoylake 10 A4
Clova 15 E4	Dalkeith 13 D2	East Retford 8 B1	**G**	Harrogate 11 D3	Hucknall 8 B2
Clovelly 2 C2	Dalmellington 12 C3	East Wittering 4 C4	Gainsborough 11 E4	Harrow 4 C2	Huddersfield 10 C4
Clun 7 D3	Dalry 12 C2	Eastbourne 5 D4	Gairloch 14 B2	Hartland 2 B2	Hugh Town 2 A3
Clydebank 12 C2	Dalton-in-Furness 10 A3	Easter Quarff 13 F2	Galashiels 13 E3	Hartlepool 11 D1	Hungerford 4 B3
Coalville 8 B3	Dalwhinnie 15 D4	Eastleigh 4 B3	Galston 12 C3	Hartley Wintney 4 B3	Hunmanby 11 E3
Cockburnspath 13 E2	Darlington 11 D2	Ebbw Vale 7 D4	Garelochhead 12 B2	Harwell 4 B2	Hunstanton 9 D2
Cockermouth 10 A1	Dartford 5 D2	Eccleshall 7 E2	Garstang 10 B3	Harwich 5 F1	Huntingdon 8 C4
Coggeshall 5 E1	Dartmeet 2 C3	Eckington 8 B1	Gatehouse of Fleet 12 C4	Haslemere 4 C3	Huntly 7 E4
Colchester 5 E1	Dartmouth 3 D4	Edenbridge 5 D3	Gateshead 11 D1	Hastings 5 E4	Huntly 15 E3

Hurstpierpoint 5 D4
Husband's Bosworth 8 B3
Hyde 10 C4
Hythe 5 E3

I
Ilchester 3 E2
Ilfracombe 2 C2
Ilkeston 8 B2
Ilkley 10 C3
Ilminster 3 E2
Immingham 11 F4
Inchnadamph 14 C2
Ingleton 10 B3
Innerleithen 13 D3
Inveraray 12 B1
Inverbervie 15 F4
Invergarry 14 C4
Invergordon 15 D2
Inverkeithing 13 D2
Invermoriston 14 D3
Inverness 15 D3
Inverurie 15 F3
Ipswich 5 E1
Ironbridge 7 E2
Irthlingborough 8 C4
Irvine 12 C3
Isbister 13 F1
Isle of Whithorn 12 C4
Ivybridge 2 C4
Ixworth 9 E4

J
Jarrow 11 D1
Jedburgh 13 E3
John o' Groats 15 E1
Johnstone 12 C2

K
Keele 7 E1
Keighley 10 C3
Keith 15 E3
Kelso 13 E3
Kelvedon 5 E1
Kempston 4 C1
Kendal 10 B2
Kenilworth 7 F3
Kenmore 12 C1
Kennacraig 12 B2
Keswick 10 B2
Kettering 8 C3
Keynsham 3 E1
Kidderminster 7 E3
Kidlington 4 B2
Kidsgrove 7 E1
Kidwelly 6 B4
Kilbirnie 12 C2
Killin 12 C1
Kilmarnock 12 C3
Kilmartin 12 B2
Kilmelford 12 B1
Kilninver 12 B1
Kilrenny 13 E2
Kilsyth 12 C2
Kilwinning 12 C3
Kinbrace 15 D1
Kineton 4 A1
King's Lynn 9 D3
Kingsbridge 3 D4
Kingsclere 4 B3
Kingston upon Hull 11 E4
Kingston 4 C2
Kingswear 3 D4
Kingswood 3 E1
Kington 7 D3
Kingussie 15 D3
Kinloch Rannoch 12 C1
Kinlochewe 14 C3

Kinlochleven 12 B1
Kinross 13 D2
Kintore 15 F3
Kippen 12 C2
Kirkby in Ashfield 8 B2
Kirkby Lonsdale 10 B3
Kirkby Stephen 10 C2
Kirkby 10 B4
Kirkbymoorside 11 E2
Kirkcaldy 13 D2
Kirkcolm 12 B4
Kirkcudbright 12 C4
Kirkintilloch 12 C2
Kirkmichael 13 D1
Kirkwall 15 F1
Kirriemuir 13 D1
Kirton in Lindsey 11 E4
Knaresborough 11 D3
Knighton 7 D3
Knottingley 11 D4
Knutsford 7 E1
Kyle of Lochalsh 14 B3

L
L'Ancresse 2 A1
Ladybank 13 D1
Lairg 15 D2
Lambourn 4 A2
Lamlash 12 B3
Lampeter 6 C4
Lanark 12 C3
Lancaster 10 B3
Langholm 13 D4
Langport 3 E2
Largs 12 B2
Lasswade 13 D2
Latheron 15 E1
Lauder 13 E2
Launceston 2 C3
Laurencekirk 15 F4
Lavenham 5 E1
Laxford Bridge 14 C1
Leatherhead 4 C3
Lechlade 4 A2
Ledbury 7 E4
Ledmore 14 C2
Leeds 11 D3
Leek 7 F1
Leicester 8 B3
Leigh 10 B4
Leighton Buzzard 4 C1
Leiston 9 F4
Leominster 7 E3
Lerwick 13 F2
Leslie 13 D2
Letchworth 4 C1
Leven 13 D2
Lewes 5 D4
Leyburn 10 C2
Leyland 10 B4
Leysdown on Sea 5 E2
Lhanbryde 15 E2
Lichfield 7 F2
Lincoln 8 C1
Linlithgow 13 D2
Linslade 4 C1
Liphook 4 C3
Liskeard 2 B3
Littlehampton 4 C4
Littleport 9 D3
Liverpool 10 B4
Livingston 13 D2
Lizard 2 A4
Llanbadarn Fynydd 7 D3
Llandeilo 6 C4
Llandovery 6 C4
Llandrindod Wells 7 D3
Llandudno 6 C1

Llanelli 2 C1
Llanfair Caereinion 7 D2
Llanfyllin 7 D2
Llangefni 6 B1
Llangollen 7 D2
Llangranog 6 B3
Llangurig 6 C3
Llanidloes 6 C3
Llanrwst 6 C1
Llantrisant 3 D1
Llanwrda 6 C4
Llanwrtyd Wells 6 C4
Llwyngwril 6 C2
Llyswen 7 D4
Loanhead 13 D2
Lochaline 12 A1
Lochawe 12 B1
Lochboisdale 14 A3
Lochearnhead 12 C1
Lochgilphead 12 B2
Lochinver 14 C1
Lochmaben 13 D4
Lochmaddy 14 A2
Lochranza 12 B2
Lockerbie 13 D4
Loftus 11 E2
London 5 D2
Long Eaton 8 B2
Long Preston 10 C3
Long Sutton 9 D2
Longridge 10 B3
Longton 7 E2
Longtown 10 B1
Looe 2 B4
Lossiemouth 15 E2
Lostwithiel 2 B3
Loughborough 8 B3
Loughton 5 D2
Louth 11 F4
Lowestoft 9 F3
Ludlow 7 E3
Luss 12 C2
Luton 4 C1
Lutterworth 8 B3
Lydd 5 E3
Lydham 7 D3
Lydney 7 E4
Lyme Regis 3 E3
Lymington 4 B4
Lymm 10 B4
Lyndhurst 4 A4
Lynmouth 3 D2
Lynton 2 C2
Lytham St Anne's 10 B4

M
Mablethorpe 11 F4
Macclesfield 7 E1
Macduff 15 F2
Machynlleth 6 C2
Maesteg 3 D1
Maidenhead 4 C2
Maidstone 5 E3
Maldon 5 E2
Mallaig 14 B4
Mallwyd 6 C2
Malmesbury 3 F1
Maltby 11 D4
Malton 11 E3
Manchester 10 C4
Mangotsfield 3 E1
Manningtree 5 E1
Mansfield Woodhouse 8 B2
Mansfield 8 B2
Marazion 2 A4
March 9 D2
Margate 5 F2

Market Deeping 8 C3
Market Drayton 7 E2
Market Harborough 8 B3
Market Rasen 11 F4
Market Weighton 11 E3
Markinch 13 D2
Marks Tey 5 E1
Marlborough 4 A2
Marlow 4 C2
Maryport 10 A1
Marple 10 C4
Masham 11 D3
Matlock 7 F1
Mauchline 12 C3
Maybole 12 C3
Meigle 13 D1
Melbourn 5 D1
Melbourne 8 B2
Melksham 3 F1
Melrose 13 E3
Melton Mowbray 8 B3
Menai Bridge 6 B1
Mere 3 F2
Merthyr Tydfil 7 D4
Methil 13 D2
Methwold 9 E3
Mevagissey 2 B4
Mexborough 11 D4
Mid Yell 13 F1
Middlesbrough 11 D2
Middleton Cheney 4 B1
Middleton in Teesdale 10 C2
Middleton 10 C4
Middlewich 7 E1
Midhurst 4 C3
Midsomer Norton 3 E1
Mildenhall 9 D3
Milford Haven 6 A4
Milford 4 C3
Millom 10 A3
Millport 12 B2
Milngavie 12 C2
Milton Keynes 4 C1
Milverton 3 D2
Minehead 3 D2
Minster 12 B2
Mintlaw 15 F3
Mitcheldean 7 E4
Modbury 2 C4
Moelfre 6 B1
Moffat 13 D3
Mold 7 D1
Moniaive 12 C3
Monmouth (Trefynwy) 7 E4
Montgomery (Trefaldwyn) 7 D3
Montrose 13 E1
Morecambe 10 B3
Moretonhampstead 3 D3
Moreton-in-Marsh 4 A1
Morley 11 D4
Morpeth 13 F3
Moss 7 D1
Motherwell 12 C2
Mountain Ash 3 D1
Mountsorrel 8 B3
Much Wenlock 7 E2
Muir of Ord 15 D3
Muirkirk 12 C3
Mullion 2 A4
Mundford 9 E3
Musselburgh 13 D2

N
Nailsworth 3 F1
Nairn 15 D3
Nantwich 7 E1

Narberth 6 B4
Naseby 8 B3
Neath 3 D1
Needham Market 5 E1
Nefyn 6 B2
Nelson 10 C3
Neston 7 D1
New Alresford 4 B3
New Cumnock 12 C3
New Galloway 12 C4
New Holland 11 E4
New Mills 7 F1
New Milton 4 A4
New Quay 6 B3
New Radnor 7 D3
New Romney 5 E3
Newark-on-Trent 8 B2
Newbiggin-by-the-Sea 13 F3
Newbridge 3 D1
Newburgh 13 D1
Newbury 4 B3
Newcastle Emlyn 6 B4
Newcastle upon Tyne 11 D1
Newcastle-under-Lyme 7 E1
Newent 7 E4
Newhaven 5 D4
Newmarket 9 D4
Newnham 7 E4
Newport Pagnell 4 C1
Newport (loW) 4 B4
Newport (New) 3 E1
Newport (Pemb) 6 A4
Newport (Wrek) 7 E2
Newport-on-Tay 13 D1
Newquay 2 B3
Newton Abbot 3 D3
Newton Stewart 12 C4
Newton-le-Willows 10 B4
Newtonmore 15 D4
Newtown (Y Drenewydd) 7 D3
Neyland 6 A4
North Berwick 13 E2
North Cave 11 E3
North Somercotes 11 F4
North Walsham 9 F2
Northallerton 11 D2
Northam 2 C2
Northampton 4 B1
Northleach 4 A2
Northwich 7 E1
Norton 11 E3
Norwich 9 F3
Nottingham 8 B2
Nuneaton 8 B3

O
Oadby 8 B3
Oakham 8 C3
Oban 12 B1
Okehampton 2 C3
Oldham 10 C4
Oldmeldrum 15 F3
Ollerton 8 B2
Olney 4 C1
Onich 12 B1
Orford 5 F1
Ormskirk 10 B4
Oswestry 7 D2
Othery 3 E2
Otley 11 D3
Otterburn 13 E3
Ottery St Mary 3 D3
Oundle 8 C3
Overton 7 D2

Oxford 4 B2

P
Padstow 2 B3
Paignton 3 D3
Painswick 7 E4
Paisley 12 C2
Pangbourne 4 B2
Par 2 B4
Patrington 11 F4
Peacehaven 5 D4
Peebles 13 D3
Peel 10 A4
Pembroke Dock 6 A4
Pembroke 2 B1
Penarth 3 D1
Pendine 6 B4
Penicuik 13 D2
Penkridge 7 E2
Penmaenmawr 6 C1
Penrhyndeudraeth 6 C2
Penrith 10 B1
Penryn 2 A4
Pentrefoelas 6 C1
Penzance 2 A4
Perranporth 2 A4
Pershore 7 E4
Perth 13 D1
Peterborough 8 C3
Peterculter 15 F3
Peterhead 15 F3
Peterlee 11 D1
Petersfield 4 B3
Petworth 4 C4
Pevensey 5 D4
Pickering 11 E2
Pitlochry 13 D1
Pittenweem 13 E2
Plymouth 2 C4
Pocklington 11 E3
Polegate 5 D4
Polperro 2 B4
Pontardawe 6 C4
Pontardulais 6 C4
Pontefract 11 D4
Ponteland 10 C1
Ponterwyd 6 C3
Pontypool 3 E1
Pontypridd 3 D1
Poole 4 A4
Poolewe 14 C2
Port Askaig 12 A2
Port Ellen 12 A3
Port Erin 10 A4
Port Eynon 2 C1
Port Glasgow 12 C2
Port Isaac 2 B3
Port Nan Giuran 14 B1
Port Nis 14 B1
Port Talbot 2 C1
Port William 12 C4
Portavadie 12 B2
Porthcawl 2 C1
Porthmadog 6 C2
Portishead 3 E1
Portknockie 15 E2
Portnacroish 12 B1
Portnahaven 12 A2
Portpatrick 12 B4
Portree 14 B3
Portrilas 7 D4
Portsmouth 4 B4
Portsoy 15 F2
Potters Bar 4 C2
Potton 4 C1
Preesall 10 B3
Prestatyn 7 D1
Preston 10 B4

Prestwick 12 C3
Preteigne 7 D3
Princes Risborough 4 C2
Prudhoe 10 C1
Puckeridge 5 D1
Puddletown 3 F3
Pudsey 11 D3
Pulborough 4 C4
Pwllheli 6 B2

Q
Queensferry 7 D1

R
Radstock 3 F1
Rainham 5 E3
Ramsey *(Camb)* 8 C3
Ramsey *(IoM)* 10 A4
Ramsgate 5 F3
Rattray 13 D1
Raunds 8 C4
Ravenglass 10 A2
Rawmarsh 11 D4
Rawtenstall 10 C4
Rayleigh 5 E2
Reading 4 B2
Reay 15 D1
Redcar 11 D2
Redditch 7 F3
Redhill 5 D3
Redruth 2 A4
Reepham 9 E2
Reigate 5 D3
Rhayader 6 C3
Rhosneigr 6 B1
Rhos-on-Sea 6 C1
Rhuddlan 6 C1
Rhyl 6 C1
Rhymney 7 D4
Rhynie 15 F3
Richmond 10 C2
Rickmansworth 4 C2
Ringwood 4 A4
Ripley 8 B2
Ripon 11 D3
Roade 4 B1
Robin Hood's Bay 11 E2
Rochdale 10 C4
Rochester 5 E2
Roghadal 14 A2
Romsey 4 B3
Rosehearty 15 F2
Ross-on-Wye 7 E4
Rothbury 13 F1
Rotherham 11 D4
Rothes 15 E3
Rothesay 12 B2
Rothwell *(North)* 8 C3
Rothwell *(W York)* 11 D4
Royal Leamington Spa 7 F3
Royal Tunbridge Wells 5 D3
Royston 5 D1
Rozel 2 B2
Rugby 8 B3
Rugeley 7 F2
Runcorn 7 E1
Rushden 8 C4
Ruthin 7 D1
Ryde 4 B4
Rye 5 E3

S
Saffron Walden 5 D1
Salcombe 2 C4
Sale 10 C4
Salen 12 A1

Salford 10 C4
Salisbury 4 A3
Saltash 2 C4
Saltburn-by-the-Sea 11 E2
Saltcoats 12 B3
Sandbach 7 E1
Sandhead 12 B4
Sandhurst 4 C3
Sandness 13 F2
Sandown 4 B4
Sandringham 9 D2
Sandwich 5 F3
Sandy 4 C1
Sanquhar 12 C3
Saundersfoot 6 B4
Saxmundham 9 F4
Scalasaig 12 A2
Scalby 11 E2
Scalloway 13 F2
Scarborough 11 E2
Scrabster 15 E1
Scunthorpe 11 E4
Seaford 5 D4
Seaham 11 D1
Seascale 10 A2
Seaton 3 E3
Sedbergh 10 B2
Sedgefield 11 D1
Selby 11 D3
Selkirk 13 E3
Selsey 4 C4
Settle 10 C3
Sevenoaks 5 D3
Shaftesbury 3 F2
Shanklin 4 B4
Shap 10 B2
Sheerness 5 E2
Sheffield 11 D4
Shefford 4 C1
Shepshed 8 B3
Shepton Mallet 3 E2
Sherborne 3 E2
Sheringham 9 E2
Shiel Bridge 14 C3
Shieldaig 14 B3
Shifnal 7 E2
Shipley 10 C3
Shipston-on-Stour 4 A1
Shoeburyness 5 E2
Shoreham-by-Sea 4 C4
Shotley Gate 5 F1
Shotts 12 C2
Shrewsbury 7 D2
Sidmouth 3 D3
Silloth 10 A1
Silsden 10 C3
Silverstone 4 B1
Sittingbourne 5 E3
Skegness 9 D2
Skelmersdale 10 B4
Skipton 10 C3
Sleaford 8 C2
Sligachan 14 B3
Slough 4 C2
Soham 9 D3
Solihull 7 F3
Somerton 3 E2
South Cave 11 E3
South Hayling 4 B4
South Molton 2 C2
South Queensferry 13 D2
South Shields 11 D1
Southam 4 B1
Southampton 4 B4
Southborough 5 D3
Southend 12 A3
Southend-on-Sea 5 E2

Southport 10 B4
Southwell 8 B2
Southwold 9 F3
Sowerby Bridge 10 C4
Spalding 8 C2
Spean Bridge 14 C4
Spennymoor 11 D1
Spilsby 9 D2
St Agnes 2 A4
St Albans 4 C2
St Andrews 13 E1
St Anne 2 A1
St Asaph 7 D1
St Aubin 2 A2
St Austell 2 B4
St Bees 10 A2
St Boswells 13 E3
St Brelade 2 A2
St Clears 6 B4
St Clement 2 B2
St Columb Major 2 B3
St David's 6 A4
St Helens 10 B4
St Helier 2 A2
St Ives *(Camb)* 9 D4
St Ives *(Corn)* 2 A4
St Just 2 A4
St Keverne 2 A4
St Lawrence 2 A2
St Martin 2 A2
St Mary's 15 F1
St Mawes 2 B4
St Neots 4 C1
St Ouen 2 A2
St Peter 2 A2
St Peter Port 2 A2
St Sampson 2 A2
St Saviour *(Guer)* 2 A2
St Saviour *(Jer)* 2 B2
Staffin 14 B2
Stafford 7 E2
Staines 4 C2
Stalbridge 3 F2
Stalham 9 F2
Stamford Bridge 11 E3
Stamford 8 C3
Stanhope 10 C1
Stanley 11 D1
Stansted 5 D1
Staveley 8 B1
Stevenage 4 C1
Stevenston 12 B3
Stewarton 12 C3
Stilton 8 C3
Stirling 12 C2
Stockbridge 4 B3
Stockport 10 C4
Stocksbridge 11 D4
Stockton-on-Tees 11 D2
Stoke Ferry 9 D3
Stokenchurch 4 B2
Stoke-on-Trent 7 E1
Stokesley 11 D2
Stone 7 E2
Stonehaven 15 F4
Stonehouse 7 E4
Stony Stratford 4 B1
Stornoway 14 B1
Stourbridge 7 E3
Stourport-on-Severn 7 E3
Stow 13 D2
Stowmarket 5 E1
Stow-on-the-Wold 4 A1
Stranraer 12 B4
Stratford-upon-Avon 4 A1
Strathaven 12 C3
Strathpeffer 15 D3
Stratton 2 B2

Street 3 E2
Stromness 15 F1
Stroud 7 E4
Sturminster Newton 3 F2
Sudbury *(Derb)* 7 F2
Sudbury *(Suff)* 5 E1
Sullom 13 F1
Sumburgh 13 F2
Sunderland 11 D1
Sutterton 9 D2
Sutton Coldfield 7 F2
Sutton in Ashfield 8 B2
Sutton on Sea 9 D1
Swadlincote 7 F2
Swaffham 9 E3
Swanage 4 A4
Swansea 2 C1
Swinderby 8 C2
Swindon 4 A2
Swineshead 8 C2
Syre 15 D1
Syston 8 B3

T
Tadcaster 11 D3
Tain 15 D2
Tamworth 7 F2
Tarbert *(Arg)* 12 B2
Tarbert *(W Isl)* 14 A2
Tarbet 12 C2
Tarporley 7 E1
Taunton 3 E2
Tavistock 2 C3
Tayinloan 12 A3
Taynuilt 12 B1
Teignmouth 3 D3
Telford 7 E2
Tenbury Wells 7 E3
Tenby 3 B1
Tenterden 5 E3
Tetbury 3 F1
Tewkesbury 7 E4
Thame 4 B2
The Mumbles 2 C1
Thetford 9 E3
Thirsk 11 D2
Thornaby-on-Tees 11 D2
Thornbury 3 E1
Thorne 11 E4
Thorney 8 C3
Thornhill 13 D3
Thornton 10 B3
Thrapston 8 C3
Thurmaston 8 B3
Thursby 10 B1
Thurso 15 E1
Tickhill 11 D4
Tigh A Ghearraidh 14 A2
Tighnabruaich 12 B2
Tilbury 5 D2
Tillicoultry 13 D2
Tintagel 2 B3
Tiptree 5 E1
Tiverton 3 D2
Tobermory 12 A1
Todmorden 10 C4
Toft 13 F1
Tomatin 15 D3
Tomintoul 15 E3
Tonbridge 5 D3
Tongue 15 D1
Topsham 3 D3
Torpoint 2 C4
Torquay 3 D3
Totnes 3 D3
Totton 4 B4
Tow Law 10 C1
Towcester 4 B1

Tranent 13 D2
Trecastle 6 C4
Tredegar 7 D4
Tregaron 6 C3
Tring 4 C2
Troon 12 C3
Trowbridge 3 F1
Truro 2 B4
Tunstall 7 E1
Turriff 15 F3
Two Bridges 2 C3
Tynemouth 11 D1
Tywyn 6 C2

U
Uckfield 5 D3
Uffculme 3 D2
Uig 14 B2
Ullapool 14 C2
Ulsta 13 F1
Ulverston 10 B3
Upavon 4 A3
Upper Largo 13 D2
Uppingham 8 C3
Upton-upon-Severn 7 E4
Usk 7 D4
Uttoxeter 7 F2

V
Ventnor 4 B4
Voe 13 F1

W
Wadebridge 2 B3
Wainfleet All Saints 9 D2
Wakefield 11 D4
Wallasey 10 B4
Wallingford 4 B2
Walmer 5 F3
Walsall 7 F2
Waltham Abbey 5 D2
Walton on the Naze 5 F1
Wansford 8 C3
Wantage 4 B2
Ware 5 D1
Wareham 3 F3
Warminster 3 F2
Warrington 10 B4
Warwick 7 F3
Washington 11 D1
Watchet 3 D2
Watford 4 C2
Watton 9 E3
Weedon Bec 4 B1
Wellingborough 8 C4
Wellington *(Som)* 3 D2
Wellington *(Wrek)* 7 E2
Wells 3 E2
Wells-next-the-Sea 9 E2
Welshpool (Y Trallwng) 7 D2
Welwyn Garden City 4 C2
Wem 7 E2
Wemyss Bay 12 B2
Wendover 4 C2
West Bridgford 8 B2
West Bromwich 7 F3
West Kilbride 12 B2
West Mersea 5 E2
Westbury 3 F2
Weston-super-Mare 3 E1
Westward Ho! 2 C2
Wetherby 11 D3
Weybridge 4 C3
Weymouth 3 F3
Whaley Bridge 7 F1
Wheatley 4 B2
Whipsnade 4 C1

Whitburn 13 D2
Whitby 11 E2
Whitchurch *(Bucks)* 4 B1
Whitchurch *(Hants)* 4 B3
Whitchurch *(Shrop)* 7 E2
Whitehaven 10 A2
Whithorn 12 C4
Whitley Bay 11 D1
Whitstable 5 E2
Whittington 7 D2
Whittlesey 8 C3
Wick 15 E1
Wickford 5 E2
Wickham Market 5 F1
Widecombe 2 C3
Widnes 7 E1
Wigan 10 B4
Wigston 8 B3
Wigton 10 A1
Wigtown 12 C4
Williton 3 D2
Wilmslow 7 E1
Wilton 4 A3
Wimborne Minster 4 A4
Wincanton 3 F2
Winchcombe 4 A1
Winchester 4 B3
Windermere 10 B2
Windsor 4 C2
Winsford 7 E1
Winslow 4 B1
Winterton 11 E4
Winterton-on-Sea 9 F2
Wirksworth 7 F1
Wisbech 9 D3
Wishaw 12 C2
Witham 5 E1
Withernsea 11 F4
Witney 4 B2
Wiveliscombe 3 D2
Wivenhoe 5 E1
Woburn 4 C1
Woking 4 C3
Wokingham 4 C2
Wolverhampton 7 E2
Wolverton 4 B1
Woodbridge 5 F1
Woodhall Spa 8 C2
Woodstock 4 B2
Woofferton 7 E3
Woolacombe 2 C2
Wooler 13 E3
Woore 7 E2
Wootton Bassett 4 A2
Worcester 7 E3
Workington 10 A1
Worksop 8 B1
Worthing 4 C4
Wotton-under-Edge 3 F1
Wragby 8 C1
Wrexham 7 D1
Wrotham 5 D3
Wroughton 4 A2
Wroxham 9 F3
Wymondham 9 E3

Y
Yarmouth 4 B4
Yate 3 F1
Yeadon 10 C3
Yeovil 3 E2
York 11 D3
Ystrad 3 D1

INDEX TO IRELAND

Abbreviations of County names used in this index.

Arm = Armagh (Northern Ireland)	Ferm = Fermanagh (Northern Ireland)	Tip = Tipperary (Republic of Eire)
Dow = Down (Northern Ireland)	May = Mayo (Republic of Eire)	Tyr = Tyrone (Northern Ireland)

A
Aasleagh 16 A4
Abbeyfeale 18 B2
Abbeyleix 19 E2
Anascaul 18 A3
Antrim 17 F2
Ardara 16 C2
Ardee 17 E4
Ardglass 17 F3
Arklow 19 F2
Armagh 17 E3
Ashbourne 17 E4
Ashford 19 F1
Askeaton 16 C2
Athboy 17 E4
Athenry 18 C1
Athleague 16 C4
Athlone 19 D1
Athy 19 E1
Aughnacloy 17 E3

B
Bailieborough 17 E4
Balbriggan 17 E4
Balla 16 B4
Ballaghaderreen 16 C3
Ballina 16 B3
Ballinagh 17 D4
Ballinamore 17 D3
Ballinasloe 19 D1
Ballinrobe 16 B4
Ballisodare 16 C3
Ballybay 17 E3
Ballybrack 19 F1
Ballycastle 17 F1
Ballyclare 17 F2
Ballycroy 16 A3
Ballydehob 18 B4
Ballygawley 17 E3
Ballyhaunis 16 B4
Ballyhillin 17 D1
Ballyjamesduff 17 D4
Ballyliffen 17 D1
Ballylongford 18 B2
Ballymahon 17 D4
Ballymakeery 18 B3
Ballymena 17 E2
Ballymoe 16 C4
Ballymoney 17 E1
Ballynahinch 17 F3
Ballyragget 19 E2
Ballyshannon 16 C2
Ballyvaughan 18 B1
Baltinglass 19 E2
Banbridge 17 E3
Bandon 18 C4
Bangor Erris 16 A3
Bangor 17 F2
Bantry 18 B4
Belfast 17 F2
Belleek (Ferm) 16 C2
Belleek (Arm) 17 E3
Belmullet 16 A3
Belturbet 17 D3
Bessbrook 17 E3

Birdhill 18 C2
Birr 19 D1
Borris-in-Ossory 19 D1
Borrisokane 19 D1
Borrisoleigh 19 D2
Boyle 16 C3
Bray 19 F1
Bridge End 17 D1
Brittas 19 F1
Bunbeg 16 C1
Buncrana 17 D1
Bunclody 19 E2
Bundoran 16 C2
Butler's Bridge 17 D3
Buttevant 18 C3

C
Cahir 19 D3
Cahirciveen 18 A3
Callan 19 D2
Carlow 19 E2
Carndonagh 17 D1
Carnlough 17 F2
Carrick 16 C2
Carrickfergus 17 F2
Carrickmacross 17 E3
Carrick-on-Shannon 16 C3
Carrick-on-Suir 19 D3
Carrigart 17 D1
Cashel 19 D2
Castlebar 16 B3
Castlebellingham 17 E4
Castleblayney 17 E3
Castlecomer 19 E2
Castlederg 17 D2
Castledermot 19 E2
Castleisland 18 B3
Castlemaine 18 B3
Castlepollard 17 D4
Castlerea 16 C4
Castletownroche 18 C3
Castlewellan 17 F3
Cavan 17 D3
Ceannanus Mór 17 E4
Charlestown 16 B3
Claregalway 18 C1
Claremorris 16 B4
Clifden 16 A4
Cloghan 19 D1
Clogher 17 D3
Clonakilty 18 B4
Clonee 19 F1
Clones 17 D3
Clonmel 19 D3
Clough 17 F3
Coalisland 17 E2
Cobh 18 C4
Coleraine 17 E1
Collon 17 E4
Cookstown 17 E2
Cootehill 17 D3
Cork 18 C3
Craigavon 17 E3
Creeslough 17 D1
Croom 17 C2

Crossmaglen 17 E3
Crossmolina 16 B3

D
Daingean 19 E1
Delvin 17 D4
Dingle 18 A3
Donaghadee 17 F2
Donegal 16 C2
Douglas 18 C4
Downpatrick 17 F3
Drimoleague 18 B4
Drogheda 17 E4
Dromod 16 C4
Dromore West 16 B3
Dromore 17 D2
Dromore (Tyr) 17 D2
Dromore (Dow) 17 F3
Drumcollogher 18 C3
Drumshanbo 16 C3
Drumsna 16 C3
Dublin 19 F1
Dun Laoghaire 19 F1
Dundalk 17 E3
Dundonald Comber 17 F2
Dungannon 17 E2
Dungarvan 19 D3
Dungiven 17 E2
Dungloe 16 C1
Dunlavin 19 E1
Dunleer 17 E4
Dunmanway 18 B4
Dunmore 16 B4
Dunshaughlin 17 E4
Durrow 19 D2

E
Edenderry 19 E1
Edgeworthstown 17 D4
Enfield 19 E1
Ennis 18 C2
Enniscorthy 19 F2
Enniskillen 17 D3
Ennistymon 18 B1

F
Fahan 17 D1
Falcarragh 16 C1
Farranfore 18 B3
Fenagh 17 D3
Fermoy 18 C3
Fethard 19 D2
Fintona 17 D2
Foxford 16 B3
Foynes 18 B2
Frenchpark 16 C4

G
Galway 18 C1
Garvagh 17 E2
Glenariff 17 F1
Glencolumbkille 16 C2
Glengarriff 18 B4
Glengeigh 18 A3
Glenties 16 C2
Gorey 19 F2
Gort 18 C1

Granard 17 D4
Greystones 19 F1
Gweedore 16 C1

H
Headford 16 B4
Holywood 17 F2

I
Irvinestown 17 D2

K
Keady 17 E3
Kenmare 18 B3
Kesh 17 D2
Kilbeggan 19 D1
Kilcock 19 E1
Kilcolgan 18 C1
Kilcullen 19 E1
Kildare 19 E1
Kildorrey 18 C3
Kilkee 18 B2
Kilkeel 17 F3
Kilkenny 19 E2
Killaloe 18 C2
Killarney 18 B3
Killenaule 19 D2
Killeshandra 17 D3
Killmallock 18 C2
Killorglin 18 A3
Killyleagh 17 F3
Kilrea 17 E2
Kilrush 18 B2
Kingscourt 17 E4
Kinnegad 19 E1
Kinsale 18 C4
Kinvara 18 C1
Knock 16 B4
Knocklong 17 C2
Knocktopher 19 E2

L
Larne 17 F2
Leighlinbridge 19 E2
Leixlip 19 F1
Letterfrack 16 A4
Letterkenny 17 D1
Limavady 17 E1
Limerick 18 C2
Lisburn 17 F2
Lismore 19 D3
Lisnaskea 17 D3
Listowel 18 B2
Londonderry 17 D1
Longford 17 D4
Loughrea 18 C1
Louisburgh 16 A4
Lucan 19 F1
Lurgan 17 E3

M
Maam Cross 16 A4
Macroom 18 B3
Maghera 17 E2
Magherafelt 17 E2
Maguiresbridge 17 D3

Mallow 18 C3
Manorhamilton 16 C3
Markethill 17 E3
Mass 16 C2
Midleton 18 C3
Milestone 19 D2
Milford 17 D1
Milltown Malbay 18 B1
Mitchelstown 18 C3
Moate 19 D1
Mohil 16 C3
Monaghan 17 E3
Monasterevan 19 E1
Moneymore 17 E2
Mount Bellew 16 C4
Mountmellick 19 E1
Mountrath 19 D1
Moville 17 E1
Moycullen 18 B1
Muff 17 D1
Mullingar 17 D4
Mulrany 16 A3

N
Nass 19 E1
Navan 17 E4
Nenagh 19 D2
New Ross 19 E3
Newbliss 17 D3
Newcastle West 18 B2
Newcastle 17 F3
Newport (May) 16 A3
Newport (Tip) 18 C2
Newry 17 E3
Newtownabbey 17 F2
Newtownards 17 F2
Newtownhamilton 17 E3
Newtownstewart 17 D2

O
Oldcastle 17 D4
Omagh 17 D2
Oranmore 18 C1
Oughterard 16 B4

P
Partry 16 B4
Patrickswell 18 C2
Port Laoise 19 E1
Portadown 17 E3
Portaferry 17 F3
Portrush 17 E1
Portstewart 17 E1
Portumna 19 D1

Q
Quigley's Point 17 D1

R
Randalstown 17 E2
Rathangan 19 E1
Rathcoole 19 F1
Rathcormac 17 C3
Rathdrum 19 F2
Rathfriland 17 F3
Rathkeale 17 C2

Rathlurirc 18 C3
Rathmore 18 B3
Rathnew 19 F1
Recess 16 A4
Rochfortbridge 19 E1
Roscommon 16 C4
Roscrea 19 D1
Rosslare Harbour 19 F2
Rosslare 19 F2
Roundwood 19 F1

S
Saintfield 17 F3
Schull 18 B4
Shannon 18 C2
Shercock 17 E3
Sion Mills 17 D2
Skerries 17 F4
Skibbereen 18 B4
Slane 17 E4
Sligo 16 C3
Sneem 18 A3
Strabane 17 D2
Stradbally 19 E1
Strangford 17 F3
Stranorlar 17 D2
Swanlinbar 17 D3
Swinford 16 B3
Swords 19 F1

T
Tallowbridge 19 D3
Tandragee 17 E3
Tarbert 18 B2
Templemore 19 D2
Thomastown 19 E2
Thurles 19 D2
Tipperary 19 D2
Tralee 18 B3
Tramore 19 E3
Trim 17 E4
Tuam 16 B4
Tuamgraney 18 C1
Tubbercurry 16 B3
Tullamore 19 D1
Tullow 19 E2
Tulsk 16 C4

U
Urlingford 19 D2

V
Virginia 17 D4

W
Warrenpoint 17 E3
Waterford 19 E3
Waterville 18 A3
Westport 16 A4
Wexford 19 F2
Whitehead 17 F2
Wicklow 19 F1

Y
Youghal 19 D3